John Mortimer

The Secret Lives of Rumpole's Creator

JOHN MORTIMER

The Secret Lives of Rumpole's Creator

GRAHAM LORD

Thomas Dunne Books
St. Martin's Press
New York

THOMAS DUNNE BOOKS.
An imprint of St. Martin's Press.

www.stmartins.com

ISBN-13: 978-0-312-33082-8
ISBN-10: 0-312-33082-0

First published in Great Britain by Orion Books
an imprint of the Orion Publishing Group Ltd

First U.S. Edition: August 2006

10 9 8 7 6 5 4 3 2 1

In memory of
Giles Gordon

Contents

List of Illustrations

Sections of photographs appear between pages 118 & 119 and 214 & 215

Between pages 118 *and* 119:
Mortimer's father, Clifford [1]
Mortimer's mother, Kath, reading to his father[1]
The Grove House, Harrow, in 1937[2]
Mortimer at Oxford in 1941[3]
Michael Fenton[3]
Michael and Barbara Fenton[3]
Mortimer's first wedding, to Penelope Dimont, 1949[4]
Mortimer with his first wife, Penelope, and family, 1958[15]
Mortimer with his first wife, Penelope, c. 1970[5]
Mortimer with his first wife, Penelope, at the Theatre Royal, London, 1960[6]
Wendy Craig, c. 1960[1]
Wendy Craig with her son, Ross, 1961[7]
John Mortimer QC, 1966[5]
Wendy Craig and her husband, Jack Bentley[8]
Wendy Craig and her sons, Alaster and Ross, 1972[9]
Ross Bentley, 2004[10]
Mortimer, 1966[6]
Shirley Anne Field[11]
Molly Parkin[12]
Susan Elliot[6]

Between pages 214 *and* 215:
Mortimer with his second wife, Penelope, and their 18-month-old daughter, Emily, 1973[13]

Every effort has been made to trace the copyright holders of the photographs included in this book but, if any have been inadvertently overlooked, the author and publisher will be pleased to make the necessary changes at the first opprtunity.

[1]Rex Features
[2]Courtesy of Richard Willis
[3]Courtesy of Ben Fenton
[4]Courtesy of Jeremy Mortimer
[5]Camera Press
[6]Corbis
[7]The Associated Press/Empics
[8]UPPA
[9]The Press Association/Empics
[10]Solo Syndication
[11]Courtesy of Shirley Anne Field
[12]John Timbers
[13]Getty
[14]Courtesy of the author
[15]Courtesy of the *Daily Express*
[16]John Ireland

One

The Temple and the Dragon
1923–1937

*O*n old age Sir John Mortimer increasingly resembled one of Britain's fat eighteenth-century German kings – with his portly Hanoverian gait, lopsided jaw and derelict teeth – so it's fitting that he was born on the same date as Queen Victoria's great-great-granddaughter, Elizabeth II, on 21 April, albeit in 1923, three years earlier than she. He chose to tell interviewers that he was born in central London, at his barrister father's flat in the Middle Temple just off Fleet Street, but he was in fact born in the North London suburb of Hampstead at 7 The Pryors, a small, rented, ground-floor apartment in a six-storey block of Edwardian flats that still stands in East Heath Road right on the leafy edge of the tranquil, rural acres of Hampstead Heath. His thirty-nine-year-old father, Herbert Clifford Mortimer, specialised in divorce and probate and practised from chambers in the Inner Temple. The baby's mother was Kathleen May Mortimer, the thirty-five-year-old daughter of a Leamington Spa debt collector, Henry Smith, a High Bailiff of Warwick County Court, so the infant's genes were infused on both sides with a whiff of the Law. He also inherited a hearty taste for alcohol from his paternal grandfather, John, a Methodist brewer from Bristol who pretended to be teetotal but often appeared to be mysteriously drunk. Less jovially the boy inherited a melancholy disposition from his maternal grandfather, the bailiff, who settled all his own debts by committing suicide.

Clifford and Kath Mortimer called the baby John Clifford but as they were atheists he was not christened. His forehead was never moistened with the sign of the cross to protect him from the Devil and he grew up to hate God and find sin amusing. His childhood was to be a strange, lonely one, for his mother had had several miscarriages, he was to be an only child, and his parents were not the sort who might be recommended as role models by psychologists or social workers. Clifford Mortimer was a tall, fair, pot-bellied man with pale blue eyes weakened by glaucoma who had been raised in South Africa – his boozy father had emigrated to Durban to become an estate agent – and had returned to England to read Law at Cambridge and spend the First World War sensibly protected by a safe job in the Inland Waterways. Clifford's own childhood was a lonely one, for his parents were cold and unaffectionate, so it is perhaps understandable that as an adult he became rude, selfish, bad-tempered and demanding. He called John dismissively 'the boy', shouted at waiters and porters, bellowed at foreigners, barked at judges, yelled at his wife if his breakfast egg was too soft or his plate too cold, complained constantly about her cooking, told her regularly that she was a cretin, and was always quarrelling with her although their son insisted later that they loved each other dearly. Regularly Clifford created scenes in public, and in the Law Courts one day when he discovered that a solicitor had forgotten an important document he swore at him loudly in the words of Macbeth: 'The Devil damn thee black, thou cream-faced loon!' He took at least two baths a day and sometimes more, perhaps to wash his unpleasantness away, yet John claimed that it was his father who inspired his liberal instincts and enthusiastic support for the Labour Party. 'My father was a kind of Lloyd George Liberal,' he told Miriam Gross of the *Sunday Telegraph* in 1986, and 'my mother was a New Woman who read Bernard Shaw. I was brought up on that middle-class idealism, if that's the right word for it, which believed that money wasn't the most important thing in life. What was important was that if you had an education and professional qualifications you used them as a kind of service to less privileged people.' And he told Paul Callan of the *Daily Express* in 1998 that his parents taught him that 'if you came from a family who had a sense of social responsibility, you cared, really cared, about the underprivileged', so when Clifford shouted at waiters and porters it must have been a great consolation that he really cared about them. As for John's claim that money was not important to him, several of his acquaintances told me that he was always extremely keen on it indeed and would do almost anything to make more, and although his mother may have worn the halo of a saintly liberal she was also a snob who admitted that although she was all for the working classes she would never invite one of them to lunch.

Kath Mortimer was a tall, gentle, dark-eyed painter who blushed easily and was, like her husband, emotionally repressed. As a young woman she had been sufficiently adventurous to teach art at schools in France and South Africa – where she met Clifford – and to ride bareback and swim naked in African streams, but she was also shy and withdrawn and came from a family that was so undemonstrative that when her father shot himself while she was in South Africa they sent her just a newspaper cutting reporting his death without any letter to accompany it. Not surprisingly her relationship with her own son was restrained. Often she forgot his name or called him Daisy, and she could never remember whether he took sugar in his tea. She made it obvious that she thought he would never amount to much, often laughed at him, never praised him either as a boy or as an adult, and he admitted that she had left him with very low self-esteem. A boy with such a mother could well grow up psychologically damaged.

Despite Clifford Mortimer's unpleasantness John insisted that he told wonderfully funny stories and would laugh until he wept. John adored him. At the age of eighty John admitted that he still felt guilty because he had felt so much affection and admiration for his father but had failed to love his mother nearly enough and had never appreciated sufficiently how talented she had been as a painter and how much she had sacrificed in giving up painting to look after his father. In later life Mortimer tried to assuage his guilt about his mother by fawning over every woman he met, seducing a great many, and finding it difficult to sustain close male relationships. Time and again he would say that women were the stronger, nicer, more intelligent and amusing sex and that men were dull and inferior in every way. It was not a balanced way of looking at the world.

John's father never played with him, not even to kick a football, perhaps because his eyesight was deteriorating rapidly. He travelled all over Europe to consult surgeons, suffered horrifying operations, and after one in Switzerland – during which an eye was removed, treated and replaced while he was conscious – he had to lie motionless with his head wedged between two sandbags for two weeks. Unforgivably he never gave his son any real guidance about life or taught him the difference between right and wrong, a pair of bewildering concepts that were to baffle Mortimer all his life.

He spent his first three lonely years in London in the family's rented first-floor flat at 4 Harcourt Buildings in the ancient ghetto of the Temple, a secluded, timeless legal haven with the hushed atmosphere of an Oxbridge college. Two hundred yards away his father's chambers occupied

the first and second floors of the south side of number 1 Dr Johnson's
Buildings, just inside the huge wooden gates opposite the southern end
of Chancery Lane that lead from the noisy turmoil of Fleet Street down
Inner Temple Lane. Here Clifford toiled daily to prepare his briefs and
appear in the Probate, Divorce and Admiralty Division of the High
Court, which the humourist A. P. Herbert once described as dealing with
'Wills, Wives and Wrecks', and he was so good at his job that his books
Mortimer on Probate and *Rayden and Mortimer on Divorce* became standard
legal reference works. At weekends the Mortimers escaped the bustle of
the city to enjoy the rustic charms of a ramshackle, ten-shillings-a-week,
rented holiday cottage – with outside lavatory and no running water or
electricity – in Buckinghamshire, at Turville Heath, a scattered little
settlement that enjoyed within a mile or so three churches, three pubs,
two schools, a post office, a regular bus service, and was inhabited by
woodsmen, farm labourers and the chair-leg turners who were known as
bodgers.

When John was three the Mortimers left the London flat and moved
back to the fresh greenery of Hampstead to live in a small, semi-detached
house a hundred yards from the Heath and three hundred from his
birthplace, at 35 Downshire Hill, which they rented for £5 a week, the
equivalent of about £152 a week when this book was published in 2005.
They lived there for three more years before moving at the end of 1929
back to another flat in the Temple, this time a third-floor apartment at 5
King's Bench Walk, part of an 1814 mansion block of lawyers' chambers
in a large, leafy square with a pretty private lawn and garden between
the square and the Embankment and River Thames. Clifford rented it
for just £72 a year (£2,283 in 2005) and the Mortimer family was to live
there for eleven years until December 1940.

Clifford ignored his son for his first few years and the boy had to rely
for company on his nursemaid, Elsie. When the family went off for a
seaside holiday he and Elsie would stay in a cheap boarding house while
his parents checked in to a luxury hotel, though they did take him to
Switzerland, Germany and France as Clifford consulted foreign doctors
about his failing eyesight with increasing alarm. These travels were not
always happy for John: when he was six he locked himself in a lavatory
at the Negresco Hotel in Nice, screamed until he was freed by a carpenter,
and never locked a lavatory door again. Later he had a succession of
governesses but once he was five his father began to take some interest
in him and to talk to him as though they were equals. He bought the
child a little tuxedo so that they could dress formally for dinner during

their holidays and once when they walked into a cinema in Lyme Regis in their tuxedos the audience clapped and cheered. Clifford had learned great chunks of Shakespeare by heart and would startle the boy by suddenly quoting for no obvious reason a line from *Macbeth* to enquire, 'Is execution done on Cawdor?' He would suddenly regale Kath with a line from *Hamlet*: 'Nymph, in thy orisons be all my sins remembered', and one of his much repeated jokes was to suggest that a line from *King John* – 'Rush forth and bind the boy' – referred in fact to a dodgy legal practice so that he would often enquire of his bewildered clerk: 'Any briefs from Messrs Rushforth and Bindtheboy?' But he did resist the temptation to frighten the boy by quoting the Duke of York in *Henry VI Part II*: 'This devil here shall be my substitute / For that John Mortimer which now is dead.'

When John was six he started school, trotting off each day with his governess to travel the five stops on the London Underground's District and Circle Line from the Temple to Sloane Square, where he attended Charles Gibbs' private Chelsea pre-prep school at 134 Sloane Street. Clifford could well afford it, expensive though it was. By now he was earning £4,000 a year (£127,000). Even so, the other children at Mr Gibbs' school came from much richer families and John was ashamed when his mother went to the school one day and looked so much shabbier than the other mothers. It was soon apparent that he was so short-sighted he could not see the blackboard, so he was given glasses and sent back to the junior class to start all over again. Equally humiliating were the boxing lessons and fights that the boys were forced to endure, which often made him cry when he was punched. He decided then, at the age of six, that never again would he take part in any sort of sport if he could possibly avoid it, and one of his proudest boasts towards the end of his life was that in eighty years he had rarely taken any exercise. He did, however, become an enthusiastic member of the Sloane Square Wolf Cubs, led by a beefy spinster who wore a vast khaki uniform sanctioned by the recently ennobled Lord Baden-Powell and would take the boys by Tube to Wimbledon Common and there entice them to play a game in which each small boy had to hide in the undergrowth and then try to crawl towards her unnoticed as she stood in her voluminous skirt with her massive legs apart. The winner of the game, who would be given a box of chocolates, was the first boy to crawl between her legs without being seen. Years later Mortimer admitted that this was the only competitive sport that he had ever enjoyed, though when at Turville Heath the gardener's daughter generously offered to show him her knickers one day, he removed his glasses, nervous of what might be revealed. His enthusiasm was soon rekindled however when the family went on holiday to Hastings, where he beheld an exotic dancer wearing fishnet stockings.

When John was nine, in 1932, his father made two decisions that were each to have a major influence on his life: he built his own cottage at Turville Heath and sent John away as a boarder to the Dragon School at Oxford, which was widely reckoned to be one of the best prep schools in England. Its pupils (ninety per cent boys, ten per cent girls) were prepared up to the age of fourteen for entrance to the greatest English public schools and among its former pupils had been the future Poet Laureate John Betjeman; Labour Party leader Hugh Gaitskell; Marshal of the Royal Air Force John Slessor; writers Nevil Shute and Naomi Mitchison; and four winners of the Victoria Cross, one of them Leonard Cheshire, who had left the school a year before John joined. Betjeman, who was at the Dragon from 1917 to 1920, had loved it. Situated idyllically beside broad playing fields on the bank of the River Cherwell, it was extremely academic, concentrating heavily on Latin and Greek, but it was also a cosy, liberal, friendly place where the boys and masters called each other by their Christian or nicknames and John's dormitory was in an imperial boarding house named Gunga Din. The headmaster, A. E. 'Hum' Lynam – he hummed loudly all the time to warn the boys that he was approaching – was the sort of teacher who would catch a couple of boys fighting, call them up onto the stage at morning prayers, and either beat them with an umbrella or make them kiss each other, which for them was probably worse. Other miscreants would be sent to the carpentry shop to ask the woodwork teacher 'for something to beat you with' and would return smiling happily and carrying a plank. Corporal punishment was rare and usually confined to two whacks with a gym shoe and Hum was given to wandering around the school in the evening playing a violin. 'Dragon School boys were allowed a freedom which seemed extraordinary to boys at other comparable schools,' wrote Bevis Hillier in his biography *Young Betjeman*. 'They did not have to wear Eton suits on Sundays and walk in a crocodile, as did the pupils of the slightly older and snootier Summerfields, higher up the Cherwell. Summerfields boys thought of Dragon boys as "oiks" [non-gentlemen] because they drank lemonade straight from the bottle.' They were allowed to bicycle into Oxford and sail boats on the river, and one of the few firm rules was that boys were not allowed to slouch around with their hands in their pockets.

'Hum was like a father to me,' Betjeman wrote to one of the teachers in 1965, forty-five years after he left. 'One always knew one could go to him if up the spout, although one never did. There was the feeling that he was there as a protection against injustice. He taught me how to speak in public and how to recite. "Hands behind your back. Eyes on the clock. Stand at the front of the stage. Now speak up."' Hum's powerful Christian faith had a deep effect on Betjeman but Mortimer was much less susceptible to religious conversion and many years later he claimed that when the other boys were saying their prayers at night he would kneel beside his chamber pot and sing songs made popular by Fred Astaire.

In September 1932 John joined more than three hundred other pupils at the Dragon, among them John Buchan's son William and two boys who were later to be his classmates: the future historian E. P. (Palmer) Thompson, author of *The Making of the British Working Class*; and Christopher Tolkien, son of the J. R. R. who was even then writing *The Hobbit*. At nine John was a year older than most of the other 'new bugs' so he was put into Lower II along with thirteen older boys and a girl, five of them over ten and one more than eleven. Clifford advised him with typical mischief to mix with the masters as little as possible because all teachers had second-rate minds, and in later years John claimed that most of the masters had served in the trenches during the First World War and were warped by shell shock and battle fatigue. He also alleged that most of them were homosexual and tended to fall in love with the boys, but his Dragon contemporaries Mark Ramage and Richard Ollard, the historian and publisher, told me in 2004 that this was quite untrue. Sir Timothy Raison, who joined the Dragon just after John left in 1937 and went on to become an MP and Minister for Overseas Development in Mrs Thatcher's government, reported that he had been very happy at the school, as were most of the other pupils, and that life there was often brightened by moments of delightful eccentricity. One of the teachers, Tony 'Rats' Retey, was disconcerted when one of the boys in his class burst into tears as he was reading out the answers to their maths prep.

'What on earth is the matter, Richard?' he asked.

'It's my damned nanny,' sobbed the boy 'She *will* do my prep and she always gets it wrong.'

'The teachers were very good,' said Ollard, and Mortimer admitted that the Dragon was a progressive school for its time but claimed in his 1982 autobiography *Clinging to the Wreckage* – in which he gave all the teachers pseudonyms – that he had hated the icy dormitories and terrible food and felt very lonely and unhappy there, and he told his first wife that he had felt utterly betrayed by his parents when on his first night away from home Clifford celebrated his absence by buying Kath a new dress and taking her to a Noël Coward revue. Typically he blamed his mother, not his father, for his exile. 'He was certainly a loner,' said Ollard, who was seven months younger but sometimes in the same class, 'and although he and I were friends for a time I can't think of any other friends he had at the Dragon, but he wasn't visibly unhappy there and he wasn't bullied or beaten. There was not much beating in any case, and I don't think he ever got up to any pranks. He was just always sceptical of order.'

John claimed that he felt no particular affection for the school – whose Latin motto was *Arduus ad Solem* (By Strife Up to the Sun) – and remarked that to feel loyalty for a place where you paid to be taught was as silly as feeling loyal to Selfridges or Marks and Spencer. He would doubtless have sniggered at the words of the second verse of the school song, 'Carmen Draconiense':

> *Let us always keep heart in the strife*
> *While our wickets or goals are defended,*
> *For there always is hope while there's life,*
> *And the match isn't lost till it's ended!*
> *But whether we win or we lose,*
> *If we fight to the very last minute,*
> *The intent of the game is always the same –*
> *To strive that the Dragon may win it!*
> *Stand up and shout with a ring,*
> *Care to the wind let us fling,*
> *The Dragon above is the Dragon we love,*
> *So to the Dragon we sing!*

He told *The Times* in 1960 that he 'hated the hearty life in prep school' and the *Daily Telegraph* in 1998 that 'school was like Elizabethan England. One minute you were a duke, the other you were being cast into a dungeon. You were always having to slime up to someone.' Yet he was confident enough while he was there to order a monocle and silver-topped cane by mail order, longing to be Noël Coward or Fred Astaire dancing across a stage. In later years he returned often to the Dragon to help raise money for the school, sent one of his daughters there as a pupil, and contradicted himself completely when he told me in 1993: 'It was an incredibly good and formative school because they were very tolerant of me. They knew I didn't like playing anything which had to do with balls flying through the air so they sent me to the theatre. The Dragon taught you very good habits of working and thinking for yourself. We were very privileged.' In 2002 he wrote in the *Daily Mail* that he had been extremely lucky to go to a prep school where the pupils learned poetry by heart and put on a Shakespeare play every year. In 1991 he told Andrew Duncan of the *Sunday Express Magazine* that the Dragon 'was incredibly exciting. I didn't learn anything after I left there,' and in 1999 he told the *Independent*: 'It's an amazing school.' It is not always easy to know when Mortimer was telling the truth, neither in his books nor in his newspaper articles and interviews. Many years later his actress daughter Emily told newspaper interviewers that her father was a compulsive liar and he often said that the English were fascinating because they were so devious and never said what they meant.

He was certainly sufficiently settled at the Dragon by the end of his first term to come top of his class in English and fourth in maths, though he was only ninth in Latin and tenth in French. Unlike Lady Antonia Fraser, who was to join the Dragon a few years later and to play a fierce game of rugby, he did his best to avoid both rugby and skating, the two main winter sports, but there were plenty of other activities to keep him occupied, from dancing classes with C. H. 'Jacko' Jaques – '*chassé*, boy! *Chassé*, damn you!' – to the debating society and Sunday-evening lectures, slideshows and concerts for piano, violin and cello.

The Dragon's annual Shakespeare play that year was *A Midsummer Night's Dream*, which was staged at the beginning of his second term in January 1933. He did not have a part but was becoming fascinated by the theatre. 'I can't remember that he had any hobbies,' said Ollard, 'but he was very keen on anything to do with acting. The parts in the school plays were almost always played by the top English division and on the whole the junior boys did not play even the minor parts.' John claimed that instead of soiling himself by joining in the rugby, soccer, hockey, boxing and shooting that were on offer that term he would cycle instead into Oxford to buy the latest copy of *Theatre World*, but once again this may be untrue. 'Sport was compulsory,' said Ollard, 'and he would not have been allowed to go to the theatre instead.'

Like many a clever boy John seems to have become over-confident in his second term and skimped his work so that he slipped to eighth place in English. The only girl in his class, Christina Muir, was already outshining all the boys in almost every subject even though she was eight months younger than John, and while she came first in Classics he was only eighth. 'Christina was very clever and nice,' said Ollard, 'a brunette, quite pretty, but in those days he didn't have anything much to do with the girls.' When she also won first prize in the Easter holiday essay competition for a piece about *The Wind in the Willows* John seems to have taken up the challenge and worked hard enough in his third term to come first in English and Classics and to win the Lower II form prize for both.

Although he tried to avoid cricket, tennis, athletics and the school sports day that summer term of 1933 he could also enjoy lazy days of swimming, boating and messing about on the river as well as an all-day picnic on the Cherwell in June, an annual school holiday in honour of Old Dragon Jack Smyth to celebrate his winning of the Victoria Cross. John was taught to swim by the traditional Dragon method where a boy was dangled in the river supported by a belt on the end of a rope attached to a pole held by a master – which may have inspired the first of his recurring childhood nightmares in which he was about to be hanged. He continued his enjoyment of the river when he returned to Turville Heath for the summer and would cycle to the Thames at Henley, swim, punt and mooch about the locks a few miles from his father's new cottage, which was finished at last at a cost of £4,000 (£150,000). Turville Heath Cottage was built in the same beech woods as the Mortimers' rented weekend cottage – looking like a Spanish roadhouse, John said later – and all three Mortimers were to live there for the rest of their lives. It was a small, white, clapboard, green-roofed cottage hidden down a stony, leafy track off the main road to Stonor on the outskirts of Turville Heath. It had twenty acres of land on which Clifford and Kath created a beautiful garden with copses, apple and cherry trees, daffodils and narcissi, peaches, nectarines and asparagus.

They hired a cook, a butler and several gardeners and began to live a privileged life. John and his father would walk together through the woods and bracken and Clifford began to tell him stories, teach him chunks of poetry, pass on to him his love of words and literature and talk about his favourite books and authors – Shakespeare, Browning, Swinburne, Kipling, Rider Haggard, P. G. Wodehouse, Conan Doyle's Sherlock Holmes stories. They went to the cinema in Henley, with its glorious levitating organ, where they saw films starring Greta Garbo, Dorothy Lamour, Bing Crosby, Fred Astaire and Ginger Rogers. They went regularly to the theatre and especially to see every production at the Shakespeare Memorial Theatre in Stratford-upon-Avon, where they would sit in the front row of the stalls and Clifford would incense the actors by declaiming their lines a split-second before they did. When they went to the theatre in London they would eat first a five-course meal at the Trocadero in Piccadilly Circus or Quo Vadis in Dean Street and then arrive late in the front row of the stalls to cause the maximum disturbance to the rest of the audience. Among the highlights of John's childhood were performances by the young Laurence Olivier on stage, John Gielgud's Hamlet at the New Theatre in 1934, and the pantomime or the Crazy Gang in Brighton every Boxing Day when they went to spend Christmas in Sussex with his rich Uncle Harold and Aunt Daisy. John wrote off successfully for Gielgud's photograph. Fifty-five years later his idol would appear in a television mini-series he had written.

By the time he was ten his father was regaling him openly with all the sordid details of his divorce cases and told him once that he had just won a case by managing to prove adultery thanks to footprints found upside down on the dashboard of an Austin Seven parked in Hampstead Garden Suburb. The boy came to worship his father, whose vibrant personality was to dominate the rest of his life, and in 2005, at the age of eighty-two, Sir John Mortimer was living still in Turville Heath Cottage and sleeping still in the bed in which his father died. Yet in 1977 he told Mark Amory of *The Sunday Times* that his father 'wasn't all that nice to me really. We got on a lot but he was anxious not to have me there too much,' and when Alan Yentob interviewed him for one of his *Imagine* television documentaries in 2003 Mortimer told him: 'Childhood is a pretty tough period of life. It's a very hard thing to live through. Nobody takes you seriously.' Mortimer's son Jeremy told Yentob that 'when my father was growing up his father was not particularly interested in him and found him quite hard to relate to and didn't really know about children, so I think he found his father distant. I don't think they confided in each other. That wasn't really their style.' Mortimer told Yentob himself: 'I don't think my father would have said he loved me. I think it became clear to me that he did, and I certainly loved him, but I would never have said that. I was alone a lot of the holidays because my father didn't like visitors, so I had to invent my own company.' It was this cool, lonely, repressed childhood that moulded him as a writer, partly to attract attention, and that made him such a detached observer that he was always watching even himself as though he were a stranger – 'oh, look at him running up that field' – and he told Yentob: 'Writing is saying, "*Look at me, I'm dancing!*" ' The boy's favourite pastimes were equally to attract attention. He made sets for his model theatre, staged Punch and Judy shows, sang and tap-danced to tunes from musical films, and performed scenes from Shakespeare on his own on the dining-room stairs or a little stage in the garden, playing both Banquo and Macbeth, both Fred Astaire and Ginger Rogers. In a scene from *Hamlet* he even duelled with himself.

He also learned to cook because his mother was not much good at it, and gave his parents little menus in French. Another hobby was to sing along to Radio Luxembourg, beating time with his little drum kit or playing his banjo or kazoo, and in the evenings he and his parents would listen to the wireless: the news from London, or *In Town Tonight*, or Tommy Handley.

Many years later his stepdaughter Madelon's boyfriend David Leitch, who was later to become a distinguished *Sunday Times* journalist, decided that there was something sinister about John's childhood. 'When I went to Turville Heath with Madelon in about 1959,' Leitch told me in 2004, 'John told us that he was accustomed as a little boy to stand on this kind of double staircase wearing some dressing-up clothes and act plays for his parents. Sitting in that room, looking at that dark staircase, hearing this story, I didn't think, Oh, what a cute little boy, how amusing he must have been, what a happy, liberal, emancipated, educated family. I felt horror. I felt an intuitive frisson of something nasty there. There was an unpleasant atmosphere in the house and it's extraordinary that he should wish to live as an adult in the place that he'd lived as a child when it was such an unhappy place.'

There was certainly something sexually unusual in John's early years. In later life, two of his girlfriends told me, he liked being spanked with a hairbrush, and most psychologists agree that a man who develops a taste for masochistic sex has invariably been deeply wounded in childhood by parental neglect, lack of affection, aggression, a cold or hostile relationship with his mother, and a strongly incestuous Oedipal feeling of jealousy and sadistic anger towards his father which makes him feel so guilty that he needs to be punished. 'Fantasies of humiliation begin when the child decides he cannot affect the intolerable outer reality in which he lives,' wrote Nancy Friday in her study of *Men in Love*, and 'the masochist learns to love what he is expected to hate ... How this happens, how pain can be used to lead to orgasm, remains a mystery.' She added that a boy may well resent parents (like John's) who seem to care so little about him that they cannot even be bothered to lay down the firm rules against which all children need to test themselves. A masochist's parents (like Clifford) are generally egocentric, moody, unpredictable, ambivalent, insensitive and simply ignorant of how to be a good parent, Cheryl Glickhauf-Hughes and Marolyn Wells reported in their book *Treatment of the Masochistic Personality*. 'Quite often,' they wrote, 'parents of masochists are uncontrolled, controlling individuals who behave like tyrannical children' – a perfect description of Clifford Mortimer. As for masochists' mothers, they are often seen by the world to be saintly – 'kind, self-sacrificing, and devoted but behave towards their child in an abusive and self-centred manner' – a perfect description of Kath Mortimer. As Esther Menaker wrote in her book *Masochism and the Emergent Ego*, 'in the absence of adequate maternal love, the mother–child relationship can become a contest, a battleground in which the weak can only win by implementing a mechanism of submissiveness.'

Alvin Rakoff, who was to direct the television film version of Mortimer's play about Clifford, *A Voyage Round My Father*, told me that John confessed to him then that his father used to assault his mother. 'He would swear at her, grab her and beat her,' said Rakoff. 'He wasn't the nice old codger you see in the film. John mentioned it more than once.' Maybe he saw his father beat his mother and connected that with sex, or maybe he felt guilty that he had not loved her enough, or maybe she used to spank him with a hairbrush. Whatever the case, there is some fascinating dialogue in the script that John was to write many years later for the first episode of his television adaptation of Evelyn Waugh's novel *Brideshead Revisited*. The Oxford undergraduate Sebastian Flyte buys a hard hairbrush in a barber's shop and says he needs it to spank his teddy bear, Aloysius. When he leaves the shop the barber chuckles that Mr Flyte is a most amusing young man and once turned up in the shop wearing a false beard, whereupon another undergraduate remarks that Sebastian is obviously jealous of his father because beards and teddy bears are Freudian father symbols and wanting to spank his teddy bear indicated guilty Oedipal feelings for his mother. Rubbish, maybe, but it was rubbish that John included in his script, and he was for the rest of his life to mistrust any sort of authority and to resist any kind of discipline or punishment, even for criminals.

Back at the Dragon at the end of 1933 he was again top of the class in English but eleventh in Classics even though he was nearly eleven and the boy who came first was only just eight. In the first term of 1934 John was first in English again but it was clever little Christina Muir who once again won the holiday essay competition. Nor did John ever win a prize for keeping a summer holiday diary and Christina won yet again in 1935. Perhaps he was too preoccupied with sex to bother to write, for by now he had developed a crush on the French actress Annabella as well as on Ginger Rogers, Deanna Durbin and Greta Garbo; he had discovered masturbation and embraced it eagerly with both hands; and he had taken a shine at school to a blond boy whom he hugged in the school museum and decided he loved.

Considering John's enthusiasm for Shakespeare and the theatre it seems extraordinary that he was never given a part in the annual Shakespeare plays that were put on at the Dragon each January nor in the Gilbert and Sullivan musicals each September until finally he landed the lead in *Richard II* in 1937. 'I really wanted to be an actor most of all,' he told me in 1993. 'It wasn't until I was about fifteen or sixteen that I decided that I would be a writer. But I wanted also to be a musical comedy star, to tap-dance and sing and wear a white tie and tails – it was the chance to show off, mainly – but I couldn't do any of those things. I was incredibly stage-struck, which I've always been, mainly because my parents took me to the theatre from the time that I was really young, and at my prep school I had the seating plans of all the London theatres.' He did win a minor form prize, a copy of *Gulliver's Travels*, for coming first in both English and French when he was eleven, but otherwise his Dragon career was curiously undistinguished until the very end – unlike the budding careers of a gang of youngsters who had just joined the school, among them Robert Armstrong, a future Head of the Civil Service; Humphry Berkeley, a future MP and author of the gloriously funny spoof letters *The Life and Death of Rochester Sneath* in 1974; Patrick Jenkin, a future Conservative Cabinet Minister; John Kendrew, a future Nobel Prizewinner for Chemistry; and Janet Young, a future Conservative Leader of the House of Lords.

In the summer of 1935 the school celebrated King George V's jubilee with a special supper, singsong and fireworks display, and published *The Dragon Book of Verse*, an anthology compiled by W. A. C. and N. H. Wilkinson, which included many of the poems that young Mortimer was learning by heart to add to those that his father loved and taught him: 'Up the Airy Mountain' by William Allingham and 'You Are Old, Father William' by Lewis Carroll. John was also building his literary foundation by reading Dickens, Wodehouse and Sapper's Bulldog Drummond, but for him the main and terrible event of that year was that Clifford finally went blind. John sometimes said that it happened when his father was climbing a ladder to prune an apple tree at Turville Heath, bumped his head against a branch, and both retinas slipped off the back of his eyes to leave him in sudden complete darkness, which is how the tragedy was depicted in the television version of *A Voyage Round My Father* in which Laurence Olivier played Clifford. But in fact it happened when Clifford was climbing out of a London taxi and banged his head against the door frame. 'The apple tree version in the film was my idea because it was more visual,' Alvin Rakoff told me. 'I talked him into it.' Nobody bothered to tell the twelve-year-old boy that his father could no longer see: he found out only when he noticed his mother putting toothpaste on his father's brush for him. Nor did anyone ever speak about Clifford's blindness. This was a seriously undemonstrative family and Clifford was determined that no one should feel sorry for him, so everyone simply pretended that nothing had happened at all. Kath gave up for ever all hope of painting seriously and devoted the rest of her life to looking after him, and he continued with unbelievable courage to work as a barrister and appear in court. To help him she would read *The Times* law reports and his divorce briefs out to him every weekday as they travelled by train from Henley to his chambers in London, startling the other occupants of the first-class compartment by describing loudly in vivid detail the latest lurid marital accusations of cruelty, adultery and disgusting practices. Clifford would learn by heart page after page of documents and appear in the Law Courts as often as before, tapping with his stick along the corridors and mesmerising witnesses with his glazed, empty eyes. His memory was amazing. 'When I was a boy I saw him in court once and it was a phenomenal performance of memory,' an eminent QC told me. 'He'd remembered an entire bundle of correspondence and particular pages and paragraphs so that he was able to say to the witness: "Turn to page so-and-so, look at the second paragraph, and you'll see that what you've just said was wrong." He was extraordinary.'

His dreadful disability and complete dependence on his wife made Clifford even nastier, less considerate and worse tempered. 'I was always rather proud of my father that when he went blind he never turned to God,' Mortimer told me once. 'He just continued to ignore God. Why didn't he curse God and throw terrible rages at the universe? But his tempers were all about soft-boiled eggs and cold plates and the tray being late!' So Clifford carried on shouting at Kath, waiters and porters, making scenes in public and behaving as selfishly as ever. In the Law Courts everyone thought he was an absolute bastard and she was an angel, yet 'what intrigued me was how a blind man could beat a sighted woman,' said Alvin Rakoff. 'My impression was that John was too young to intervene. It must have affected him terribly.' John was in fact almost a teenager, an age when most boys who saw or heard their father assaulting their mother would at least protest, and if John failed to do so out of cowardice it would have left him with a lifelong psychological scar.

Instead of cursing God, Mortimer claimed, Clifford took his revenge by sitting in the garden on summer evenings, despite his blindness, trapping and drowning dozens of earwigs at a time in a bucket of water.

As the years went by he began to ease off his legal work and spend more
and more time in his beloved garden, where he would sniff the flowers
and hide in the shrubbery if he heard visitors. There was a terrible
poignancy about his fate and stoicism. When lost for words or deeply
unhappy he would suddenly sing in a tremulous voice one of the old
music hall ditties of his youth, perhaps his favourite one of all, 'Pretty
Polly Perkins of Paddington Green':

> *She was as beautiful as a butterfly*
> *And as proud as a queen*
> *Was pretty little Polly Perkins*
> *Of Paddington Green.*

John helped to carry some of the burden of his father's blindness. He read
to him for hours – books, newspapers, divorce papers – and took his hand
on his arm to guide him on their walks, describing the colour and texture
of the flowers in the garden when his father urged him to 'paint me the
picture'. Clifford's blindness was to have a huge impact on his son's life
because it was to make John feel that it was his duty to follow in his
footsteps and try to achieve all the things that his father could no longer
achieve himself. 'He might have done so much had he not gone blind,'
John told Peter Fiddick of the *Guardian* in 1970. 'He was about to take
silk and become a judge. He was a much better lawyer than I am.
Sometimes I sit as a judge and I ask myself why I do it, and I think the
answer is because he should have done and couldn't.'

As a weapon against the darkness Clifford became at times even more
outrageous than before. 'Travel narrows the mind,' he would announce.
'All advice is useless ... Love has been greatly over-estimated by the
poets ... I've never had a mistress with thighs like white marble ... All
education's quite useless but it fills in the time ... You don't mean anyone
actually *likes* music?'

Years later John's first wife, Penelope, complained that Clifford and
John never said anything serious to each other but hid their feelings by
making jokes, telling stories and playing silly games. 'But I don't regard
that as an insult,' John told Melvyn Bragg on *The South Bank Show* in
1986, 'because that's a very English way of behaving. The English way
of dealing with disaster, which was my father's way of dealing with his
blindness, was to make jokes and sing songs and never discuss it under
any circumstances, and that seems to be an admirable way of coping with
those things. I really do believe that a certain levity in the face of life is

not only important and appropriate but quite courageous.'

John returned to the Dragon at the beginning of 1936 to discover that Christina Muir had now won yet another prize, for an essay on *Lorna Doone*, as well as a drawing prize, and in the summer term she won no fewer than four more prizes for writing and art. John took up painting himself and in the final term of 1936 bounced back by coming first in Classics and second in English and Maths, though this may have been because he was by now far and away the oldest in the class, well over thirteen and a half – old enough to be given a checked sports coat and a silk tie that Christmas – and most pupils of his own age had moved on to their public schools so that his strongest rivals were no longer at the Dragon. He had grown very tall and gangly and while he was nearly fourteen all but two of the others in his class were only eleven or twelve. Perhaps because he had no real opposition of his own age John was made a prefect at last and chosen to play the lead in Shakespeare's poetic tragedy *Richard II*, the story of the sensitive, intelligent but weak, egotistical, untrustworthy and self-pitying king who was murdered at Pontefract Castle in 1400. 'It was very exciting,' he told me in 1993 – so exciting that more than fifty years later, despite all his books, plays, legal triumphs, sexual conquests and knighthood, he claimed that it was the single most important achievement of his whole life. 'There has been no happiness like it,' he told Andrew Duncan. 'I heard the other day that my rival for the part has never been happy since.' His rival was Mark Ramage, the twelve-year-old son of the celebrated actress Catherine Nesbitt, who was nearly a year younger than Mortimer and indeed furious not to land the lead but to have to play Bolingbroke instead. 'I remember being *deeply* wounded at the time,' Ramage told me in 2004. 'I've never forgiven the master responsible, "Cheese" Vassall, who did the casting. The year before I had done Shylock and Vassall said that the following year I could do Richard II. For all I know I might have been cast entirely because of my mother but I began to learn bits of the part and then he rang me in the holidays and said, "I've changed my mind, I'm getting Mortimer to do it instead." I was *livid* with him. I've no idea why he changed his mind. Mind you, I remember that Mortimer was exceptionally good. He *looked* the part terribly well because he was so tall and thin.' Ramage was to become a Colonial Office civil servant and then an advertising executive.

John's two appearances in *Richard II*, a matinée and an evening performance on Saturday 23 January 1937, were memorable, reported 'Jacko' Jaques in his history of the school, *A Dragon Century*. 'Is it possible that of all Shakespeare's leading characters King Richard comes nearest to being within the compass of an intelligent thirteen-year-old actor?' he asked. 'Perhaps the answer is that in this second Richard we had a king who never grew up.' Mortimer himself wrote in the Royal Society of Literature's magazine *Letters* in 1992 that his death scene was the greatest triumph of his life – 'Mount, mount, my soul! Thy seat is up on high / Whilst my gross flesh sinks downward, here to die' – and more than fifty years later he could still recite all thirty-four lines of Richard's soliloquy that includes the lines:

> *For God's sake, let us sit upon the ground*
> *And tell sad stories of the death of kings:*
> *How some have been deposed, some slain in war,*
> *Some haunted by the ghosts they have deposed,*
> *Some poisoned by their wives, some sleeping killed;*
> *All murdered: for within the hollow crown*
> *That rounds the mortal temples of a king*
> *Keeps Death his court, and there the antick sits,*
> *Scoffing his state and grinning at his pomp; . . .*

The Draconian magazine of April 1937 carried four pages of photographs and no fewer than four reviews of the play, an astonishingly professional production with lavish costumes and scenery, a fourteen-piece orchestra, and Richard Ollard playing the First Gardener. Mortimer was 'excellent', said a local Old Dragon, John Gamlen, in his review. 'He understood the poetry of his lines, spoke them beautifully, and was every inch a king.' Miriam Bullard agreed although she felt that at times his performance was a little cold and remote: he 'gave a kingly and beautifully spoken interpretation of the part [and] his ease on the stage was good to watch; so was his absolute composure in those picturesque but irksome robes in which the kings of those days – presumably – went to battle with Irish rebels or tossed on breaking seas [and] in the final prison-scene he *was* warm, flinging away his life with a careless gallantry that struck just the right note.' The third reviewer, Neil Wylie, another Old Dragon, wrote that John 'looked every inch a king' and that it was impossible to speak too highly of his performance: 'He provided the title and the poetry and all that was best in the play. He may disapprove of my saying all that without spicing it with a word of criticism, but there my ingenuity fails me and I cannot think of anything to criticise.' The writer and publisher Frank Sidgwick commended the 'striking brilliance' of Mortimer and Ramage as the two main characters: 'The School is to be congratulated on having discovered Mortimer and cast him for the King. He looked the part, every inch; stood and moved well, and wore his robes nobly.' He also spoke well and demonstrated 'a fine appreciation of blank verse and – a still rarer gift – an admirable skill in rendering the rhythm, the rise and fall, the pulsations of the long poetical speeches. I am told that this is likely to be his only appearance on the Dragon stage, which is much to be deplored.' Even the university dons' journal, the *Oxford Magazine*, reported that John's performance had 'much pathos and dignity … he had learned how to move like a king'. Clifford must have felt a sharp twinge of bitterness that he could not see his son's acclaimed performance in one of his beloved Shakespeare plays.

Less happy were John's academic results in that final term at the Dragon. Although he was so much older than most of his classmates he came only third in English, ninth in Classics and tenth in French. In January he did have a very short story published in *The Draconian* – a two-paragraph squib called 'The Night Mail' in which a sinister stranger boards a train and terrifies his fellow passengers with ghoulish stories about murder – and in March it printed another piece of his writing, just one paragraph, 'Night', describing a dark, sinister country scene. But otherwise John's career at the Dragon was surprisingly dull for a boy who was considered extremely bright and it seems odd that in 2004 none of his surviving Dragon contemporaries except Richard Ollard and Mark Ramage could remember anything about him. Even Ramage said: 'I can't remember him particularly except that he was very tall and thin.' Except for his final burst of glory in *Richard II* he left barely a ripple. 'No, he didn't shine,' said Ollard. 'He was undistinguished at the Dragon.'

Before he left the school in March 1937 he and the other leavers were given a sex talk by Hum Lynam's father and predecessor as headmaster, Charles 'Skipper' Lynam, who warned them to beware of 'dreams' at night and of boys who wanted to be 'friends', and especially of anyone who might offer them a seductive piece of cake. Cake, especially, said Skipper sternly, should always be resisted. Thus armed against the big, wide, wicked world, John Mortimer stepped confidently into adolescence, and Christina Muir sailed on to become a Leading Wren in the Royal Navy.

Two

Sex, Lies and Harrow
1937–1940

Mortimer was baffled that his father chose to send him to Harrow after the Dragon, despite its reputation as a major English public school and its roll-call of distinguished Old Harrovians, among them Sheridan, Palmerston, Byron, Peel, Manning, Trollope and Churchill. It was not nearly as intellectual or aesthetic as Eton, and John was both; it was extremely sporty, which John was not; and it was renowned for turning out louche, slightly disreputable young men. Yet Mortimer was 'a classic Harrovian', David Leitch told me, and John admitted to Lynda Lee-Potter of the *Daily Mail* in 1988 that Old Harrovians 'are all vulgar, wear suede shoes, drive fast cars'. Even so, he said, 'I'm not averse to vulgarity. I don't condemn people for having coach lamps around their swimming pool. I quite like awfulness, anything that makes me laugh is absolutely fine with me. I can forgive anybody if they make me laugh.'

As a committed hater of God he must at least have been delighted to learn that the school had been built on a spot that had been famous in the sixth century as the foremost site of heathen worship in all England. It is a scattered north-west London village of impressive old buildings that sit astride the High Street of Harrow-on-the-Hill and perch on a healthy hilltop between Wembley and the open countryside of Hertfordshire, where on a clear day you can see to the south the Houses of Parliament and St Paul's Cathedral ten miles away and to the west and south as far as Windsor Castle and Hampton Court if you use binoculars. Young Mortimer joined five hundred other boys for the second term of 1937 on 30 April, a week after his fourteenth birthday, and was enrolled in the Grove boarding house – where his housemaster was Leonard Henry, a wounded veteran of the First World War – and the Classical Shell class, where he was to study Greek as well as Latin, English, French, History, Geography and (horror of horrors) Divinity.

Sandy Wilson, who was a year younger than John, joined the school a term later and would become famous as a lyricist and composer of several musicals, among them *The Boy Friend*, was greatly impressed by the school. 'Harrow seemed incredibly free,' he wrote in his autobiography *I Could Be Happy*. 'It was wonderful to be able to go out into the street whenever one felt like it, visit a shop or have a meal in a café. Instead of sleeping in a dormitory, I shared a whole room with one other boy, in which we could have our own furniture, pictures and books, and where we slept in beds which folded up behind a curtain by day, so that one had the feeling of a grown-up sitting-room.' For Wilson, a scholarship boy, even the work was relaxed. 'We did have to do Early Morning School for an hour before breakfast, but we had three half-holidays a week ... and instead of classes in the evening we only had preparation in the house. During our ample leisure we were free to do as we pleased, without being spied upon, and there were numerous clubs and societies to join.' He admitted that there was some bullying 'and some of the monitors made "fagging" for them an unpleasant chore; but on the whole, for most of the time I was there, I found Harrow a tolerant and easy-going place, where individuality was rarely discouraged and where, provided you did not flagrantly break the rules, you could live life pretty much as you pleased'. When a boy reached the age of fifteen he was even allowed to drink alcohol and at least it was rare for a monitor to beat younger boys as they had in earlier decades, when a junior could be thrashed by a senior for letting his fire go out or burning a piece of toast. 'As in any institution of such age, there were some absurd traditions, particularly in respect of dress,' Wilson added, 'and a complicated system of privileges for seniority; but ... that could be taken as being part of our education.' In 2004 Sandy Wilson told me: 'I had reservations about Harrow, the compulsory sport and all that, but looking back on it I think it was wonderful and I owe a great deal to it, particularly to the teachers.'

The school's myriad dress codes were indeed ludicrous. The formal uniform consisted of a white flannel shirt with a stiff collar, black tie, light-coloured cashmere trousers, black waistcoat, tailcoat or blue blazer and top hat or straw boater. Each summer term a boy was allowed to unfasten another button of his blazer. After three years he could wear coloured socks, a flower in his buttonhole and a white scarf, and after

four years he could sport a flower with leaves. A member of the elite
sporting Philathletic Club committee was allowed shiny buttons, bow
tie, coloured waistcoat and to show more than eight inches of shirt
front. Each sport, house and house team had its own distinctive
clothing and every year the boys were expected to excite the ridicule
of their fellow Tube passengers by travelling into London to watch the
annual cricket match against Eton at Lord's wearing top hat and tails
and carrying a silver-topped cane with a blue tassel. A beady-eyed,
left-wing cynic like young Mortimer must have considered all this
folderol to be utterly ridiculous and he rebelled by joining the
Communist Party, which was particularly popular in Britain at that
time because of public outrage at the ruthless bombing of Guernica
during the Spanish Civil War by the German Nazis on 26 April, just
four days before he joined Harrow. 'I had a one-boy Communist cell,'
he told Nigel Farndale of the *Sunday Telegraph* in 2001, 'and I got
instructions to slow down production on my factory floor. So I told
my fellow pupils to translate Virgil more slowly' — a story that sounds
more like a Mortimer joke than reality.

Harrovians also spoke a distinctive slang in which a sports star was
a 'blood', a bath a 'tosh', a blazer a 'bluer', a swot a 'groize', a senior
boy a 'priv', a quick snack a 'swipe'. Another tradition that he found
irritating was the singing at least three times a term of hallowed
school songs that oozed with nostalgia, sentimentality, love of sport
and pride in the school. Mortimer boasted all his life that he had
never felt any team spirit or loyalty towards any institution, not even
the Labour Party, and the school song, 'Forty Years On', an anthem
that managed to combine a worship of God, football and Harrow and
was sung on most big school occasions, made him cringe with
embarrassment:

> *God gave us bases to guard or beleaguer,*
> *Games to play out, whether earnest or fun;*
> *Fights for the fearless and goals for the eager*
> *Twenty and thirty and forty years on! . . .*
> *O the great days, in the distance enchanted,*
> *Days of fresh air, in the rain and the sun.*
> *How we rejoiced as we struggled and panted*
> *Hardly believable forty years on!*

Then there was a song about rugby:

Play up! Does it matter who wins or who loses?
Play up and play hard all the same.
There's plenty of bumps and plenty of bruises:
They'll teach you much more than a game.
On, on, on, on,
Take strength and good temper and courage and speed.
On, on, on, on,
They're not a bad outfit for life and its need.

A military song called 'Left, Right' began thus:

Young Brown, he was a little boy and barely four foot four
But his manly bosom burned to join the Harrow Rifle Corps.

Mortimer's own manly bosom burned only with a deep dislike of Harrow right from the start and later he claimed that because its pupils were all rich and male it had seriously delayed his emotional development. 'I hated it,' he told Lynda Lee-Potter in 1970. 'There were long, boring periods when nothing happened. I was bored to hell. I used to grow mustard and cress in my top hat and nobody took any notice, which was maddening.' He decided to become a dandy, bought a silver cigarette case, and claimed that from time to time he wore a monocle, but his contemporary Tony Murray told me that 'he wouldn't have been allowed to wear a monocle and I don't believe the story about the mustard and cress'. Nor did Sandy Wilson, who said 'that's just absolute idiocy', and another schoolfellow, Dick Willis, agreed: 'I think that's fiction, just wishful thinking.' Although smoking at Harrow was forbidden 'I thought I was very elegant smoking cigarettes and tapping them on the side of a silver case,' he told Caroline Bridgwood of the *Sunday Mirror* in 1987. 'I thought I was Lord Peter Wimsey' – yet he claimed to loathe the class-conscious snobbery at Harrow, where at roll-call the boys all had to answer to their surnames alone but the son of a Lord would be called 'Mr'. He shared his first study with a boy about whom another warned him not to make friends because 'his parents have side plates at dinner', which came as a major shock to John because his own parents always had side plates at dinner.

In later years he complained often about his parents' cold-heartedness in sending him to Harrow and liked to tell the story of the British officer in a Japanese prisoner-of-war camp who remarked to another: 'Cheer up, it's not nearly as bad as Harrow', which was why 'public schoolboys are always so calm when they're being tried at the Old Bailey', he told the *Daily Mail* in 1982. 'They know nothing can be so bad as their schooldays. Working-class boys shake and burst into tears at the thought of leaving home and going to prison.' He hated the food – 'terrible fish,' he said – and told Chloe Diski of the *Observer* in 2004: 'The food was simply disgusting. I remember the footman, wearing a blue tailcoat with gold buttons, bleeding into the cabbage as he served it to us.' He hated the head boy, who was also head monitor of the Grove, a 'blood' who played for the school rugby and football teams, and whom Mortimer called 'Keswick' in his autobiography, describing him as a bully and a fascist even though he was to go on to reach the rank of Major while fighting fascism during the Second World War. Mortimer said he also hated having to share his study with a wild, violent boy whom he called 'Tainton' in his autobiography and who by some curious coincidence also apparently grew mustard and cress on his top hat. 'I joined the Grove the same term as Mortimer and there wasn't anyone there like "Tainton",' David Henley-Welch told me. 'We would have heard about it. And I don't think he ever wore a monocle. I think John made up quite a few things about Harrow.'

You would think that if young Mortimer were indeed an eccentric who wore a monocle, carried a silver cigarette case, grew mustard and cress in his top hat, and received orders from the Kremlin, he would quickly have become famous in the school, but two of his contemporaries – Nico Craven and Captain Tony Hunter – do not remember him at all even though both were in his house. 'He must have made remarkably little impact,' said Capt. Hunter. One who did remember him well was Angus Stroyan, who was eighteen months younger, also in the Grove, and went on to become a QC and judge. 'I don't think people noticed Mortimer very much,' Stroyan told me in 2004. 'He was never a tremendously popular boy and never became a house monitor, still less a school monitor, and he never really got anywhere in the House. He was obviously a very bright boy, a little sarcastic and very chippy, a bit of a loner. Harrow wasn't a brutal school but I think Mortimer would have said it was philistine. I don't think it *was* but his view was that there were an awful lot of oiks there. I think he hated it because there wasn't anybody who loved him, really. I didn't like him and I don't suppose he liked me. I don't think he liked many people, which is why not many people liked him. He didn't find any real friends and he was rather pitied because he wasn't any good at games, and he didn't like being pitied, and he may have felt that he was being looked down on.' Yet Sandy

Wilson pointed out to me that although he had never been any good at sport either he had not been made to feel inferior because of that: 'I don't think it was anything to do with that, it was just that Mortimer's personality was very forbidding.'

Sir Rupert Buchanan-Jardine, who was two months older than Mortimer and in the same class during his first term, told me: 'He was highly intelligent but a loner who always seemed to be on his own and didn't mix with others.' Seven other contemporaries – Forest Ellvers, Godfrey Royle, David Henley (who later changed his name to Henley-Welch), Sir Dermot de Trafford, Brian Straton-Ferrier, Dick Willis and Sandy Wilson – also remembered that John was very much a loner. 'He was standoffish,' Wilson told me. 'We were only in the same form for one year, in 1939, and he sat at the back and didn't seem to want to communicate with anybody. Once the class was over he disappeared. He didn't seem to talk to anybody or to be interested in anything and he made no effort. I didn't dislike him, I just felt, well, if you feel like that, to hell with you.' Straton-Ferrier agreed: 'He was very supercilious,' he told me, and Forest Ellvers said that John 'would hang about in the corridors and give a cynical grin now and then. He was also scruffy and not very clean, and some people thought he was a bit of a shit.' Godfrey Royle agreed. 'He wasn't terribly popular because he was always making snide remarks,' he said, 'and he was a troublemaker and two-faced. When you told him off for something he'd blame someone else. He was also a bit unclean.'

Each house had a butler and two footmen who served meals. 'We used to have these open fires in our rooms at night,' said Royle, 'and Mortimer banked his fire up so high that when the house butler, George, came round John had made the poker red hot and poor old George suffered a burned finger. He was full of schoolboy pranks like that.' Mortimer told a different version of the story: in two of his autobiographies he claimed that the sadistic villain had been his roommate 'Tainton'.

David Henley, who was three months younger than John but a monitor (prefect) in the Grove and went on to captain Harrow at cricket, to play football and rugby for the school and cricket and golf for Oxford University, was less critical. 'Mortimer was rather colourless at Harrow and very strange,' he told me. 'He was a nonentity there and not really noticeable, and I can't think of anybody who was one of his friends, but I've always envied him his brain power and when I got to know him I quite liked him. He was quite amusing to talk to. Because I was a monitor I had to make him play games sometimes and it was a nightmare to see the poor chap hanging about behind the scrum, not knowing what to do. He had to play once a week and I remember him looking totally miserable and feeling rather a cad for making him play. But he was always against authority, and if he hated Harrow it was probably just because there was some authority. I and most of my friends enjoyed it.'

Sir Dermot de Trafford, who was two years younger than Mortimer but also in the Grove and went on to play rugby for Harrow, agreed that John 'was the sort of person who objected to authority, very much an odd man out and unpopular because he didn't like sports. He tended to look scruffy and he was once given a compulsory house tosh – thrown into the bath – because they thought he wasn't clean enough and didn't bath enough.' Sandy Wilson agreed that Mortimer was 'rather scruffy' and Sir Rupert said that he had been unhygienic. 'He never looked very clean,' he said, and another contemporary, Tony Murray, confirmed that 'he *was* a bit dirty but it all went with the gangly image. His trousers were always flying at half-mast and he was not exactly good-looking, very thin with a slightly crooked face in that his teeth and jaw were slightly Hapsburg, and very thick pebble glasses.'

John had in fact at least four friends at Harrow – Christopher Bulstrode, Gerald Howard-Smith, Michael Whidborne and Rupert Waterlow – but by 2004 they were all dead and I could find only two of his Harrow contemporaries who got on really well with him, Dr Ted Bott and Dick Willis, an artistic boy a year younger than John who was also in the Grove and had two pictures exhibited at the Royal Academy while he was still at the school, the youngest person to have done so then. 'John was the only person that I could consider congenial in my house and we got on very well together,' Willis told me. 'Nor did I like Harrow at all. I thought it was a dreadful place. I liked him because we were both iconoclasts on principle and we hated the fagging business. It was degrading having to work for other people when you despised them and they weren't very much older than oneself. John was very cunning and managed to get away with it without actually getting beaten. I liked him because we were both outsiders because I was in the arts school all the time and he was an academic and very clever. We used to fill ourselves up in the house lunch and then go down to the tuckshop and fill ourselves up even more with two eggs, bacon and chips. At one stage he couldn't get his usual tangerine drink and said to the girl: "What is this place? A concentration camp?" We would spend endless amounts in the tuckshop, where you could spend as much as you liked. He never became a prefect but hovered like me in the hinterland where people younger than he were giving him orders.'

When it came to the teachers at Harrow Mortimer admitted that some of them were excellent. He admired his English master, the Revd. Ian Venables, who stimulated him and introduced him to Wordsworth, whose poems stirred Mortimer to an almost religious pantheism. He also liked the teacher who ran the Art Society, John Nash, who would cycle off with his pupils to draw churches, paint watercolours and (according to two of Mortimer's autobiographies) to drink gin and lime in country pubs. 'That's quite untrue,' I was told by Dick Willis. 'He didn't take us to pubs. We had cream teas, not gin,' and Sandy Wilson, who also took art, told me that Mortimer's gin-and-lime story was sheer invention. John also got on extremely well with his frail housemaster and history teacher, Leonard Henry, a history scholar who had studied at Brasenose College, Oxford, joined the Inns of Court Regiment in the First World War, and been invalided out of the army after being gassed. 'He looked bloody sick, with a nasty yellow skin,' Capt. Hunter told me, but 'Leonard Henry was a very nice chap and the Grove was a very happy house,' I was told by another contemporary, Bryan Routledge. Harrow's headmaster, Paul Vellacott, was also a genial fellow, another history scholar who had played hockey for Cambridge University and come down with a first-class degree, become a Brigade-Major during the First World War, and been wounded and taken prisoner. 'He was very popular and easygoing,' said Sir Rupert Buchanan-Jardine.

There is always the possibility that Mortimer may have had an unpleasant homosexual experience at Harrow that might explain his lifelong dislike of the school, his wariness of men and his adoration of women. He claimed that homosexuality was rife at Harrow and told Alice Thomson of the *Daily Telegraph* in 1998 that 'it was a totally gay world. You could have any boy for a box of Cadbury's milk chocolate.' Boys in the Grove would bath together naked, two in a bath – 'the whole thing was fraught with danger!' said Dick Willis – and one of John's schoolfriends once said to him 'I don't know if I'm ever going to be able to take breasts' so that John reckoned that for many Old Harrovians the ideal woman was a boy with a bosom. So did Mortimer ever succumb to the temptation of a box of Cadbury's milk chocolate? 'I can't think so,' said Sandy Wilson. 'He was desperately unattractive!' But Sir Dermot de Trafford told me that homosexuality was indeed widespread. John admitted in his autobiography that he went through a homosexual phase at Harrow and in 2004 he told the *Mail on Sunday* magazine that 'homosexuality was the only thing on offer at public school. Yes, I suppose I did indulge in a mild sort of way.'

The highlight of his first term should have been the coronation of King George VI on 12 May and the celebratory firework display three days later, but much more memorable was the school chaplain who advised him that if he started to feel fond of another boy he should jump into a cold bath and cry, '*Down, Stan!*' He was delighted to discover that another rebel, Lord Byron, had written poetry as he lay on a tombstone in the churchyard and that his Turkish slippers and dagger were kept in the library, and he consoled himself by buying a first edition of Byron's work from a local antiquarian bookseller.

At the end of his second term one of the five Old Dragons at Harrow wrote to *The Draconian* to report that 'Mortimer, our newest recruit, is very reticent about his doings, but we hear from other sources that he is an English scholar of no small renown'. When he returned to Turville Heath for Christmas his father was disappointed to hear that Harrow was not at all like Rugby and *Tom Brown's Schooldays*. 'Don't they roast you at school at all?' he asked. 'Can't imagine what I'm paying all that for in school fees if they don't *roast* you a little from time to time.'

In John's third term, at the start of 1938, 'we had to play football', said Sandy Wilson in his autobiography – Harrow Footer, a complicated version of football – 'but only if we were picked for a team; other afternoons, provided we were out of the house for an hour or so, we could take what exercise we pleased.' John's idea of taking exercise was to hide in the art room or read in the lavatories under the Fives court, though the threat of a war with Hitler's Germany did encourage him to join the Officers' Training Corps and to go on unlikely manoeuvres at Aldershot with the Brigade of Guards. Not that he would have been much use against the Nazi tanks. As he loitered on one imaginary field of battle a Guards officer rode up on horseback and cried: 'Bang, bang! You're dead!' Now and then he was forced by his head of house to play footer but usually, since he was so bad at the game, he was allowed just to change into footer clothes and forbidden to enter the house for an hour until the games were over.

At the start of John's second year at Harrow in May 1938 he was promoted to the Classical Remove class but although there was a school production of *The Tempest* in June and a new edition of the annual literary magazine, *Harrow*, he featured in neither, though he did enter unsuccessfully for the Junior Crompton Prize for Clear Speaking and *The Draconian* back in Oxford reported that he was 'still working hard for the

School Certificate and still retains a reputation for being a beautiful speaker and a good English scholar'.

It was a tense summer as Hitler threatened to march into Czechoslovakia and Europe teetered on the brink of war. 'We were all of us thoroughly scared,' wrote Sandy Wilson in his autobiography. 'We had seen newsreels of aerial bombing in Spain and China and we were terrified that it might soon happen here,' but a week after the start of the new term in September the British Prime Minister, Neville Chamberlain, signed an agreement with Hitler at Berchtesgaden and flew back to London to announce 'peace in our time' and to be hailed for a few sad months as the saviour of Europe. Mortimer and Wilson had both been promoted to the Lower Fifth, where their form master was Ronald Watkins, a Shakespearean scholar who was guiding them that term through their School Certificate set play, *Macbeth*. 'One afternoon soon after the beginning of term we were sitting in our classroom, waiting for him to arrive,' said Wilson. 'Suddenly we heard a sound of cheering from the other rooms in the building. The door flew open and Ronnie burst in. "Chamberlain has signed a pact with Hitler and Mussolini," he announced jubilantly. "He says it's Peace in Our Time!" The feeling of relief was indescribable. We all joined in the cheering.' In later years Wilson, like so many other Britons, was ashamed of his reaction to what turned out to be a betrayal of the Czechs. 'Of course there were political reasons,' he wrote. 'There was betrayal, conspiracy, compromise and sheer muddle. But the over-riding motive was plain, abject fear.'

It was during the next year, 1939, that Mortimer suddenly started to make an impact at Harrow even though none of his contemporaries could remember his triumphs sixty-five years later. In February he won second prize in the junior section of the Lady Bouchier Reading competition, which was judged by Sir Arthur Quiller-Couch, the professor of English Literature at Cambridge, who had edited *The Oxford Book of English Verse*. John read two pieces – one of them particularly appropriate considering his future profession as a barrister, 'The Honourable Profession of the Law' by Jonathan Swift – and 'Mortimer's restrained interpretation of Tennyson's "The Splendour Falls" had a special appeal, for he seemed appreciative of the slender quality of this ever-delightful piece,' reported the school's weekly four-page newspaper *The Harrovian* the following week.

At the start of the summer term, in the first week of May, Ronnie Watkins gave each of his Lower Fifth English class a section of their School Certificate Greek set play *Medea* to translate into English blank verse and announced that they would then produce it on the stage. 'I'll never forget it,' Brian Straton-Ferrier told Sandy Wilson. 'You'd get about fifty brilliant lines by Mortimer and then suddenly you'd get me.' Wilson remembered that John's contribution was very good but that he was not given a part in the play: 'I didn't realise he wanted to be an actor and he showed no sign of it.'

In June John spoke in the debating society from the floor on the motion that 'the modern generation believes what it is told rather than thinking for itself'. ' "Backchat" was once more the order of the day,' reported *The Harrovian*. 'It was nimbly led by J. C. Mortimer, *The Grove*, who was consistently amusing.' Three days later an oil painting that he had entered for the Henry Yates Thompson Art Prize was given an honourable mention and a couple of his watercolours were displayed in the school's annual art exhibition and praised in *The Harrovian*, whose reviewer said that unlike many of the other pictures, where the use of paint was too thick, untidy and ugly, 'two figure designs by J. C. Mortimer, *The Grove*, with a light touch and a finish of their own, were notably free from this fault'.

On Speech Day at the end of June the school's literary magazine, *Harrow*, published John's first short story, a witty, typically sardonic and devilishly irreligious tale entitled 'The End of the World', in which a notably good man believes that the world will end at midnight, gives everything away, waits piously to be wafted up to Heaven, and is then so devastated when the world does not end after all that he commits suicide. The magazine sold for 2/6d and John was paid ten shillings (£16.50) for his contribution, which encouraged him to start writing a novel about Harrow and to decide that he would rather be a writer than an actor. He told his father so during the summer holidays. Clifford was not enthusiastic. It would not be fair on his wife, he said, because writers always mooched around the house in a dressing gown trying and failing to come up with the right words. He would be much better off divorcing people, an easy job that required a bit of common sense and clean fingernails. John's fingernails were notoriously dirty but his steps were pointed firmly though reluctantly towards the Law.

In July he sat seven exams for his School Certificate and passed them all, coming first in the English Language paper, but on 1 September Hitler invaded Poland, Chamberlain declared war against Germany two days later, and the question of whether to become a lawyer, writer or actor suddenly seemed unimportant. John told his father that if he were called up to join the army he would claim to be a conscientious objector, which would inevitably attract contempt from people who would call him a coward. 'Do you really think you're *brave* enough for that?' asked Clifford wickedly. 'You should always avoid the temptation to do anything heroic.'

The new term at Harrow began three weeks later with John in the Upper Fifth specialising in history and with his own study. Early lessons and many evening activities had to be suspended because of the blackout – all the windows had to be covered at night by dark cloth – and each house had its own basement air-raid shelter. Some of the masters had already been called up into the forces and most of the clubs and societies were put into abeyance but the debating society kept going and in October Mortimer made his first major speech to propose the motion that 'this house considers that man has not yet discovered his purpose'. According to *The Harrovian* he 'painted a vivid picture of the chaotic state of the world at present. Education and government have utterly failed in their ideals – we have not even avoided another war.' With hindsight it is amusing to read that he 'depicted the evils of the society and *Tatler* life, the fox-hunting life', since he was later to revel in his own socialite, glossy-magazine existence and support fox-hunting, but as a fully paid-up Communist he asked, 'how can man have found his purpose, when we are content to sit smugly in the family pew, oblivious of the mine-workers and the factory-workers?' His speech, reported *The Harrovian*, 'was witty and eloquent, and relied on these qualities for its appeal rather than on logical argument'. A month later he spoke again, this time from the floor during a debate to decide that if you were stranded on a raft and had to eat one of your fellow survivors which would you choose: the Member of Parliament, the barrister, the schoolmaster or the painter? John said he would eat the MP because he would obviously be the fattest – a claim that would not be true thirty years later when he was himself a plump barrister – and at the end of the debate the MP was voted onto the menu.

In later years Mortimer claimed more than once that the School Songs gathering in the Speech Room at the end of that term was graced by the presence of Winston Churchill, who had just been appointed First Lord of the Admiralty, a member of the War Cabinet, and would become Prime Minister five months later. In an article in *The Sunday Times* in 1977 he sneered at Churchill's 'ancient and quavering voice' which was slurred 'from too much brandy or ill-fitting teeth', and claimed that after the singing the decrepit, trembling Churchill had to be helped onto the platform, where he peered at the boys 'like a misty-eyed tortoise'.

Mortimer decided that if Churchill were ever put in charge of the war it would be a disaster 'as he appeared to me to be about ninety-nine and totally thick', he told Mark Amory of *The Sunday Times Magazine*. This contemptuous description of Churchill was complete fiction. Churchill did not go to the Harrow singsong at the end of 1939, when he was far too busy worrying about the Soviet invasion of Finland, the mining of the seas off Norway, planning a British invasion of Sweden, and trying to prevent attacks on British shipping in the South Atlantic by the German pocket battleship *Graf Spee*. There was no mention of a visit by Churchill to Harrow at the end of 1939 in *The Harrovian*, and eight of Mortimer's contemporaries told me that it was in fact a year later that Churchill attended the Songs, on 18 December 1940, months after Mortimer had left to go to Oxford – a date confirmed by Martin Gilbert's magisterial biography of Churchill. All denied too that Churchill was at all frail when he did come. Sir Rupert Buchanan-Jardine, who was to join the Horse Guards two years later and to win the Military Cross in 1945, told me that 'it was definitely 1940 and Churchill was not at all doddery but delivered an excellent, most amusing speech, during which he said, "When I was at Harrow I was not only in the bottom form but at the *bottom* of the bottom form." Then he peered at us over his spectacles and said: "Well, *some*body has to do it. It's a very honourable position." Mortimer wasn't there.' Dick Willis agreed: 'John just made it up,' he said. Sandy Wilson told me that 'Mortimer's description of Churchill was absolute nonsense', and David Henley-Welch said, 'I was rather impressed by him. He wasn't at all frail and he had a strong voice and spoke well. He came again in 1941 and even then I didn't feel that he was tired or doddery. He seemed confident.' Brian Straton-Ferrier added: 'He was vigorous and went on to make one of his rousing speeches in which he said "we shall never, never, never, never give in".' At the end of 1939 he was only just sixty-five and was soon to deliver his most inspiring wartime speeches and to spend nearly six gruelling years saving the world from Hitler and the Nazis. So why did Mortimer make such a false claim, especially one that was so easy to disprove? Could it be that his dislike of any authority, even when Britain was fighting the monstrous evil of Hitler, was enough for him to bear false witness against a great British hero? If so, his career as a Devil's Advocate was off to a diabolical start. Yet when Churchill *did* visit the school at the end of 1940 he made a speech that Mortimer should have welcomed as a socialist had he been there. 'When this war is won by this nation, as it surely will be,' said Churchill, 'it must be one of our aims to work to establish a state of society where the advantage and privileges which hitherto have been enjoyed only by the few shall be far more widely shared by the many and the youth of the nation as a whole.' Ironically it was Mortimer himself who was in old age to become a doddery, trembling, quavering, boozy geriatric with dreadful teeth.

In March 1940 he delivered a socialist speech of his own when he proposed yet another motion in a debate about whether public schools encouraged class distinction. Mortimer, 'now familiar to many of us', reported *The Harrovian*, 'always has much to say; he is so eager to have it all out and done with, however, that he is sometimes hard to follow, and his arguments thus lose some of their persuasiveness. He drew a comparison between the Harrow boy and the footman who serves him; the latter must find it very hard to understand the fezzes, the beatings, the privileges, and the host of other such integral parts of the public school system. Between these two, therefore, there springs up a hatred – a class hatred. Thus the public schools engender a distinction, and the lower classes become increasingly embittered towards the upper.' Despite his eloquence the motion was defeated.

'There were a lot of air raids in 1940 and we could see the whole of London burning, all the docks,' Sir Rupert Buchanan-Jardine told me. 'We all slept in the basement and had regular fire-watching, and I put out an incendiary bomb that landed on the roof of our house. We continued to play sports against other schools but the food was a bit short and it was rationed and not very good.' Mortimer claimed years later in his autobiography that his brightest memory of Harrow was of Sandy Wilson sitting in their class blithely knitting mufflers, socks and balaclavas for the soldiers at the front, but that was another lie. 'It's absolute nonsense,' Wilson told me. 'I can't even sew on a button. When Mortimer's autobiography was published in 1982 I wrote to him to complain about it and say it was untrue and he apologised and said he would take it out of the next edition. I've really no idea why he did it. It was pure invention, just ridiculous.' Mortimer never kept his promise to remove the story from later editions of the book, which was republished in paperback in 1983 and reprinted nine times that year, three times in 1984 and twice in 1985 but the lie never corrected.

The following term Mortimer spoke again in a debate to propose that 'this house considers the evacuation of children to Canada to be detrimental to public morale'. The war was not going well and Britain was by now in grave danger, for the Germans had overwhelmed Norway, Denmark, Belgium and France, and the British Expeditionary Force had only just managed to escape annihilation by evacuation through Dunkirk. Mortimer, however, avoided being serious as usual and began a typically mischievous, tongue-in-cheek speech by describing 'the dangers of a torpedo-infested Atlantic', reported *The Harrovian*, and then 'painted a lurid picture of an England without children; a gloomy fortress, peopled by unemployed schoolmasters, where such medieval practices as wife-beating abounded'. With another gratuitous dig at Churchill, who had become Prime Minister a few weeks earlier, he 'touched on the effect such an exile would have on our "Little Winstons", citing with an extraordinary propensity to bad language such examples as the ... lack of culture in Canada'. Mortimer made 'an admirable summing-up' but to no avail: he lost his motion again, by fifty votes to twenty-one. He had not yet polished to perfection the silver-tongued knack of persuasion that he was later to display as a barrister addressing a jury.

At the end of his last term he had a poem published in 'Harrow 1940', an article in *The Harrovian*, and won a Coward History Prize for the Upper Fifth form, but he did not stay on at school for a year in the Sixth, as Wilson, Straton-Ferrier and most of his contemporaries did. Instead he left a year early to go to university at the age of seventeen. 'I think we might run to Oxford,' said his father, 'provided you fall in and read Law.' John's housemaster, Leonard Henry, had been a scholar at Brasenose College and the principal of Brasenose was himself a renowned legal scholar, so John went off to Oxford for an interview and entrance exam-ination. Because of the war and falling numbers of undergraduates, 'if you had a cheque to pay the fees – which my father had – they were pretty interested in seeing you,' he told Jonathan Sale of the *Independent* in 1999. 'The vice-principal of Brasenose put me in the library with some Latin to translate and left me. The library was full of Latin dictionaries so I translated the passage. He came back, looked at it and said: "Come along to Brasenose." ' In his autobiography he told a different story: that as he was trying to translate the passage a friend from Harrow who was doing the same test 'slipped out unnoticed' and bought a Latin dictionary which allowed them both to pass the exam. Once again it is difficult to know when he was telling the truth or whether either version came even close to the truth.

He left Harrow on 29 July 1940 after making 'few friends but many enemies' he told Heather Dixon of the *Yorkshire Post* in 1990. It sounded almost like a boast. 'He didn't make enemies amongst us in his class,' said Sandy Wilson, 'but I would not be surprised if he made enemies by his behaviour.' But Brian Straton-Ferrier was unconvinced. 'I don't know of any enemies,' he said dismissively. 'People were just indifferent to him.' Barely noticed at Harrow, Mortimer was to spend the rest of his life trying to draw attention to himself.

Three

Oxford and the Troublesome Organ
1940–1942

When Mortimer left Harrow that glorious summer of 1940 *Rebecca*, *The Grapes of Wrath* and *Gone With the Wind* were on in the London cinemas and *Thunder Rock* and *Margin for Error* at the theatre. Gracie Fields was singing 'Wish Me Luck As You Wave Me Goodbye', the top of the pops was Judy Campbell's haunting, romantic hit 'A Nightingale Sang in Berkeley Square', and Mortimer's own long life of romance began, he claimed, when he lost his virginity at the age of seventeen when a couple of lesbians invited him to a party at their cottage at Turville Heath. 'They're very interesting,' he told his father. 'They knew Jean Cocteau and said he smoked opium.' Clifford was dismissive. 'Never smoke opium,' he said. 'Gives you constipation. Look at pictures of the wretched poet Coleridge: green about the gills and a stranger to the lavatory.'

At the lesbian party the guests played a blindfold kissing game and Mortimer claimed that he found himself being kissed with serious intent by a heart-faced girl with different coloured eyes and a gammy leg. In *Clinging to the Wreckage* he called her 'Sarah' and said he was amazed when she soon led him to a spare bedroom, but as they got down to business the door crashed open. 'What do you think you're doing?' barked one of their hostesses. 'This is a decent lesbian household!' John and 'Sarah' were thrown out but he claimed that they repaired to the common to continue their negotiations in the bracken. It was just a one-night stand but years later, he said, after 'Sarah' had married and divorced, they met again in Hampstead and conjugated for a while.

He went up to Oxford in October 1940 to join more than seven hundred freshmen and women who were also matriculating that term, among them the eighteen-year-old poet Philip Larkin and the writer Alan Ross, who was later to edit the *London Magazine*. In peacetime Oxford had usually housed 4,500 undergraduates but now there were only two thousand and most would be allowed to spend only one year there – or two at the most – before being called up for military service, so that none would enjoy a full three-year university career. Nor was this the smart, sparkling, hedonistic Oxford of his Dragon School childhood and *Brideshead Revisited*. This was wartime-economy Oxford: drab, rationed, blacked-out after dark, with streets full of people carrying gas-masks and the hitherto glamorous summer Commem Balls suspended for the duration. 'The nights passed quietly enough,' wrote D. E. Mount in the university's undergraduate magazine *The Cherwell*, 'but everywhere there was an atmosphere of watchful tension, heightened by the furtive pad-pad of crepe soles along the darkened gutters, and the sound of a piano in Christ Church, on which somebody was pensively picking at the strains of "The Internationale".' The Royal Air Force was winning the Battle of Britain in the air but for eight months British cities were to suffer the horrors of German bombing, the Blitz. For almost all of Mortimer's two years at Oxford the news from the battlefronts was depressing except for that from the Middle East, where the Allies took control of Iraq, Syria and the Lebanon. Mussolini had joined Hitler in June, attacked Albania and Greece and driven the British out of Soma-liland. The Germans invaded Bulgaria, Yugoslavia, Greece and Russia, reaching the outskirts of Moscow, killing and deporting millions. German U-boats sank hundreds of ships in the Atlantic and the Japanese overran most of South-east Asia, including Hong Kong, Singapore and the islands of the western Pacific. It was no time for light-hearted high jinks. Petrol was severely rationed, so few people had a car. Under-graduates sat up at night fire-watching on roofs and towers. Food and coal were often in short supply and although Mortimer did his best to show off and attract attention by smoking black Balkan Sobranie cig-arettes and wearing purple corduroy trousers, cigarettes and clothes were scarce, let alone exotic ones. Under government regulations no one was allowed to spend more than five shillings in a restaurant (£7) and the meat was likely to be whale – 'Moby Dick and chips' – the wine Algerian diesel, the omelettes made out of dried eggs. Under university regulations no undergraduate was allowed to drink in a pub and although many did the bars were deserted between eight and nine at night when the uni-versity proctors patrolled the town. Any student caught more than once in a pub might be sent down and although it was possible to drink in the bar of the Union or the college buttery the beer often ran out, wine was scarce, and Mortimer and some of his contemporaries resorted to drinking gin mixed with communion wine – a foul brew known as Gin and Altars. 'The enormous impact of war has given Oxford a fundamental shock, so that its axis has been shaken from the Radcliffe Camera to Carfax,' wrote Philip Larkin to his childhood friend Jim Sutton in May 1941. 'Army lorries thunder down Cornmarket Street in an endless procession . . . I gain the impression of being at the end of an epoch.' Later he wrote: 'There was not a great deal of scope for personal development in the sense of high living . . . You couldn't even have meals in your own rooms. You had one bottle of wine a term from the buttery – that was your lot . . . You didn't have marvellously furnished rooms because you were all doubled up.'

Some colleges had been taken over by civil servants from the Ministry of Food and Agriculture, and Brasenose – commonly known as BNC – had been commandeered by the army as a military training school, so that John and other BNC men found themselves housed in the grandest and most snobbish of all the Oxford colleges, Christ Church, 'The House'. Dating from 1546, planned by Cardinal Wolsey and founded by Henry VIII, it was perhaps the most beautiful college with its honey-coloured stone walls, cold, gloomy, monastic corridors, medieval cloister with worn, ancient steps and flagstones, and little courtyards and battlements. It had its own lofty, magnificent, twelfth-century cathedral with a stunning tower with seventeenth-century fan-vaulted ceiling, ancient tombs and stone effigies, and a clock that was always five minutes slow because in the Middle Ages the time in Oxford was five minutes later than that in London. Christ Church had a vast dining hall with superb hammerbeam ceiling, stained-glass windows and numerous depictions of *Alice in Wonderland*, which had been written there by the college's mathematics don Charles Dodgson under the pseudonym Lewis Carroll. A tranquil fishpond with a delicate statue of the Roman god Mercury lay amid the lawns of its huge central square, Tom Quad, so named after the seventon bell Great Tom that hangs over the gatehouse designed by Sir Christopher Wren. Charles I lived there during the English civil war from 1642 to 1646 and among its alumni had been John and Charles Wesley and Sir Robert Peel, though when Mortimer went up the college's most famous undergraduate was the witty actor, lyricist and singer Michael Flanders, who was eventually with his stage partner Donald Swann to take the London theatre by storm with their hilarious revue *At*

The Drop of a Hat. So grand was Christ Church that 'we were not always welcome', I was told by John Browning, a grammar school boy from Tyneside who went up to Brasenose the same term as John. 'Some of The House men used to call us "the vulgar herd of BNC"!'

Mortimer's rooms were on the second floor of staircase five at the far end of the Meadow Buildings, a large, Gothic, Venetian-style edifice designed by John Ruskin in 1863 with a panoramic view over a broad field that reaches to the banks of the River Cherwell and was often so flooded that it looked like the Venice lagoon. His rooms – a vast sitting room, huge bedroom and shared lavatory outside on the landing – were right above those of the German-born physicist Dr Frederick Lindemann, Oxford's professor of experimental philosophy and director of the Clarendon Laboratory, who was Churchill's friend, personal assistant and military guru, later joined his government and eventually became a Companion of Honour and Viscount Cherwell. To Mortimer's heathen dismay, however, he found he was sharing his rooms with a fervent Christian – whom he called 'Parsons' in his autobiography – who tried to save him from the Devil by urging him to join the Bible Society. His roommate was in fact Patrick Freeman, an eighteen-year-old freshman from Tonbridge School who was reading Politics, Philosophy and Economics. 'I was fairly religious then but there's a malicious twist to his description of me,' Freeman told me in 2004. 'It's very unfair. I have a vivid memory of John Mortimer. I don't know why he went to BNC, which was a very sporty college, because he was aesthetic rather than sporty. He wore thick pebbly glasses and used to wear rust-coloured corduroy trousers and velvet ties and things like that, and tan shoes with yellow soles, bow ties made of velvet. He tended to dress a bit like Oscar Wilde but he was untidy and dirty. I didn't see much of him. He seemed to go off to parties and he used to get tight quite regularly. Our scout, Bustin, would come in and say, "Mr Mortimer, sir, is not very well this morning again." He would get up at about eleven o'clock and lie in bed having had a good night out the night before. I don't think he went to lectures and he didn't work very hard. In fact I don't remember him studying or working at all. He preferred chasing girls and having parties.' Among the lecturers whom Mortimer should have heard but probably missed were Edmund Blunden on his favourite poet Wordsworth, Lord David Cecil on the romantic poets, Nevill Coghill on Chaucer and Shakespeare, C. S. Lewis on medieval and renaissance literature and J. R. R. Tolkien on Anglo-Saxon poetry, though in the case of Tolkien he did not miss much. Tolkien 'was an appalling lecturer', reported Kingsley

Amis, who went up to St John's the following year. 'He spoke unclearly and slurred the important words, and then he'd write them on the blackboard but keep standing between them and us, then wipe them off before he turned round.'

Freeman had little in common with Mortimer: 'There was no conflict between us but he just wasn't my type. I was much more serious and hard-working. He used to put cakes down on the floor for the mice to eat! When I was sharing the rooms with him in our first term his father came up to see him and he was desperately keen that I should be out of the rooms when his parents were there. He was not quite ashamed of his father but rather reticent about him. They came in and I shook hands with them and vanished immediately. I didn't dislike Mortimer. I think he was talented but I would never have guessed that he would have gone as far as he has.' Another contemporary freshman, Arthur Bone, who was eighteen months older than Mortimer and reading Classics at BNC, remembered him wearing a red bow tie with white spots and agreed that he was 'rather aesthetic and intellectual in the hearty, beefy, Blues-ridden atmosphere of the place, not a typical Brasenose man, and pretty lazy and lackadaisical. He had a florid personality but I thought he was very young, and we called him the ugliest man in the university! We moved in different circles and although we were neighbours along the same Old Library corridor in our second year we didn't go into each other's rooms. If he'd been at all affable we would have spoken to each other but we never did. He was standoffish and snobby, and seemed to look down on me because I was a grammar school scholar and hadn't been to public school. He walked about with his nose in the air.' Another grammar school boy who had come up on a Chemistry scholarship, John Holmes, never got to know him at all even though their rooms were right next to each other, and James Silvester, who went up to Brasenose on a scholarship a year later and became a friend of Kingsley Amis, told me that at Oxford Mortimer 'was not very popular. I also found his appearance rather repulsive. He still has that off-centre lower jaw and some projecting teeth which look as though they need to be worked on.' John Browning confirmed that 'Mortimer was gaunt, gawky, lanky, an unlikely looking man for Brasenose, not handsome'.

Brasenose was however an ideal college for a future lawyer. Its Principal, William Stallybrass, who taught Mortimer the Law, was a barrister who had edited several editions of Sir John Salmond's standard reference book *The Law of Torts* and went on to become Vice-Chancellor of the university in 1947. 'BNC was very much a legal college,' said Silvester, 'and there was an intellectual leavening among all the hearties.' Mortimer was however soon bored studying Law and wished he had chosen to read History instead. He forced himself to plough through books about tort, property, libel and slander but found it all extremely dull and soon realised that most of it would be of no use at all to him as a barrister. He learned how to manumit an Ancient Roman slave and adopt a geriatric senator but reading Law was 'a big mistake', he told Jonathan Sale of the *Independent* in 1999. 'Law isn't a proper academic subject, not creative, and ... it only becomes interesting when you start doing cases. I didn't read much of it; I read my way through Proust and Dostoevsky.'

From the start of his first term at Oxford – indeed, for the rest of his life – Mortimer's great obsession was girls. 'He was excessively conscious of his lack of looks,' I was told by the novelist and critic Francis King, who was reading Classical Moderations at Balliol. 'He said to me once, "You're lucky, you don't know what it is to be ugly." I think that Mortimer was determined to show that his ugliness need not preclude him from sexual conquests.' The fashion at Oxford in 1940 was to be homosexual, Mortimer reported in his autobiography, but he said he was no longer interested in homosexuality and preferred to pursue boyish girls from the women's colleges and androgynous, virginal, tennis-playing 'waifs' in the WAAF, the Women's Auxiliary Air Force. Oxford's theatres and cinemas were still open so any of them might offer a handy venue for seduction. At the end of October you could take a girl to hear Billy Cotton and His Band at the New Theatre or the West Indian variety star Hutch (Leslie Hutchinson) with Don Rico and his Ladies' Swing Band. *The Marx Brothers at the Circus* was on at the Scala, Gary Cooper in Sam Goldwyn's *The Westerner* at the Ritz, *Baa, Baa, Black Sheep* by Ian Hay and P. G. Wodehouse at the Playhouse, and Malcolm Sargent conducting the London Philharmonic Orchestra at the Sheldonian. Or perhaps you could impress some pretty undergraduette by speaking powerfully in a debate at the Oxford Union, where Mortimer rose to his feet just two weeks after his arrival and launched an attack on snobbishness against the motion 'that this House believes that the House of Lords in its present form has a valuable influence on the country'. Even the dons' yawningly dreary weekly publication the *Oxford Magazine* reported that 'there were happily a number of maiden speakers last Thursday, and the majority showed greater promise than in many instances in past years. Among the best were Mr J. C. Mortimer (Brasenose), who deplored snobbishness' – which must have amused those victims of Mortimer's own snobbery Arthur Bone and John Holmes.

Another speaker against the motion was a twenty-year-old Balliol undergraduate, Roy Jenkins, the future Labour Home Secretary and Chancellor
of the Exchequer, who had stood the previous term for election as President of the Union but had lost by just five votes even though *The Cherwell*
described him as 'self-possessed, well-informed and unfailingly sincere'.
Jenkins attacked 'bankers, industrialists, landowners, reactionary forces'
and thanks to his and Mortimer's eloquence the motion was easily
defeated. Twenty-five years later the two were to become allies in the
vanguard of the movement that founded the Permissive Society, but
strangely Mortimer never spoke again in a Union debate.

It was the twilight of a blazing era for politicians at Oxford. Roy
Jenkins' twenty-one-year-old future Labour Cabinet colleague Anthony
Crosland had left Trinity the previous term to join the army. Another
future Labour Chancellor of the Exchequer, twenty-one-year-old Denis
Healey, was at Balliol, had been elected chairman of the university Labour
Club the previous year and had just resigned after years as a loyal member
from the discredited Communist Party, which was in disarray after the
Soviet Union's pact with Hitler and invasion of Finland – although
twenty-year-old Iris Murdoch of Somerville College was still an enthusiastic member and blind to the cynical treachery and totalitarianism of
the Russians. Yet another Balliol man, twenty-two-year-old Edward
Heath, the future Prime Minister, had been President of the Union the
previous year and was in the words of the Tory politician Julian Amery
'the leading Conservative figure in the university'. Amery was also at
Balliol, as were two other prominent future Tory politicians, Maurice
Macmillan and Hugh Fraser, the future husband of Lady Antonia, whose
thirty-five-year-old father Frank Pakenham, the future Earl of Longford
and Labour Cabinet Minister, was a history tutor at Christ Church. 'We
were perhaps the most political generation in Oxford's history,' wrote
Healey in his autobiography. Like Healey, Mortimer was disillusioned
with Communism and became instead a committed socialist although as
a non-joiner he still resisted the temptation to ally himself formally with
any political group, even the Labour Party or its Jenkinsite offspring the
Democratic Socialist Club. Jenkins tried once more to become President
of the Union when he joined the Labour MP Aneurin Bevan to support
the motion 'that this House does not want to hear of the Conservatives
again' at the end of November, but although he spoke impressively and
they won the debate he was beaten in the presidential election the next
day by I. J. Bahadoorsingh and abandoned his ambition to be President.

In the first week of December *The Cherwell*, which regularly published poems by Edward Blunden, listed Mortimer on its cover as a contributor and printed four of his lovelorn verses – under the imaginative title 'Poem' – in a metre reminiscent of Longfellow's 'Hiawatha' that began:

> *Insensible, my darling,*
> *To the way the world is whirling,*
> *While the static past is burning*
> *Through the cold and jaded morning . . .*

During that first term at Oxford, Mortimer claimed in his autobiography, he used Patrick Freeman's electric kettle to boil a mixture of Algerian wine, sherry and Bols to make a punch, drank it, passed out, and came round to find Freeman kneeling at his side and praying for him. 'That's not true at all,' Freeman told me. Mortimer also claimed that Freeman was so annoyed that his electric kettle had been ruined that he asked to be moved to a different set of rooms. 'That's not true, either,' said Freeman. 'After the first term *he* moved out of the set of rooms we were in and I stayed. He got the next-door rooms allocated to him and after he moved I saw very little of him except for the vibrations of his parties which would come through the walls. I was never invited to one of his parties and I don't know how he paid for them because he didn't seem to be overflowing with money.'

The parties were of course the best way of meeting girls. 'I can remember girls being at his parties but he didn't sleep with them, to my knowledge, in the rooms,' Freeman told me. Sexually Oxford was still remarkably naive and Denis Healey reported in his autobiography that when he told Edward Heath that a mutual friend was taking his girlfriend to Bibury for the weekend Heath was horrified. 'You don't mean to say they are sleeping together?' he whispered.

'I suppose so,' said Healey.

'Good heavens!' said Heath. 'I can't imagine anyone in the Conservative Association doing that.'

'The majority of young men and women coming up to Oxford at that time, at the age of eighteen or so, were virgins, and often remained so for several years,' reported the only man at Oxford who was allegedly uglier than Mortimer – the poet John Heath-Stubbs – in his autobiography, and the women's colleges did their damnedest to keep the wolves away from their doors. It was difficult for undergraduettes to get permission to stay out late or accept parts in plays produced by the men's colleges, and they were forbidden to entertain men in their rooms, so Mortimer adopted the cunning ploy of inviting them round for tea. Tea was considered impeccably respectable: what could one possibly get up to in the afternoon over the Earl Grey and cucumber sandwiches? Robert Runcie, the future Archbishop of Canterbury, told his biographer Humphrey Carpenter that when he went up to Brasenose in April 1941 at the age of nineteen and was given ground-floor rooms near Mortimer's he asked their scout, Bustin, why so many pretty girls kept tramping up the stairs in the afternoons. 'Mr Mortimer, sir,' said Bustin, 'he's a man wiv wot you'd call a troublesome organ.'

'But did you get your leg over?' the *Mail on Sunday* interviewer Craig Brown asked Mortimer in 2001.

'Yaaarp, I suppose I did a bit,' he fibbed. 'There were all these art students at the Slade school, which helped.' It was quite untrue and he was to confess in his autobiography that all his attempts at seduction at Oxford were in vain, though he did become chastely engaged to a quiet, gentle Welsh girl who was studying book illustration at the Slade, which had been evacuated from London to the Ashmolean Museum in Oxford for the duration of the war, when he joined it to draw nudes and ogle naked women. His engagement ended, he told Craig Brown, when he had lunch with the girl and her mother at the George restaurant 'and I thought I was feeling her leg under the table, but it turned out to be her mother's. It was a pure mistake. But the mother was appalled and that was the end of my invitations to her family home in Yorkshire.' This story was probably another invention because it is quite unbelievable that a man sitting at a table with two women could possibly squeeze by mistake the leg on his left instead of the leg on his right.

Despite his relentless pursuit of female flesh Mortimer embarked that term on one of his rare close male friendships, with eighteen-year-old Michael Fenton, who had been at Lancing School, whose rooms were on the same floor and staircase and whom he came eventually to consider his moral guide. In his autobiography, in which he called Fenton 'Henry Winter', Mortimer wrote that their friendship was warmed by sexual frustration, and Fenton's son Ben told me in 2004: 'My father loved Mortimer. There was nothing homosexual about their relationship but you will never understand Mortimer unless you understand their friendship. When he went on *Desert Island Discs* sixty years later and chose one of my father's favourite pieces of music, Brahms' Fourth Symphony, they had to stop the recording because John burst into tears.' In his autobiography John wrote that it was Fenton's quiet serenity and moral certainty that appealed to him so much and it was in fact Brahms' Fourth that first attracted Mortimer to Fenton. He heard the music wafting across the corridor in Meadow Buildings and was fascinated to discover that whereas Clifford had never given him any advice or moral bearings as to what was right and wrong, Fenton had no doubts at all despite being an agnostic, though it is difficult to believe that he really did know right from wrong since he opposed the war and was prepared to go to prison as a pacifist if necessary – a stance difficult to respect at a time when it was obvious that Hitler and the Nazis were evil and could be stopped only by force. But Fenton did introduce Mortimer to music, they went for long walks together and stayed up late into the night talking and drinking, and eventually became so inseparable that when Mortimer occasionally did something on his own he felt as though he were guilty of infidelity. This did not stop him years later trying to seduce Fenton's second wife, Barbara. 'Fenton also wore velvet bow ties and a rather aesthetic look,' said Freeman, 'and they and Michael Beazley, who was on the next floor up, went about quite a bit together.' Fenton was to remain Mortimer's only really close male friend for nearly thirty years. 'What they had in common was that they were both bright lads who had been to public schools, and both the only children of much older parents,' I was told by Ben Fenton. Barbara Fenton, who met both men ten years later, confirmed Mortimer's aloof, snobbish reputation. 'John was very arrogant,' she said, and in typical public school fashion 'Michael always called him Mortimer or Old Mort. I never heard him call him John.' Fenton was a shy man, I was told by the poet James Michie, who met him at Oxford after the war and became another close friend of his. 'They were both also classical scholars and keen on jazz and Michael liked the unconventional, and I'm sure John was that. I certainly don't think there was anything homosexual about their relationship.'

In his autobiography Mortimer claimed that he acted regularly in Shakespeare at Oxford but there is no mention of him or the plays in *The Cherwell*, the *Oxford Magazine*, BNC's magazine *The Brazen Nose* nor Humphrey Carpenter's history of the Oxford University Dramatic Society. Mortimer did however have two more four-verse poems published in March and June in *The Cherwell*, which was by now printing also the poetry of Philip Larkin and Roy Porter, that earned him more mentions on the cover of the magazine. The first, again entitled just 'Poem', began:

> *The castle of yourself is hard to keep,*
> *And many, starting, lost their heads,*
> *Panicking because they could not stand*

The shot off face, the X-ray photograph,
And dripped effetely off to fairyland.

The second, 'Nocturne', was equally pretentious and began:

The amber cups where strangers discover
Dark strangers are pallid and empty. 'Thank you so much'
(They are sucked white the amber eyes of this morning's lover).
Gloved hands thank you and hover ...

In April eighteen-year-old Kingsley Amis, himself a poet, came up to
join his future chum Philip Larkin at St John's – and to join the Oxford
Communist Party, where the secretary, Iris Murdoch, was writing letters
to Roy Jenkins addressed to 'Dear Comrade Jenkins' – and it would be
illuminating to know what Amis and Larkin thought of Mortimer's arty-
farty doggerel. Surprisingly Mortimer seems not to have met Amis or
Larkin at Oxford, nor did they mention him in autobiographies or diaries
despite a common interest in writing, poetry, jazz and left-wing politics,
though both Amis and Mortimer probably went along to the Union in
June to hear the fiery young left-wing Labour MP Michael Foot speak in
a debate against the Tory Under-Secretary for Foreign Affairs, 'Rab'
Butler, on the motion 'that this House deplores the view that Con-
servatism is a vice in a young man'.

   In June too Mortimer took part with an undergraduate called Lloyd
in a mock trial before the annual dinner of the Brasenose lawyers' club,
the Ellesmere Society, of which *The Brazen Nose* reported that 'the leading
counsel, Lloyd and Mortimer, distinguished themselves'. Later in the
year he also read a paper entitled 'Auden on 52nd Street' to the college's
literary Pater Society, and he was still dreaming of becoming a writer
and had started to write another novel, this time about Henley and its
regatta, from which he read extracts to his father in the evenings during
his vacation at Turville Heath Cottage. Clifford and Kath had given up
the tenancy of their flat at 5 King's Bench Walk at the end of 1940,
driven out by the dangers of the Blitz, and were now living permanently
in the country – a wise move because in May 1941 the Inner Temple
suffered a devastating German bombing attack during which their old
flat at 4 Harcourt Buildings was destroyed. Clifford did his best to
undermine John's dream of becoming a writer by sneering at his novel
and eventually, reluctantly, John followed his advice to get a proper job
and practise Law, and on 15 October 1941 he was admitted to the Inner

Temple as a student although he was to stay on at university for another nine months.

By now he was deeply bored and disillusioned by Oxford and escaped with Michael Fenton as often as possible to London to revel in the louche pubs and coffee bars among the prostitutes, poets and day-long drunks of Soho where sometimes they bumped into Stephen Spender, Cyril Connolly, Roy Campbell or Dylan Thomas, who told him once in an alcoholic haze that he was looking for a woman with a vagina as tight as the earhole of a mouse. Fenton decided to go before a tribunal to explain why he should be excused national service in the forces as a conscientious objector, so early in 1942 they took a bus from Oxford to the nearby village of Wootton to discuss Fenton's tactics with a renowned pacifist, Charles Dimont, who had been Reuters' feckless, alcoholic correspondent in Vienna before the war but been sacked for fiddling his expenses and was now working as a porter at the Radcliffe Infirmary. Dimont told Fenton that he would probably lose his case because he did not believe in God, so Fenton devised his own tactics: when he was asked by the tribunal the usual question about what he would do if he saw a German raping his grandmother, he would reply: 'I'd wait until he had finished, and then I'd bury the dear old lady again.' In due course Fenton did persuade his tribunal that he was sincere in his opposition to the war and was put to work with a pacifist service unit in London where he cleaned up the mess after air raids and took victims to hospital.

Sitting silently in the living room at Wootton that day was Dimont's strikingly attractive twenty-three-year-old wife, Penelope, who was to seduce Mortimer five years later and to marry him two years after that. When they met that day he was 'a nervous boy, thin with a damp handshake', she wrote fifty-one years later in her autobiography *About Time Too*. In his own account of that first meeting John wrote in his autobiography with his usual exaggeration that she seemed to have a lot of small children but in fact there was only one toddler, three-year-old Madelon, and a baby, Caroline, who was just a few weeks old and in a pram. It was the prologue to an obsessive, tempestuous relationship that was eventually to destroy Penelope and to scar Mortimer for life.

He decided that he would take his father's advice not to do anything heroic like claiming to be a conscientious objector himself but would try to find a comparatively safe bolt-hole with RAF ground staff, but he need not have worried about being called up: the RAF rejected him as totally unfit for service because he was so thin and had such poor lungs and eyesight.

His university career ended with a yawn and a whimper. He sat his final Jurisprudence exams in the summer of 1942, after just two years at Oxford instead of three, and claimed later in his autobiography and interviews that he was given an unclassified degree because different degree classes were not awarded during the war, but once again it seems that he was not telling the truth. According to his college magazine, *The Brazen Nose*, he was in fact given a poor Class III degree, the equivalent of a 2:2 today, a decidedly feeble result for a man considered to be very clever. 'That's astonishing,' said John Browning, 'but it could have been that his mind was elsewhere, either on the girls or the theatre.' His degree was not actually awarded until more than a year later, in October 1943, and not surprisingly he did not bother to go to Oxford to collect it.

Mortimer also claimed inaccurately in his autobiography that his 'ancient' tutor William Stallybrass died during the war when he opened a train door in the blackout and fell onto the track. In fact when Mortimer went up to Oxford in 1940 Stallybrass was only fifty-six and he did not die until 1948, long after the last blackout. So was Mortimer's claim a deliberate fib to spice up his story or simply due to a lazy disinclination to check the facts? It is a question that one has to ask over and over again.

Four

Propaganda, Probate and Penelope
1942–1949

One of the Mortimers' neighbours at Turville Heath, Jack Painton, had been so impressed by John's childhood solo plays and puppet shows that when John left Oxford and Painton was head of the Ministry of Information's wartime propaganda films section he offered John a job helping to make propaganda documentaries with the Crown Film Unit at Pinewood Studios at Iver Heath in Buckinghamshire. As Fourth Assistant Film Director he was just a gofer whose only real glimpse of film-making was when he had to cry 'quiet, please!' as the cameras were about to roll. He was paid £2 a week (£52) and spent three-quarters of his wages to rent a room in the house of an aircraft fitter and his wife a couple of miles away, in Slough, which left him with just ten shillings a week (£13) to live on. He claimed in his autobiography that he was so incompetent that his fellow workers, like his mother, thought he was a joke, and that when he had to take fifty electricians by train to Liverpool he lost them all. In other versions of the story he claimed that they were never seen again. It was yet another of his transparently unbelievable stories. *Fifty* electricians? What were they all doing? Shooting a remake of *The Charge of the Light Brigade*? And why were they never seen again? Were they kidnapped? Abducted by aliens? Seven pages later in the autobiography he admitted that he *did* find the electricians in the end, but every time he told the story the number of electricians was different. In 1977 he told *The Sunday Times Magazine* that he had lost not fifty but fourteen. In 1979 he told the *Daily Mirror* that there had been seventeen. In 1986 he told Melvyn Bragg on *The South Bank Show* that there had been twenty. So did it happen at all?

His film career was given a boost by the unit's resident scriptwriter, Laurie Lee, who was to write *Cider With Rosie* seventeen years later. Lee was becoming restless in the job, suggested that John might replace him, and persuaded the head of the unit to send Mortimer off to see if he could write a script about one of the dreariest subjects possible: Watford railway junction. When he came up with a story about a station master's wife's unhappy affair with an American soldier Lee proclaimed it such a success that John was promoted to replace him. They gave him a khaki army uniform with SCRIPTWRITER neatly sewn across his shoulder, a bicycle, and so much money – £11 a week (£289) – that he was able to leave the aircraft fitter's house in Slough and rent instead a room in north London in the house of an engineer and his wife on Haverstock Hill, Belsize Park. According to his second volume of autobiography, *Murderers and Other Friends*, this allowed him to take girls to his father's chambers in the Temple at night, help himself to Clifford's vintage port, and make love to them. Given John's gaucheness and inexperience this sounds more like fantasy than fact although he did perhaps manage to seduce one of Michael Fenton's girlfriends at about this time. 'John was just down from Oxford and had a limp-wristed, homosexual manner and rather extravagant feminine traits,' I was told in 2004 by Dr Alan Gildersleve, one of Fenton's conscientious-objector friends in the same Pacifist Service Unit in London. 'Mortimer seemed to want to be taken as being homosexual but he wasn't and it was a false impression. Michael was one of her lovers and John another. She was a flamboyant girl and never appealed to me at all but she was a promiscuous young woman who had flings with three or four of the unit. The French would call her a *grande horizontale* and *bien usée*. She was always available and liked variety and John's affair with her was a very brief, carnal liaison.'

He soon left the engineer's house, driven out by the dreadful food, bawling infants and lack of hygiene, and rented a room in the fashionable King's Road in Chelsea, at World's End, where he could afford to eat rabbit in restaurants and go to bottle parties as the air-raid sirens wailed and bombs crashed all around. In *Clinging to the Wreckage* he claimed that he persuaded the small, fragile, long-haired daughter of a retired general, who worked at the Air Ministry, to move in with him, and insisted that her name was Angela Bedwell, which seems unlikely, especially since he gave fictional names to almost every other character in the book. He said that 'Angela' was his first great love and he courted her by taking her to their favourite pub, where they played bar billiards, and to restaurants and parties. Even though the bombed streets might be strewn with rubble, shattered glass and bodies every morning he said later that those dangerous wartime days were among the happiest of his life.

The documentaries on which he worked – *Target For Tonight*, *Listen to Britain*, *Fires Were Started* – starred not actors but ordinary people going about their normal patriotic wartime duties as soldiers, firemen, factory workers, nurses, farmers or fishermen. 'By and large I reacted against the documentary movement because we weren't really telling the truth,' he told Melvyn Bragg – somewhat cheekily considering that he was not exactly devoted to telling the truth himself. 'We were making films which told you that bombs actually fell on their targets and never killed a single civilian. And we were pretending that on the home front everyone was only thinking about the war and not indulging in the black market or making love to each other's wives, which seemed to be their main occupations, so it wasn't really a truthful way of approaching life.' But making the films brought him into contact for the first time with ordinary working-class people – carpenters, cameramen, electricians, technicians, prop men, continuity girls, canteen ladies and matey people who called him 'comrade' and 'brother', played cards and dragged him off to the pub. For more than two years he travelled by train all over the country to coal mines, factories, airfields and barracks to mingle with production-line workers as well as soldiers and airmen, and he began to believe that if only Britain would elect a socialist government after the war it might be possible to reform society, build a Utopia, and give the common man and woman a decent break in life at last. He also came to feel that he should be nicer to people and not so snobbish and standoffish. 'I was very intolerant as a young man,' he told Ginny Dougary of *The Times* nearly sixty years later. 'There's enough trouble in the world without people going around not being nice.'

His dream of becoming a writer was given a boost in October 1942 when the pocket magazine *Lilliput* published a very short story he had written about the war, 'It's Nobody's Fault!', under the pseudonym 'Nicholas Mortimer'. It was a mischievous, iconoclastic little yarn set in a shambolic operations room at Duty Command, where servicemen and women are trying to deal with the drama of a convoy being attacked, telephones not working, chaotic bureaucracy and an official attempt to send a pointless message that says simply 'nothing to report'. It was a mildly amusing tale that depended too much on coincidence, but its publication – opposite a pin-up of a smiling, seductive black woman – encouraged him to begin to write a jokey novel about the Crown Film Unit that he called *Charade*. Like most first novels it was strongly autobiographical and gave a vivid picture of his life at the time, telling of a shy, self-effacing young assistant director who joins a military film unit making a documentary about army training, falls for the director's wife, determines to solve the mystery of a sergeant's fatal accident, and is arrested as a possible spy. It described the unit and its work as an absolute shambles, the hours spent hanging around in pubs, the late-night games of cards, beer and cigarettes in hotel rooms, the taboo on discussing anything at all 'artistic'. And the narrator succeeds one idyllic afternoon in seducing the director's wife only to discover that he has just cuckolded his own father – an interestingly naughty twist considering John's possibly Oedipal hang-ups about his parents.

On 30 April 1945 Hitler committed suicide, Germany surrendered eight days later, the streets of London exploded in an orgy of celebration, and 'everyone was having sex in Hyde Park', Mortimer told Craig Brown in 2001. It is said that when Churchill heard that an elderly civil servant had been arrested in Hyde Park for celebrating up against a tree trunk with a woman he had never met before, the Prime Minister growled: 'It makes you *proud* to be an Englishman!' Mortimer's own celebrations got 'Angela Bedwell' pregnant and although he said he offered to marry her he sounded so reluctant that she induced a miscarriage by having a hot bath and a lot of gin. He claimed later that he should have married her because he loved her so much, but their affair was fatally damaged and she soon left him and married another man. John was devastated, mourned her for months, resigned from the Crown Film Unit, moved back to Turville Heath to live with his parents, abandoned his dream of becoming a writer because the manuscript of *Charade* kept being rejected by publishers, and decided to obey his father and become a barrister after all. His only solace was the General Election on 5 July when he drove Labour Party supporters from nearby villages to the polls in his father's battered old Morris Oxford and helped Labour to win a landslide victory. Clement Attlee became Prime Minister with almost twice as many seats in the Commons as Churchill's Conservatives and a huge majority of 146 seats over all other parties. 'That was the great political event of my life,' Mortimer told Melvyn Bragg. 'I thought a great new world had started, a new world where there was going to be no further unemployment, no more class distinctions because we'd all worked together during the war and there probably weren't going to be any more Conservatives. It was the age of the common man. It was a paradise I wanted and I did believe in that and I really thought it would happen.'

Reluctantly he began to take the Law seriously, studying at home, attending lectures in Chancery Lane a few yards from his father's chambers – where he paid one of the senior barristers £100 (£2,580) to take him on as a pupil – eating the required number of dinners at the Inner Temple so as to qualify for the Bar, and passing some Bar exams but failing the Real Property exam. His writing ambition flared brightly again when at last a publisher, the Bodley Head, accepted *Charade* and he celebrated by spending several weeks in Paris where he checked into a cheap hotel, met one of his theatrical icons, the seventy-four-year-old artist and stage designer Gordon Craig, and landed briefly a dream job teaching English to a group of delicious Christian Dior models who resisted all his lumbering attempts to seduce them.

Back in England *Charade* was published at last in 1947. His aim in writing it and all his subsequent novels was 'to make people more sceptical of authority, of people who seek to rule us or make laws for us or seek to be the top dog, and more sympathetic to the underdog', he told Bragg. The book, which he dedicated to his parents, was obviously a first novel. The characters tend to make speeches at each other and some of the similes are bizarre: 'a pale sun appeared over the clouds like an invalid sitting up in bed'; 'her voice broke bravely round me like the ring of a wine-glass, or the distant cry of a hunting-horn through iced woods in winter'; 'the waiters move among the white tables like dirty merchantmen navigating an icefloe'. John Gielgud's novelist and playwright brother Val, who was head of BBC radio drama, sneered that 'the book contains the sort of fumbling round the skirts of sex which passes for sophistication in adolescent minds'. Even so it was an excellent first novel, sensitive, well written, amusing and extremely readable and rightly earned some very good reviews. In the *Daily Express* Daniel George wrote 'I urge you not on any account to miss it. A brilliant first novel' and praised the book's 'humour, tenderness, satire, compassion, insight'. *Time and Tide* said it was 'brilliantly done. It combines the sparkle and freshness of an observant newcomer with the poise of a practised old hand.' Pamela Hansford Johnson reported that the book had 'all the freshness of a sharp spring morning' and commended it as unpretentious, engaging, funny, shrewd and subtle. Peter Quennell agreed that 'the point of view is fresh, the style and the turn of wit are genuinely distinctive', and forty years later *Punch* reported that 'these reviewers weren't overstating the case. *Charade* is a little masterpiece ... marvellous.' He sent a signed copy to 'Angela' but received no reply. Eventually he was to earn about £150 from the book (£3,600).

Hugely encouraged, he started to write a second novel, *Rumming*

Park, about a thirty-five-year-old solicitor who has been adopted as a
parliamentary candidate and moves to his almost feudal constituency in
the country to prepare for an election. Simultaneously John sweated at
Turville Heath over his dreary law books and for recreation drove his
father's old car around, went horse riding and with a few friends to dances
in the nearby villages, and drank in the local pubs and at gymkhanas
with a couple of artists and a thirty-eight-year-old Communist poet,
novelist, reviewer and broadcaster, Randall Swingler, whom he had met
at a party. Swingler, who had won the Military Medal for his courage
during heavy fighting in Italy and was emotionally and physically shattered, commissioned him to write a few film reviews for a magazine he
edited, *Our Time*, and often mentioned a beautiful, twenty-nine-year-old
married woman with whom he was having an affair. She had left her
husband after ten years of marriage and was living in a tiny rented cottage
in the nearby village of Southend, and John realised with a shock that
this was the same beautiful Penelope Dimont whom he and Michael
Fenton had met at Wootton five years earlier when they went to consult
her pacifist husband Charles about Fenton's military tribunal. Swingler
was married too but his wife Geraldine, a concert pianist, led a separate
life with their twelve-year-old daughter Judith in Essex while he endured
a restless, chaotic, pub-crawling, manic-depressive existence, mainly in
a flat in London, and spent far too much time beer-swilling in Soho with
other writers, among them Patrick Hamilton, Flann O'Brien and Dylan
Thomas. Mortimer decided that he would very much like to meet the
strikingly good-looking Mrs Dimont again, rode his horse past her
cottage one lovely summer's day and saw her painting a coal scuttle in
the front garden. He introduced himself, said he was a friend of Swingler's,
and when she said she needed some bread he rode off to buy her a loaf. It
was the start of an extraordinary love affair.

By now Penelope had three daughters: two by her husband, nine-year-
old Madelon and five-year-old Caroline, who were both away at boarding
school; and two-year-old Julia, the illegitimate result of an affair that
Penelope had had with a man who worked at the chemical warfare
laboratory at Porton Down in Wiltshire, Kenneth Harrison. Julia was
living with Penelope's parents at Willersey in Worcestershire because
although Penelope loved being pregnant she was not at all keen on
looking after children, preferring to drink with men in pubs and clubs
and to have love affairs. She had met Swingler in the Gargoyle Club in
Soho but she was not just some selfish, boozy nymphomaniac, for although
her first novel, a huge historical saga set in Austria between the wars,

had been rejected, her second, *Johanna*, was about to be published and she had just sent her third, *Holiday*, off to her publishers, Secker and Warburg. She was startlingly casual about her adulteries and illegitimate child and was able to write dismissively in her second volume of auto-biography, *About Time Too*, that she knew very little about Julia's father and that when she told her husband that Kenneth Harrison was the child's father 'I have an impression of weeping, and don't think it was mine'. To make the situation even more bizarre, Harrison was homo-sexual, according to the journalist Christopher Booker, who told me that he met him in 1957 at Cambridge, where Harrison had become a maths don. Harrison did not acknowledge the child publicly – Dimont was named on the birth certificate as the father – but he was rich, kind, supported Julia generously for years, gave Penelope a car, and visited them regularly.

Penelope, Swingler and twenty-four-year-old Mortimer soon became a regular threesome in the local pubs and would sometimes go together to the theatre or cinema in London. Evenings often ended with Penelope playing the piano and the three of them singing, though John's voice was dreadful. Swingler wrote love poems for her but was often depressive and moody and for Penelope young Mortimer was welcome light relief and made her laugh, especially when he did his party-piece impersonation of an irritable old barrister – the first hint of Rumpole of the Bailey. John could be hilarious, she wrote in *About Time Too*: 'He was a clever, skinny, excitable youth – a more apt description, actually, than "young man" – and I enjoyed being taken to pubs where he was treated indulgently as the young Squire, a bit of a lad, always ready for a bottle of Scotch or can of black-market petrol.' She had no idea why he fell in love with her: 'My belief is that he was virtually inexperienced with women and that the girlfriends he told me about, if not exactly figments of his imagination, were much embellished by it. He certainly had two clear fantasies, neither of which had anything to do with me. The first was of a bouncing, good-natured semi-boy, slightly grubby, always ready for a lark ... The second was of high heels busily tapping to work in some executive office.'

Swingler was frequently away and Mortimer would take Penelope to a pub in his father's jalopy and they would talk about everything even though she was nearly five years older than he. One night on the way back he stopped the car and said, 'What about a quick fuck and then home?' She was astonished and turned him down but it was inevitable that one day they would become lovers. Swingler was still her man of the moment and in November she became pregnant by him after a romp in

an armchair at her parents' house in Willersey. She went up to London
to the Gargoyle Club to tell him, he left the club immediately, and she
did not see him again for seventeen years. She returned to live with her
parents and Julia in Willersey for a while but found life with her mother
claustrophobic and soon wangled an invitation to spend a weekend with
the Mortimers at Turville Heath. 'I certainly wasn't in love with John at
that time,' she wrote in *About Time Too*, 'but comforted by his attention
and enjoyed his company.' During the night, 'against all my high-flown
principles about loveless sex' and despite being pregnant 'I found myself
tip-toeing into his room, leaving Julia soundly asleep. Whatever else he
may have felt, I know he was amazed.'

At the end of 1947 John was about to be called to the Bar and
generously his father rented for him a two-room flat in the Inner Temple
so that he could live near his chambers instead of travelling in from the
country every day. The flat was on the second floor of 11 King's Bench
Walk and cost Clifford £193 (£4,950) a year. John was called to the Bar
on 26 January 1948, bought himself a wig, gown, bowler hat and striped
trousers, and went to work every day as a barrister in his father's chambers,
where Clifford paid him £5 a week (£120) to help with his probate work
and to draft his clients' divorce petitions and allegations of adultery,
cruelty and unreasonable behaviour. He started his legal career by urging
Penelope to break the law and have an abortion and she claimed that he
took her to see an abortionist in Chelsea, but the idea of killing her child
revolted her and she ran from the house with John pursuing her down
the street crying, 'What's wrong? What's the matter?' To make the
situation worse her alcoholic husband, who was now working as an
information officer for the BBC, was drying out in a psychiatric hospital
and would need somewhere to live when he was released, so in the spring
of 1948 John found a tiny cottage in Turville for her to rent, the White
Cottage, once a butcher's shop, and she moved into it with all three of
her children and was eventually joined by Charles, who stayed only a few
days before disappearing again. Despite the fact that Penelope was very
pregnant by now John walked every weekend the mile and a half from
Turville Heath, arriving sexually 'over-excited', she said, 'to grapple with
me as I cooked or washed up or persuaded the children to bed'. One
evening when they gave a party he took her outside and rogered her in a
haystack and she returned to the cottage dishevelled and sprouting pieces
of hay. Her brother Paul looked at her sadly. 'You are a chump,' he said.
This surfeit of shagging seems to have induced the birth of Swingler's
child, Deborah, who was born two months early and weighing only four

pounds in the Hermitage maternity hospital in Henley in June. Once again poor old cuckolded Charlie Dimont was registered on the birth certificate as the father. 'I was in no sense an earth mother,' Penelope told Catherine Stott of the *Sunday Telegraph* in 1979, 'and as each child arrived it was something of a surprise to me. The whole situation now seems to me extraordinary and deeply irresponsible.' Swingler sent her a box of peaches but did not visit her in hospital and made no effort to see her or the baby. He may have won the Military Medal but accepting lifelong responsibility for your child requires a different kind of courage.

At the end of July John took Penelope and the shrieking six-week-old infant to Ireland, where he managed to get lost in the bogs of Connemara as their car ran out of petrol. Less amusingly they went to a beach where Penelope gazed moodily out to sea and wondered whether to commit suicide, which may have been due to post-natal depression and should at least have warned him about the darkness in her character, but by now he was so besotted that nothing would stop him living with her. Together they rented a cottage in the village of Southend and over several months Penelope began to fall in love with him until eventually they decided to marry as soon as she could persuade Charles to divorce her. 'She was very beautiful and quite dangerous,' Mortimer told Andrew Billen of the *Evening Standard* in 2000, 'and she had all these children. As an only child, that was quite exciting for me. And she seemed capable of anything.' He was too young and naive to realise that much as he adored her she was not a great marriage prospect. Not only had she been constantly unfaithful to her first husband and had four small children by three different men, she had also suffered a bizarre, wildly unstable background. Her father, the Revd. Arthur Fletcher, was a short, fat, desperately unhappy, potentially suicidal, sexually tormented Anglican vicar who no longer believed in God, the virgin birth or the resurrection and so grabbed desperately at any possible alternative belief, from spiritualism and Communism to free love and nudism. Her mother, Amy, was possibly lesbian, said Penelope, refused to sleep in the same room as her father and shrank whenever he tried to touch her, so that early in their marriage he slept outside in an army hut and walked about the garden at dawn naked. Penelope claimed that he was so frustrated sexually that he had molested her regularly from the time she was eight until she was seventeen, kissing, fondling and groping in her knickers, until she was strong enough to fight him off when he tried one night to rape her. 'So she *said*, but I don't know,' Mortimer told Craig Brown disbelievingly in 2001, but their son Jeremy told me in 2004 that he believed his mother because her father also molested his granddaughter Madelon. Yet Penelope claimed that she was not at all traumatised by her father's taste for incest and was so unconcerned about the indecent assaults – or maybe about her children – that incredibly she let her small daughters go and stay with her parents on their own.

She came to hate her father, who disrupted her childhood further by sending her to six different schools across southern Britain, from London to Wales, one of them an 'anthroposophist' school where there were no rules and the children were encouraged to walk around barefoot, do what they liked, and nurture their 'astral bodies'. Her stability was further undermined when she discovered at the age of twelve that her name was Penelope, not Peggy, which was what everyone had called her until then. She was bright enough to win a place at University College, London, to do a journalism course, but with such a flaky childhood it is not surprising that she stayed only a year and never took any exams. As for her mother, she wrote in *About Time Too*, she was frigid and not at all maternal. To keep her randy husband away Amy hired a decoy, an unneeded nineteen-year-old 'governess' with whom the vicar proceeded to have an affair, and the Fletchers were so dysfunctional that not one family photograph was ever taken. Not surprisingly Penelope grew up emotionally unstable, insecure, neurotic and suicidal, weaknesses that had been made even worse by ten years of marriage to a weak, unreliable drunk and by giving birth to the daughters of a homosexual and a boozy, manic-depressive, undependable poet. 'With my mother the *thought* of suicide was constant,' said Jeremy. 'She was genuinely quite interested in the concept.' An added problem was that Penelope 'liked men very much but she didn't like women', he said. 'She had problems maintaining friendships, partly because I think she always believed that people would let her down in the end. She would make impossible demands on people, almost willing them to default so that she could then write them off. She was a tormented woman. I don't think it was the fact that her father molested her as a child, I think it was that she was very beautiful and sought after. She was *fun* when she was younger, and she had a wild life. People wanted to be with her.' Even the way her eldest daughter Madelon was born and named in March 1938 was beautifully barmy: the child was born on a train between Vienna and Switzerland, and when Penelope read in a newspaper that a local horse race had been won by a beast called Madelon, that was it. She named her first-born after a racehorse.

With such a background it is little wonder that she had given herself so carelessly to so many men. 'I was so grateful to anybody who loved me, that was the least I could do,' she told Caroline Phillips of the *Evening Standard* in 1994. 'I had a great longing to be loved.' Naive and inexperienced though he was, twenty-four-year-old Mortimer deluged her with affection and cosseted her by giving her breakfast in bed, presents and treats, and that was enough. Penelope 'was an amazingly beautiful woman', their daughter Sally told Alan Yentob during a TV interview in 2003, 'and he was very young and just joined in like a big child, and it was fun for a while.' Penelope's own explanation for falling in love with John was that he was *there* and their affair allowed her to be childish, share his naughtiness, play forbidden games with a 'spice of incest', and because he was talented, funny and surprisingly tolerant of her children. 'She had four children to support,' said Jeremy, 'and she found this young man, not just *very* young but naive, and I think he was as surprised as anybody that she actually wanted to be with him. There's no doubt that she did love him. I don't think it was on the rebound from Swingler. She was really happy with my father.' As for John himself, he was by now having all the sex that he had dreamed about for so long and with a beautiful, experienced, older woman. 'I think Penelope was bananas,' the author Celia Brayfield, who became a friend of John's many years later, told me, 'but he married her because he was extremely ugly and couldn't get laid.' Had he been older and more experienced he would have realised that Penelope was seriously unbalanced and would have bolted. He should at least have been alerted by the casual, selfish way she treated her children. All she really cared about was her writing, so whenever her mother was available Penelope would lie in bed late and then spend all day at her typewriter, leaving her mother to look after the children, bathe them, play with them, take them out, and do all the housework, shopping and cooking. Her first three daughters were virtually raised by their grandmother, who believed reasonably that Penelope was a dreadful, thoroughly irresponsible mother. It was not a happy omen for John and Penelope's marriage, which he kept proposing throughout 1948 until eventually she agreed over lunch and a plate of *sole véronique* at the Queen's Hotel in Sloane Square in 1949.

John's parents failed him badly by making no real effort to warn him that it would be disastrous if he married this damaged, unstable, rackety older woman with four children by three different men. Clifford joked that he was baffled that a woman 'with a car and furniture' should see anything in his callow son and told her that John would be a dreadful husband because he had no money or prospects, was utterly lazy, drank far too much, and would offer no sympathy if she was ill because he hated illness. As for John's mother, Penelope was disconcerted to discover how secretive and remote she was, detached from the rest of the world, including her son, and her only reaction was to remark that Penelope had 'really nice eyes, not at all the eyes of a divorced person'. Penelope was startled to find that John's parents thought he was a joke, and often when she was in the garden at Turville Heath she would hear through the window Clifford yelling at him and John's cowed, mumbling reply. 'A lot of people are embarrassed by love,' she told Lynda Lee-Potter of the *Daily Mail* in 1993, 'and they were the kind of parents who could only show it by putting him down, making a joke of it.'

Yet Clifford, who hated visitors or noise, soon became a loving sur- rogate grandfather and let her children crawl all over him and play with his fob watch, though Madelon, who was now ten, confessed years later that he frightened her because he was blind and everyone pretended that he wasn't. When they went to Turville Heath he would bark 'let me see you all' and would 'see' them by feeling them and pronouncing who was who by their size. As for Penelope's father, whom John came to like – probably because he was an atheist priest, which appealed to John's God-hating sense of humour – he did warn John that if he married Penelope he would have to 'keep a firm hand on her tiller', but John was so helplessly cunt-struck that he ignored the advice.

His other great excitement in 1948 was that his second novel, *Rumming Park*, was published by the Bodley Head. It was meant to be part comedy of errors, part political satire, but it was sadly dull, laboured, unbelievable and unfunny and not nearly as good as *Charade*. The characters never came alive, the dialogue was stilted, and once again he concocted some weirdly inappropriate descriptions: 'In the wind the trees creaked and laboured as old women pant and creak in stays'; 'The hawthorn trees were gnarled and shapeless furniture, the leaves oppressive upholstery, and the cow parsnips reminded her of yellowing, unwashed antimacassars'. Most embarrassing of all was an overwritten two-page scene about a woman dying in childbirth. Still, at least the book was published, whereas Penelope's novel *Johanna* sank without trace and her publisher, Fred Warburg, rejected her next one, *Holiday*, telling her cruelly to go off and read Thucidydes' history of the Peloponnesian wars instead, a suggestion that undermined her confidence so badly that she did not write another word for five years.

Charles Dimont reacted to Mortimer's affair with his wife by trying to commit suicide and then refusing to divorce her, though eventually he was persuaded to agree. Since Mortimer was a practising divorce barrister himself this should not have been as difficult as it turned out to be. For more than a year, for just a guinea a time (£25), naive and inexperienced though he was, he had been listening to men and women more than twice his age complaining about their spouses and sex lives and telling them how to end their unhappy marriages, but now he was reduced to hiring a private detective to spy on Penelope and himself as they stayed together openly in hotels to provide evidence that they were committing adultery. This went on for weeks because whenever the detective questioned chambermaids and waiters afterwards none could remember either Penelope or John. Eventually they managed to persuade the private eye that they were indeed sleeping with each other and on 4 July 1949 Dimont was awarded a decree nisi that became absolute on 18 August. Nine days later, on 27 August, Penelope and John were married at Chelsea Register Office. He was twenty-six, she thirty. Their parents were all there but strangely none of Penelope's children, not even eleven-year-old Madelon nor seven-year-old Caroline. They celebrated with a party that went on until dawn at John's flat at 11 King's Bench Walk, which from now on was to be their home, and the happy couple went off to St Malo in northern France on a honeymoon that cost John a frightening £11 (£257), which he could not really afford after having to pay all the costs of the divorce. Immediately they had the first of the hundreds of blazing rows that were to engulf their marriage right from the start – this one about money – and they returned to England after just three days, much earlier than they had planned. It was the start of twenty turbulent years for both of them.

Five

From Poverty to Pacific Pallisades
1949–1959

The flat at 11 King's Bench Walk overlooked the pretty garden of the Middle Temple but although it had a large living room the bedroom, kitchen and bathroom were tiny and it was much too cramped for two adults and four children. Madelon was away for much of the time with Penelope's parents or at boarding school, where Charles Dimont was still paying her fees, but John and Penelope had to sleep in a cupboard recess that was just big enough to take a double bed and Caroline, Julia and Deborah slept on bunks in the bedroom. The living room was usually draped with wet laundry and infused with the pungent ammonia stench of soaking nappies, and the lawyers who worked in neighbouring chambers – twenty-three of them at the same address and dozens more on either side – were constantly complaining about the racket of the Mortimer offspring. When a woman barrister from the floor below could finally bear no longer the creaking of the rocking horse Penelope informed her loftily that there was a statue in the garden with an inscription that said 'Lawyers were children once'.

John escaped as much as possible to work in his father's chambers a couple of hundred yards away now that Clifford was sixty-one, delegating much of his work to him and coming up to London much less often. John claimed later that he would rise at four o'clock each day to supplement his meagre legal income by reviewing more films for *Our Time* and writing a short history of costumes for the clothes store Moss Bros as well as another novel for a small advance of £100 (£2,336). He began to write romantic short stories for women's magazines and was advised by one editor to make his heroines meet their dark, handsome lovers by glorious chance –

in a lift or the street – so that readers would sigh and go off to work with hope in their hearts. Luckily Clifford was paying the rent for the flat, Penelope's mother bought most of the children's clothes and had them to stay during the holidays, and Penelope's father contributed to Caroline's and Julia's fees as soon as they were old enough to be packed off to boarding school. 'They all seemed to get sent away to school because Penelope needed quietness to write,' John told Judith Palmer in 2001 for her book *Private View: Artists Working Today*. Kenneth Harrison was still supporting Julia and paying Penelope a small allowance, but despite all this financial help John was for some reason so hard-up that he sponged constantly off his father, regularly pawned his silver cigarette case and was nervous of his tight-lipped bank manager. 'He was awfully young when we got married,' Penelope told Lynda Lee-Potter in 1993, 'and I don't think he had any idea of what living with four kids and a writer entailed. His home life had been very smooth, everything laid on, there was plenty of money. Getting married was mad, absolutely crazy. It's not surprising that later he suddenly thought: I've been missing out on something.'

To add to their financial woes Penelope became pregnant immediately and nine months and a day after they had married she gave birth to their daughter Sally on 28 May 1950 at Queen Charlotte's Hospital in Hammersmith, so that now there were seven people living in the tiny flat. 'You're like a train,' Clifford scoffed. 'Stop at the next station for children to board.' The shortage of money led to more and more rows with Penelope and John soon consoled himself by having an affair. Whenever Penelope went to his chambers, she wrote in her autobiography, 'my familiar husband seemed strange, clammy, over-anxious. His barrister's uniform smelled of sweat, semen and cologne.' It was the start of twenty years of blatant adulteries that were to cause a huge number of vicious rows and to damage the marriage beyond repair.

The amazingly generous Kenneth Harrison came to the rescue again by giving Penelope the freehold of a farmhouse in Essex which the Mortimers started to use for weekends and holidays, Burnt House Farm, as well as a Ford V8 station wagon to allow them to drive out into the country. In the fresh air of East Anglia, away from the claustrophobia of the tiny flat and the Inner Temple, John was able again to enjoy horse riding and painting and to nurture his feminine side, happily cooking, cleaning, changing the baby's nappy, cutting Julia's hair, and playing convincingly the part of the doting stepfather. He would cook breakfast, take the children for walks, boating, swimming and riding, tell them stories and write little plays for them. 'He would have made an excellent mother,' wrote Penelope in *About Time Too*. 'Masculine jobs such as starting the electric generator, putting up shelves or cutting the grass depressed him enormously. "Get a man in" became one of those family sayings that can be applied to almost anything.'

The first few years of Mortimer's legal career involved a dismal round of trying to suck up to solicitors and their clerks by hanging around the Law Courts and buying them cups of coffee or the occasional pint in a pub in the hope that they might brief him to divorce one of their clients. At first he was hired to do undefended divorces but still had to prove adultery, cruelty or desertion and persuade the judge that his client was the innocent party and the spouse the guilty one. To prove that they had committed adultery the husband or wife might have to repair to an hotel, perhaps with a professional 'co-respondent', so that they could be found apparently committing sin – yet both they and their barristers would have to pretend that the whole charade was genuine. In those days a husband or wife might go to court to force the other to restore 'their conjugal rights' – resume sexual intercourse – and a husband still had the right to sue his wife's lover for damages. One lascivious old judge became so aroused by all the titillating evidence of sexual misbehaviour that he would sketch the outline of an enormous penis, hand it to a female witness, and ask her if it had looked like that.

Divorce briefs were scarce and the glum world of probate and contested wills where heirs fought each other with naked greed was depressing but Penelope helped by typing out his divorce petitions for him and he tried to produce every day at least five pages of a new novel before the children awoke. His third book, *Answer Yes or No*, was published by the Bodley Head in 1950 and was much more fun and better written than *Rumming Park*. Dedicated to Penelope, it was again autobiographical and told of a hard-working divorce barrister who falls for a married woman with a complaisant husband and begins to come alive. Like John the hero has been a lonely only child who is dominated by his father, finds it difficult to make friends, lives in an Inner Temple flat close to his chambers, and rises before dawn each day. He gives free legal advice to the poor in the East End of London – as John had begun to do – and is appalled to meet so many humble people who are not just hard-up but deeply mired in desperate poverty: sick, broken, old working-class men and women; exhausted young wives whose drunken husbands beat them when not in prison or raping their daughters; thin, grimy urchins; an endless queue of underclass hopelessness that arouses his angry socialist instincts. The book relies again on some ridiculous coincidences but it is well written, thoughtful, very readable, and Mortimer's ear for colloquial dialogue was excellent. Towards the end one paragraph reads as though it was an ominous warning to Penelope that while a woman can be happy if she is loved and secure, a man needs to believe in something more important to him than his woman and bigger than himself.

Answer Yes or No eased their financial burden a little when it was selected as a Book Society choice and published also in America under the title *Silver Hook*, and in 1951 John made a bit more on the side by writing captions for the Hall of Coal at the huge Festival of Britain exhibition of national achievement. But the upkeep of Burnt House Farm, the cost of getting there and continual repairs to the electricity generator all proved to be too much, and the Temple flat was far too small now that the girls were thirteen, nine, six, three and nearly two. Early in 1952 they left King's Bench Walk and swopped the Burnt House freehold for the last seven years of the lease of a big, narrow, four-storey, semi-detached house in north London where they were to spend the next thirteen years, at 23 Harben Road. It was an old Victorian house in a rundown street a couple of hundred yards from Swiss Cottage underground station with six bedrooms, high ceilings and a long back garden. The rent was just £7 a week (£133) because the railway company that owned the house planned to demolish it soon. They never did and the house still stands today although it has long been converted into two large maisonettes, but the possibility of imminent eviction hung over the Mortimers all the years that they were there, adding an extra uncertainty to Penelope's insecurity. She did however come to love the area because it was home to hundreds of Central European wartime refugees and seemed glamorously cosmopolitan with its delicatessens, German restaurant, a shop that sold nothing but coffee and a big Odeon cinema. The Mortimers were also delighted to have so much space after the tiny Temple flat and together they painted the hall a dark, violent red – an unwise colour for a couple who were so often fighting – and as John's legal practice began to prosper they hired the first of a series of au pairs and a treasure of a cleaning woman, Mrs Medway, who was to work for them for fourteen years.

That summer of 1952 the two youngest girls went to stay with Kath and Clifford while John and Penelope took the three oldest for a holiday in a rented bungalow on an island in the Thames, where both he and she started to write new novels, for her the first that she had dared to tackle in seven years. John's book was *Like Men Betrayed*, a thriller about a London solicitor, Christopher Kennet, who discovers that his son is 'borrowing' money from a rich, widowed client to finance a big deal to buy obsolete weapons from the British government. When the widow dies in a car crash her heirs threaten to expose his embezzlement but Kennet saves him by sacrificing himself and is murdered by the arms dealer. Penelope's novel, *A Villa in Summer*, set in an English country cottage, was a searing account of their increasingly dreadful marriage. A howl of anguish that was barely fiction at all, it was the first of her seven blatantly autobiographical novels. Both she and John admitted that her novels were factual and about themselves and their marriage. 'Oh yes,' John told Mark Amory of *The Sunday Times Magazine* in 1977, 'I'm the husband all right and all those other unpleasant husbands.' The husband in *A Villa in Summer* is Andrew Addams, a hard-up, thirty-year-old, Inner Temple divorce barrister who lives with his wife Emily and their children in an overcrowded flat and is often moody, unkind and offensive to her: rude, selfish, short-tempered, inconsiderate and always nagging, critical and starting rows, yet also naive and at times pathetically childish. They move to the country, where Andrew falls for the schoolmaster's wife, Alice, tells Emily that he wants to go to bed with Alice, and is surprised when Emily refuses angrily to condone his adultery. He reckons that she is being unreasonable, that if she really loved him she would let him be free to deepen himself by exploring other women without lessening his love for her.

'Are you asking for my permission?' Emily asks him. 'Is that why you told me? Do you want me to say go on, have an affair with her, give you my blessing?' (The same question was to recur throughout the Mortimer marriage, with John driving Penelope to the boundaries of despair as he flaunted his infidelities and told her about them.) They have yet another of their dreadful rows:

> 'I'm sick of it,' [*he said*], 'sick of everything. I want to get away from work, the children, this bloody house. I've had it. Finished.'
> 'And me?'
> 'Yes. And you. You've changed. You're no longer the person you were in London. I hate the whole business. Hate it.'
> 'And you'd sooner be with Alice?'
> 'For a time, yes.'
> 'And then?'
> 'Oh, I don't know. Live. Just be somewhere and live.'

She slaps him viciously, he grips her wrists and gazes calmly into her eyes, and she runs to the bedroom to cry. He leaves her but eventually returns for a happy ending which Penelope later admitted was false and sugary, but the sensible moral of the story seems to be that if a man needs to commit adultery he should at least be polite enough to keep his infidelities secret from his wife. *A Villa in Summer* was melodramatic, clichéd and every character was unsympathetic, but it gave a vivid snapshot of how unhappy the Mortimer marriage had already become after just three years – yet Penelope still dedicated it to John, hoping he would heed its lesson and give up his philandering. 'I used to leave home after a *terrible* row with my wife,' he told Melvyn Bragg, 'with my shirt torn, bleeding at the nose. I used to stumble down the stairs, all the children had infectious diseases and were sick, the au pair girl was pregnant, the mat was absolutely covered with bills foreclosing the mortgage, shutting off the overdraft, the car had been stolen [yet] I was absolutely capable of advising fifty-year-old company directors on exactly how they should conduct their married lives!' Apart from the fact that he had no mortgage he paints a pretty credible picture, and it seems quite possible that it was John himself who had impregnated the au pair girl. In Penelope's most agonisingly autobiographical novel, *The Pumpkin Eater*, which she was to write seven years later, the wife accuses the husband of seducing their twenty-four-year-old lodger, Philpot. He admits it, and it seems that he may also have made her pregnant. 'Penelope always used to say that if they went to the cinema with the au pair girl he used to sit in the middle and hold hands with both of them!' Barbara Fenton told me. 'I think he jumped on all the au pairs as well.'

Mortimer's naive dream that Penelope might become a complaisant wife and condone his infidelities was mirrored in Nancy Friday's book about male masochism, *Men in Love*, by the case of 'Peter', a masochistic husband of whom she wrote: 'If only he could have other women, with no threat that it would cause his wife to leave him, then it would be "great to get home to mama." He wants what he wants – but he needs his wife's permission to want it. If only she would commit adultery, too, she would be revealed to be just like him. They would be united even in their dirty desires. Men like Peter illustrate a common facet of the masculine conflict. They long for the swinging life, but want to hold on to "mama", too. Their solution is often to go in for orgiastic scenes, having talked their wives into going along with them.' Mortimer simply could not understand why Penelope wanted him to be faithful and was said in later life to have been to at least one orgy. 'Boringness and lack of generosity and cruelty are worse sins than infidelity,' he told the *Mail on Sunday* magazine in 2004, adding unconvincingly: 'I think infidelity can be a help in a marriage, because it renews the passion between husband and wife.'

The Mortimers' marriage was not all misery. Sometimes it was tame and domesticated. Caroline told *The Sunday Times Magazine* in 1973 that she remembered her mother was 'very beautiful and glamorous, smelling of French perfume, going to somewhere called the French Club', but she also had a Singer sewing machine with which she made clothes for herself and the children and in the evenings she would sew and repair while John wrote or worked on his briefs. Sometimes they would slip out of the house while the children were asleep to go to the pub or cinema. At weekends they might visit John's parents at Turville and he would take the older girls riding or out on the river, and they gave parties and danced to the records of Louis Armstrong, Bing Crosby and Fats Waller. Despite all the rows they were still in lust, made up with passion after their fights, and John made a real effort to be a good parent. 'He was a wonderful stepfather to me when I was a child,' Julia told me in 2004, 'and for this I always think of him with great love and affection.' Madelon was amazed when he went up to her boarding school in the Midlands to attend her confirmation in a draughty cathedral despite the fact that he was an atheist and had a temperature of 103 degrees, and 'he was very nice to me,' Caroline told *The Sunday Times Magazine*. Penelope felt so committed to John that she changed Caroline's, Julia's and Deborah's surnames from Dimont to Mortimer. One weekend when John had earned a surprise £100 (£1,900) for just one divorce they took Madelon and Caroline to Paris, where he insisted on taking them to a strip club. Penelope typically complained that the Champs-Elysées was too wide and was devastated to hear a fortune teller in the Place du Théâtre tell John that he would never be really happy until he was fifty. The forecast was very nearly accurate.

John finished his novel *Like Men Betrayed* so quickly that it was inevitably slapdash and much less readable than *Charade* and *Answer Yes or No*: a wordy, waffly book in which the reader is lectured rather than shown developments by the use of character and dialogue. It needed serious rewriting – a task that John was to avoid only too often in his writing. He was to become renowned for dashing off a novel or play and grabbing the money without taking time to polish his first drafts. In *Like Men Betrayed* the characters are ill-defined, difficult to differentiate, rarely come to life, and once again are so unsympathetic that it is not easy to care about them, but he was already making such a name for himself that it was picked as a Book Society choice and he was asked to adapt it as a radio play that was broadcast two years later, which encouraged him to write a second radio play, *No Hero*. Despite the unhappiness of his marriage he dedicated the book again to Penelope even though the hero's wife hates and despises him because he is so coldly unfaithful. Equally treacherous was John's old friend Michael Fenton, once his moral beacon, who was still in Oxford studying medicine but in 1954 abandoned his first wife, Jean, and their two tiny children and left them in their cramped bedsitter while he ran off with the woman who was to become his second wife, Barbara, in April. The Mortimers went to the wedding, which reinforced John's belief that adultery was an unimportant trifle if a principled moralist like Fenton had no qualms about it.

While Penelope was taking more than a year to write her novel John dashed off another, *The Narrowing Stream*. Dedicated to her yet again, this was another thriller in which a bored, lonely, disappointed wife, Julia, in her late thirties like Penelope, faces up to her husband's lies and infidelity with a beautiful young girl who has been murdered. When she asks him why he has been unfaithful to her he says it was because he would soon be old. It was a short book, again knocked off quickly to make some money, but this time fast, well written and gripping. By coincidence it was published on the same day in May 1954 as Penelope's *A Villa in Summer* and both books attracted excellent reviews. In the *Guardian* Norman Shrapnel praised John's 'energy, wit and sheer professionalism', Kingsley Amis said that he 'has a great gift of fixing character by a few scraps of dialogue and he has a very fine sense of place', and the *New Statesman* reckoned that 'what really distinguishes Mortimer from his rivals is . . . a humane morality of his own and a rare gift for avoiding the obvious'. Penelope probably snorted at the suggestion that John had any sense of morality at all but she compromised her own by letting her new publisher, Michael Joseph, pretend that the novel was her first, arguing speciously that it was the first she had written under the name Mortimer – a ploy which attracted better reviews than she deserved because reviewers are usually kind to beginners. *A Villa in Summer* was picked as a Book Society choice and John Betjeman wrote in the *Daily Telegraph* that it was 'really excellent' and said that 'such a book as this needs to be written. It is disillusioned and angry, but written with heart and skill.' *The Times* said it was 'masterly' and Daniel George reported in the *Bookman* that it was 'a novel that makes much other fiction look false'. According to Penelope, John was jealous of her good reviews. 'He was always tremendously competitive with me, though he knew it was stupid,' she told Lynda Lee-Potter in 1993. 'When my second novel was published on the same day as one of his bloody novels, some ghastly magazine reviewed me rather well and him rather poorly. He minded terribly. He can't stand criticism.' A year later John admitted to Helena de Bertodano of the *Sunday Telegraph* that 'two writers together are a recipe for disaster. One of you is always doing better than the other,' and in 1977 he told Mark Amory of *The Sunday Times Magazine* that 'there was a lot of competition in my first marriage, competition about everything'. Penelope's own opinion of John's novels was dismissive. 'Frankly, I've never managed to finish one,' she told Lee-Potter.

Her book was so much admired that she became an instant literary lioness and to celebrate their dual success – and a welcome double boost to their finances – they drove that summer to Rome, stopping off in Parma and Pisa. In Switzerland she crashed the car and in Besançon in July she conceived yet again, their only son, Jeremy, who was born in London on 27 April 1955. At first the Mortimers were ecstatic to have a son at last after five daughters and John wrote her a loving letter the next day exulting that now they had everything they could possibly want and promising that they would embark together on a great new adventure, but having another noisy, demanding baby in the house reinfected the marriage and left Penelope feeling post-natally depressed, dull and too tired even to go to the pub, and John feeling trapped and that he was wasting his life. They rented a small house in Cornwall for a summer holiday but the sewage tank overflowed in the front garden and they discovered that none of the local hotels had a bar. In 2004 Jeremy told me that when his parents had married an important part of their decision was that they should 'continue to have *fun*, but I think that the fun element of it was perhaps something that he'd been banking on a little bit more'. To Penelope's huge distress John 'began coming home later', she wrote in her autobiography, 'making furtive phone calls, being extravagantly affectionate for no reason. When he finally told me he was having an affair – though I doubt whether it was much more than an interesting flirtation – my grief bewildered him.'

He was still divorcing people and sorting out disputes over wills but one of the traumas of his early legal career was to do with murder: the hanging of the nightclub hostess Ruth Ellis in July 1955, three months after Jeremy was born. Ellis had shot her racing-driver lover, David Blakely, outside a Hampstead pub a few weeks previously but he had been a cruel, violent lover and many were horrified that she should be executed. There was a storm of protest and Mortimer was so appalled by her death that he vowed to fight for the abolition of capital punishment, and his disgust was to fuel his attempts to help bring about a gentler, more tolerant, understanding society.

To diminish Penelope's depression and listlessness she started taking pep pills, 'uppers', that fired her to rush off to parties and nightclubs with John and still be able to write afterwards late into the night, crash out for a couple of hours' sleep, and then take another pill to keep her going through the day. It was a dangerous way to live and began to damage both her mental and physical health and she had a nervous breakdown. John hired a German nanny, Helga, to look after the children and sent Penelope and Caroline off to the Austrian Alps for a convalescent holiday. When they returned he persuaded her to consult a psychiatrist, Dr Fieldman, but she found it difficult to take him and his questions seriously. They took another holiday together, this time to the South of France, where they drove through the Camargue and looked out for the famous wild horses and flamingoes, but even here they fought so much that when Penelope spotted a flamingo at last she kept it to herself because they had been having a row. Her poor mental condition coloured a dark novel that she began to write during those unhappy days. Depressingly entitled *The Bright Prison*, which was how she saw her marriage, it was another howl of grief at the state of their relationship. This time the husband was a weak, unstable solicitor in his forties, a childish, selfish, bad-tempered, vicious man who drank too much, slept with any woman he could, and hated the four rude, horrible children who dominated his life. The wife was a lonely, nervous, melodramatic worrier who was constantly tearful or depressed, a disturbed, obsessive woman utterly disconnected from normal life, who comes to realise that she no longer loves her husband and starts an affair with a neighbour. Her husband's latest adultery is with a pale, skinny, flat-chested, childlike, gormless girl – probably Penelope's savage portrait of John's latest conquest – but the married couple's lovers dump them both and marry each other, forcing the husband and wife together again. In a desperately bleak, hopeless ending they realise they are stuck with each other.

The book suffers from too many unbelievable moments, coincidences and instances of incredible behaviour. Even in the 1950s people just did not behave like this. It is also grossly overwritten and melodramatic: the characters are always screaming at each other, mouths hang open with disbelief, and the four main characters are utterly amoral and supremely unattractive. It is a thoroughly silly, hysterical book and *The Times* reviewer reckoned that Penelope had overreached herself: 'when it comes to adults Mrs Mortimer's touch is less sure, and her quadrangle of unhappy lovers seem to behave in a most implausible way.' Even Michael Joseph disliked the book, considering it too cynical and gloomy. Yet Penelope earned her high reputation in the mid-1950s because she was the first female novelist to write with absolute candour and brutality about the deep unhappiness suffered by hordes of married women, so when it was published in September 1956 *The Bright Prison* was again a Book Society selection. Bizarrely she dedicated the book again to John – and he dedicated his new one, *Three Winters*, to her once more. How could they possibly believe that they would enjoy what they were writing about each other? Yet in novel after novel they would both pick away at the scab of their marriage and expose the raw pain beneath. Something very strange was bubbling deep in this miserable yet obsessive relationship. John's infidelity was so blatant that when in 1956 he went to visit Michael Fenton and his new wife he tried to seduce her. 'John was actually staying with us and we were out walking,' Barbara Fenton told me, 'and he made a lunge and I said, "I don't think so." He seemed to think all's fair in love and war even though I was married to his best friend. I'm sure he tried it on with anybody and everyone. It didn't seem very important, and when my husband heard about it he just said, "Typical Mortimer." John was a tremendous charmer and very funny and he told Michael that when he wanted to seduce a woman it took him half an hour to talk away his face!' As for Penelope, 'She was terrifying,' said Mrs Fenton, 'and I think Michael was frightened of her too. She was very arrogant intellectually, very demanding both emotionally and materialistically, and she didn't like women at all.'

John's new novel, *Three Winters*, was a love story about compulsive sexual obsession. It started by telling of the lonely, thirteen-year-old only son of strange parents who takes a shine to a girl called Diana, the daughter of a doctor who he suspects is his mother's lover. In part two, now aged twenty-three and working with a wartime film unit, he meets Diana again, becomes obsessed by her, and manages at last to seduce her. In part three he is thirty-three, married to her, and they are back at his family home for Christmas, where Diana storms from the dinner table when his uncle reveals that her father was renowned for seducing his women patients. It becomes apparent that Diana has herself been obsessed all her life by her father and that maybe her childhood was stained by incest. Much of the very readable story is blatantly autobiographical: the father in the novel is selfish, demanding, constantly quotes Shakespeare, treats the boy like an adult, warns him never to do anything heroic and tells him that love has always been hugely overrated. And John was surely thinking of his problems with Penelope when he wrote that the hero had given up trying to be nice to his wife because he was tired of always making the huge effort necessary to make her happy. They were duplicates of each other, he wrote hopelessly, and trapped together like prisoners. *Three Winters* was the best of John's six novels to date, and again a Book Society choice, but it was the last he would write while still married to Penelope. Two novelists in one marriage were too many and it rankled that Penelope was more famous than he was. 'You write about your life,' he told Judith Palmer, 'and if you're having the same experiences as the person you're living with, and both writing about them, then there isn't enough to go round, really. Also, when one person's writing, you hear this typewriter clicking click-click-click while you can't think of what to say. It's quite difficult to live with a writer because writers are very, very selfish and live in a world of their own. You need someone who lives in the real world.'

Under the pseudonym Geoffrey Lincoln he started to write a series of light-hearted articles about being a barrister for Malcolm Muggeridge, editor of the humorous magazine *Punch*. They were collected and published the following year, 1957, as an anecdotal guidebook for novice lawyers entitled *No Moaning of the Bar* and illustrated with John's own simple little ink sketches. If, for example, a magistrate should ask you at the start of a case 'what are you here for?' it is unwise to reply 'two guineas': the correct response should be 'for the defendant', though it is said that when a judge barked at the legendary barrister F. E. Smith, 'What do you think I'm here for?' Smith replied: 'Who am I to question the inscrutable ways of Providence?' Smith it was too who gave a long explanation in court about a tricky legal point, was told by the judge, 'I'm afraid I am none the wiser, Mr Smith,' and replied: 'No, my lord, but better informed.' Sadly not much of the book was that amusing. *No Moaning of the Bar* was a thin, facetious little potboiler that Mortimer would prefer to forget.

On 15 May 1956 Penelope's father died of lung cancer, smoking until the very end, aged seventy-five, leaving just £404-15s-1d to her mother – a paltry £6,700 in modern values, though he would have left much more had he not been helping with the girls' expensive school fees. Penelope's reaction was to write a cold, unloving portrait of her father, *The Parson*, which she sold to the *New Yorker* magazine. When she wrote her autobiography thirty-six years later she had trouble remembering the year of his death. Apparently more important for her was the outcry after the Egyptian leader Colonel Nasser nationalised the Suez Canal on 26 July and Britain and France invaded the canal zone to protect the free flow of their shipping before they were forced by America and the United Nations to withdraw. Many Britons supported the invasion, fearing that Nasser might become another Hitler, but during the crisis the Mortimers joined the left-wing demonstrations in Downing Street and Grosvenor Square against the Prime Minister, Sir Anthony Eden.

Michael Joseph paid for the Mortimers to rent a house at Positano, just south of Naples, for a two-month family holiday in August and September and commissioned them to write jointly a book about taking so many children abroad. They called it *With Love and Lizards* and compiled it by keeping diaries and writing separate passages of the book rather than fighting over every word. When they reached Positano they found to their dismay that the house had only two bedrooms, no telephone, and was perched on a hill a twenty-minute climb and hundreds of steps above a small, insanitary beach. It was the first place they had ever stayed abroad for more than a fortnight and they made the best of it by visiting a church museum where the exhibits were all skulls and bones, taking a steamer to Amalfi, watching a *son et lumière* Saracen invasion on the beach, visiting Paestum, Capri, Naples, Pompeii and Sorrento, and accepting invitations to several expatriate writers' and painters' parties. At one lunch John was horrified to find himself sitting next to the British Fascist leader Oswald Mosley and taken aback to discover that this chum of Hitler's was charming. Madelon, now eighteen, and Caroline, fourteen, were pursued constantly by Italian men, even the old ones, and the whole family was savaged by mosquitoes, the smaller children got sunstroke and badly sunburned, Penelope caught an eye infection, and she and four of the girls went down with fever. But John tried hard to be a good father, I was told by David Leitch, who was to become Madelon's boyfriend two years later. 'Positano was then *the* most fashionable place to go,' said Leitch, 'and he did all the things little girls like to do, which were not necessarily what an extremely randy thirty-three-year-old divorce lawyer would find the ideal way to spend his holiday, especially when they weren't his kids.' For all that, *With Love and Lizards* was not a great success when it was published the following year. The style was jaunty but the book was dull and bloated with pointless anecdotes that had probably been made up by John since Penelope admitted later that he wrote most of the book because he had 'more agile powers of invention'. It was not a book of which either of them could be proud though it led the *Evening Standard* to sign Penelope up to write a regular column about her life as a mother of six entitled *Five Girls and a Boy*.

In October Madelon went up to Newnham College, Cambridge, to read Law and John met a BBC radio producer, Nesta Pain, who asked him to write another radio play, and he decided to stop competing with Penelope by writing novels but to write for radio and television instead. One of the subjects that he had discussed in *No Moaning of the Bar* was the dock brief, a legal custom which allowed an accused person who has not yet appointed a lawyer to look around the court and pick to represent him any one of the gowned, bewigged, unemployed barristers sitting there like a rank of taxis plying for hire. The fee for taking on a dock brief was only two guineas (£36) and the case might last for several days, so the taxi-barristers parked in court and trying to catch the accused's eye tended to be the old, desperate or incompetent. It was this that inspired the radio play that was to launch Mortimer as a celebrated playwright, *The Dock Brief*, in which Herbert Fowle, a shopkeeper accused of murdering his wife, has looked around the court and chosen just such an old hack barrister to represent him despite his tattered gown, frayed cuffs and the hole in his sock. Fowle tells the broken-down old barrister, Wilfred Morgenhall, that he did kill his wife because she was always infuriatingly cheerful and kept laughing at dreadful 'jokes', and the first scene, set in a prison cell, consists of a comic discussion between the two men as to how Morgenhall is going to get Fowle acquitted even though he is guilty. Scene Two is set in the same cell after the trial, during which the incompetent Morgenhall has made such a dreadful mess of his defence, failing to ask the right questions and flunking his final speech, that Fowle has been found guilty – but has then been reprieved because his barrister has been so useless that he has not had a fair trial. Morgenhall has won the case and saved a guilty man not because he is brilliant but because he is useless. *The Dock Brief* was not particularly amusing and when John read it to his father Clifford was unimpressed, but the mischievous twist at the end was to make it a classic and in Morgenhall John had created the prototype of the most famous of all his characters, Horace Rumpole. After ten years of writing novels he felt that he had suddenly found his true voice and that writing for radio was exhilarating and challenging because you had to tell the entire story simply with voices.

When the play was broadcast on the BBC Third Programme in May 1957 Michael Hordern played the old barrister and David Kossoff the murderer, and both took the same parts again four months later – along with a singing warder – in a BBC television musical version for which Hordern won the Television Actor of the Year Award. The play 'was a perfect little jewel', said Hordern – and it 'touched that rare dramatic level at which comedy and tragedy are indistinguishable', said *The Times*. It was to transform Mortimer's life, for it won a prize, the Italia, inspired London's leading theatrical agent, Peggy Ramsay, to take him on as a client and a theatrical producer, Michael Codron, to commission him to adapt it for the stage.

Penelope's writing was extremely successful too. In the spring of 1957, when she contributed the short story about her father to the *New Yorker*, she was paid a huge amount for it – $970, which in 2005 would be worth about £3,700 – and was given a lucrative contract to write six stories for the magazine every year. Both she and John were suddenly making decent amounts of money from their writing and she used some of hers to hire a cook to help at 23 Harben Road. She also rented and furnished one wing of a baronial stately home in Norfolk so that they had somewhere for weekends and holidays where Penelope could write in peace while her mother looked after the children: Cromer Hall – a huge, pseudo-Gothic castle, built in the 1830s, with vast halls, giant antique furniture, and two servants.

Michael Codron was only twenty-six but he had just taken over the Lyric Opera House at Hammersmith, was soon to stage *The Birthday Party* by an unknown playwright called Harold Pinter and was later to become the most prestigious producer in London. He commissioned Mortimer to write another short stage play, *What Shall We Tell Caroline?*, to be staged at the same performance as *The Dock Brief* after the interval. Suddenly John was as famous as Penelope – so famous that when twenty-five-year-old Arnold Wesker's Uncle Solly wrote a letter to Wesker in October to try to persuade him that he would never make any money as a playwright he wrote: 'There are hundreds of people writing scripts and stories, hundreds and hundreds. Take John Mortimer. He's published six novels and he still has to be a barrister – though what he spends in a day could keep you for a week.'

In November another of John's short plays was broadcast on the BBC Third Programme. *I Spy* was a lively, amusing piece in which a private detective is hired to prove that a missing wife is committing adultery, falls in love with her, and gives false evidence against her so that he can marry her himself. Two months later a television version of the play was broadcast on the BBC and suddenly the Mortimers were fashionable, the golden couple of the London literary scene, and invited to the smartest literary parties and dinners. Penelope's mother took charge of the house and children while her daughter wrote and smoked and drank and smoked again. 'My grandmother was a tiny woman but a force to be reckoned with,' Jeremy told me. 'My mother *adored* having children and we were desperately important to her, but my parents had a bit of money now and were able to employ au pairs and helps in a way that they hadn't before, and they were in a kind of literary set, being featured in *Vogue*, having parties, having a good time, and they were out to enjoy themselves, which is not necessarily an easy thing to balance with having six children. I'm not entirely sure whether I was unhappy or insecure. I didn't know any other childhood and didn't have anything with which to compare it.' An added problem was that although John and nine-year-old Deborah seemed quite fond of each other she was 'fiery tempered', Penelope wrote in *About Time Too*, 'and as she grew older they had savage fights, nails, teeth and the flat of John's hand.'

The Mortimers began to give smart parties themselves and among the regular visitors to Harben Road was Madelon's first serious boyfriend, twenty-year-old Christopher Booker, whom she had just met at Cambridge at the end of 1957. 'She was a charismatic, bubbly, absolutely super girl with lots of energy and was running a magazine at Cambridge called *Broadsheet*,' I was told by Booker, who was to become the first editor of the satirical scandal magazine *Private Eye*. 'I fell head over heels and we became engaged. Penelope and John couldn't have been more friendly and kind, and I have nothing but glowing memories of how pleasant they were. I was aware there were arguments and nowadays I would probably suss out the tensions in the marriage, but I was young and John was his usual genial self. For years I got on perfectly well with him without knowing him really at all. I don't think I ever had a meal out with him, never one of these champagne lunches.' I pointed out to Booker that John had always found it difficult to befriend men and much preferred the company of women. 'I'm sure he's a fascinating psychological study,' said Booker. 'I'm quite into father/daughter/mother relationships and John's absolutely obsessive relationship with his father means he's never escaped from the shadow of his dad at all – but he never adored his mother, like most men do, so he's quite an unusual case. There was a phrase he used to use which gives quite an interesting insight: if something went wrong with the plumbing or electricity John would always say, "We must get in a proper man," and that, I think, says an awful lot about him. If you've got a strong feminine streak when you're young you do have to work quite hard becoming masculine and the whole masculine/feminine thing is absolutely crucial in understanding storytelling. His remark about "a proper man" is very revealing. But Madelon and Caroline got on well with him and I don't remember Madelon being anything other than pretty favourable about her mother. Because she was pretty bright herself she had respect for the fact that her mum was bright too. Penelope was a very difficult lady, quite funny and acerbic, interesting to know. She was quite highly strung. She must have been ravishing when she was young.'

Caroline, who was nearly sixteen and 'a tortured teenager' according to Booker, had recently landed a job as assistant stage manager at the Royal Court Theatre in Sloane Square, Chelsea, where John Osborne's revolutionary play *Look Back in Anger* had opened a year previously, and she must have felt that it was decidedly spooky that her stepfather should now be writing a play about her called *What Shall We Tell Caroline?*. In the play Caroline Loudon is celebrating her eighteenth birthday and her mother and headmaster father, who still treat her like a child, are discussing with one of their teachers what advice they should give her about life. The irascible father is obviously based on Clifford, the mild mother on Kath, but Caroline Mortimer can hardly have been flattered that although the Caroline in the play is gorgeous she is a bore who says nothing until the very end but just sits there, utterly impassive, vacuous, and reacting to nothing. At the end she says eight brief sentences and leaves home to work in a bank in London. She has grown up without her parents noticing. It is a lively, jaunty, highly entertaining play that Mortimer wrote extremely quickly, inspired by the heady excitement of hearing actors speaking his words. *What Shall We Tell Caroline?* was 'very unusual and quirky, one of my favourite plays of his', Michael Codron told me. 'He had a literary talent then and a very oblique view of life which Peggy Ramsay called Mortimeresque, and to an extent he still *does* have that but he hasn't remained as idiosyncratic as I hoped he would in his writing. He had the most extraordinary flair for phrase.'

Peggy Ramsay represented many of the most talented playwrights in Britain, from Alan Ayckbourn, Robert Bolt and David Hare to Peter Nichols, Joe Orton, J. B. Priestley and P. G. Wodehouse. Hers was 'the most potent and influential play agency the theatrical world has ever seen', wrote her biographer Colin Chambers, the literary manager of the Royal Shakespeare Company. 'Through her magnetic allure and her blazing, forthright personality, she transformed herself into a legendary figure, a towering landmark of her time.' She was a short, pop-eyed, heavy-smoking redhead – Mortimer described her once as being 'like an excited and intelligent cockatoo' – and sizzled with energy. She was also amazingly forthright and indiscreet. The actor Simon Callow recalled in his autobiography going into her chaotic office in the heart of West End theatreland, in Goodwins Court just off St Martin's Lane, to hear her saying into the telephone, 'Well, you'll just have to tell them to fuck off, dear. I shall tell Merrick that we *must* HAVE a million.' Then Robert Bolt came on the line. 'But your play's *no* GOOD, dear,' she told him – and then in a loud aside to Callow: 'It's Bolt; I'm telling him his play's no good.' Back to Bolt: 'I've got *Simon Callow* here and I'm telling him your play's *no good*.' Then she chuckled. 'Well, it isn't, dear, is it?' She addressed all her clients by their surnames – Mortimer was Morti*maire* – and would often forget to whom she was speaking. Chambers reported that Christopher Hampton walked into her office once as she was on the telephone to an American theatre discussing a play written by another of her clients. 'Oh, don't do *that* play, dear. He never got it right. He never solved the ending. I'm here with Hampton. Why don't you talk to him and do his play instead?' On another occasion he arrived to hear her telling another writer: 'You don't want to end up like Hampton, darling. One success and he imagines the world owes him a living.' 'I heard that,' said Hampton. 'Well, it's *true*, isn't it, dear?' she said. Robert Bolt once overheard her telling a producer who was enquiring about Bolt's latest play: 'Can't you think of anything more interesting than that, dear? You don't want that bourgeois crap.' When she wasn't calling Mortimer Morti*maire* she was calling him Mercer and told him once that 'Morti*maire* has fallen in love again and can't write a word.' Yet her clients valued her hugely because she encouraged young writers, gave them excellent advice, went into battle with rich producers on their behalf, and was so full of vitality and enthusiasm that she fired them with new purpose and made them feel wonderful as well as useless. Mortimer reckoned that it was she more than anyone else who revitalised the postwar British theatre.

What Shall We Tell Caroline?, produced by Codron – whom Peggy Ramsay called Codfish – opened at the Lyric with *The Dock Brief* in April 1958. Michael Hordern and Maurice Denham were in both plays, as Morgenhall and Fowle respectively in *The Dock Brief* – 'it was a *wonderful* performance by Michael Hordern,' said Codron – and as the teacher and father in *What Shall We Tell Caroline?*. Caroline was played by Marianne Benet, her mother by Brenda Bruce. The play earned such excellent reviews – John was a brilliant new playwright, said John Barber of the *Daily Express* – that it transferred to the West End six weeks later, to the

Garrick Theatre, only to close early because of a transport strike that shut several London theatres.

The first night was very difficult for Penelope, Jeremy told me, because the play was about her daughter, and later first nights of John's plays were equally uncomfortable because they were always about their own experiences. Heady with the success of his first two stage plays, he announced that he was leaving the Bar to write full time but four days later, realising that writing plays was a precarious business if a theatre could be closed suddenly by a transport strike, he changed his mind.

The Mortimers were now such a celebrated literary couple that five days after the opening the *Daily Express* devoted half a broadsheet page to a huge, smug photograph of them poseuring with all six children amid the grandeur of Cromer Hall with John adopting a Napoleonic stance and smirking at the camera, Madelon gazing into the distance, and three-year-old Jeremy sitting on Penelope's lap and sucking his thumb. The caption read pompously 'The Author in the Bosom of his Family' and the accompanying text was admiring although it drew attention to his crooked teeth and reported that when he claimed to rise at six each morning the children jeered and called him a fibber. His fellow barristers in chambers considered all this publicity to be so vulgar that they fined him a case of champagne.

That same week he was fêted in the *Spectator*, telling the magazine that his plays were comedies because he felt that comedy was a much more effective weapon than frontal attack and 'the only thing worth writing in this despairing age, provided it's comedy which is truly on the side of the lonely, the neglected and unsuccessful and plays its part in the lone war against established rules, and against the imposing of an arbitrary code of behaviour on free and unpredictable human beings'.

After just two stage plays he had made such an impact that the arts magazine *Encore* included him in a group photograph on the cover of its September issue to illustrate an article about the young new-wave 'Angry Young Men' playwrights along with Osborne, Pinter and Wesker. However, Michael Codron told me that 'John wasn't really part of any theatrical movement' and Wesker told me that 'to describe the new wave of playwrights as "Angry Young Men" was nonsensical because there was no such group. It was the creation of George Fearon, the press officer of the Royal Court Theatre when they put on *Look Back in Anger*, who asked Osborne if he would mind if he described him as an "angry young man", and we were then lumbered with the label for ever. But we had very little in common with each other and I don't think John Mortimer was really part of that group.' The director, producer and writer Ned Sherrin agreed. 'John was the slightly more elegant side of the New Wave,' he told me. 'He was never quite "kitchen sink" but at the same time one did feel that his work was contemporary, relevant and amusing.'

While John was being hailed at thirty-five as a shining new theatrical talent Penelope was writing savage book reviews for *The Sunday Times* and stories for the *New Yorker* – all based on incidents in her own life; not one was fiction, she confessed – as well as yet another depressing novel. *Daddy's Gone A-Hunting* is about a lonely, neurotic, whining woman who is married to a selfish, bullying, constantly unfaithful dentist in his forties who is beginning to get fat, thinks his poor jokes are funny, is always criticising and sneering at her, and drives her to talk to herself, drink, weep, hate him, a nervous breakdown, and yet another bleak, hopeless ending.

Penelope was about to turn forty, a challenging age for a beautiful woman, but she was earning decent money of her own at last and could afford to escape her dreadful marriage for a while by going back to Positano on her own that summer of 1957 in search of her lost youth and a stocky Belgian painter with bandy legs, Hermann Minner, whom she had met there the previous year. With Minner she took at last her revenge for all John's infidelities by having an affair herself for the first time during their marriage. John even encouraged her, telling her that he was incapable of jealousy, and she wrote to him daily to tell him that she loved and missed him but was lounging in bed until noon every day and that Minner was painting her naked. Perhaps she too was a masochist because there was something deeply weird about their marriage and her unhealthy obsession with her faithless husband even while she was betraying him with another man. 'John and I were still engrossed in each other,' she wrote in her autobiography, 'but his flirtations – infatuations, whatever they were – were becoming an almost constant part of my life. Though bucket-and-spade holidays in a sharp east wind were some of our happiest times, staying in England would later become intolerable – there was always some reason for him to nip off to London, returning with sour offerings of guilt and remorse. I welcomed his eagerness to go abroad, even if the children didn't. In the future we traipsed further and further away, the South of France, Austria, Italy, Morocco, Spain, Bermuda. The moment the 'plane took off or the ferry sailed I had the illusion of safety, thinking that for the next few weeks we could live free of the unknown, invisible "someone" who haunted my life at home.'

Although John's fame had now outstripped hers Penelope was still one

of the fashionable (though over-praised) novelists of the end of the 1950s
and when her latest grim effort *Daddy's Gone A-Hunting* was published
in September 1958 it was praised inexplicably by *The Times Literary
Supplement* as 'a remarkably fine novel' that was 'pellucid, tart, poetic and
compassionate [and] written with considerable distinction'. *The Times*
said it was 'one of those rare modern novels that can be discussed and
enjoyed', and although *The Sunday Times* admitted that its characters and
subject were 'repellent, dreary and sad almost beyond belief' it claimed
that she had brought them to 'vivid, appalling life' with 'tender hatred
and ironical compassion' and added optimistically that Penelope had
'done a characteristic, tiny slice of English life with such terrible precision
that she can never return to it'. She did return to it time and time again
in five more novels and several short stories – and whenever she asked
John for his opinion of something she had written and he said it was very
good she would tear it up, not trusting him or his judgement.

By 1959 the Mortimers felt so secure financially that they bought two
cars, ensured that they always had a foreign live-in au pair girl, sent
Deborah and Sally off to Christopher Booker's parents' expensive prep
school for girls in Dorset, Knighton House, despite their apparently
socialist ideals, and spent a fortune installing a fancy new kitchen with
pine beams and concealed lighting at 23 Harben Road. 'They spent
£10,000, a huge amount (£154,000), on this kitchen which was designed
by Terence Conran,' I was told by David Leitch, who was then a twenty-
year-old undergraduate at St John's College, Cambridge, and had succeeded Christopher Booker as Madelon's boyfriend. 'It looked rather like
a restaurant in Bali. It had all kinds of hanging things and was very
sophisticated, not like any kitchen I'd come across, and the whole idea
of having a designer kitchen in those days was unknown. I was puzzled
and thought, How could you spend so much on this thing and why
would you want to, anyway? It added to my feeling of general alienation
from John and Penelope. They were an extremely bizarre pair, the first
sophisticated, literary, urban, swinging couple. They were like that cari-
cature couple in the Mark Boxer newspaper cartoons, the Stringalongs,
who were always in pursuit of the contemporary. The Mortimers were
the archetypal trendies. He wore expensive, uncared-for clothes and ties
bought for him by Penelope and his various girlfriends, and they lived
like film stars rather than professional people, with a lot of caviar and
champagne, and they were always going off to stay in their castle. But
they used to quarrel about everything and didn't give the impression of
a couple who were sexually well adjusted. The atmosphere was awful and

it was a very unhappy house. I think Penelope was mad. She was manic-depressive and had fits of depression helped along by drink and his infidelities. I was jealous of their extreme, very conspicuous wealth, yet they were always very short of money.'

Leitch did however admire John's efforts as a stepfather. 'It's jolly difficult to be the stepfather of teenage daughters,' he said, 'but they got on well and I don't think Madelon was angry at John for the way he treated her mother although he was very waspish. It was more complex than that. I think they hated Penelope but were devoted to her as well. It went up and down.' Madelon turned twenty-one in March and John and Penelope gave her a lavish birthday party at the Caprice which 'was typical of them', Leitch told me. 'The guests were Noël Coward, Margaret Leighton and her husband Laurence Harvey, who arrived late looking like a snake in a snakeskin dinner jacket. Leighton was wearing a kind of French outfit and Harvey said to her "a fucking old tottie like you shouldn't show so much of her tits!".' Not surprisingly they were to divorce two years later.

In the spring of 1959 Penelope was surprisingly delighted when she found she was pregnant again but she miscarried in July and tried to lighten her sadness by seducing her daughter's boyfriend. 'There was a bend on the staircase at Harben Road,' Leitch said, 'and she made a pass at me. She expected me to kiss her or to make some physical approach and although she was very good looking I flinched away, the worst thing I could have done. To me then a woman of forty was like a woman of a hundred and forty would be now, and she was vicious to me after that and caused me a lot of trouble. She felt rejected and was very nasty in a variety of spiteful, stupid ways, and told people untrue, unpleasant things about me.'

Caroline, now seventeen, left home to live with Tom Kempinski, a young actor who was studying at the Royal Academy of Dramatic Art, and to try to become an actor herself. Madelon completed her three years at Cambridge, came home, found a job as a statistician with a cigarette company, but she and Penelope did not get on and she left to live with Leitch, who had become a journalist in Rome, where she was to stay for ten years. In August the Mortimers rented a house in the South of France where Penelope wrote a very good, tense short story about a neurotic mother's desperate attempts to free her five-year-old son from a rented holiday villa in the South of France in which he has been trapped, 'The Skylight', which she decided later she had written in subconscious mourning for the lost baby of her recent miscarriage. The unrelenting anguish of her marriage, which she had described so vividly in her books, inspired the *Daily Mail* to hire her to write its agony aunt column under the pen-name Ann Temple. She was now almost as busy as John, reviewing books for the *Bookman* and adapting one of her short stories for television, 'The Renegade', an extremely autobiographical story about her father in which a bored, lonely vicar plans to take his thirteen-year-old daughter to a nudist colony and she runs away from school.

John was himself deeply occupied with adapting his radio play *I Spy* for a stage version, which was to open at the Salisbury Playhouse in March 1959; writing a radio script based on his novel *Three Winters*; adapting *The Dock Brief* and *What Shall We Tell Caroline?* for television; and writing four short sketches for a stage revue that was to open at the Lyric in July, *One to Another*, for which Harold Pinter and N. F. Simpson also wrote two sketches each. He was taking on too much work with the result that his contributions to the revue – 'Triangle', 'Cleaning Up Justice', 'Collector's Piece' and 'Conference' – were all thin, corny or just silly. Even so the revue transferred five weeks later to the West End, to the Apollo Theatre in Shaftesbury Avenue. His new fame and wealth allowed him to embark on a wild sexual spree with a series of young girlfriends, apparently without caring at all how Penelope might feel about his constant infidelities and his immature insistence on confessing and talking about them afterwards. 'He felt that our marriage would be perfectly satisfactory if I could understand this and give him my blessing,' she wrote in her autobiography, 'but I couldn't. Actual sexual infidelity was the least of it, provided I wasn't expected to sympathise, but I furiously resented hints and confessions, implausible excuses, furtive muttering on the 'phone, a flowering of Carnaby Street shirts and medallions. I despised him for needing my sympathy as much as for the minor and clumsily conducted affairs ... At the same time there was a new kind of loneliness, supportable only because I knew that in the intervals between affairs there would be a short time of hectic reconciliation; and always, through every activity except work, there was an undercurrent of apprehension and mourning.'

John's reputation as a writer was now so exalted that the Hollywood film producer Anatole 'Tolly' de Grunwald, whose past successes included *French Without Tears* and *The Windsor Boy*, asked him to fly to California to write a screenplay for him and arranged for him to stay in the salubrious Los Angeles suburb of Pacific Pallisades. In ten years John had risen from comparative poverty, living with a wife and five children in a tiny flat in the Inner Temple to the glamorous glitter of Hollywood. He was only thirty-six, rich and famous at last, and would never be poor again.

Six

Wendy and *The Pumpkin Eater*
1959–1962

*J*ohn soon tired of Hollywood, where he was forbidden to leave the studio lot, had to attend numerous story conferences with dreary executives and to scratch out a script all day in a cramped hutch in a building appropriately named the Writers' Block. His script stood only the tiniest chance of ever being filmed, he quickly despaired of de Grunwald's idea, and was delighted when his name was eventually removed from the film's credits because another writer insisted that he alone should be credited. He did earn one film credit by writing some additional dialogue for the comic thriller *Ferry to Hong Kong* in which Curt Jurgens played a drunken passenger trapped aboard a ship that is skippered by a prim Orson Welles and boarded by pirates, and he did enjoy parts of Los Angeles and Malibu. He also met some interesting people – the director George Cukor, the actor Trevor Howard – but after a few months he could stand it no longer and returned to London, the divorce courts and his first full-length, three-act stage play, *The Wrong Side of the Park*.

He set the play, which was once again highly autobiographical, in a replica of 23 Harben Road, on 'the wrong side of the park', where the husband, Henry, is always quarrelling with his wife, Elaine, and always tells her to 'get a man in' if anything goes wrong. Their dreadful marriage is not improved by the arrival of an attractive lodger whom Elaine fancies because he reminds her of her dead first husband, Peter, whom she idolises. Eventually it transpires that Peter was in fact a hopeless drunk – shades of poor old Charlie Dimont – whom she never really loved, and that all her happiest memories have actually happened during her marriage to Henry. The play ends soppily and unconvincingly with Henry and Elaine reconciled. Michael Codron agreed to produce it, twenty-nine-year-old Peter Hall to direct it, Margaret Leighton and Richard Johnson to play Elaine and Henry, Robert Stephens to play the lodger, and it opened in London at the Cambridge Theatre in February 1960.

Playing Elaine's sister was a perky, pretty, twenty-five-year-old redhead, Wendy Craig, with whom John began an affair that was to result in a son whose paternity was to be kept secret for forty-two years. She appeared in the first act playing appropriately a girl who is eight months pregnant with an illegitimate child. Wendy had been married for four years to a much older man, forty-six-year-old Jack Bentley, a trombonist – 'the man with the velvet tone' – who had played with the Ted Heath Band until the early 1950s but now wrote a weekly showbiz column in the *Sunday Mirror*, and they had a two-year-old son, Alaster. Bentley was 'a small, plump, swaggering chap with a slight Fifties Teddy boy haircut and a slightly showbiz, mid-American accent', I was told by an ex-editor of the *Daily Mirror*, Mike Molloy. 'He was very jolly,' said another *Mirror* colleague, Felicity Green, and the artist Andrew Vicari, who knew the Bentleys well in the 1950s, told me: 'I'm amazed that Wendy had an affair with John Mortimer. She was madly in love with Jack and they were devoted.' However, a third *Mirror* man, Tony Delano, said, 'Bentley was an unpleasant drunk. He and Wendy were often fighting and falling out,' and Shirley Anne Field, who was then a stunningly beautiful twenty-two-year-old actress who had just appeared in *The Entertainer* with Laurence Olivier and *Saturday Night and Sunday Morning* with Albert Finney, told me: 'Wendy was nice but Bentley was a bit of a showoff who was a little too familiar with us young actresses. I didn't particularly care for him. He was like a wide boy – but not with her, apparently. He was *wonderful* to Wendy. He loved her and I think she loved him.'

Mortimer, who was thirty-six, was enchanted by her and his passion inflamed further when she had to unbutton her shirt and breast-feed her baby on stage and then appeared in skimpy pyjamas. Despite her apparently wonderful marriage John charmed her into bed by making her laugh. Their affair was to last for more than a year and the atmosphere at rehearsals must have been stiff with lust, for Margaret Leighton and Robert Stephens were also having an affair. Her husband Laurence Harvey was also pursuing Joan Cohn, the rich widow of Hollywood mogul Harry Cohn, whom he was to marry eight years later.

'The Mortimers were by now a very glitzy couple,' I was told by Barbara Fenton, who was living in the Cotswolds at Moreton-in-Marsh, where her husband Michael was a general practitioner. 'We still used to see John once or twice a year and to go with them to the theatre. *The Wrong Side of the Park* had a preliminary run at Stratford-upon-Avon and that's when we had supper with him and Wendy Craig. Michael said to me after that meal that it was obvious Mortimer was doing his normal thing with Wendy!' Mortimer's adultery was so blatant that Barbara Fenton began to suspect that he might be leading her husband astray. 'Barbara was an incredibly attractive woman,' Fenton's old pacifist friend Dr Alan Gildersleve told me, 'but she said to me that she was very worried that Michael was going up to London a lot and staying with John Mortimer and she feared that John was introducing Michael to actresses.'

The play earned excellent reviews and the *Radio Times* included Mortimer in a list of leading playwrights along with Brendan Behan, Willis Hall, John Osborne, Anthony Shaffer, Arnold Wesker, 'and perhaps also J. P. Donleavy and Harold Pinter – whose future is still a controversial question'. Michael Codron had no doubt about John's talent. 'As a playwright of his time he was very good,' he told me. 'He was *immensely* practical and I wish playwrights now would write good, strong leading parts, which is what he did.' Not everyone was impressed. In the *Spectator* Alan Brien called Mortimer 'the Christopher Fry of prose drama' and wrote: 'There are some tours de force which can only be described as ghost art. I mean those productions of men with quicksilver talents – Kodak eyes, stereo ears and a copywriter's fluency – which never quite add up to genius. I mean the paintings of Annigoni, the verse plays of Christopher Fry, the poetry of Dylan Thomas, the novels of L. P. Hartley – all these okay names are creators of middle-brow masterpieces.' John's old Harrow classmate Sandy Wilson, who was being invited to the Mortimers' smart theatrical parties now that he was famous for having written *The Boy Friend*, told me that although he had liked *The Dock Brief* very much 'I didn't think *The Wrong Side of the Park* was good at all'. Arnold Wesker thought that the play was 'a little lightweight' and told John so: 'It was in the very early days when I felt driven to be honest about everything. He extended a smile the graciousness of which stayed with me and badly bruised my self-esteem.' John Gielgud, however, saw the play soon after it opened and wrote to the writer and lyricist Hugh Wheeler in February that he was 'mad about it. It is a big hit, but no one seems to like it except me.' The writing and acting, he said, were 'very good. But Binkie, J. P. and Paul all loathed it, and I hear the Royal Court boys as well.'

The play failed to fill the Cambridge Theatre and was moved to the smaller St Martin's Theatre, where 'it went pretty well', Codron told me, 'until Margaret Leighton told me that she was going to leave the play to try to rescue her marriage to Laurence Harvey. She failed but we were not able to replace her and closed shortly after that.' The play had run for seven months, but after just one Mortimer was sufficiently confident to tell *The Times* that he had given up writing novels to write instead one stage play and two for television every year. He said that he felt particularly drawn to writing about characters who were worldly failures. 'It's an attitude I've had since childhood,' he said, 'and in court I was always sympathetic with the "guilty party". Now it's instinctive. When characters become successful I lose interest in them.' He also announced that he would like to write a horror filmscript about the sort of dreadful, bloodthirsty, English person who rides to hounds and hunts foxes – a 'barbarian in boots, hacking jackets behind the door, all that blood'. Twenty years later, when his second wife became keen on hunting, he suddenly became a vociferous supporter of blood sports.

By now writing plays was taking precedence over the Law. 'I was a writer who did barristering in my spare time, not a barrister who did writing in my spare time,' he told me in 1993. 'Barristering was my day job, like waitressing when you're an out-of-work actor.' As he explained to Melvyn Bragg on *The South Bank Show*: 'The process of a barrister appearing for a client is the antithesis of what a writer is: you don't have a personality of your own; you are part of your client and you're there to protect your client, and you're really a puppet on a string. The personality, which is the most important thing for a writer, is constantly suppressed. And the main preoccupation of a writer is to tell the truth of the world as you see it. The great preoccupation of a defence barrister in a criminal case is to prevent too much of the truth leaking out!' Again he considered leaving the Bar but decided that might still be imprudent and hung on while he wrote another television play for the BBC, *David and Broccoli*, and another one-act stage play, *Lunch Hour*, which allowed him to give Wendy Craig another part, as a twenty-three-year-old girl who has an assignation in a small hotel during her lunch hour with one of her company's directors – an older man who spends the entire lunch hour trying in vain to get her into bed. Emlyn Williams played the would-be seducer when the play opened in Salisbury in June 1960.

Not to be outdone by John's fertile productivity, Penelope published a collection of her *New Yorker* stories in September, *Saturday Lunch With the Brownings*, and as always they were highly autobiographical and revealing. The title story describes one day in the life of a family where the husband is a bad-tempered writer who is the same age as John, thirty-seven, 'but in bed he looked older, the thin hair straggled over his forehead, the face heavy and loose like an old man. In the eight years of their marriage, forced to support two stepchildren and one of his own, he had become successful and careless. His fingernails were dirty and he hadn't shaved for two days.' He fights childishly with his wife over her two daughters by a previous marriage, turns violent and threatens to leave her, but after a long afternoon sleep he calms down, expects her simply to forget the vicious incident, and the story ends with his wife staring hopelessly into the evening gloom. Almost every story tells of a trapped, bickering married couple who are always sniping at each other: the woman weak, neurotic and terrified; the man selfish, bad-tempered and unloving; the children whiny and demanding. Even in the final story, 'What a Lovely Surprise', an unusually affectionate husband and his three children give their mother a series of special treats on her thirty-ninth birthday but the day still ends with the parents shouting at each other and sleeping apart. Penelope's constant gloom, suspicion and depression made her very difficult to live with and it is understandable that John sought refuge in the arms of other women.

Saturday Lunch With the Brownings was praised by *The Times* and *Times Literary Supplement* but *The Sunday Times* complained that the stories were monotonous and that her married couples, 'trivially embittered, chronically quarrelling about nothing, obsessive, filled with a fatigued desperation ... seem repetitious, and one wishes that, since they are so unhappy as well, they would step into Harrods for fifty aspirins, and end it all'. When John Fowles read the book he wrote in his journal that it was 'a perfect example of the mid-century smart style ... the total withdrawal of the artist from the canvas. No heart, no persona even; the creator absconditus.' To be fair, four of the twelve stories are excellent and one, 'Such a Super Evening', is actually amusing, poking fun as it does at a glamorous couple of fashionable writers, the Mathiesons, who are just like the Mortimers. When they are invited to dinner their hostess says admiringly to Mr Mathieson: 'I read somewhere that you get up at six every morning.'

Mrs Mathieson snorts. 'You know what time he gets up? Midday. Just in time for lunch at the Caprice. Although, of course, there are occasions when he gets up at ten. Then he has to have a snooze in the afternoon.'

In October an important trial began at the Old Bailey when Penguin Books was charged with obscenity for publishing an unexpurgated edition of D. H. Lawrence's sexually explicit novel *Lady Chatterley's Lover*. Newspapers still state that Mortimer was a member of Penguin's defence team along with Gerald Gardiner. In fact he was not involved in the case at all though it was certainly to be vital for him as a barrister and writer because it was the first case brought under the Obscene Publications Act of the previous year, which had been introduced to Parliament by Roy Jenkins, who was now an MP. Under this 'Jenkins Act' the defence could argue that a book was not obscene if it had literary merit and 'an article shall be deemed to be obscene if its effect ... is, if taken as a whole, such as to tend to deprave and corrupt persons who are likely, in all the circumstances, to read, see or hear the matter contained or embodied in it'. Penguin was acquitted after thirty-six 'experts' swore that the book had great literary merit, among them E. M. Forster, Rebecca West, Cecil Day-Lewis and the Bishop of Woolwich. *Lady Chatterley's Lover* went on to sell three million copies in three months because of all the publicity, and the gates of literary permissiveness were thrown open so wide that writers and publishers felt free at last to publish anything they liked.

It was the first trumpet call of the Permissive Society, the moment many believe that British morality, manners and family life began seriously to deteriorate, and it was to lead Mortimer in later years to fight several important obscenity cases during which he was to argue that a writer should be free to publish anything at all, no matter how shocking or indecent it might seem to some. He and Jenkins were to become midwives of the Permissive Society and from the end of 1960 the growth of literary licence became unstoppable: *Lolita* was filmed, *Fanny Hill* and Frank Harris's *My Life and Loves* published, Kenneth Tynan was saying 'fuck' on television in 1965. By the end of 1989 *Lady Chatterley's Lover* was being broadcast as BBC Radio 4's cosy Book at Bedtime, and by 2000 every British newsagent sold kinky magazines and the most offensive hard-core pornography was easily available even to children.

In January 1961 Mortimer represented Margaret Leighton in the High Court when at last she divorced Laurence Harvey, and Michael Codron presented *Lunch Hour* on the stage again – with Wendy Craig again playing the girl – as one of a trio of one-act plays at the Arts Theatre Club along with *A Slight Ache* by Pinter and *The Form* by N. F. Simpson, which did well enough to be transferred to the Criterion Theatre a month later. 'Well,' said Emlyn Williams, who was once again playing the would-be seducer, to John, 'you just got into the New Wave as the

Tube doors were closing.' Understudying Wendy Craig was Mortimer's stepdaughter Caroline, who was now at RADA and must surely have known that he and Wendy were having an affair. And then that month Wendy and Penelope both became pregnant by Mortimer – just as he began to pursue the gorgeous Shirley Anne Field, choosing her to replace Wendy in the screen version of *Lunch Hour*.

'John Mortimer, James Hill, my agent Jean Diamond and I all had tea at the Dorchester,' Shirley Anne, still strikingly good-looking, told me in 2004. 'John offered us seven per cent of the film and it was wonderful to be treated so fairly. I liked him enormously straight away. It was hard not to like someone who so obviously liked me – he made that quite clear. He made me feel beautiful and special and kept making me laugh. He was a total life enhancer, and irreverent. I was a youngster in London trying to set the town alight, and he looked like a twinkly older businessman to me, eminently respectable, suit and tie. I didn't look at him in a romantic way at all: it wouldn't have occurred to me in a million years. He was always a bit rushed and untidy. I was spoilt for choice, life was full of fun and it wouldn't have occurred to me to have seen John in a romantic way at that time.'

For the film, in which Robert Stephens played the would-be seducer, John included several more characters and rewrote scenes each day as he dashed in and out from the divorce courts. 'It was a very creative, quick, low-budget film and the happiest experience workwise I've ever had,' said Shirley Anne. 'One could only admire how clever he was. You would have a conversation with him at lunchtime and the next day it would be included in the script, still in the character you were playing, of course, but with your own rhythms of speech. No wonder he has had such a success since then. From what I saw of Penelope Mortimer, which was rare, she was a strikingly handsome woman, and to my young eyes almost masculine in appearance, whereas John was unlike any man I'd ever encountered in my short life, not macho or interested in sport. He had many feminine qualities, a "New Man" before it was even thought of. They must have been fascinating to watch together. However there was no reason for her to feel threatened by me because I never even considered John in that way in those days. I'd have lunches with him, and sometimes I went to tea in Harben Road, maybe three or four times for supper, where I met most of the family. Sometimes one would feel a tension in the air. I'd hear doors banging, and there would be raised voices when I assumed Penelope came in. It must have been a difficult time in his life.'

After a family holiday in Austria, when John wrote all the time to finish two new television plays for the BBC, *Twenty-Four Hours in a Woman's Life* and *The Encyclopaedist*, he began to work on two filmscripts for Susan Hayward and Sophia Loren for which he boasted to the *Evening Standard* that he would be paid £20,000 (£294,000). He also finished the screenplay for a film starring David Niven, Leslie Caron and James Robertson Justice, *Guns of Darkness*, an excellent thriller in which Niven played a British planter in a South American republic who rescues the country's wounded president after he has been overthrown in a coup. John and Penelope flew out to see the film being shot in Spain. 'David was a huge star,' Mortimer told me in 2001. 'He was thirteen years older than me but we became great friends and spent a lot of time together and went to see the Alhambra, which was not really his thing because it was a bigger star than he was! He was very funny. We drank a lot of cheap Fundador brandy, so he called me Fundador, and we sang "Fundador is a Perfect Night for Love" instead of "Wunderbar is a Perfect Night for Love" out of *Kiss Me, Kate*. Afterwards we would always meet when he came to England.' Both men were mischievous, lecherous, boozy and loved telling tall stories that bore little resemblance to the truth, and they were to remain firm friends for twenty-two years until Niven died in 1983. Niven's Swedish wife, Hjördis, however, claimed 'that she had been disgusted when she met John Mortimer in the Connaught Hotel in London and he propositioned her', one of her friends told me. 'She said, "I thought you were a friend of my husband," and was surprised and deeply affronted by his overt pass' even though she was no prude and had several affairs herself, one of them a quickie with President Kennedy.

Now that Mortimer was making so much money he took the family off to Elba for a summer holiday and bought his first house, Southend Cottage in the small hamlet of Southend, less than a mile from Turville Heath – a pair of converted Georgian farm cottages with four bedrooms, three bathrooms, an acre of garden, tennis court, three-car garage and orchard. And then Penelope and Wendy both found they were pregnant.

Unwanted pregnancies were common in 1961, before the contraceptive pill was widely available, but for Penelope to become pregnant yet again, at the age of forty-two, after six children and a miscarriage, was remarkably careless for such an intelligent woman even though her four eldest daughters were away from home most of the time now and Jeremy had just started going to day school at the age of six. 'She just *loved* being pregnant,' he told me, 'and would have gone on to have more children had she been able to. I'm sure that must have been a source of arguments between her and my father, but you'd have thought that *he* could have taken a bit of responsibility for that too.' Her doctor told her that at her age she ought to have an abortion and be sterilised. John agreed, telling her that another child would destroy all their hopes of beginning to have fun again, as he promised they would, so she had the operation reluctantly in March, hoping that by sacrificing their unborn child she might make John kinder and save their marriage. 'Being sterilised,' said Jeremy, 'and later having a hysterectomy, were of great significance and led to psychological problems for her.' But what threw her emotional stability completely off-balance was to return home to find a mauve envelope addressed to John and containing an adoring letter from Wendy which made it horribly clear that they were lovers. When he came home, she said, he confessed not only that he was having an affair with Wendy but also that she was pregnant, and for Penelope the knowledge that he had allowed her to abort a baby and to be sterilised at the very time that Wendy was carrying his child would surely have been the ultimate betrayal. On 9 May she wrote in her diary: 'And the bitter thought that with her there was wine for lunch and the afternoon planned.'

In her autobiography Penelope described her desperate misery and Mortimer's cruel lack of sympathy or understanding:

> John was writing one of his elegant, light-hearted plays about his affair, though not about my involvement in it. He would recite the choicer passages to the producer over the 'phone and couldn't under-stand why I minded so much. His confused feelings were more than he could bear but I lumbered him with them; the sight of my sickness and wretchedness was intolerable. There were bitter quarrels, savage recriminations. His invective was more brutal than he intended – why didn't I just get out, go, I was useless to everyone, I was hideous, why didn't I *die?*

Penelope told Jack Bentley that his wife was pregnant by John, Wendy ended the affair but decided to have the baby, and Mortimer started to pursue Shirley Anne Field. 'I knew he had had a fling with Wendy Craig,' Shirley Anne told Laura Collins of the *Mail on Sunday* in 2004 when the story of Mortimer's secret child first became public, 'but it slowly became clear to me as a result of what John was telling me that she was going to have a child. Bentley, John said, had said to him that this brat, as he put it, is going to suffer and that Wendy was going to know every day of her life what she had done. John said that Bentley had said Wendy was never going to be able to forget how this child came to be born. It was hideous.

I remember being utterly shocked when John recounted the conversation. I don't think John was alarmed or even frightened by the words and brutal nature of Bentley's phone call. He was almost amused.'

Penelope resigned from her job as the *Daily Mail*'s agony aunt – she was suffering quite enough agony of her own. She escaped to the country to spend most of that summer at Southend Cottage trying to forget her unhappiness by entertaining glamorous weekend guests with tennis and dinner parties – actors, producers and directors who laughed at what Penelope called John's 'often cruel stories'. One day she followed him secretly up to London to spy on him at work in the divorce court. On another she vowed to leave him and spent three days on her own in the empty house in Harben Road, but she could not bring herself to go for good. She was consoled briefly when her first television play, an adaptation of her *New Yorker* story about the time she ran away from school as a child, 'The Renegade', was broadcast in September, with Jane Asher playing Penelope and Andrew Cruickshank as her father. Peggy Ramsay telephoned to say how good it was, the reviews were excellent, and Michael Gowers wrote in the *Daily Mail* that she was just as fine a playwright as John. '*The Renegade* teemed with more ideas, throbbed with more compassion, struggled with more psychological concepts rendered in terms which no one could fail to understand, than anything I have seen on either channel for a very long time,' he wrote.

But none of this was enough to raise her spirits, which sank even lower when John's father fell seriously ill towards the end of September and it became obvious that he was dying. John went to stay at Turville Heath and was at his bedside on his last day, 29 September, when Clifford suddenly became enraged when he was told that he could not have a bath. Kath begged him not to be so angry. 'I'm always angry when I'm dying!' he shouted. He died of a heart attack at 3.30 a.m., aged seventy-seven. 'It can't be true!' cried Kath. 'It can't!' He was buried in Turville churchyard and left her a surprisingly small amount: just £3,593-1s-0d (£52,900).

Depressed by the funeral on 3 October and just four days before Wendy Craig's baby, Ross, was born in London on 10 November, Penelope was overwhelmed by a geyser of grief, rage and despair that drove her to her typewriter in Southend Cottage to pour out the best of all her novels, *The Pumpkin Eater*, another searing account of her nightmarish marriage and John's selfishness, heartlessness and treachery. It is a brilliant book, seething with anger, bitterness and unhappiness, and it seems that every word in it is absolutely true. 'There's not one of her novels which is not autobiographical,' Jeremy assured me. 'It's impossible to read *The Pumpkin Eater* without seeing the relationship between my mother and father,' he told Alan Yentob during a television interview in 2003. Even the letter from Wendy to John that Penelope had discovered is apparently reproduced word for word in the novel where the actress calls him 'John baby ... lamb ... poor darling ... my love' and warns him not to 'let your eyes stray to those luscious bits hanging around the set, they're no good when it comes to it as well you know. I'm saving myself for you like you told me, although it's pretty difficult.' It ends: 'See you on Monday *and then*!!'

The Penelope character, the narrator, is not named in the book but John is called Jake Armitage, Jack Bentley and Wendy are Bob and Beth Conway, and the book describes a telephone conversation between the cuckolded Conway and the betrayed narrator which is remarkably similar to Shirley Anne Field's account of Mortimer's telephone conversation with Bentley and a call that Bentley made to Penelope about the possibility of Wendy having an abortion: 'Oh no, Mrs A. Oh no. I'm not giving her that pleasure ... She's going to have this kid in a public ward and if there's any way of stopping her getting a whiff of gas, I'll find it. She's going to wipe its bottom and stare at its ugly mug for the rest of her young life. There's going to be no more movies, no more champagne, and no more hair-dos, no more sexy clothes for my little Beth. This kid's going to kill her. I've told her that. This kid's going to make her curse Jake Armitage for the rest of her days. I'm going to see that this kid turns her into an old hag, and if you saw her now you'd know that's not too difficult.'

In the film of *The Pumpkin Eater* the narrator was to be called Jo, and in the book her compulsively adulterous husband is startlingly similar to Mortimer: a sad, lonely, only child whose father nagged and bullied him, treated him with contempt, and warned Jo not to marry him because he was lazy, poor, unreliable, unsympathetic, bad-tempered and drank too much. Nevertheless Jake has become a very rich scriptwriter who earns about £50,000 a year (£736,000). His wife is undoubtedly Penelope's double: a neurotic whose first husband was an alcoholic, who thought Jake was homosexual when she first met him, whose father told Jake that she would need a firm hand on her tiller, and whose three eldest children by other men have come to hate Jake because he insisted they should go to boarding schools when he married her. The Armitages live in a house exactly like 23 Harben Road and their marriage is a constant battlefield.

'You don't give a damn for me, and you know it,' Jake shouts at her:

'Shut up! You don't care about *me*, all you care about is the bills being
paid and the bloody children, that great fucking army of children that
I'm supposed to support and work my guts out for, so I can't even take
a bath in peace, I can't eat a bloody meal without them whining and
slobbering all over the table, I can't even go to bed with you without
one of them comes barging in in the middle. If you cared about me
you'd try to understand me, wouldn't you? All right, I'm a bastard!
All right, I'm no good to you! But what joy do you think *I* get out of
this god-awful boring family life of yours? Where do *I* come in?'

Jake has written a lucrative filmscript for a new thriller, *The Sphinx*,
starring Beth Conway and a young Italian actress, Maria Dante, but Jo
has a nervous breakdown in Harrods and is sent to see a psychiatrist. She
tells him that although she loves Jake she does not like him because 'he
is a coward, a cheat, he is mean, vain, cruel, he is slovenly, he is sly'. He
is also 'a violent man who wears a sluggard body for disguise. Sleepy,
amiable, anxious to please, lazy, tolerant, possibly in some ways a little
stupid: this is the personality he wears as a man in the world. His
indestructible energy, aggression, cruelty and ambition are well protected.' Jake starts drinking too much, Jo becomes pregnant yet again,
and he tells her he can't bear the thought of having to support yet another
child. She writes:

He's been terrified by the task of supporting us all. For years he's been
driven on by panic, taking on ghastly scripts he didn't want to do,
accepting everything he was offered; destroying, incidentally, his own
talent in the process, but that doesn't matter, the point is that he's
kept us, we've come out of it alive. But the irony, the bloody irony of
it is that just at this point when he has realised how much he loves
me, when we could for the first time start planning a happier, more
sensible life, just at the point when we could start thinking of a little
freedom – I'm pregnant again.

She realises that he wants her to have an abortion even though he denies
it forcefully, so to save her marriage she has the operation and is sterilised,
but when she returns home, determined to build a new life with Jake
and to make him happy, she finds the mauve letter that Beth has sent
him, and to add to her torment and misery she discovers that Beth is

pregnant by Jake and refusing to be aborted herself. The Other Woman is going to have Jake's baby instead.

After the birth of the child Jo/Penelope and Conway/Bentley meet in a teashop to discuss the upheaval in their lives. 'He's been bashing around for years,' says Conway, 'but I suppose you know that.'

'Bashing around?'

'Author's perks. He gets the ones the stars don't want. There's a pub quite near the studio – well, I suppose there are pubs quite near any studio. Pricey, I should think, for a couple of hours, but that wouldn't matter to him, would it?'

Later Conway tells her:

'It was Dante before this, it seems they were always necking on the set until she got fed up with him. He's not much good in bed, I understand. A bit on the small side . . . You know *why* you had an abortion? Because Beth's a good girl at heart, she would have left him. He made you have it, so he could keep Beth. It's a charming thought, isn't it? . . . He's not a grown man, your husband, he's a puking boy. He can't even lay a girl without the whole world knowing it. Beth says he made her sick with his slop. I made her swear on the baby's head that she was telling me the truth. I brought the baby in and I told her to swear on its head. That's how I feel about it. If he tries to get in touch with her, I'll *know*, you understand? So tell him to keep off.'

'You must tell him yourself.'

'I don't want to speak to him. I don't want to hear his pansy voice.'

'Yes, John's very nancy, isn't he?' I was told in 2004 by Molly Parkin, who was to become Mortimer's mistress a few years later. 'It *is* a fairy voice.'

In the novel Jo/Penelope tackles Jake/John about all his infidelities over the years and he admits that he had slept often with their lodger, Philpot, as well as at least a dozen other women, too many to count. And what about Beth/Wendy?

'Why did you go to bed with her?'
'Oh, for God's sake.'
'Why?'
'Out of curiosity. Vanity. Wanting to keep young.'

'Did you love her?'

'I found her ... appealing.'

'But did you love her?'

'I love you. I don't know what it means, love.'

'Didn't you ever, any of the times ... try not to?'

'You know I have no self-control.'

And finally, brutally, Jake says to his wife: 'Why don't you shut up? Why don't you *die?*' She takes to drinking brandy in the afternoons, leaving the receiver off the hook, and then she gets the vicious telephone call from Bob Conway to tell her that he will make his unfaithful wife's life a misery for the rest of her days. When the drama is all over Jo takes her revenge by going to bed with her first husband but that is not the answer and she goes back to Jake, without hope, to a bleak, unloving future. She writes:

> To Jake, living is necessarily defective, vicious, careless, an inevitable time of activity between two deaths; to him the world is a little spinning piece of grit on which sad and lonely human beings huddle together for warmth, sentimental but unfeeling, always optimistic, but embarrassed by any real hope. That is the basis on which he works, and loves, and will eventually die. It's enough for him.

'I think the story in *The Pumpkin Eater* must have been about the four of them, there's no doubt about that,' said Shirley Anne Field. 'John used to tell me about it and he talked to me about the child – it seemed general knowledge. He mentioned it to me years ago and told me about Jack Bentley ringing him up and saying "you bastard!" and all sorts of hideous things that had gone on. He was going on about a child and this man phoning him, and I just thought, how sad, and I wasn't really interested. Why would I be? I didn't really know the people involved. John used to go on about this horrible phone call but in a jocular way. "Oh," he said, "this man rang up and said, 'This child is going to pay.'" As he repeated this mean conversation about this small child, I remember thinking that Jack Bentley must be very distressed.'

Molly Parkin told me: 'Later, after my affair with John was over, I became a friend of Penelope's and we liked each other immensely, and she told me about the child too. John is utterly selfish and unreliable, a faithless man, not a man of good character. He's been particularly treacherous to women and many people say that he destroyed Penelope's life. I think she was the valuable one in that marriage.'

What was so odd about Wendy's affair with Mortimer was that she was in fact 'extremely ladylike and notably prudish', Mike Molloy told me. 'She once threatened to leave Bentley if he published in his *Sunday Mirror* column a picture of Ross playing with the illegitimate child of some aristocratic woman.'

Seven weeks after she had given birth to Mortimer's son Wendy Craig was starring on television in a BBC version of Bernard Shaw's classic drama *Candida*, which ends when the heroine has to choose between her two admirers and says: 'I give myself to the weaker of the two,' knowing that it is the weaker man who needs her most. In real life, by giving herself to Bentley rather than John, she had chosen the stronger of the two. Unselfishly she gave up work for two years so that she could devote herself to Mortimer's child, but went on after that to become extremely successful as a television actress specialising in playing daffy, airhead women in comedy series such as *Not in Front of the Children*, *Nanny* and *Butterflies*, in which poignantly she played a loyal housewife who was tempted every week to commit adultery with her rich admirer, Leonard. She was to win a BAFTA Best Actress award in 1968, to be voted BBC Personality of the Year in 1969 and ITV Personality of the Year in 1973, and the critic Kenneth Tynan once described her as 'one of the six best actresses in the Western world'. In 1972, ironically, she was to be voted Mother of the Year, and maybe she deserved the title for the way she had devoted herself to Mortimer's child, but in the early 1980s, tormented perhaps by guilt over her infidelity, she suffered a midlife crisis before recovering and becoming a born-again Christian in 1984. She was to have no more children nor any contact with Mortimer for forty-three years, until 2004, even though she lived for decades at Cookham Dean, just nine miles from Turville Heath, and they sometimes found themselves at the same showbiz gatherings. Despite the long silence between them Ross would have reminded her constantly of Mortimer because the boy came increasingly to resemble him with his small, shrewd eyes, mischievous expression and lopsided jaw. He had also inherited some of Mortimer's more attractive traits: when Ross was nine Wendy told Peter Dacre of the *Sunday Express* that he was 'rather brainy, with a dry sense of humour. He's the funniest kid I've ever met. He kills me.' Two years later she told Clive Hirschhorn of the same paper that Ross was 'a real little monkey, the comedian in the family', and Bentley himself agreed that the boy was 'a caution'.

Bentley seems to have behaved with astonishing decency and dignity, giving Ross his surname, raising him as his own son and forgiving his unfaithful wife so generously that in gratitude a few years later she gave him a baby-blue Rolls-Royce. In 1972 she told Hirschhorn that 'what matters most in a marriage is trust, devotion and understanding. If you've got that everything else is incidental,' and two years after Bentley's death of cancer in 1994, when she was asked by Moira Petty of the *Daily Express* how she and Jack had coped with all the temptations of showbiz life, she replied: 'None of us is perfect. I think loving each other and forgiving is more important. People shouldn't feel bound and gagged in their marriage. I didn't and, because of that, loved him more. The core of our love never changed. I felt safe with him and loved.'

Mortimer soon embarked on another affair – apart from his ongoing campaign to seduce Shirley Anne Field – and did not even hint at this traumatic episode in his autobiography. When the story of Ross's paternity was finally published in a deluge of newspaper reports in 2004 he claimed that Wendy had never told him she was pregnant, that Ross had been born, nor that he had spoken to Bentley about it. He insisted that he had found out only a few weeks previously when she had telephoned him for the first time in forty-three years to warn him that I was asking questions. Although Penelope Mortimer, Shirley Anne Field, Molly Parkin, Michael Codron, many others in the theatre, and even I knew about Ross's paternity – I was told by three people within six weeks of starting to interview witnesses for this book – apparently Mortimer himself did not after forty-two years. 'I knew and assumed he did too,' Codron told me and Shirley Anne Field told me just before the story broke that 'there's a different side to John. When I spoke to Wendy Craig last week she said, "I haven't seen or heard from John Mortimer for forty years."'

There was an amusing sequel to the Wendy Craig saga. At the beginning of 1961 Tony Delano was the *Daily Mirror* correspondent in Paris. He told me: 'Bentley asked me if I could get him and Wendy a room at the Ritz because they'd been having another row and he wanted somewhere to have a glamorous reconciliation. I got them into the Ritz, she became pregnant, and after that he always blamed me for the conception of their second child. He always said I was responsible!'

None of this emotional turmoil stopped Mortimer working and yet another of his plays, *Collect Your Hand Baggage*, was staged at the London Academy of Music and Dramatic Art in December 1961. It was a little one-act twist-in-the-tail jest in which a middle-aged Peter Pan invites an unattractive girl as a joke to go off to Paris with him, never thinking she will accept, and is stunned when she turns up at London airport with a ticket. He is so shamed by her trust in him that he decides he has to take her after all and buys a ticket for himself, only to find that she never heard his invitation and is actually meeting another man. It was a slight piece but amusing enough to be broadcast on Anglia Television in August 1963 with the rakish Kenneth More playing the lead. More had recently left his wife Billie for the perky young actress Angela Douglas, who was many years his junior, and felt that the part mirrored his own naughty life. Mortimer's plays 'always have two themes', wrote More in his autobiography fifteen years later: 'sex, and a middle-aged man chasing his youth ... Once more, I was playing the eternal juvenile, the man who could not face the thought of growing old. Was I playing myself? A lot of people thought so.'

Mortimer was even more productive in 1962, writing two filmscripts, a two-act stage play and a portfolio of sketches for television as well as appearing regularly in the divorce courts. The play, *Two Stars for Comfort*, which was dedicated yet again to Penelope as though nothing had come between them, was based on the novel about Henley that he had tried to write years earlier and opened in Blackpool in March and then in the West End at the Garrick Theatre in April. It depicted a lecherous but charming, jovial ex-solicitor, Sam Turner, played by Trevor Howard, who runs a jolly, two-star, riverside hotel. Sam is a cheerful, life-enhancing fellow who goes out of his way to make people happy by telling them always what they want to hear, even if that means telling lies, but when he brightens the life of an ugly, lonely, unpopular college student by making love to her and asking her to live with him she learns the truth about him, becomes hysterical, and walks out. It was an unusual, amusing piece but the production started nervously when its opening night in Blackpool coincided with the local students' rag week and Howard was kidnapped as he left his hotel, locked in a broom cupboard, and made it onto the stage only just in time. In the West End it ran for a healthy six months and earned plaudits from the critics. 'It was a very good part for Trevor,' said Michael Codron. *The Financial Times* reviewer T. C. Worsley wrote that Howard was 'one of our really superb actors', and W. A. Darlington wrote in the *Daily Telegraph*: 'I have never seen Trevor Howard do anything better or more understanding than his Sam.'

Others were less impressed. '*Two Stars for Comfort* was not good at all,' I was told by Sandy Wilson, who had by now become a friend of the Mortimers. 'I don't reckon him very much as a playwright, more as a novelist, and his television scripts were also amusing.' Peggy Ramsay was also beginning to feel that John's plays were too lightweight and to doubt that he was as good a playwright as she had hoped he would become. Her biographer Colin Chambers reported that she told the play's director, Michael Elliott, that 'the trouble with Sam is that there is too much periphery and not sufficient indication of what he *is*. This is what makes it so tremendously hard for Trevor to play him. Yes, he's unsympathetic, but so is Iago; the latter is riveting because one sees the movement of his mind. We should see more of the movement of Sam's. This is, actually, Mortimer's big failing to my mind. He himself hasn't got a true philosophy and wouldn't know, if you asked him, where he *stands*. In the old days it didn't matter in the theatre, because we were only interested in surface, but now we want to try and see how people tick ... The only thing I'm really interested in is *what drives a man*, and it's discernible in quite a short time in real life.' She felt that Mortimer had lost his way because his 'big weakness is a passion for success and the trappings of success, and the awful part of it is that success, when indulged in, saps people's character and drains their true potential talent away – the people who love successful people exploit them, take them up, throw them away, and sometimes only a shell is left. Mortimer has a rare and touching talent, a remarkable sense of atmosphere, deep sympathy and a moving plaintive voice – he could be a superb artist, not merely a successful one, and it's this which makes me sad.' She complained to Codron that 'John only wants to socialise' and told Mortimer: 'Darling, you're just a *whore*. You're a harlot of literature. If you're going to be a whore then at least before you open your legs make sure you're properly paid.' Although she remained fond of him and was to represent him for the rest of her life, and his scripts made a lot of money for them both, 'Peggy lost real interest in Mortimer's development as a writer at this point,' wrote Chambers, and, 'she thought that his writing for the screen was better than his writing for the stage.'

He was certainly being given a great deal of work for the screen. The film of *Lunch Hour* never reached the cinemas because it was only an hour long and was eventually seen only in small clubs or on late-night television, but he worked with Jack Clayton on *The Innocents*, which was partly written by Truman Capote and based on a spooky Edwardian ghost story by Henry James, *The Turn of the Screw*. The film would star Deborah Kerr and Michael Redgrave, who said later that the script was excellent. John also adapted *The Dock Brief* for a film starring Peter Sellers as the bumbling old barrister Wilfred Morgenhall, Richard Attenborough as the wife-killer who gets away with it because Morgenhall is so incompetent, and Beryl Reid as the jolly wife. Instead of having just two characters, like the original play, John invented six others for the film, which was retitled *Trial and Error* in the United States. He discovered that Sellers was a sad, almost desperate man who did not know who he was until he could adopt the role and camouflage of someone else. He was also paranoid, believing that the Mafia was after him because he had fallen in love with Sophia Loren, and he kept imagining that Princess Margaret and Nanette Newman were equally besotted with him. At first he wanted to play Morgenhall with a thin northern accent until Mortimer and the director, James Hill, persuaded him that the character really was a southerner.

John also adapted Shelley Smith's novel *The Ballad of the Running Man* for Carol Reed for a film with the title shortened to *The Running Man*, which told the glossy story of a pilot who crashes his private plane in the sea, fakes his death, tells his wife to collect the life insurance and then, when she joins him in Spain with the loot, is seriously worried when they bump by chance into an insurance investigator who may be on his trail. Laurence Harvey played the pilot, Alan Bates the insurance man, and Lee Remick the pilot's wife, but despite the numerous twists and turns of the script the critics were unimpressed and *Newsweek* compared the plot to a rackety old engine 'clanking away [and] in need of oil'. In London *The Times* said that the film was too obvious and old-fashioned and the *Sunday Telegraph* lamented that 'something awful has happened to the cool professionalism of Carol Reed'. Reed's biographer Robert Moss wrote that the plot was ludicrously unbelievable and relied too much on 'contrived situations'. He added waspishly that 'Mortimer could not be counted on for much help in strengthening credibility, judging by his work in other mediums; in his novel *Like Men Betrayed*, for instance, the course of the plot is determined by the wrong character receiving a phone call'. Mortimer's reliance on unlikely coincidences was always to be one of the major weaknesses of his writing, especially in his novels, but Moss did concede that 'there is a good deal of fine detail and workmanship to admire in the plot: an ingratiating mix of wit, suspense and pungent dialogue; and several piquant surprises'.

Finally that year Mortimer wrote several short television sketches as one of a team of occasional contributors to Ned Sherrin's witty, revolutionary, satirical comedy programme *That Was the Week That Was*, on which the star performers were David Frost, Bernard Levin, Roy Kinnear, Lance Perceval, William Rushton and Millicent Martin. 'I liked him

enormously,' Sherrin told me. 'You light up when you see John and he
lights up to you. He wrote for us quite often. I'd ring him up and ask if
he'd got an idea and he was wonderfully fertile and his mind worked fast.
His scripts were always funny and either political or about racial or social
problems.'

When Penelope finished *The Pumpkin Eater* in the spring she was asked
to review books regularly for the *Daily Express*. She had become so sad
and insecure that she was not to write another novel for four years.
Amazingly John told her that the book was brilliant, even though it was
a raw, savage cry of despair about him, Wendy Craig and the bastard
baby. Equally amazingly Penelope dedicated it to him yet again. Astonishingly she still dreamed that she could win him back, that he would
give up his promiscuity, that one day they would be happy together.
Even as she was in the middle of typing some devastating passage in the
novel she would telephone him lovingly at work. They seemed to be
playing some obsessively unhealthy game but there was never any doubt
which of them would win: Penelope cared too much to have a chance.

John was still advising unhappy husbands and wives, appearing in the
divorce court, and the barristers at number 1 Dr Johnson's Buildings still
specialised in divorce and probate but the head of chambers, John Latey,
thought it was time to broaden the practice to embrace criminal and
other civil cases as well and invited a young Welsh QC, thirty-seven-
year-old Emlyn Hooson, to join them and eventually succeed him as
head. Hooson shared Mortimer's room, where they worked on opposite
sides of an old desk that had once belonged to Hartley Shawcross, the
one-time Labour Attorney-General, and although Hooson was two years
younger than Mortimer and Mortimer was still a junior barrister, 'he
wasn't jealous', Lord Hooson told me in 2004. 'I had nothing but
cooperation from him and he was a tremendous worker – he would work
all night if necessary – but he was always a loner, never very chatty, and
didn't go out drinking with the boys, though he had numerous girlfriends.' Mortimer was thinking seriously again of leaving the Bar. Why
should he waste his life dissecting strangers' sad domestic disputes and
tired accusations of adultery, cruelty or unreasonable behaviour? There
was quite enough adultery, cruelty and unreasonable behaviour in his
own life, and one particular case in the Appeal Court brought him to the
brink of abandoning the Law: the parents of an eight-year-old girl were
fighting for custody of the child and the father accused the mother of not
teaching her to read properly. The judge called the girl into court, told
her to read aloud a passage in a weighty legal volume, and when she read

it perfectly he awarded custody to the mother. Mortimer was appalled that a child's whole future should depend on whether she could read an abstruse paragraph of Law. He dreamed of living somewhere sunny, in Italy perhaps, where he could write contentedly, unencumbered by strangers' miseries, yet it was to be twenty-two more years before he stepped off his legal treadmill. He delayed for so long partly out of loyalty to his father but also because the Law brought him into contact with clients whom he might use as characters in his plays.

Caroline, now twenty and calling herself not Mortimer but Fletcher – her mother's maiden name – had landed a part as an understudy in a West End play and started to have an affair with a fellow member of the cast – the comic actor Leslie Phillips, who was eighteen years older and married with four children – and had left home to live with him nearby. The rest of the family spent most of that summer of 1962 at Southend Cottage, where Kath's cook Dora fed them and the children played tennis with John and frolicked in a big, blue, above-ground plastic swimming pool. In August John and Penelope took seventeen-year-old Julia, fourteen-year-old Deborah, twelve-year-old Sally and seven-year-old Jeremy off on holiday to Malaga, where Julia fell for a rich young American, Ben Sonnenburg, and decided to stay there with him when the others returned to England. Penelope was distraught. On top of all the traumas of the past year Julia's defection was just too much. On 9 September, three weeks before *The Pumpkin Eater* was due to be published, Penelope left the children at Southend Cottage, drove up to London, let herself into 23 Harben Road, and took an overdose of Soneril sleeping pills, which she swilled down with a large glass of neat brandy. She was found in a coma and rushed to New End Hospital in Hampstead, where she came round after two days and was chided by a nurse for having abandoned 'all those lovely children', whom John took to Turville Heath for his mother to look after. 'My wife has been receiving medical treatment for insomnia for some time,' he told the Press smoothly. 'She must have taken a few pills too many. She has been working very hard.' She was taken to a nursing home where her brain was zapped with electro-convulsive treatment in the hope of shocking her back to a sort of sanity. Nobody bothered to tell Julia that her mother had tried to commit suicide and suggest that she might like to come home.

Leslie Phillips and Caroline had been invited to join a publicity cruise to Istanbul on a Turkish liner, the *Ackdeniz*, and Penelope went with them although she disliked Phillips, leaving her mother to look after the children in Harben Road. On board she tried to take revenge on John and heal herself by having an affair with a German journalist, Richard Kaufmann, but it did not help. Unbelievably she was still obsessed by John. She had however a brief burst of happiness when *The Pumpkin Eater* was published in Britain on 1 October, the day the ship reached Genoa. The book took its title from the nursery rhyme,

> *Peter, Peter, pumpkin eater,*
> *Had a wife and couldn't keep her.*
> *He put her in a pumpkin shell*
> *And there he kept her very well*

and many of the reviews were ecstatic. It was 'quite the best of Mrs Mortimer's excellent novels', said *The Times Literary Supplement*. *The Times* agreed: 'The best she has written ... one of the best novels of the year.' It was 'impressive and powerful ... remarkably intelligent and compassionate', said *The Sunday Times*, 'one of those novels which seem to be written with real knowledge of the brink of the abyss, taut almost beyond endurance.' One reviewer said perceptively that it was 'an odd, unhappy, painful work that seemed to be conceived in the womb and not the brain'. It was 'a compelling and tragic new novel', said Robert Pitman in the *Sunday Express*. 'Mrs Mortimer is perhaps the most brilliant of all the younger women novelists writing in Britain today. She has made herself expert in picking away the surface gloss which covers the life of the rich, new middle classes. She is the family historian of the smart, go-ahead, two-car household, which has a double load of private misery packed in each boot.' Pitman hinted heavily that the shit of a husband in the novel was a perfect portrait of John.

Some women were appalled by the book because it suggested that a mother may resent or even hate her children. *The Pumpkin Eater* was 'about as compassionate as a flick-knife', wrote a columnist in the *Daily Mail*. 'The heroine, far from being sensitive, is a callous egotist, who uses husbands, children and friends as fodder for her self-indulgence ... It is not often that a woman novelist writes a book completely devoid of charity about her own sex.' Even so it shot to the top of the bestseller list and Caroline reported later that as they drove through Istanbul Penelope was singing, 'I'm a genius! I'm a genius!' But in October she returned to London to discover that John was having yet another affair, this time with a woman called Bobbie. Unable to take any more of his infidelities and convinced that her marriage was finally over, she escaped to Switzerland with Caroline, who flew back to London after a couple of days in

Zurich while Penelope drove on south to Ascona, near Locarno, on Lake Maggiore, where she rented a flat. Unable to keep away from John, she telephoned him and he announced that Bobbie was going away for a week and suggested that he might pop out to Switzerland for the weekend to see her. He did, and when he arrived said blithely, 'Let's go to bed and forget all this nonsense.' Amazingly Penelope agreed and they returned to London to resume their dreadful old life as though nothing had happened.

'Happiness has something to do with simplicity and seclusion,' she told the *Daily Mail* optimistically. 'It certainly has nothing to do with the desperate kind of life everyone I know leads – the London life of too much money, too much competition, too much success, too much fear. I'm determined now to shed, to strip off the insane complications.' In Ascona, she said, she had lived so simply that she had not bothered even to buy a kettle. She had just boiled water in a saucepan because 'why do people need kettles?' and she added: 'For the first time in my life I lived completely alone. I'd at last escaped from the noise and rushing that drive you demented. I know now that I can do without the kettle – and without many other things that appeared important.' Perhaps she thought that her marriage had become so awful that it could only improve. If so, she was whistling into the wind.

Seven

'The Casanova of the Sixties'
1963–1969

As the Swinging Sixties blossomed in all their hairy Technicolor glory in 1963 Mortimer turned forty and embarked on a wild, delayed adolescence. While Penelope consulted doctors and psychiatrists, swallowed fistfuls of pills and suffered more electric-shock treatment to try to control her depression, John bought a Volvo sports car, Rolling Stones LPs, grew his hair long, wore flared velveteen trousers, bright flowery shirts, matching kipper ties and Nehru jackets. He decked himself out in necklaces, bangles and beads, and tried marijuana although he was nervous of LSD, cocaine and heroin. 'I hung out with the Beatles in the Sixties,' he claimed in a *Mail on Sunday* magazine interview in 2004 – unconvincingly since he never mentioned it in any of his autobiographies, but he did go to trendy London clubs like the Arethusa in the King's Road, came home late night after night, and was for years to pursue pretty, miniskirted girls much younger than himself, realising that he was already middle-aged and might not be able to keep it up much longer. Penelope went off to America in March to publicise the American edition of *The Pumpkin Eater* but in New York she suffered a crisis when she froze with terror, wandered the threatening streets of Manhattan for a day, and flew back to London after just four days. 'For most of her adult life my mother suffered from depression,' Julia told Alan Yentob in 2003, 'and I think she had probably the wrong sort of husband in the end who couldn't deal with it either and was rather a coward and she needed to get away from him.'

One of Mortimer's many young mistresses in the Sixties was a vivacious, mischievous, thirty-one-year-old Welsh divorcée, Molly Parkin, a painter with naughty green eyes and two small daughters, who had been the mistress of the actor James Robertson Justice, was now the fashion editor of *Nova* magazine and would later become fashion editor of *The Sunday Times*. 'John had what I'd put at the top of the bill, a sense of humour and an ability with words,' she told me in 2004. 'His banter was very sexy and he had a wonderful voice that could get you into bed apart from anything else – a high-pitched voice, very light and fairy, but always mellifluous and he used wonderful words. He had a waspish, almost gay, quality of humour and everything about him was lovely except that you knew he would never be faithful to you, but I didn't want any strings either, so he was a perfect companion. Mind you, I had to fit him into a very busy schedule because I was between marriages and had three regular lovers already and I was also busy shagging whoever else was passing by as well!' When Molly left *Nova* and ran a bistro near Sloane Square called the Red Brick – from which some wit removed the lower curve of the B – 'it was a nightmare because all my lovers used to come and wait until the end of the evening, all wanting to go home with me, and there was no back entrance. John would always come in with *excruciatingly* groomed, glossy, Sloane Rangery, top-of-the-market girls who turned out to be his "secretaries". They were *totally* out of place because the air was thick with hurled brandies and we didn't close until four in the morning and the police used to join in, so there were complaints and I was knackered by the time we got home.' In her autobiography she confessed thirty years later that she had 'screwed a sanitary inspector at the back of the filthy kitchen when he expressed doubts about renewing our licence. We got the licence, but he came back for more. I gave him a discreet hand job every time he happened to be in the area, which for some reason was quite often. A nice man. I don't believe his other clients were so obliging.'

As for her affair with John, she told me, 'there was genuine affection and we always laughed and laughed, but he wasn't a good lover – it was all about his own enjoyment – and he'd done a lot of drinking, and when it came to the love-making what he most liked me to do was to smack him on the botty. If I'd had a whip that would have suited him admirably, but one night – when I had to slap his arse until he came, and he couldn't have come without it – I said, "Oh, I've had enough." He wanted a dominatrix but he wanted me to mother him as well. He's like a little baby, really, very sweet, but I was really used to a bloody good rogering rather than smacking!' In his book *Masochism in Modern Man* Dr Theodor Reik noted that most male masochists are either impotent or partly so.

'The desire to be punished or humiliated is just another expression for wanting to adopt a passive feminine attitude towards the father,' he suggested. 'Thus to be beaten means for the masochist to be loved.' Freud identified a 'feminine masochism' in a man with a weak ego that made him want to be treated like a helpless, dependent but naughty child – a finding reported also by Cheryl Glickhauf-Hughes and Marolyn Wells in their book *Treatment of the Masochistic Personality*, in which they wrote that 'what the masochist seeks is not the mature love of a healthy adult-to-adult relationship [but] to be nurtured, gratified, and emotionally held as a parent would a child'. Molly Parkin was not Mortimer's only mistress to tell me about his enjoyment of smacking and it was enough to put Molly off him as a lover. 'Our fling didn't last very long,' she said. 'I wasn't interested in all this slapping of the buttocks.'

Mortimer's compulsive pursuit of women, late nights and heavy drinking seem to have sapped his creative energy and he wrote nothing of significance that year. With his income dwindling he put Southend Cottage on the market for £17,000 (£235,000), while Harold Pinter – who was by now famous for having written *The Birthday Party*, *The Caretaker*, *The Collection* and the filmscript of *The Servant* – was writing a brilliant screenplay for Jack Clayton's moving black-and-white film of *The Pumpkin Eater*. John was to be played by Peter Finch, Penelope by Anne Bancroft, Jack Bentley by James Mason and Wendy Craig by Janine Gray. Pinter remained almost completely faithful to the book and its dialogue but Penelope was displeased with the film, complaining that the ending was too happy. She said that if she had been married to a gorgeous man like Peter Finch rather than John she would have had nothing to complain about. Finch was certainly too handsome, suave and kind to play Mortimer but young Maggie Smith was superb as the dreamy lodger Philpot, Finch's possibly pregnant lover, of whom the children shriek in the film: 'She smells of fish. She *stinks* of fish.' James Mason too was wonderfully slimy and vindictive as the cuckolded Jack Bentley and revelled in the gossip that Finch's character had a kinky perversion and liked beating women. Despite Penelope's reservations the movie won an award at the Cannes Film Festival, was voted the Film Critics' Guild Film of the Year, Bancroft was nominated for an Oscar and Pinter won the British Film Academy award for the best screenplay of 1964.

By now Penelope had had several affairs herself, one with the thirty-six-year-old Yorkshire working-class playwright David Mercer, the author of

A Suitable Case For Treatment. Mercer was a huge man with a wild shock of hair, beard and moustache, unhappily married for the second time, often drunk, whom Penelope met when she and John flew to Scotland in September for the Edinburgh Festival. He was deeply lovable, she wrote in *About Time Too*, even though he was difficult, thin-skinned and sometimes deceitful and cowardly. Mercer could also be a stupendously boring alcoholic and was given to telling everyone, including Mortimer, that he was deeply in love with Penelope, but although she desperately wanted some man to free her of her sexual obsession with John none did. She even thought of trying lesbianism but could never bring herself to embrace another woman. 'She was very attractive,' Ned Sherrin told me, 'and I remember Peggy Ramsay being highly amused because Penelope thought Mercer was this great working-class fellow who would give her a good rough rogering, but then she couldn't get him to do it until one day she stopped the car in the Mall and got him into the bushes in Green Park!' Despite her affair Penelope 'always remained obsessed by John', I was told by Robin Dalton, who had just become her agent. 'It was a traumatic relationship because she was a very, *very* difficult lady – on her bad days a vicious character who became a viper – but she could be very funny and on her good days she was vulnerable, generous and fun. And I liked John enormously – he was outgoing, courteous and pleasant – but he was ugly and very unattractive and I could never see his sexual attraction – never never never.'

Caroline – who was about to appear in her first major part in a professional West End play, *The Photographer* – was now living in a nearby flat with Leslie Phillips, whose wife, Penelope Bartley, was to divorce him the following year, citing Caroline as the other woman. Julia had left Spain and her rich boyfriend and was living at home with Debbie and Sally. The girls were now nineteen, sixteen and fourteen and nine-year-old Jeremy 'was aware that the marriage was under huge strain and it was quite an explosive household', he told me. 'I was quite withdrawn and wept a lot. It wasn't a jolly childhood, it was an *eventful* childhood. My parents didn't know how to deal with us at home so that the first day of the holidays we would go abroad and we wouldn't come back until the end of the holidays. I didn't really know how to make friends and was never given a chance to develop a *holiday* life at home. They'd hire houses in Italy or Spain and fill them with people. What they wanted was to go somewhere and sit down and write and enjoy the wine and the sunshine. At home there was some friction between my mother and the au pairs because I became more friendly with them than I did with her.

The key thing was to arrange things so that she could write. My father could write anywhere but she needed to get somewhere away from the hustle and bustle.'

Penelope became so angry with John during their rows that she would throw the telephone at him or smash her car into the garage wall, back it up, smash it again, and keep on as long as her rage lasted. On one occasion she hurled a bowl full of dirty plates into the street and in October she attacked him in a heartfelt article in the *Sunday Mirror* about his slothful helplessness:

> The male Sloth tends to retire into some cloud-cuckoo-land where he is responsible for nothing . . . The Sloth's car is always breaking down, his watch doesn't go, his cigarette lighter doesn't work . . . the merest thistledown of a demand on him reduces him to a state of bewildered panic. He is obsessed by the problem of avoiding the Herculean tasks required of him, such as buying a new razor blade, making a telephone call, deciding whether to take a bath . . . the most tragic mess the Sloth allows to happen in his life is his marriage . . . he has to convince himself that his wife doesn't exist. This is absolutely necessary for his survival, for she, of all the burdens he has to bear, the dangers he has to defend himself from, is the greatest. Not only is he expected to maintain her, give her shelter, understand more or less how the frightening little object *works* – he is expected to love her as well . . . He concludes, therefore, that his wife's need to be loved is trivial, tiresome and unjustified.

The Hollywood producer Otto Preminger was so impressed by *The Pumpkin Eater* that he flew Penelope to New York to write the screenplay for a thriller about a five-year-old child who is kidnapped in Hampstead, *Bunny Lake is Missing*, but once again she hated New York and flew back to London without finishing it, telling Preminger that she could do it only if John helped her, so he flew them both out to work on the script in Hawaii, where he was shooting a film about the Japanese bombing of Pearl Harbor. Penelope contributed little to the film but John knocked it off so quickly in just two weeks that she told Robin Dalton that she would write no more screenplays because 'she didn't want to overshadow John and thought that would ruin their relationship. She felt she was a better writer than he was and that her marriage was more important than her career.' The film eventually starred Laurence Olivier, Noël Coward and Keir Dullea – pronounced Delay – who was mortified when Coward crept up behind him one day and murmured cruelly, 'Keir Dullea, gone tomorrow.'

Mortimer wrote three scripts for BBC radio – *Personality Split, Education of an Englishman* and *A Rare Device* – and more sketches for Ned Sherrin's new television show, *Not So Much a Programme, More a Way of Life*, which starred David Frost, John Bird, Eleanor Bron, John Fortune and Roy Hudd as well as Patrick Campbell, Denis Norden and Harvey Orkin. The irreverence of programmes such as Sherrin's and the new iconoclastic mood of the Swinging Sixties contributed to the Labour Party's victory over the Conservatives in the general election of October 1964 when Harold Wilson became the first Labour Prime Minister since Clement Attlee, much to Mortimer's delight, albeit with a tiny majority. To compound his pleasure Mortimer's standing in the theatre had become so high by the end of 1964 that he was appointed a governor of the Royal Shakespeare Company, and to crown a triumphant year he persuaded Shirley Anne Field to go to bed with him at last. She was twenty-six and about to reach the height of her beauty and career when she filmed *Alfie* with Michael Caine, and Mortimer was an ugly, paunchy forty-one, but she had been raised in an orphanage and was particularly vulnerable to anyone who showed her affection and Mortimer showered her with it. 'After three years without any hanky-panky at all,' she told me, 'he told me all about himself one day and suddenly I saw a very sensitive, caring, less flippant side of him, and our relationship became more physical although it wasn't anything that I took too seriously. He was fun, enormously charming and made me feel so special and safe. However he had this thing about spanking with hairbrushes! I thought, God, what a strange one we've got here! I was in my middle twenties, the world was my oyster, I was going through a very racy time myself and I just thought that the spanking was a public school sort of thing.'

They were to remain close friends and part-time lovers for several years, though this did not stop him soon embarking on another affair, with Jane McKerran, a journalist who was working with Michael Foot on the left-wing paper *Tribune*.

'Our office was near John's chambers,' she told me in 2004, 'which made it very convenient. Our affair lasted for two years, from 1965 to 1967, until I met and married Brian Walden,' the Labour MP and television presenter.

Mortimer faced a new challenge when Ken Tynan, the literary manager of Laurence Olivier's new National Theatre, which was little more than a year old and still based at the Old Vic, suggested that he should

translate into English for the National a French farce by the eccentric
Parisian playwright Georges Feydeau, who had died in 1921. They
decided on the 1907 play *La Puce à l'Oreille*, a perfect choice for John
because it was a breathless, helter-skelter romp of misunderstanding,
mistaken identity, lust, adultery and sexual jealousy. He decided not to
translate the play literally but to invent an English equivalent of Feydeau's
French slang and to add some jokes of his own. In English the play was
entitled *A Flea in Her Ear* and told of an ugly, impotent Parisian insurance
executive whose wife suspects him of infidelity because his braces have
just been posted back to him from a seedy hotel called (of course) the
Coq d'Or. She gets such a flea in her ear about her suspicions that she
persuades a woman friend to write to him to suggest an illicit meeting
at the hotel, and slapstick chaos ensues.

In a final desperate attempt to save their marriage Penelope and John
both consulted psychiatrists. One, a jolly Scotsman, advised him to take
up golf but none of the advice was of any use and Penelope began at last
to prepare to leave him and live alone, a prospect that frightened her at
the age of forty-six but seemed inevitable since he showed no sign of
mending his ways and she simply could not bring herself to condone his
constant blatant infidelities. 'If I had been prepared to put up with it,'
she told Lynda Lee-Potter in 1993, 'we would possibly still be together.
He thought that the girls were unimportant. He felt that our marriage
would be perfectly satisfactory if I could understand this and give him
my blessing. But I couldn't.' She had earned a great deal of money from
The Pumpkin Eater and took her first step towards independence by renting
cheaply a painter's studio near Harben Road where she could escape,
write, and begin to believe that she might be able to survive on her own
even though John kept telling her that they should stay together for the
sake of Jeremy, who was now withdrawn, insecure and apprehensive. In
January she agreed to rent a flat four streets away from Harben Road, in
Aberdare Gardens, and decided that it would be best for Jeremy if he
went to boarding school. She chose the progressive, co-educational
Bedales School's prep school, Dunhurst, which had a high reputation for
making children from dysfunctional families feel at home, and she bought
a small semi-detached house near by, Stable Cottage, so that Jeremy
would not feel that she had abandoned him. In September they both took
him to start his first term – astonishingly considering the fuss Mortimer
had made himself when he was sent to boarding school – and coolly
Jeremy accused them of dumping him because he had become an incon-
venience to their selfish lives. The next day Penelope moved out of

Harben Road into the flat in Aberdare Gardens. Julia was living with a boyfriend in a basement flat in Knightsbridge and Deborah and Sally had gone back to their boarding schools too, so Mortimer was on his own. Yet even now Penelope and John telephoned each other constantly and met almost every day. He invited her to join him and his latest girlfriend at Harben Road for dinner, which he cooked himself, and told Penelope absurdly afterwards: 'If you were living with someone else I would begin to court you.' They even spent occasional weekends together in a country hotel that was near both Sally's and Jeremy's schools. Their separation was as bizarre as their marriage.

Bunny Lake is Missing was finally finished – 'it is a thrilling picture and I am very good,' wrote Noël Coward in his diary – and John continued to write television sketches for Ned Sherrin, this time for his latest witty series *BBC3*, which starred Robert Robinson, John Fortune and Alan Bennett. He was still also toiling away in the divorce and probate courts and Judge Stephen Tumim remembered a day when Mortimer panted into court to represent a woman who was not contesting her husband's petition.

'What on earth are you doing here?' asked Tumim.

'I *always* represent her in her divorces,' gasped Mortimer.

In another case he acted for a vicar whose wife had been having a lesbian affair with the district nurse and Mortimer felt that he could at least persuade the judge to grant the vicar custody of the children because they would need a male role model while they were growing up, but he lost the case when the wife's counsel declared that the district nurse had now changed sex and so was perfectly capable of providing whatever masculine influence was necessary. Mortimer's basic rule as a barrister was that like a taxi driver he should take on anyone who wanted to hire him but he broke his rule once when he discovered that his client was a part-time hangman. He was so disgusted that he refused to carry on with the case.

Dreary though divorce and probate cases were, especially now that it was no longer necessary to prove adultery, they could be highly lucrative. One, a dispute over the estate of a young German millionaire called Fuld, lasted for nine months as his mother, wife and harem of mistresses battled over several wills he had left while Mortimer and teams of lawyers rubbed their hands as the daily refreshers rolled in. To rejuvenate his legal career he applied to the Lord Chancellor, Gerald Gardiner of *Lady Chatterley's Lover* fame, for 'silk', which would make him a senior barrister, allow him to put the letters QC (Queen's Counsel) after his name, and bring him all sorts of criminals to defend, including murderers. He had appeared already in his first murder case as a last-minute replacement for Emlyn Hooson, who told me: 'I had a husband-and-wife murder case at the Old Bailey and got a desperate phone call from our clerk, who was going berserk because this case had been brought forward to the next day, when I had a very difficult civil case fixed in the Court of Appeal, and he could not find any criminal silk available to do it. I suggested he got John Mortimer, even though John was not yet a QC, because he'd be ideal for this case, he'd make sure half the jury were women, and he'd say the wife had been justified to murder her husband. He was very good with juries, at creating the right, friendly atmosphere. It was the first criminal case he'd ever done and he got an acquittal.'

In October 1965 a thirty-one-year-old Nigerian author and political activist, Wole Soyinka, who was in 1986 to become the first black African to win the Nobel Prize for Literature, was accused of breaking into the radio station at Ibadan and forcing an engineer at gunpoint to broadcast a tape attacking the Prime Minister of Western Nigeria, Chief Samuel Akintola. To ensure that Soyinka was given a fair trial Amnesty International hired Mortimer to fly out to Nigeria to sit as an observer in the court, where he learned that one local barrister sometimes resorted to a powerful form of witchcraft by removing his shoes in court and waggling his naked toes at the judge. For recreation John drove out one night to a bush village where he picked up some African girls, took them back to his hotel, and bought them Guinness. Soyinka was acquitted and John returned to London impressed that the best traditions of British justice were being upheld by polite, bewigged, begowned, black barristers and judges deep in the bush of a violent, unstable West African country.

To make him even happier, the Commons abolished capital punishment for a trial period of five years in November although it left three archaic capital crimes on the statute book: treason, piracy with violence, and arson in Her Majesty's dockyards.

That Christmas was the last that any of the Mortimers would spend at 23 Harben Road. Deborah agreed that she would live with Penelope, Sally that she would live with John in the temporary flat that he was about to rent little more than a mile away in Little Venice. Penelope mourned his absence, drove aimlessly around the streets, unable to write, and started again to consult her psychiatrist, Dr Heinz Wolff, who prescribed powerful, debilitating drugs and suggested she should go to hospital. In despair, unable to keep away, she went to see John in his new flat and wrote in *About Time Too*, 'I have an impression of girls sitting about, plain, good-natured, grubby, wearing down-at-heel sling-backs. John snapped at them and they giggled, making mock-contrite faces.' To torture her further he called her 'my little touchstone, magical Penelope', and asked her to move back with him, saying: 'It would all be so simple if I didn't love you.' In some weird way that seemed to be true. 'It was obviously intense,' Shirley Anne Field told me. 'They were strangely besotted by each other and both strange people who didn't have any sense of conventional morality.' John, however, soon made himself at home in his new flat. 'He was as domesticated as any man could be,' said Shirley Anne. 'He was unbel*ievable*, his apartment, all this pine furniture, and then he'd cook lunch. There was no suggestion that he was gay but he was like some avuncular uncle. He'd tidy the table, put the flowers around, and cook. At the time I was going through disastrous romances at least twice and told John all about them and he'd say, "Would you like a cuddle? Shall I cuddle it better?"'

A Flea in Her Ear, directed by the portly, mischievous Jacques Charon, the veteran director of the Comédie-Française, scored such a helter-skelter triumph when it opened in February at the Old Vic that it moved into the West End for a ten-week season at the Queen's Theatre, went on tour around the country, and was later televised. Twenty-nine-year-old Albert Finney and thirty-three-year-old Geraldine McEwan – who played the part of the suspicious wife as if she were Groucho Marx – were superb in the main roles but Mortimer claimed inaccurately in his book *Murderers and Other Friends* that the small part of the butler, Etienne Plucheux, was played at the National by Olivier himself: Olivier did not take on the part until the company toured Canada more than a year later. Ken and Kathleen Tynan celebrated the play's success by throwing a louche party – with lifesize fibreglass models of women in erotic poses, black stockings and suspender belts – at their home in London on the night of the second general election in eighteen months, 31 March, when Labour won again with a much bigger majority and Harold Wilson was re-elected Prime Minister. Mortimer was overjoyed and delighted again a few days later when he became at last a Queen's Counsel and was able to dress up in a tailcoat, knee breeches, silk gown, full-bottomed wig, winged collar and bands, ruffled lace shirt, patent leather shoes with buckles and black silk stockings. From now on he could 'lead' the defence in all sorts of high-profile criminal cases at the Old Bailey, ignore boring cases on the provincial circuits, hire junior barristers to look up legal precedents and do most of his donkey work for him, and charge his clients a fortune. 'I think my father would have been glad I became a QC,' he told me in 1993. 'I've followed his life so closely he'd better!'

He began to take on cases that allowed him to deploy to the full his greatest legal skill, his ability to sway juries, and his orotund eloquence was such that when he found himself at Uxbridge magistrates court defending a woman charged with smuggling marijuana through Heathrow airport he heard himself exhorting the worthies on the Bench to 'give her justice, but let it be justice tempered with that mercy which is the hallmark of the Uxbridge and Hillingdon district magistrates court!' Soon he was appearing in court in all his QC glory to defend serious criminals. One of his first murder trials was that of a young man who stabbed his mother with a knife in their London flat and remarked before being sent to Broadmoor: 'I have either buggered a prostitute or killed a peacock in paradise.' Another bizarre trial was that of a young male prostitute who fell in love with another who was changing sex, flirted with a third man on the dance floor of a London club, and was battered to death with a child's plastic piggy bank by the jealous boyfriend. Amazingly Mortimer persuaded the judge that the killer had been provoked beyond endurance and should be found guilty only of manslaughter.

'Judges liked having John before them. He was a charmer,' Lord Hooson told me, and Mortimer told Scarth Flett of the *Sunday Express* in 1990 that he had always 'made a point of looking scruffy' because 'I didn't want juries to think I was some sort of smarmy lawyer'. Some judges, however, took pleasure in putting him down. One of his earliest courtroom ploys was to mesmerise the jury by walking up and down as he asked questions of the witnesses until one judge eventually barked: 'Do keep still! It's like watching ping-pong.' When Mortimer told another jury that they had just listened to the dreariest prosecution speech he had ever heard the judge purred: 'Members of the jury, it may come as something of a surprise to know that the sole purpose of the English criminal law is not to entertain Mr Mortimer.' Some judges, however, were very strange indeed. In one case Mortimer was defending a husband who had tried to drown his wife when they were both in the bath – he was let off with a warning when the judge learned that for twenty years the wife had always made her poor, henpecked husband sit at the tap end of the bath. Another judge confided that to keep his silk stockings up he wore a woman's suspender belt that he had bought from a shop that sold clothes to outsize hospital matrons. Another used to take his childhood Paddington Bear into court. Not that Mortimer's clients were always the full shilling themselves: one defendant trembled when he entered the dock at the Old Bailey and saw the scarlet-clad judge and sword-wielding court officials in all their colourful medieval finery. 'The Day of Judgement is at hand!' he cried in terror and was duly sent to an asylum.

The broadening of Mortimer's legal career brought a new buzz into his life. 'If you're doing a criminal case and talking to a jury, and then waiting for the result with your heart in your mouth, it's very exciting,' he confessed to Judith Palmer in 2001. He claimed too that criminals, even murderers, were generally much nicer than greedy beneficiaries fighting over a will or vicious husbands and wives getting divorced, who he told Deborah Ross of the *Independent* in 1999 would 'ring you at 2 a.m. and say: "You'll never guess what he's done now. He's gone off with the toast rack!" But murderers – because they've killed the one person who was really bugging them – have a certain peace about them.' His new criminal practice also gave him a hoard of legal anecdotes that he was able to save for use in a play, story or novel. One, which he was to use in one of his Rumpole stories, was about the Welsh Labour Attorney-General Elwyn Jones, a friend of Emlyn Hooson, who was leading Hooson in a murder case in Cardiff. 'Emlyn loved going off on Parliamentary jaunts to other countries,' said Lord Hooson, 'and when he went to Tripoli to see King Idris he was anxious that I should get the case fixed for the Thursday after his return. In Tripoli he was discomforted to find that there was a guard outside his bedroom door every night and he thought he was being followed everywhere he went, so he complained to the authorities, who admitted having him watched because of a cable I had sent to him which said "murder fixed for Thursday".'

Another favourite tale was the one about the newly appointed judge who was unsure how severe a sentence he should pass on two men who had been arrested for pleasuring each other in a public lavatory. He telephoned a more experienced judge to ask what he usually gave for buggery. 'Oh, never more than a pound,' said the judge.

There was the tale of the deaf old judge who asked a convicted defendant whether he wanted to say anything before being sentenced.

'Bugger all,' said the defendant.

The judge turned to the defence barrister. 'Did your client say something?' he asked.

' "Bugger all," my Lord,' said the QC.

'Strange,' said the judge. 'I could have sworn I heard him say *something*.'

Mortimer also loved to tell the story of a young woman victim in an indecent assault case who could not bring herself to say out loud in court what the accused had said to her. 'Write it down,' said the judge. She was given a piece of paper, wrote 'would you care for a screw?' and the note was passed to the foreman of the jury to read and then from one member of the jury to another until a pretty young jurywoman nudged the twelfth juryman, who seemed to be half asleep, and passed it on to him. He read the note, grinned, nodded at her and put it in his pocket. 'Would you pass that note up to me,' said the judge. The juryman shook his head. 'It's a purely personal matter, my Lord,' he said.

Mortimer was himself asking an increasing number of girls if they would care for a screw now that he was living alone in Little Venice. An astonishing number succumbed, including several famous actresses, after he had taken them out for an expensive lunch, dinner or dance at clubs like the Arethusa or Ad Lib or Annie's Room and had spent the requisite first half-hour making them laugh and forget his face. He took great pride in his seduction technique and loved to tell a story about a randy but pathetic author who was travelling around the country to publicise his latest book accompanied by one of his publisher's nubile young publicity girls. One evening he plucked up the courage to proposition her. 'I'm not much good at sex,' he said, 'but with you I'll really try.'

Not that Mortimer's own attempts at seduction were always successful. He pursued a beautiful young Australian journalist, Jill Neville, who lived near by in Clarendon Gardens, but 'although she put it about quite a lot with other men she drew the line at him', I was told by Tony Delano, one of her lovers. 'Mortimer would ring her late at night from a public telephone box and say that he would be coming round to her flat in ten minutes, and she told me she'd have to vomit in his lap or something to avoid having sex with him. She didn't like him at all and thought he was greasy.' Mortimer also determined one night to ravish a smouldering young English actress, rang the doorbell of the mansion block in which she had a flat, and removed his strong glasses because he had heard that she wore a wig and could not face seeing her bald. The outside door of the block opened and he took the lift to the top floor, where a blurred, bald figure stood in the doorway of the flat. 'Darling!' cried Mortimer. 'You look wonderful!' He threw his arms around the bald person only to discover that he was embracing an alarmed elderly man. He had picked the wrong flat.

Another embarrassing moment was when he staggered out of bed just before dawn to drink a glass of water and realised too late that he had swallowed a pair of mink eyelashes. 'It was amazing how John managed to bed so many girls,' Sandy Wilson told me, 'including one from the cast of *The Boy Friend* even though she was very happily married. And he treated them very badly and just chucked them over when the next one came along.' Another enchanting girl whom Mortimer is said to have pursued was the twenty-seven-year-old Canadian ballerina Lynn Seymour, who Dame Ninette de Valois said was the greatest dramatic dancer in the first fifty years of the Royal Ballet. But Miss Seymour told me that she had never met Mortimer although 'I'm sure it would have been delightful being one of his girlfriends'. He even renewed his affair with his first love, 'Angela Bedwell', who was now a widow with two children.

'I think he was rather proud of being the Casanova of the Sixties,' Penelope told Elizabeth Grice of the *Daily Telegraph* in 1993. 'He never showed the slightest shame or guilt about it. He didn't take it seriously and he didn't expect me to.' David Leitch, who was to live with Jill Neville for twelve years and marry her in 1970, told me that he reckoned Mortimer's success with women was similar to that of the literary critic Cyril Connolly. 'They were both very unattractive,' said Leitch, 'yet Connolly was probably the most successful womaniser of his time other than Aly Khan. I met John somewhere with Shirley Anne Field and here was this *incredibly* beautiful girl, looking sixteen, and this nondescript chap who looked like a middle-aged tax collector. He was in those days a good deal shabbier than he is now, and in his middle years he was overweight and a bit dishevelled, and he lisped as if his dentures didn't fit very well, and he had a kind of mumbling address, a funny squeaky voice, and he had green mould on his teeth and smelled very heavily of tobacco. I'm sure that he, like Connolly, was so successful with women because although they were both very English they conducted themselves in a weird way like Continental boulevardiers out of P. G. Wodehouse.' At a party Mortimer's stepdaughter Caroline met a couple who said they had recently bumped into him at an orgy. 'Well, everybody knows he was screwing half of London by then,' she told Alan Yentob with a cackle in 2003.

But 'I don't think John has had as many women as he likes to pretend', I was told by John Timbers, a photographer who came to know him well in the 1960s, 'and he certainly doesn't mind if people exaggerate the number.' Shirley Anne Field agreed: 'I don't think John had as many girlfriends as he liked to pretend. Sex wasn't the most important thing for him. What he wanted was just to be close to someone. He wasn't this great big ladies' man even though he wants you to think he was. All this stuff about girls is a bit of bravado. They were just delicious things to flirt with. It was all very lightweight and without substance. My relationship with him was really a deep friendship. I don't believe that John was especially sexy. He was persistent and loving and had this quality of making a woman feel special or safe, and he made me feel like a priceless piece of art. Mind you, I knew there was another side to him because I saw another way he treated various people. For instance, he had this girl of about twenty-six who worked for him as his sort of secretary-cum-helper and he'd take her upstairs at lunchtime. I'd arrive at his flat in Little Venice with my girlfriend Romey and he'd come down and then the girl would come down with a flushed face. I asked her once about her red face and she said, "Well, how would you feel if you had just been spanked?" I was quite taken aback but John just said, "Don't be hysterical, dear." '

Despite their separation John would still take Penelope out for lunch, dinner and to the cinema, where they still held hands even though she confessed to yet another psychiatrist, Dr Barrington Cooper, that she was actually cheerful when John was hundreds of miles away but that she began to shake and go to pieces when he was near. Their marriage was a constant battlefield, she wrote in her autobiography, and she claimed that he loved to humiliate and hurt her. If she was ever to be whole again she was going to have to escape this vicious marital battle for good. John's behaviour resembled that of a cat playing with a mouse. 'I feel I must for ever be holding you at arm's length, then pulling you to me,' he told her. The doctor prescribed more pills, then pentathol, then methydrine, and eventually advised her to find a nice new lover. 'You're not depressive,' he said, 'you're obsessional.'

Penelope tried to match John's infidelities over the next four years but few of the boyfriends meant much to her and her adulteries were self-destructive. One old lover who came back briefly into her life was Randall Swingler after she decided it was time to tell Deborah – a sulky, door-slamming seventeen-year-old who had just taken her A-level exams – that he, not Charles Dimont, was her real father. Now living in Essex and drinking heavily, Swingler 'turned up at the flat, fifty-eight-years-old, toothless, weeping, with the head of an old woman', she wrote in *About Time Too*. 'All day he talked and wept and drank and read his poetry, much of it beautiful, [and] he and Deborah flung themselves into [an intense father–daughter] relationship. I could only think how awful it would be when he died, and how for Deb's sake I hoped he wouldn't die too soon.' He decided that he was in love with Penelope again and showered her and Deborah with letters and love poems which deeply annoyed his wife Geraldine and their two children. Deborah spent that Christmas with the Swinglers and went to a couple of Swingler weddings, but on her nineteenth birthday Swingler took her out for lunch in Soho, collapsed on the pavement and died.

Despite Penelope's unhappiness she still managed to keep writing and in August her television play *Ain't Afraid to Dance* was broadcast at peak time by Associated Television. As usual it was strongly autobiographical, telling of a lonely, ten-year-old boy (like Jeremy) with busy, glamorous, absentee parents (like John and Penelope) who turns for love and fun to the family's kind German au pair girl (played by Lynn Redgrave) but sinks back into a bleak, unloved loneliness again when she has to leave. It was hardly a load of laughs but 'all the characters were seen through the mind of a real writer', wrote Peter Black in the *Daily Mail*.

None of John's time-consuming horizontal activities prevented him taking Deborah and Jeremy to Greece for a summer holiday in August and writing during the year three television plays – *The Choice of Kings*, *The Exploding Azalea* and *The Head Waiter*, which starred Donald Pleasence – as well as a new stage play, *The Judge*, in which an elderly High Court judge who is about to retire returns to the small English cathedral town where he was born to preside over the last Assize of his career. Renowned all his life for his severe sentences, he is now seeking masochistically to be punished himself for impregnating all those years ago a girl who was under the age of consent and still runs a shop in the town. He has never admitted to being the father of her child but has long felt so guilty about it that he doubts his fitness to judge others, and now needs desperately to atone for what he has done and failed to do. Mortimer's purpose was to show that judging is fallible, but since most of his plays were inspired by his own life he may well have been suffering twinges of guilt himself about Wendy Craig and the four-year-old son whom he had abandoned.

In September he flew to Hollywood to write a filmscript for Twentieth Century Fox and Rex Harrison for a movie version of *A Flea in Her Ear*. The studio put him up at the Beverly Hills Hotel, gave him a yellow Mustang to drive, and let him scribble happily by the hotel pool with the help of a humourless, grey-haired secretary who was certain he was French because of his English accent. He was appalled to discover that the Republican Party considered the actor Ronald Reagan fit to stand for election as the new Governor of California; intrigued by the restaurant on Sunset Strip where the waitresses were bottomless as well as topless, and by the sexy small ads in the newspaper; amazed to find that in a delicatessen he could buy cannabis and lumps of sugar soaked in LSD;

and at night he sought fresh young flesh at the Whisky a Gogo and Galaxy clubs. In Hollywood he also bumped into the forty-year-old English film director Clive Donner, who was shooting his eleventh film, *Luv* with Jack Lemmon, and was soon to become Penelope's lover. Before that, however, she flew to Canada to write a preview of a big international exhibition in Montreal and had a brief but passionate fling with a dapper little thirty-six-year-old French Canadian lawyer, Philippe Jannes, who drove her in his E-type Jag across the border into the United States and instantly inspired her next novel – the first since *The Pumpkin Eater* – *My Friend Says It's Bullet-Proof*, which is what a small boy had said as he admired Philippe's car.

Despite all these infidelities it still seemed at times as if the Mortimers had never separated at all. At Christmas they took Sally and Jeremy to Bermuda, enjoyed a family picnic on the beach on Christmas Day and went on to New York to do all the usual touristy things. To escape John and write her new novel in peace she joined Clive Donner in Hollywood and finished it in six weeks – a barely fictionalised travelogue account of her trip to Montreal and affair with Philippe. It is a bizarre, rambling, disjointed book with a hint of madness in which the heroine, who has had a mastectomy, is darkly neurotic, introspective, and hears voices. She is moody, fearful, manic-depressive, self-destructive, indecisive, constantly sorry for herself and deeply irritating. To read it is to wonder how Mortimer could have put up with such a nightmare of a woman for so long and why he was still trying to keep their relationship alive. She was however still such a fashionable writer that *The Times Literary Supplement* called it 'brilliantly planned, taut, intelligent', and in 1989 the feminist publishers Virago reprinted it in their series of modern feminist classics.

Plays by British writers, like *The Dock Brief*, were surprisingly popular in Germany in the 1960s and Mortimer was greeted like a film star when *The Judge* had its world premiere at the vast Schauspielhaus in Hamburg in January 1967. He was wined, dined and treated to the sleazy strip clubs of the Reeperbahn, but when he appeared on stage to take a bow after the first performance he was booed. Nor was the play much more successful when Michael Codron staged it at the Cambridge Theatre in March with Patrick Wymark playing the judge and Patience Collier the woman whom he had wronged so many years ago. 'We had a very traumatic opening because we couldn't get it quite right,' Codron told me. 'Patrick Wymark drank a lot and Patience Collier was *miserable* in it. The twist in it, about the judge fathering the child, wasn't totally believable.' Mortimer reckoned that his mistake had been to write about characters he did not know well enough and vowed to write in future only about people he knew. His fiction, like Penelope's, needed to be based on fact.

In April Clive Donner asked Penelope to marry him but although she was fond of him he was too much the fussy bachelor for her and she said no. Unbelievably she still hankered after John and although she knew that to go back and live with him would be disastrous she did just that in May when they moved together into a spacious maisonette in a stylish part of Kensington, just a stroll from the beautiful gardens of Holland Park, at 73 Holland Park, an elegant, five-storey, detached house with a roof garden and glass-and-wrought-iron canopy entrance in a wide avenue lined with tall trees and broad pavements. They agreed to live together for the sake of Jeremy and Sally, who left her boarding school to go to the excellent local state school, Holland Park Comprehensive, but Mortimer insisted that he and Penelope should still lead separate lives.

That year he wrote two plays for BBC Television: *The Other Side* and *Infidelity Took Place*, the second of which gave a second early glimpse of the down-at-heel lawyer who would one day become Rumpole of the Bailey. It was commissioned by a BBC producer, Irene Shubik, and told of Molly and Bill Panett, a happily married couple who decide to save tax by divorcing and living together as single people. Molly hires a seedy, untidy, Rumpolesque lawyer, Leonard Hoskins, but he falls for her and plans to marry her himself only to be deeply disillusioned when he discovers that her divorce is just a ploy to evade tax. Hoskins even has a bossy mother who is recognisably Rumpole's wife, Hilda, She Who Must Be Obeyed, and he was also partly a portrait of Mortimer himself. 'John was always very scruffy and dirty,' Irene Shubik told me in 2004. 'His tie always had food stains on it, his teeth were always very yellow and seemed to have some sort of mould growing on them, and his sartorial elegance was never of the highest order but he didn't seem to care very much about that. Like many who met him I thought he was the fat, jolly man par excellence and very good-hearted, kind and nice. I liked him and his ready wit and witty writing, and he *adores* women. I've often wondered how somebody who is not exactly an Adonis could get so many women to . . . you know . . . cooperate. The answer is flattery. I once went to a party at his house and he was throwing his arms around every woman and saying "darling, you look so beautiful", the same thing to everyone but they were all lighting up with pleasure. And fame and money are the greatest aphrodisiacs, and he had both, and he could give actresses parts and took them out to nice places. I've always thought that he might have had such a complex about his looks that he wanted to prove to himself that that didn't matter. He was still married to Penelope and she was destroyed completely by the sheer heartlessness of his attitude towards her, so I'm glad to say I was never one of his girlfriends.'

When Ms Shubik took Mortimer out to lunch he suggested the expensive White Elephant in Curzon Street, where she found him sitting with a beautiful Israeli girl and a bottle of champagne. 'He said he was sure I wouldn't mind if she joined us to talk, nor that he had already ordered some drink,' she recalled, but in the middle of lunch, which went on and on, she became so worried about the size of the bill that he was running up that she slipped away to telephone her BBC head of department to warn him 'before my week's wages vanished down the throat of John's uninvited guest'. The Israeli girl was a glamorous model as well as a sergeant in the Israeli army. 'She was one of his lovers and extremely beautiful,' Molly Parkin told me. 'He asked me out with her once and took us to see the biggest private collection of pornography ever, and I'm sure he would have liked a threesome but at that time I hadn't experimented.'

In 1967 Shirley Anne Field, now in her late twenties, married a young aristocrat, Charles Crichton-Stuart, a relative of the Marquess of Bute, and Mortimer sent them a cutesy telegram that read 'ISN'T GOD LUCKY MARRYING THE TWO OF YOU TODAY?' After the wedding he still telephoned her often and when she had a daughter, Nicola, later in the year he was very supportive, especially when her husband was away all day training to become a private pilot instructor and sometimes would not arrive back home until late. 'With Charlie being away for such long hours I got lonely and scared,' she told me. 'Then the phone would ring and it would be John saying "We haven't seen you around, darling. We haven't had London enhanced by your beauteous presence." He was great. He would come round and because I didn't have a carrycot he'd put the baby in a vegetable box with a shawl draped over it and he'd talk to her and mash up some spinach and feed her. He was fantastically domesticated, and to cheer me up he took me out every Friday lunchtime sometimes to his home at Turville Heath. Sadly my marriage did break up when my daughter was two, but John came round and made me feel safe. His friendship and affection saved me from feeling like the world had collapsed on me. I was so lonely but he was such a good friend and sometimes he'd say, "You could have anything you want – you could marry me." I think he was serious and I did think about it but I was still desperately hoping that Charlie would come back. I said to John that I couldn't marry him – I didn't know if I could remain faithful. He replied: "It doesn't matter. That's not everything."'

One afternoon early that summer John's old Oxford chum Michael Fenton, who had been practising for years as a general practitioner in Moreton-in-Marsh in the Cotswolds, turned up unexpectedly to ask his advice. They had kept up their friendship, visiting each other once or twice a year and going to the theatre with their wives, but now Fenton said he had fallen in love with a thirty-five-year-old married woman, Pauline Bowden, when she had worked as a cleaner at the hospital in Moreton. She was now a part-time shop assistant at the local Co-op and lived with her painter-and-decorator husband Cyril and three teenage daughters in a humble council house in the village. To allow her to slip out of her house late at night to make love with him in his surgery Fenton prescribed powerful sleeping pills for her husband that knocked him out for hours. Fenton's wife, Barbara, caught them in flagrante at the end of April but Fenton was so besotted by Mrs Bowden, even though she was overweight and not beautiful, that he wanted to divorce Barbara and go off with his mistress to live in Chile, where he had inherited a sheep farm, and he wanted Mortimer to tell him how much he would have to pay Barbara after the divorce. Mortimer was astonished because Fenton had always seemed to be a model husband to Barbara and a doctor of impeccable rectitude, morality and wisdom, and he warned him that a court would order him to give Barbara at least a third of his income and to support his three young sons until they were adult. Even that did not dissuade Fenton, who returned to Moreton to persuade Mrs Bowden to elope with him. But on 12 July, when she told him that she could not bring herself to leave her husband and daughters, he went to her house, found her in the living room, shot her in the stomach with a sawn-off shotgun, drove down a remote track into some woods eight miles away, scribbled several letters including one to his wife, swallowed fifty-seven tablets from his medical bag with the help of a can of beer, and committed suicide. He was forty-five. In the glove compartment of his red Triumph Vitesse were his passport, £300 and two airline tickets to Buenos Aires and Patagonia.

Mortimer was stunned. He went to Moreton to console Barbara Fenton, whose son Ben, then six, told me in 2004: 'My mother said he was in tears and blaming himself, which several of my father's friends did too, not to mention the psychiatrist who had seen him about four days earlier.' In London Mortimer lunched with another of Fenton's closest friends, James Michie, to try to find out why he had ended his life so terribly.

'We were completely puzzled by it,' Michie told me in 2004, 'because Fenton was an apparently extremely relaxed, phlegmatic, unflappable person, an ideal doctor, whose marriage to Barbara seemed to be a good one, yet he was clearly completely over the top when it happened. Eventually John said, "Well, I can only think of one thing which might be a clue, which is that Michael was a pacifist." I laughed because I was a pacifist too, but afterwards I thought that was quite an interesting remark because I think some pacifists *do* suppress violence in their ordinary lives and therefore if they blow a valve it's more likely to be serious.' In the note that Fenton left for his wife he quoted two lines of Catullus –

Odi et amo: quare id faciam, fortasse requires.
Nescio, sed fieri sentio et excrucior

– which means 'I hate and I love. You may well ask me why. I don't know, but I feel it's true and I'm being crucified.'

'That does suggest madness,' said Michie. 'The Michael I knew cannot have imagined he was going to be happy with a hospital cleaner in Chile. I still find it incredible, especially in a man who had such a strong sense of morality, unless you assume a really certifiable disorder.'

The Mortimers retreated to the South of France where they rented the actress and writer Yvonne Mitchell's house and invited Harold Pinter and his first wife, Vivien, to stay. When they returned to England John was asked by David Frost to appear on his television show at the end of September to quiz the Beatles John Lennon and George Harrison about their fascination with Eastern mysticism, their giggling Indian guru Maharishi Mahesh Yogi, and his gospel of Transcendental Meditation, TM. When Frost suggested that TM was a selfish, introverted creed compared with religions that aimed to help others, such as Christianity, the Beatles denied it but Mortimer agreed. 'What I think one needs,' he said, 'is a little well-aimed loathing at things like President Johnson and Ronald Reagan and so on, and not sitting in San Francisco watching the flowers grow and letting Governor Reagan be elected perhaps as the President of the United States'. The universe, he said, was 'a soulless biological thing, and it is for us to improve it, and we're not going to improve it if we're going to stay quite still enjoying peace and perfection.' What he aimed to do himself, he said, was 'to do an imperfect best to improve the lot of other people' – a claim that may well have had Penelope hurling something at the television set. The following Sunday he made amends by writing in the *News of the World* an article in which he said how much he admired the Beatles and that Lennon was one of the best English poets 'since W. H. Auden went soppy'.

October 1967 was a memorable month for both the Mortimers. Penelope's novel *My Friend Says It's Bullet-Proof* was published to general approval, she succeeded Penelope Gilliatt as the *Observer*'s film critic and was interviewed at length by Peter Lewis of the *Daily Mail*, telling him that 'men want it both ways. They often want their wives to work so they are relieved of responsibility but they also want to be looked after. I think all men and all women want to be looked after. They are all looking for their fathers and mothers.' She admitted that she did not like women much because they were so intolerant and materialistic, tended to ruin their children, and that maybe she had invented the man that John had become. 'The majority of women are deeply masochistic,' she said. 'If they can't find someone to hurt them, they'll invent someone. Women in their hearts still really want to be kept. If you start treating a woman as an equal you'll get a great many hot tears. I just don't think they're up to it.' She concluded that monogamy was impossible for most people yet infidelity was terribly destructive.

John's landmark that month was to join the board of the National Theatre, where Laurence Olivier and Ken Tynan had just tried to stage a play close to Mortimer's anti-Churchillian heart: Rolf Hochhuth's *Soldiers*, which claimed that Churchill had connived at the assassination in 1943 of the Polish wartime leader General Sikorski. *Soldiers* was dropped because of objections by several of the board including the chairman, Lord Chandos, who had been Churchill's friend and in his war cabinet, though it was produced later in the West End. Mortimer's appointment was a hint that the National was leaning towards a more liberal, permissive future, and working closely with Olivier and Tynan, two highly influential giants of the English theatre, would be invaluable for him as a playwright.

Another accolade that confirmed his burgeoning fame was his first appearance on *Desert Island Discs* in January 1968 to choose eight favourite records. He selected 'Voi che sapete' from Mozart's *The Marriage of Figaro*, Stravinsky's 'Firebird Suite', Glenn Miller's 'Moonlight Serenade', Boccherini's 'Quintet No 2 in C Major', Gershwin's 'Summertime' from *Porgy and Bess*, Louis Armstrong playing 'Loveless Love', Shostakovich's 'Piano Trio in E Minor' and John Gielgud delivering Prospero's farewell speech from *The Tempest*. As his luxury he chose a marble bath with constant hot water and his book was Proust's *À la recherche du temps perdu*.

In May he invited several of his girlfriends to dinner and to watch *Infidelity Took Place* on television. Judy Cornwell played the wife, Paul Daneman the husband, and John Nettleton the early Rumpolesque lawyer. One of the guests was Molly Parkin. 'He had some very Sloane Rangery girls doing the food, so it was very grandiose,' she said. She cackled. 'I'm sure he'd shagged everybody at the table because there was that kind of bonhomie, and it was the way he lightly touched people in an intimate way. Shirley Anne Field was there and lots of others. She was a *big* star at that point and absolutely delicious. They all were. After dinner we were asked to sit and look at the television, and John beckoned me to sit next to him and hold his hand. His play came on and to my *horror* everything that I had told him about my marriage was in it. The main character's name was even Molly and if my ex-husband had been looking he would have been very upset. That put me off John totally because I felt abused. I didn't trust him and thought it was a betrayal, a predatory, exploitative coarseness in his character which made me realise that he was not a true artist, just an opportunist with an eye to the main chance. It seemed unloving. There's a cruel streak in John.'

Infidelity Took Place attracted eight million viewers and he was commissioned to write another play for the BBC, *Desmond*, a scenario for a ballet, *Home*, and the screenplay for *John and Mary*, a film based on a novella by Mervyn Jones. He also enjoyed a jaunt to Paris when Rex Harrison began filming *A Flea in Her Ear* there and relished the long French lunches, delicious dinners and evenings in nightclubs like the Elle et Lui, where the waitresses dressed up as boys in dinner jackets. 'Sexy Rexy' Harrison loved the script but insisted that his fans would never believe that any character he played could possibly be impotent and refused to play his part that way. The film was not a success. 'There is a tremendous difference between French farce on the stage, and on the screen,' wrote Harrison in his autobiography, 'and on the whole it is a form which doesn't work on film.'

More important than any of Mortimer's writing that year, however, was a brief that was sent to him by Prime Minister Harold Wilson's favourite lawyer and adviser, the hugely influential solicitor Lord Goodman, the chairman of the Arts Council, who wanted him to conduct an appeal in the most important literary trial since the prosecution of *Lady Chatterley's Lover*. It was to shape Mortimer's legal career for the next ten years and to build him a heady reputation as a champion of free speech and authors and publishers who were accused of obscenity. One of Goodman's clients, the publisher Calder and Boyars, had been found guilty by an all-male Old Bailey jury a few months earlier of publishing an obscene book, a collection of American short stories, *Last Exit to Brooklyn*, and Goodman asked Mortimer to conduct the appeal. 'I thought that an approach of less orthodoxy might be more successful,' explained Goodman in his autobiography. Mortimer was at first reluctant because he did not expect to win the appeal, but when he met the publisher, John Calder, he agreed. *Last Exit to Brooklyn* was a disgusting book that described in graphic detail the brutal, degraded lives of teenage and homosexual prostitutes, transvestites, rapists, perverts, drug addicts, criminals and seedy down-and-outs in the squalid slums of 1950s New York. The author, Hubert Selby Jr, had himself been a heroin addict and the book contained such explicit scenes of bestial events – a gang rape, a homosexual orgy – that the England Test cricketer David Sheppard, who was later to become the Bishop of Liverpool, admitted in court that he had been depraved and corrupted by the book because it had inflamed old homosexual lusts with which he had struggled as a young man. Yet thirty witnesses had also come forward at the Old Bailey trial to swear that the book had literary merit, among them Anthony Burgess and Professor Frank Kermode, who compared Selby to Dickens. Others mentioned Dostoevsky.

The Appeal Court hearing was scheduled for Monday 22 July 1968. 'We had been nervous about John Mortimer,' wrote Calder in his autobiography in 2001, because he only 'reluctantly agreed to listen to the tape of the most important parts of the trial on the Sunday afternoon before the case came to the Appeal Court, and we felt at the time he was more interested in the attractive secretary he had brought with him. But in the court itself he was brilliant.' He told the three judges that in art nothing should be taboo, that it was a writer's duty to examine even the most bestial and depraved behaviour, and that a writer who censored himself for fear of shocking or offending people was betraying his muse. But the argument that clinched the case was when he said that *Last Exit* could not possibly be legally obscene because it would never 'tend to deprave and corrupt those likely to read it'. On the contrary, he declared ingeniously, the book was so revolting that any normal reader would be nauseated by it, disgusted rather than depraved by it, so that it would actually strengthen rather than weaken the reader's morality. This brilliant argument was to become known as the Repugnance Theory or the Aversion Defence and was to underpin almost every defence in future cases where publishers were prosecuted for obscenity. After a three-day hearing the judges allowed the appeal, *Last Exit to Brooklyn* was reprinted, became a bestseller, and opened a new era of literary, theatrical and cinematic permissiveness.

Over the next few weeks Terry Southern's pornographic novel *Candy* was published, theatre censorship was abolished, an actress called Jennie Lee appeared on stage as the first full-frontal theatrical nude, the naked musical revue *Hair* was performed, a play called *The Beard*, which featured oral sex, was staged at the Royal Court theatre, and in London in 1969 the cast of the American Living Theatre company wandered naked through the auditorium haranguing the audience. Mortimer was appointed to an Arts Council working party set up to investigate the obscenity laws and when it reported back a year later and urged their abolition he told *The World This Weekend* radio programme that this was 'a necessary step to adulthood ... everybody should have their own standards, but freedom of speech and thought is not divisible and it is impossible to draw a legal line'. It was however to be several years before prosecutions of books for obscenity were abandoned completely, and soon afterwards a case was brought against Paul Ableman's *The Mouth and Oral Sex* during which one of the 'expert' witnesses, the novelist Margaret Drabble, was asked by the judge, Alan King-Hamilton, 'we have got on for over two thousand years without any mention of oral sex, so why do we need to read about it now?' When the defence counsel, Jeremy Hutchinson, came to address the jury he reminded them of the judge's question. 'Poor His Lordship!' he said. '*Poor* His Lordship! Gone without oral sex for two thousand years!'

In November John and Penelope took Deborah, Sally and Jeremy to Kenya and Tanzania where they travelled in a minibus striped like a zebra and visited Mombasa, the Lake Manyara game reserve, the Serengeti, the great volcanic Ngorongoro crater and several Masai villages. Back in London John heard that thirty-one-year-old Dustin Hoffman – who had just made *Midnight Cowboy* and was one of the hottest stars of the time – was interested in appearing in *John and Mary*, John's film about a young couple's quickie love affair in Swinging London, with the equally fash- ionable twenty-three-year-old Mia Farrow, who had just made *Rosemary's Baby*. John and the film's director, Peter Yates – who had recently directed Steve McQueen in *Bullitt* – flew to Philadelphia, where Hoffman was appearing in a stage play, *Jimmy Shine*, saw the play and then met Hoffman in his hotel just after midnight. Mortimer was due back at the Old Bailey the next day and had to return to New York to catch a 6 a.m. flight back to London, but Hoffman chatted endlessly about everything except the film and asked for ideas to improve his play. Mortimer and Yates obliged, drawing diagrams for him to consider, and only then could they persuade him to talk about the film. More in gratitude for their advice than enthusiasm for the script, Hoffman agreed to take the part – though 'I'm not even sure I understand the character,' he said – and Mortimer just managed to catch his flight back to London.

To accommodate Hoffman and Farrow the setting for *John and Mary* was changed to New York and the film told the story of a young couple who meet in a singles bar in Manhattan one Friday night and go to bed and spend the weekend together without knowing each other's name. To ensure the authenticity of the dialogue Mortimer lived for a while in New York, taking a room at the Carlyle Hotel, hiring two young American actors to read the script aloud to him and comment on it so that he could get it right, attending rehearsals at the Biograph Studios in the Bronx, and ogling the fey Mia Farrow, who had recently divorced Frank Sinatra and embarked on an affair with André Previn, the conductor of the London Symphony Orchestra. Mortimer fancied her rotten even though she appeared at times to be away with the fairies, turning up for rehearsals clutching a bottle of wine, wearing a blanket, and occasionally gazing up to Heaven to tell Mozart that she loved him. Hoffman was less enchanted by her because she went on and on about meditation and the Maharishi Mahesh Yogi, with whom she had just spent a month in India, and one night he exploded with irritation when a limo was taking them into Manhattan and she insisted on jumping out because she had seen a wishing star and wanted to recite a poem to it.

The author of the original *John and Mary* novel, Mervyn Jones, was not impressed by the film, claiming that it bore little resemblance to his book, which he said was a trivial little novel anyway. Nor were the reviewers impressed. 'It's like an old comedy of the Thirties – minus the comedy,' said Judith Crist. Pauline Kael wrote in the *New Yorker* that 'reviewing this perfect nothing of a movie is rather degrading', and Hoffman's biographer Ronald Bergan judged the film 'too thin and too contrived, and rarely amusing or touching enough ... these two people spend the weekend together communicating on as superficial a level as the movie itself.' Another Hoffman biographer, *The Sunday Times* film critic Iain Johnstone, felt that the script was decidedly frail, but even so Mortimer was nominated for the Golden Globe award for the best screenplay of the year and Hoffman and Farrow were such big stars that *Time* and the *Observer* colour magazine both devoted cover stories to the film. They filled the cinemas, despite their failure to conjure up any real warmth between them on the screen, and the movie eventually made a profit of $1.2million (more than £3¼ million).

Mortimer's next film project came to nothing at all. The Hollywood mogul Sam Spiegel asked him and Penelope to cooperate on yet another filmscript for Rex Harrison, *The Right Honourable Gentleman*, based on Roy Jenkins' biography of Sir Charles Dilke, the radical Victorian politician, barrister and friend of the Prince of Wales whose chance of succeeding Gladstone as Prime Minister was ruined after he was cited as the co-respondent in a notorious divorce case in 1885. Spiegel invited the Mortimers to spend several days drinking Bullshots (beef soup and vodka), 'spit-balling' (chatting) and scribbling aboard his yacht, the *Malahne*, during the Cannes Film Festival in May, where he was on the jury and would tell John each evening that what he had written that day was magic but would somehow decide it was garbage the next morning. Back in London Penelope had a brief tearful fling with Spiegel, who asked her to marry him even though he was still married to his third wife, had an eleven-month-old illegitimate son by a twenty-three-year-old, and was now lusting after sixteen-year-old Lynne Frederick, who was about to play the Russian Grand Duchess Tatiana in his $8 million epic about the murders of the Russian royal family, *Nicholas and Alexandra*. 'He asked lots of people to marry him,' said Jeremy Mortimer.

Another abortive film project was an attempt to persuade the Soviet Union to allow a movie of Anthony Burgess's novel about smuggling nylon underwear into Russia, *Honey for the Bears*, to be shot there. John took Penelope with him to Moscow but this was the age of the Cold War and despite numerous polite meetings in government offices and a side trip to Leningrad, where it took three hours to order an egg for breakfast, permission was eventually denied and the film was never made. Yet even though writing a filmscript was often a waste of time and too many came to nothing, John enjoyed working for Hollywood producers because they paid him a great deal, flew him first class to exotic locations, provided limousines and lavish entertainment, and showed him the sort of extravagant lifestyle that he relished. He thought of films as mistresses, he told the *Mirror* in 1979 – glamorous but finally unsatisfying – which cannot have endeared him to his real mistresses.

Much more satisfying than movies was the theatre, for which he started to translate a second Feydeau farce, *Cat Among the Pigeons*, a knockabout three-act piece of nonsense about a French turn-of-the-century singer, Lucette, who adores a young man who is already engaged while Lucette is herself adored by a comic, pantomime Mexican general who vows to kill his rival. The play is packed with the usual sexual shenanigans, undressings, innuendo, misunderstandings, confusion, rushing about, hiding in cupboards, asides to the audience, and although it was notably unfunny it opened at Wimbledon in March 1969 and then a month later in the West End at the Prince of Wales Theatre with Elizabeth Seal, Richard Briers and Victor Spinetti.

Life in the theatre was not however always benign and Mortimer found himself in the middle of a row between Olivier, Tynan and some members of the National Theatre board, which was being pressed not to renew Tynan's contract because of derogatory remarks he had made about the board during the earlier row over *Soldiers*. Lord Chandos wanted Tynan to be fired, Olivier wanted him to stay, Tynan asked for Mortimer's help and Mortimer managed to broker a compromise.

That summer he spent several bizarre weeks in Wales defending six of eight men who were accused at Swansea Assizes of being members of an illegal terrorist organisation of Welsh nationalist 'freedom fighters' that called itself the Free Wales Army. At the start of the trial, as the jury was being empanelled, he decided that his best hope of winning was to object to any potential juryman who looked too respectable and was about to challenge the choice of a bank manager when he noticed the man winking at the defendants, so he let him be sworn in. Later he realised to his chagrin that the juryman was still winking and obviously suffered from a nervous twitch rather than sympathy with the accused. The trial, during which the defendants began each day by bellowing patriotic Welsh songs, dragged on for fifty-three days and heard all manner of unusual evidence including the allegation that the defendants had planned to fly a helicopter filled with pig dung over the ceremonial investiture of the young Prince Charles as Prince of Wales at Caernarvon Castle and dump its load from a great height onto the royal family. On the very day that the investiture was being held two of the 'terrorists' were acquitted and six given sentences ranging from three to fifteen months in prison.

In August the Mortimers rented a house at Ravello, near Naples, and invited John's mother, who was now eighty-two, to join them. It was the first time she had ever been on an aeroplane and although John had visited her regularly ever since his father's death, and his children had often gone to stay with her, he claimed that it was only now that the warmth of Italy melted at last the edges of their chilly relationship and that they became friends for the first time. Kath was even able to tease him when he told her that nowadays he was occasionally sitting in minor courts as a junior judge. 'You!' she giggled. 'A judge! How killing!' She still disapproved, however, of an hour-long television play that he was writing about her, Clifford and his childhood, *A Voyage Round My Father*, and refused to watch it when it was broadcast with Mark Dignam as Clifford and Ian Richardson as John. She thought it was incredibly vulgar to write publicly about his parents 'but I don't think my father would have minded', Mortimer told me in 1993. 'He was very encouraging about what I wrote.' The Writers' Guild later voted it the best original teleplay of 1969 and when he expanded it for the theatre the following year it was swiftly acclaimed as the best of all his plays.

He wrote five more plays that year – half-hour, one-act squibs with the same three or four actors in each – that were to be staged together at the New Theatre early in 1970 under the joint title *Come As You Are!*. Each was about middle-aged sex and was an amusing, light-hearted variation on the eternal triangle in which the relationship between a man and woman was threatened or bolstered by a third party. Each play was set in a different part of London. In *Mill Hill* a married woman's lover can become sexually excited only if she dresses up as Elizabeth I and he pretends to be Sir Walter Raleigh – her bit of ruff – but when they are interrupted by her husband's early return home he plays the part much better. In *Bermondsey* the marriage of a cockney couple who run an East End pub seems to be threatened on Christmas Eve by the husband's affection for the pretty young barmaid until it becomes obvious that he is homosexual. In *Gloucester Road* – a quirky jape about a husband's jealousy over his wife's blatant flirtation with their lodger – the equilibrium of their *ménage à trois* is disturbed by the arrival of another lodger, a fey girl who wears a blanket and granny glasses, is into yoga and meditation, burns incense, intends to have a child by Shakespeare, and was obviously inspired by Mortimer's recent passion for Mia Farrow. In *Marble Arch* an ageing actress wakes to find to her horror that her married lover has died in her bathroom, so that she needs quickly to dispose of the corpse, and the nightmare develops into a fast, knockabout farce, crammed with misunderstandings, confusion and opening and closing of doors, of which Feydeau himself would have been proud. And finally in the highly amusing *Knightsbridge* a young woman is appalled when she suspects that her middle-class, Conservative, Harrods-and-Harvey-Nichols mother has secretly been a prostitute for years.

It was difficult to find four actors to play several different, demanding parts in one evening but eventually an excellent cast was assembled: Glynis Johns, Denholm Elliott and Joss Ackland, who were all in their forties, and perky twenty-nine-year-old Pauline Collins. When they opened in Edinburgh at the start of a three-week, pre-West End tour in November, the producer, director and Mortimer decided to stage only the first four plays and to drop *Knightsbridge*, which was eventually to surface as a BBC television play three years later with Googie Withers playing the prostitute mother. John became deeply involved in the production and rehearsals of *Come As You Are!* but although he befriended Joss Ackland and Denholm Elliott this did not stop him ravishing Elliott's wife, Susan, on a British Railways bunk when they travelled together to Edinburgh on an overnight sleeper. 'Susan had a raging affair with Mortimer, not just that bunk-up on the train,' I was told by a friend. 'When she was writing her biography of Denholm in 1993 she wrote to Mortimer to ask if he minded her including their affair but he objected and it was taken out. I think he objected because it looked mean that he was bonking Denholm's wife even though Denholm was a friend of his and away on tour in his play. It made him look like a bit of a shit. He's actually quite a ruthless bastard.' One of Susan's friends was Caroline Mortimer/Fletcher, who had recently appeared in a revival of *Look Back in Anger* at the Royal Court, knew that her stepfather and Susan were having an affair, and told her at a party one evening, 'I don't really care what you decide to do as long as I don't have to call you Mother.'

Denholm Elliott was notoriously, promiscuously homosexual and enjoyed bisexual orgies, and he and Susan were both very heavy drinkers, but when he found out about her fling with Mortimer he became very jealous and frightened that it might become serious, she said, 'because he had such a huge admiration and liking for him. In his moments of pure honesty he could not imagine why I did not take up with John.' She soon replaced Mortimer with another lover with a splendidly appropriate name, Marcel Boffin, and Mortimer and the Elliotts remained friends until Elliott's death in 1992.

According to Joss Ackland the tour of *Come As You Are!* was chaotic. Two days before it opened in Edinburgh the production was still a shambles, he said in his autobiography, and he rang Mortimer in the middle of the night to beg him to come and help. At the dress rehearsal the stage's revolve, which was vital for each play to blend smoothly into the next, refused to turn. The first-night audience was appreciative but a row exploded backstage between Mortimer and the producer, Alexander H. Cohen, because Cohen felt that the out-of-town run should be extended from three weeks to seven to give them more time to polish the production. Mortimer lost his cool, marched into Elliott's dressing room, where Elliott was entertaining his cousin, shouted at the director, Allan

Davis, grabbed him by the lapels and shoved him up against the wall. The cousin fled. Elliott then launched into a row with the unfortunate Davis, who retreated nervously to Ackland's dressing room where he remarked unwisely 'well, that went all right then, didn't it?', upon which Ackland picked him up by his jacket and dragged him down the corridor. Elliott's cousin, who had never been backstage before, gaped in amazement and declared that he could not understand why the audience paid good money to watch the show from the auditorium when they could have much livelier entertainment for free backstage.

Eventually the rumpus subsided and Elliott's cousin, Forest Ellvers, who had been in the same house as Mortimer at Harrow, invited them for a drink the next day. 'Mortimer didn't seem to realise who I was,' Ellvers told me, 'and as they were leaving he saw a picture of the Bourne Library at Harrow. "Were *you* at Harrow?" he said, and suddenly I was in his vision, and I thought, you're a strange chap.' The tour was extended to seven weeks so that it could be perfected in places such as the Theatre Royal in Brighton before *Come As You Are!* opened in the West End at the New Theatre in January 1970, when it was given rave reviews, but their real troubles were only just beginning. Elliott resented Glynis Johns tagging along after him and Ackland, accusing her of never having any money to pay her share of the restaurant bills and telling her she was drunk. She complained to Cohen and after a few weeks 'started to get a trifle neurotic', reported Ackland in his book, 'and had a breakdown and was unable to cope. She became so insecure that she would telephone me at least ten times a day. The record was eighteen times, and that was through the night as well. For two or three weeks the show became a nightmare ... Nearly every night, ten minutes before the show, she would leave the theatre and I would have to run after her down St Martin's Lane and haul her back. Then I would have to coddle her and cuddle her to make her go on stage. I have even slapped her and pushed her into her make-up chair.' Often she never even arrived at the theatre at all, or dropped out in the middle of the show, and had to be replaced by an understudy. 'The worst night was when Glynis could hardly manage to get a line out and Denholm and I had to take over. As the curtain came down at the end of the first half Denholm slammed down the piano lid and said, "That is the last time I appear on any stage with you, babe."' When Ackland finally got home that night his hair had turned white in a couple of hours. Amazingly the show survived long enough to be transferred to the Strand Theatre after its run at the New.

As the Swinging Sixties came to an end the Mortimers' marriage too was finally all but over. On 25 November Penelope crashed her car a few yards from their house in Holland Park, cut her head and had to go to hospital for ten stitches, but by now the marriage was beyond repair. John should have been extremely cheerful because the House of Commons had just confirmed one of his dearest dreams, the abolition of capital punishment for good, but on Christmas Eve he and Penelope wrapped the children's presents in silence, John announced that he was going to spend New Year's Eve in Paris and went out, leaving Penelope alone.

She said goodbye to the sad old decade by taking Jeremy to join the producer Jack Clayton and director Karel Reisz and their wives who were skiing in Switzerland. John then decided not to go to Paris after all and rang her every day to complain that she had abandoned him and that he was unhappy and had nothing to do. But on the last night of the Sixties, while Penelope was at Deborah Kerr's New Year's Eve party in Klosters, John was desperate for company, wangled an invitation to a party in Edwardes Square, and met the girl who was to become his second wife, Penny Gollop. She was only twenty-three and he was forty-six but they were to stay together for the rest of his life. The Parisian fortune teller's prophecy that he would not be happy until he was fifty was about to come true.

Eight

Penny 2, Oz and Emily
1970–1972

Penny Gollop – Penny 2 as Mortimer called her to distinguish her from Penelope – was the slim, brunette daughter of a rich Kentish pig farmer. She looked about sixteen, but she had a degree in languages from Exeter University and worked in London as a models' booking agent for an agency run by Peter Hope Lumley. The same agency represented Mortimer's beautiful Israeli mistress, who had gone to America for the New Year. Hope Lumley died in 2004 but left notes for an autobiography which describe how John and Penny 2 met at his partner Jill Rushton's party after Mortimer had begged to be invited because he was so lonely on his own. His eyes 'kept wandering over my shoulder', said Hope Lumley, 'and eventually he mouthed the words: "Who is that?" It was our new booker, a very attractive girl called Penny Gollop, whose back was turned to us. In those days extremely short skirts, or "pussy pelmets", were worn by every girl with good legs and Penny's legs were charming, as was her rounded bottom then being presented to John. Later Penny asked my advice – John had invited her to go out with him! She knew from colleagues in the office of his reputation and his affair with the Israeli model, and whilst she was very flattered she needed to be *advised*. All I could tell her was that it really was up to her, but that I knew and liked John. A couple of days later she told me that she had been out with John, had found him fascinating – and that was the start of a very happy relationship.'

John gave her a lift home from the party, took her to lunch at the White Elephant the next day, 2 January, and said later that for him it was love at first sight although she needed a couple of weeks to forget his face. She confessed that she had once worked in an Italian nightclub where the punters were not allowed to touch the girls but one had once given her a huge £100 tip (more than £1,000), but Mortimer did not care about her past and told Emily Bearn of the *Sunday Telegraph* in 2004 that he fell for her 'because she was such a good person. She was a farmer's daughter and they're very sensible, I've always found. They realise that animals are eaten for lunch.' He told Moira Petty of *The Times* in 2003 that 'throughout my first marriage I'd hoped that, somewhere in the world, there was a calm, sensible, lovely person waiting for me, and she has remained just that.' She was however 'very *jeune fille*', he admitted. Penny had read *The Pumpkin Eater* 'and thought how awful to marry a bastard like the one in the book', she told Alasdair Riley of the *Evening Standard* in 1973. 'Then, of course, I went and ended up with the original – and have no regrets about it, either.' At that first lunch she reminded John that at forty-six he was twice her age and only a year younger than her parents, and her mother was furious when she learned that Penny was being pursued by this randy old goat whom she called The Wicked Man. 'But he was so funny,' Penny told Pauline Peters of the *Evening Standard* in 1994. 'What's irresistible is that he still makes me laugh.'

In later years they disagreed about how their affair developed. She told Alasdair Riley that John went to Los Angeles to work on another filmscript – *Casanova* for Rex Harrison, which was never made – but that he did not bother to telephone her for two weeks and then flew off to Greece with Jeremy while she went to New York with two girlfriends. Six weeks later, she said, John turned up in New York, asked her to live with him in London, and she agreed.

His version was much more glamorous although he did take Jeremy, now fourteen, to Rhodes where he adapted *A Voyage Round My Father* for the stage and they rediscovered each other by riding motorbikes, taking donkey rides and sailing to Turkey. He said that after Penny went to New York he flew to Hollywood, stopped off in New York, persuaded her to spend the night with him at the Plaza Hotel and then to fly on with him to Los Angeles, where they stayed for two weeks at the Beverly Hills Hotel. In LA, he said, they went to several glitzy parties, at one of which he recognised that the terribly English, good-looking butler had been a brilliant, very sporty head boy at Harrow and expected to become Prime Minister – an unlikely story that needs to be taken with a sackful of salt because not one of his Harrow contemporaries had ever heard of a head boy who became a butler. 'It sounds most unlikely,' said Sir Rupert

Buchanan-Jardine and 'I don't think that story holds any water at all,' said Godfrey Royle. John and Penny did however go to Los Angeles because the director Michael Lindsay-Hogg saw them brunching at the hotel. 'She was very young looking and very attractive,' he told me, 'but of course he was quite funny, quite rich and he had that nice sheen of fame on him.'

Whichever version is true, John left Penelope for good in February and rented a flat in Little Venice on the upper floor of 16a Blomfield Road – a big, semi-detached house on the bank of a quiet canal with brightly painted houseboats and colourful pots of flowers, and he and Penny moved in with little more than a Bob Dylan album. It seemed that his compulsive Sixties philandering was over. 'I was having my youth at a very inappropriate time,' he told the *Daily Mail* in 1982. 'I don't regret any of it, but I don't think I could have gone on. I couldn't stand going back to ringing people up to see who I was going to have dinner with each night. I knew that it would come to an end. I always knew that somebody would come along with whom I could settle down and have a very placid life.' He made sure that everyone knew he was living with a pretty young mistress, the youngest he had ever had. 'I saw them at the Old Vic,' I was told by the television producer Derek Granger, 'and he was chewing Penny's ear in a way which was unbecoming even for an eighteen-year-old schoolgirl. I felt like Disgusted of Tunbridge Wells. It was very vain to behave like that in public, very undignified exhibitionism.'

Two of his television plays were broadcast that year, both with highly appropriate titles, *Married Alive* and *Only Three Can Play*. For Penelope the final ending of her marriage after twenty years was devastating even though she had known for years that it was inevitable. She did, however, derive some consolation from an astonishingly dismissive remark that John made to her soon afterwards when he belittled Penny 2 off-handedly as though she meant nothing to him at all. 'Oh, she does the rough,' he shrugged. 'I suppose she'll have to go.' *She does the rough*? What, the household chores? The smack of hairbrush on buttock? It was an extra-ordinarily derogatory remark to make about a woman he claimed to love. He also allowed Penelope to remark airily when he introduced her to Penny: 'If you'd turned out to be a talented, articulate, interesting woman I'd've been jealous, but now I've met you I don't mind at all.'

Mortimer suggested ludicrously that Penelope should live next door but wiser counsels prevailed and they spent £28,500 (£291,000) to buy a big, four-bedroom, Regency house for her, Sally and Jeremy to live at

St John's Wood, in Loudoun Road, less than a mile from his flat in Maida Vale. Even so Penelope was terrified of being alone again and John still kept dropping in to see her, once kissing the top of her head and announcing cruelly, 'I'm sure we'll be back together in the autumn.' She continued to write about films for the *Observer* and started a new novel but her stability was jolted again when her occasional lover David Mercer, who was now forty-two, openly began an affair with her daughter Deborah, who was only twenty-two. 'My mother's and Deborah's affairs with Mercer were not *quite* simultaneous,' Jeremy told me, 'but it couldn't have been very easy for her.' It seemed as though all the men in Penelope's life were conspiring to drive her out of her mind.

Penny 2's mother, Anne, was eventually won round by The Wicked Man when he joined her on her daily naked swim in the chilly seas off Whitstable, and from then on she and Penny's father, Bill, accepted John as a friend though it took others longer to acknowledge Penny and John as a couple. At dinner once a bishop was placed beside Penny and remarked how happy he was to meet 'the clever lady who wrote all those lovely novels' and was deeply embarrassed when she put him right.

In May Mortimer appeared in court to defend the novice entrepreneur Richard Branson, a nineteen-year-old ex-public schoolboy who had recently launched *Student* magazine, a mail-order company called Virgin, and a student advisory centre after finding how difficult it was for his girlfriend Debbie to find a doctor to abort his child. Branson was charged with contravening the Venereal Diseases Act of 1917 and the Indecent Advertisements Act of 1889 – and threatened with two years in prison – because the centre was handing out leaflets telling young people where they could get treatment for VD. Mortimer offered to defend Branson for free because he considered the prosecution to be an absurd attack on civil liberty and argued in Marylebone Magistrates' Court that if Branson were guilty then the government was also guilty for displaying posters about VD in public lavatories. Branson was acquitted of the indecent advertisements charge but fined £7 for transgressing the VD Act and Mortimer announced that he would prosecute the government over its own VD notices unless the archaic law was quickly repealed. The House of Commons duly obliged, and although Mortimer was depressed when Labour lost the general election in June he felt vindicated when the new Tory Home Secretary, Reggie Maudling, apologised to Branson for the prosecution even though it had happened under the Labour government.

In July Julia, now twenty-five, married the author and playwright Wolf Mankowitz's son Gered and Penelope held a reception for a hundred people in her new garden. Julia's father, Kenneth Harrison, was there along with her twenty-seven-year-old stepsister Caroline, who was now a highly successful actress and had just appeared in two BBC television plays in two days and was soon to appear in another as well as a film with Ian Hendry, *The Mackenzie Break*. Mortimer was not as genial as usual, judging by Penelope's next novel, *The Home*, in which she wrote a chilling description of the heroine's estranged husband's reaction to her daughter's wedding: 'He hates . . . He resents every mouthful of food we eat. We are his enemies.'

His ambivalence continued to torment her. Even though he was living with Penny he still called Penelope 'sweetheart' and invited her to lunch, which drove her again to see her psychiatrist, Barry Cooper. He told her to stop behaving like a masochist, to break with John completely, once and for all, and sent her to the Greenways nursing home where she was kept sedated for days. John telephoned to tell her that 'we must all be great friends', brought her a bottle of champagne, and said he was going somewhere sunny after Christmas but then 'I'll come back and live with you and have a string of girlfriends' and 'I love you always'. Was he constantly giving her hope so as to stop her committing suicide, or was he playing some sadistic game with her fragile emotions? No wonder she wept a great deal.

He was deeply involved that autumn in rehearsals for the stage version of *A Voyage Round My Father*, which was to open at the Greenwich Theatre in November 1970 with Clifford played by sixty-one-year-old Mark Dignam, who had appeared in thirty-five films and already starred in the television version. 'John told me that he was having to subsidise the production of *A Voyage Round My Father* from his earnings at the Bar,' reported Lord Hooson, yet he was now such a force in the theatre that three days before the first night the *Guardian* published a huge photograph of him to illustrate an interview by Peter Johns. 'Mr Mortimer is a large man,' wrote Johns. 'He is heavily built and fairly tall and the line of demarcation between his neck and his chin has become indistinct in a generous roll of flesh. He seems to look at you a bit blearily through his glasses.' Johns was sceptical when Mortimer claimed that he rose at four o'clock every morning, played the record player loudly while he did the washing up – which seemed a bit rough on his sleeping mistress – and that this enabled him to finish a play in twelve days.

John's mother had always disapproved of the play so it seemed appropriate that she died of a stroke in Amersham General Hospital the day before it opened. She was eighty-two and left everything to him –

£21,993.84 (£225,000) – except for a painting, teapot and tea service that she bequeathed to her sister. In her will she asked him to spend some of the money on a headstone for Clifford's grave but it seems that he ignored her final request because in 2004 I could find no trace of it in the Turville churchyard, nor could the vicar, the Revd. Amanda Bloor, who told me that there is no mention of it in the church's records. When Mortimer wrote about his mother's death in *Clinging to the Wreckage* he could not be bothered to check the date and got it wrong.

A Voyage Round My Father was a clever two-act kaleidoscope of John's relationship with his parents, especially Clifford. In brief, episodic, scenes it drew a vivid portrait of the old monster and revealed a great deal about himself. Writing it was powerfully cathartic and eventually Mortimer could not remember what was true and what he had made up, and by putting Clifford on the stage he lost him as a father. 'He doesn't belong to me so much any more,' Mortimer told me in 1993. 'He belongs to everybody that sees the play and I'm not quite sure whether he's him or whether he's something I've half invented.' The first night was plagued by technical difficulties and the stage machinery refused to work but the reviews were superb and it is generally agreed that it was easily the best play Mortimer ever wrote. 'It was one of the most pleasurable experiences I've ever had,' Michael Codron told me. 'It was wonderful,' said Arnold Wesker, and Sir Richard Eyre called it 'an immaculate piece of work, one of the three or four best accounts of father and son in English literature'. The Canadian director Alvin Rakoff, who was to film it for television ten years later, said: 'I cannot praise the play enough. I think it will last well into this century.' Less enthusiastic was Penelope, who had to watch herself being portrayed onstage. She was in any case never a fan of the theatre, Jeremy told me, 'and *A Voyage Round My Father* was an uncomfortable experience for her.'

When John and Penny went down to Turville Heath Cottage to tidy his mother's life away and move in themselves he felt that he had no right to buy anything new or even shift the furniture, and for many years they left it as it was. His father's ghost was to linger there for the rest of Mortimer's life.

While Penny spent Christmas with her parents John joined Penelope and the children in Cornwall where Deborah, now twenty-two, had rented a house. Penelope 'looked at him and thought how strange, my husband: an overweight, vain, talented man with no idea how to behave or what to do,' she wrote in her autobiography. He gave her a locket and confessed that the root of all his problems was that he was so easily bored.

Afterwards he sent a telegram of thanks 'and great love', and when they decided on a legal separation he agreed to pay her a generous £292 a month (£2,990) – as well as the cost of all rates, repairs and insurance on her house in Loudoun Road and Jeremy's school fees. Nevertheless, Julia and Deborah both wept when they read the heart-rending typescript of her new novel, *The Home*, which described how weak, afraid and vulnerable she felt now that she was alone and had lost the home she had always loved. Like her heroine she considered suicide:

> The idea of death was appallingly attractive and she played with it dangerously, letting it fill her mind to the exclusion of all reality ... She lived with death, an evil and beautiful companion ... her heart was broken ... She was dreadfully sad, and dreadfully frightened ... I'm dying. Help me, please ... She stared at him and knew, for the first time, that their relationship was completely hopeless. It was as though she had never really seen him before. He was a stranger, whom she happened irrevocably to love; whom she would always love ... Goodbye, my darling; goodbye, my darling.

In the novel John's alter ego tells his wife cruelly that 'when we are separated we'll have a huge affair. It's just being married that's so impossible.' He has always been like this, she says, assuming right from the start 'that he was going to be looked after, like the children, for the rest of his life. Even at the height of his uxoriousness, when [she had] entirely possessed him, he dreamed of asking her permission to go to bed with someone else, of bringing his mistress home to nursery tea in full assurance of her blessing.' Penelope's alter ego in the novel is called Nelly and Penny 2 appears with an almost identical name, Nell, and is depicted as a passive, gormless, twenty-two-year-old bimbo, 'a kind of gap, a nothing ... sitting about all day brushing her hair'.

To try to escape her misery for a while Penelope went to Kenya in January with her choreographer friend Eleanor Fazan, but although she made new friends, slept in a tent and went exploring, sailing and flying in a light aircraft, she returned to London unhealed. She consulted yet another psychiatrist who prescribed even more powerful drugs and electro-convulsive treatment at Greenways nursing home, where eventually she spent six months. John visited her there and tortured her yet again by telling her that he loved her, calling her 'darling sweetheart' and promising to return to live with her – yet despite all her suffering she was still able to use the experience to write another BBC television play, *Three's One*, in which Caroline appeared with Hywel Bennett in a story about two young people who consult the same psychiatrist. Caroline was now twenty-nine and famous, had just played Hitler's mistress Eva Braun in an ITV production and was about to take on a major role in the BBC's classic new twenty-six-part Anthony Trollope television series *The Pallisers*.

At the end of March amazingly Penelope spent the weekend with Mortimer and Penny at Turville Heath – 'Penny with cosmetic blush on each cheek and John marching about in boots being a gentleman landowner,' she wrote in *About Time Too* – and inevitably hated it. She returned to Greenways for more shock treatment and in May learned in despair that Penny was pregnant. A week later John turned up again to moan about his lack of work and money and to ask for a divorce because of the baby, telling her glumly that he did not particularly want to marry Penny but that she 'doesn't want to have the child of another woman's husband'. Even so, he said with staggering naivety, 'we'll always be terrific friends, won't we?'

In fact he had a great deal of work and money, so his moaning was obviously a ploy to persuade Penelope not to ask for more maintenance now that they were to divorce. Michael Codron wanted him to rewrite parts of *A Voyage Round My Father* so that he could bring it into the West End. A collection of his first short *Five Plays* was about to be published by Methuen. In March his translation of the German playwright Carl Zuckmayer's *The Captain of Köpenick* for the National Theatre opened at the Old Vic and he was translating another Feydeau farce for the National, *Cat Among the Pigeons*. The director Tony Richardson wanted him to write a screenplay of Robert Graves' *I, Claudius*, and in June he was to appear in two lucrative trials that were finally to make his name as a celebrity QC. Mortimer was earning a fortune.

To translate *The Captain of Köpenick*, a German classic that had first been staged in 1931, was a brave venture because Mortimer knew little German and it was a very long play with dozens of characters and scenes, one of them in thick dialect, and veered from tragedy to farce to tragedy. It was said to be untranslatable. Olivier asked him to produce a very free adaptation and he reduced its three acts to two, cut and invented entire scenes, introduced his own dialogue and jokes, and changed the ending much to Zuckmayer's dismay. The play was based on the true story of Wilhelm Voigt, a middle-aged, semi-literate, down-and-out Prussian cobbler who in 1906 kept trying to get a passport, finding himself rebuffed by bureaucrats and tangled in red tape, and eventually in desperation bought an army captain's second-hand uniform, ordered a squad of real soldiers to follow him, captured the town hall in Köpenick and held the mayor to ransom. The play was a gentle satire about the slavish German willingness to obey any man in uniform and it had been especially effective because Zuckmayer, the author of *Blue Angel*, had written it just before Hitler came to power and when the Nazis realised its message they banned it. When it opened at the Old Vic in March, Voigt was played by Paul Scofield and seventy-four-year-old Zuckmayer was in the audience to see what this non-German-speaking English barrister had done to his famous play. He was cross about the new ending, claiming that it was a feeble anticlimax, unhappy about several other changes that Mortimer had made, and felt that John's version was less subtle than his. But when Mortimer's version was published he wrote magnanimously in the preface: 'I admire his scenic skill, his good crafts-manship and his wise insight into my "hero's" character.' Zuckmayer felt that Scofield had been brilliant, 'the greatest I have seen in this part since the wonderful Werner Krauss who created it', and the first-night audience gave Scofield a standing ovation and twenty curtain calls. This aroused the jealousy of Olivier, who always feared that Scofield might be a better actor than he. After Scofield's rapturous reception Olivier went to his dressing room and, according to Scofield's biographer Garry O'Connor, patted him condescendingly on the back and said wickedly: 'You mustn't worry about our first nights, Paulie. They're never very interesting. But don't worry, Paulie, we'll get it right.' The play was an immediate hit but Olivier let it run for only thirty performances.

Inevitably word of Penny's pregnancy reached the *Sunday Express* gossip columnist Peter McKay, who dispatched a lady reporter to the flat in Blomfield Road. 'I knocked on the door and asked for Penny Gollop,' she told me, 'and the cleaning lady let me in. I went upstairs and there was this huge man, Mortimer, standing at the top. I blurted out who I was and he became enraged and ordered me out: "*Get out! Get out!*" He was so angry because if I'd seen Penny I'd have realised immediately that she was pregnant. He tried later to claim that I'd got in under false pretences, that I'd broken into his house – he did it on the air during a radio broadcast and told anyone who would listen – but that was com-pletely untrue. His anger was very evident and for ever afterwards, for years, he was always very denigratory about me. He's not a man to cross.'

Shirley Anne Field was upset by Penny's pregnancy. Although she had said 'no' when John used to talk of marriage she felt sad when he introduced them at a party given by Tony Richardson in Little Venice.

'I remember crying at this supper because I felt as though I was going to lose my dearest friend, John,' she said. 'Penny 2 was always wary of me and I felt that's why I didn't see much of John once they were married. One funny thing, I remember him saying to me when he was still married to Penny 1: "I can't be unfaithful to my wife without her knowing because when you've got a deviation like mine she'll notice when her hairbrush is missing!"'

John and Penny went off on holiday to Greece and he returned to London to do battle at the Old Bailey in his second important obscenity case, the defence of *Oz*, a mischievous, rebellious 'underground' magazine with a circulation of 40,000 that had been launched in England in 1967 by three young Australians – the twenty-nine-year-old editor Richard Neville, thirty-three-year-old Jim Anderson, himself a barrister, and twenty-four-year-old Felix Dennis, the sales manager. It aimed to question the older generation's outdated beliefs and standards of behaviour and morality, and for its twenty-eighth issue about twenty teenagers aged from fifteen to eighteen were invited to contribute anything they chose and to edit it themselves. Entitled the *Oz School Kids Issue*, it consisted of forty-eight A4 pages with a cover that was green and blue in both senses of the word. The front showed part of an erotic montage from a rude French book, *Desseins Erotiques*, of four naked black women, one of them licking the neck of another – who had a rat's tail protruding from her vagina and a long, thin object up her anus – and a third woman burying her face between the legs of a fourth. The back cover depicted four more naked black women, one of them licking the nipple of another as she inserted a dildo into her vagina. Inside the magazine were articles about homosexuality, lesbianism, sexual perversions, sadism and a naughty cartoon-strip collage, put together by a fifteen-year-old boy, which showed the *Daily Express*'s famous Rupert Bear with a huge erect penis explicitly ravishing a 'Gipsy Granny' who somehow managed to be a virgin as well as a grandmother. There was a cartoon of an elderly male teacher fingering a boy's buttocks and masturbating, and another of a middle-aged man caning the naked buttocks of a second man while a third inserts a cane into his anus. Another cartoon depicted characters saying 'cunt cunt cunt!' and 'Bollocks you cunt', another showed a man pleasuring a dismembered woman, another a naked woman urinating on a penis-shaped cactus. One cartoon strip depicted the unsavoury drug-dealing activities of the Fabulous Furry Freak Brothers, and at the back of the magazine were numerous dubious small ads about prostitutes and homosexuals. It was all decidedly sleazy and juvenile, but was it any worse than that or just an example of tiresome adolescent sniggering?

The editors and solicitors of *Oz* had great trouble finding a QC prepared to defend the *School Kids Issue*. First they approached Emlyn Hooson. 'I didn't think I was the chap for that case,' he told me, possibly because he was an MP as well as head of chambers. Another QC accepted the brief but backed out eleven days before the trial was due to start, saying that he could not take the risk of jeopardising his career by defending in such a case. In desperation Neville and his twenty-four-year-old Australian friend Geoffrey Robertson, a Rhodes Scholar and Oxford postgraduate law student, remembered Mortimer's success in the *Last Exit to Brooklyn* case and approached him just four days before the trial. Mortimer was defending an axe murderer at the Old Bailey that day and they found him having lunch nearby with Penny and her sister. They handed him the Rupert cartoon, expecting him to be appalled, but he giggled and showed it to the young women, who laughed as well. He agreed to defend Anderson and Dennis while the highly intelligent Neville, a university graduate, defended himself so that he could address the jury. Twenty-six years later Robertson, who went on to become a QC and close friend of Mortimer, wrote in his book *The Justice Game*: 'I suspect John Mortimer thought of sex as an amusing but bemusing fact of life, not to be taken entirely seriously ... his willingness to sacrifice his precious writing time to save these provocateurs from prison gave reason to hope that there was yet some life left in old liberal England.' As Mortimer's junior barrister the *Oz* team chose a lawyer who was practising from nearby chambers in the Middle Temple at 1 Garden Court: thirty-one-year-old Jonah Walker-Smith, later Sir Jonah.

As in the *Last Exit to Brooklyn* case, the key to whether *Oz* was legally obscene was not whether it was shocking or in bad taste but whether it tended to deprave and corrupt a significant number of those people who were likely to read it. The defendants were also charged with intending and conspiring to corrupt public morals and with sending an indecent object through Her Majesty's Royal Mail. The trial began at the Old Bailey on 22 June 1971 before His Honour Michael Argyle, a stern, fifty-six-year-old judge who had won a Military Cross during the war, had stood in two elections as a right-wing Conservative candidate, and was renowned for his ferocious sentences. A devout Christian, Argyle was appalled by the loose standards of the Permissive Society, firmly in favour of capital punishment, and his favourite breed of dog was the Rottweiler, so predictably he was extremely unpopular with liberal, radical barristers. 'We were up against it with one of the most unpleasant judges of those years,' Sir Jonah told me. 'I suspect he was the original of Judge Bullingham in the Rumpole stories. He was a nasty piece of work and his conduct throughout that trial was monstrous. He was totally for the prosecution, made his own views abundantly clear, and was quite the wrong judge to try the school kids' *Oz*. It was smutty, yes, and there was sex in it, yes, but it had a small circulation and was just cocking a snook at authority, and if the powers-that-be had had any sense at all they'd have just let it be.'

The trial was seen as a contest between the generations. 'The young are in the dock, judged by the old,' said the publisher Anthony Blond, who commissioned a television producer, Tony Palmer, to write a book about the trial – and so it seemed when about a hundred young *Oz* supporters wearing long hair, kaftans, beads, bells, and T-shirts showing randy Rupert rampant marched on the Old Bailey on the first day accompanied by a lorry carrying a twenty-foot papier mâché figure of a nude woman. Each day dozens of weirdly dressed youths and girls queued for the fifty seats in the public gallery and the defendants stood in the dock with their long hair and casual, colourful clothes and faced the judge in his formal wig and medieval fancy dress. The charge of conspiracy to corrupt public morals carried an astonishing maximum penalty of life imprisonment and the security measures were extraordinary. Day and night four armed Special Branch officers and two Alsatian dogs and their handlers guarded Judge Argyle, who received death threats, obscene telephone calls and letters, and retired each night to a secure suite at the Savoy Hotel. Describing Mortimer in court that day, Jonathan Dimbleby wrote in the *New Statesman*: 'A shaggy yellowing wig fails to hide shaggier hair; his waistcoat is ill-fitting. A man of sharp wit, he has an air of world-weary tolerance.'

He began his opening speech to the elderly jury of three women and nine men on the afternoon of the second day by saying: 'This is a very, very important case because it is this case, and cases such as these, which stand at the crossroads of our liberty, at the boundaries of our freedom to think and say and draw and write what we please.' It was a case, he said, 'about those who are critical of the established values of our society, who ask us to reconsider what they believe to be complacent values, and are anxious, on that basis, to build what they think (and what we may not think) is a better world. Members of the jury, we are all of us totally entitled to disagree with their views, but this is a case about whether or not they are also entitled to disagree with us.' He urged them to accept that 'freedom of expression is at all times preferable to censorship' and concluded by saying that it was important for the public good that the older generation should know how school children feel, think and behave, unencumbered by inhibition or school or parental discipline, even if they were shocked by what they learned.

The trial lasted six weeks and he revelled in it. 'Few things are more exciting than appearing for the defence in an important and sensational criminal trial at the Old Bailey,' he said once and invited both Penny and Shirley Anne Field to attend the trial. 'He loved being seen performing,' said Shirley Anne. Walker-Smith's wife Aileen used to join them for lunch in a pub opposite the Old Bailey and 'was covered in confusion', said Walker-Smith, 'because Penny was pregnant and Aileen thought that she was John's daughter.' Half of the six-week trial was devoted to Rupert Bear's gargantuan erection and the virgin granny, which resulted in one of many memorable passages of cross-examination:

'What sort of *age* would you think Rupert is, to your mind?' the prosecutor, Brian Leary, asked one 'expert' witness, the psychologist Dr Michael Schofield. 'What sort of aged bear?'

'Oh. I'm very sorry. I'm not up to date with bears.'

'You don't have to be, because he doesn't change, Rupert, does he?'

Judge Argyle intervened. 'I think the question is "what age do you think Rupert is intended to be: a child, an adult, or what?" '

'It's an unreal question,' said Schofield. 'You might as well ask me "how old is Jupiter?" '

'He's a young bear, isn't he?' said Leary. 'He goes to school. That's right, isn't it?'

'I don't know whether he goes to school or not,' said Schofield. 'I'm sorry, but I'm obviously not as well informed as you are about little bears. I'm a psychologist.'

Mortimer called ten psychiatrists, psychologists and educationalists to testify for the defence, one of them Professor Hans Eysenck, who said that a recent American study showed that even hours of watching pornographic films did not deprave or corrupt the people who watched them. 'What, thirty hours of oral sex and still no detrimental effect?' asked Mortimer.

'This is right,' said the professor.

A week after the *Oz* trial began Mortimer disappeared south across the river for three days to defend twenty-seven-year-old Richard Handyside in the Lambeth Magistrates' Court in another obscenity case that Mortimer felt was even more important than that of *Oz*. Handyside was the publisher of another publication that was aimed at school children, *The*

Little Red School Book, a 30p English edition of an anarchic Danish guidebook about sex, contraception, pupils' rights, and left-wing politics that urged children to strike, rebel and ignore their teachers, and suggested that all schools should have a sex shop and a contraceptive vending machine, that venereal disease was irritating but not serious, and that drugs could be fun. The prosecution had been inspired by the Christian moral campaigner Mrs Mary Whitehouse, who was to find herself increasingly during the 1970s crossing swords with Mortimer in trials for obscenity and pornography that she and her followers considered to be vital for the preservation of decency in Britain. The magistrate found Handyside guilty, fined him £50 and £110 in legal costs, and afterwards Mortimer complained that the book had been banned because of its left-wing political opinions rather than because it was obscene. It was 'amazing', he said, 'that the prosecution has been allowed to single out just twenty-three pages dealing with sex out of a 208-page book ... dealing with politics and other matters. It is characteristic of those seeking censorship to concentrate on sex' when children were already living in a society dominated by sex on television and in books and magazines.

Back at the *Oz* trial Neville called as a witness George Melly, the ebullient jazz musician who had succeeded Penelope as film critic of the *Observer* and who said he was quite sure that his sixteen-year-old son would not be corrupted by reading *Oz 28*, not even by the description of cunnilingus. 'Well, pardon me,' said Judge Argyle. 'For those of us who did not have a classical education, what do you mean by this word "cunnilinctus"?'

' "Sucking" or "blowing", your Lordship,' beamed Melly, 'or "going down," or "gobbling" is another alternative. Another expression used in my naval days, your Lordship, was "yodelling in the canyon".'

Neville also called as a witness the pop-eyed comedian Marty Feldman, who thought the Rupert cartoon strip was hilarious but refused to take the oath because 'there are more obscene things in the Bible than in this issue of *Oz*'. He insinuated that Judge Argyle was asleep, saying, 'Am I waking you up? Shall I speak louder?' and as he left the court he told reporters loudly that the judge was 'a boring old fart'. Argyle could have had him committed immediately to prison for contempt of court but realised that Feldman was trying to boost his career by becoming a martyr in such a notorious case. He pretended not to hear and even Neville was not amused by his witness's behaviour.

Another defence witness was the disc jockey John Peel, who found himself discussing with Leary whether it might be possible to induce an orgasm by listening to the music of Mozart or Beethoven. When Peel referred to 'making love' Leary pounced: 'So we take it that you would consider it bad taste to use the word "fuck" rather than "making love"? Which would you prefer?'

Peel shrugged. 'The expressions are not different,' he said. 'I just felt because I was in court I should say "make love" but everybody else seems to say "fuck" so I will say "fuck" as well.'

[Laughter in court.]

Judge Argyle: 'Once again I have to remind people that this is not a theatre.'

One day the seats in the public gallery were packed with American judges and their wives who howled with laughter at some of the evidence. 'Silence!' bellowed the ushers and Argyle barked: 'This is a courtroom, not a theatre' as he threatened more than once to clear the public gallery. 'Are we going to have continual laughter and cross-talk? Are we going to be allowed to smoke and have drinks?' Later he told the court: 'No doubt these people thought they were in Chicago.' Another American visitor found the trial so entertaining that he asked: 'Are they running this thing right through the tourist season?' When Peel admitted in the witness box that he had once contracted a venereal disease Argyle ordered the court usher to smash the glass from which Peel had been sipping water in case it were infected, and when the mother of the boy who had produced the Rupert cartoon admitted that she had taken him to see the nude revue *Hair* Judge Argyle asked, 'Is "hair" an article?'

Mortimer sighed. '*Hair* is a play,' he said hopelessly. 'It's been running in the West End for the last three years.'

'Argyle was an ogre of a judge,' said Walker-Smith, 'but John was never *rude* to him. That would have been counter-productive.' And Mortimer did have an important safety valve: every evening, when the court adjourned, he would escape to the Haymarket Theatre to help with rehearsals of Codron's West End production of *A Voyage Round My Father*, now starring Alec Guinness.

After nearly five weeks in court Mortimer's summing-up was masterly. He pointed out wearily that the prosecution had not called even one expert witness to suggest that *Oz* might deprave or corrupt anybody. 'Ladies and gentlemen of the jury,' he said, 'we have sat here through a very large number of days and thousands and thousands of questions while the best part of the summer has passed us by. Wimbledon tournaments have been and gone, and we have almost entered the Common

Market. And meanwhile we have turned over and over and over again the pages of a little underground magazine. We have done it so often that we may feel that the Furry Freak Brothers have entered our sleeping as well as our waking hours. A huge quantity of public time and money has been spent in the ardent and eager pursuit of – what? . . . a schoolboy prank. In pursuit of that prank, ladies and gentlemen of the jury, and to squash this little outburst, to gag a little cheeky criticism, to suppress some lavatory humour and some adolescent discussion of sex and drugs, we have had rolled out before us the great, majestic engine of the criminal law. The threat to our nation of forty-eight blurred pages of schoolboy ebullience has been countered by the rolling prose of the indictments, by the tireless researches of Inspector Luff, by the inexhaustible cross-examination of my learned friend Mr Leary, and by the deep and carefully preserved, sonorous solemnity of a great criminal trial. And one may be tempted to feel, members of the jury, that the prosecution is like some nervous public official who, when a child puts out a tongue at him in the street, calls in the army.' And then he flattered the jury shamelessly, telling them that they had been specially chosen to judge this case 'because it is you who have the experience of the outside world. It is you who live in it. It is you who know, better than anybody, what the world is like today – a world by whose standards we must judge this particular magazine. Perhaps it is most important that a case like this *should* be judged by ladies and gentlemen such as yourselves. Lawyers, traditionally, are suspicious of change ... You, ladies and gentlemen, with your common sense and your experience of the outside world, are there to restore to us our sense of fairness, our sense of proportion and, above all, our sense of humour.'

Mortimer concluded his oration with a powerful statement on the vital importance of freedom of speech that was to underpin the defence in all his future obscenity cases. 'The real division,' he said, 'between the philosophy of those who have given evidence for the defence and the views put forward by Mr Leary is this: are there certain subjects which are taboo? Are there certain things about life which we mustn't discuss, however honestly? ... Or do you not think that human dignity and human responsibility to our fellow citizens enjoins us to discuss every-thing as honestly and frankly as possible? It's very easy and simple to be tolerant and to allow freedom of speech when what people are saying is that with which we agree. But if free speech and democracy mean anything at all, they imply tolerance and freedom for people with whom we disagree.' It was an impressive speech that went on for six hours, though Shirley Anne Field must have raised an eyebrow when Mortimer referred to the *Oz* cartoon of the elderly men caning each other's naked buttocks. 'No one is going to be lured into flagellation by the picture of the three old schoolmasters with canes,' he said. 'They are going to be disgusted and think that to be a disgusting experience.'

Geoffrey Robertson was appalled by what he saw as Judge Argyle's blatant bias throughout the case. 'If during the trial he regarded evidence as irrelevant,' Robertson wrote in *The Justice Game*, 'he would put his pen down with a clatter, fold his arms and lean back in his seat.' In Argyle's final summing-up 'whenever he dealt with the defence his tone could not help but be scathing and contemptuous: the prosecution arguments he repeated with respect. Frequently he expressed his own opinion – usually to the detriment of the defence ... He could hardly have made his views more clear had he actually held his nose and raised his arm as if pulling a toilet chain.'

The jury found the defendants not guilty of conspiring to corrupt public morals but guilty of obscenity and indecency by a majority of 10–1 after one woman had to drop out. Argyle refused to grant bail but remanded the defendants to Wandsworth prison for medical and psychiatric reports. 'It really is inhuman to keep them in suspense any longer,' protested Mortimer. Several Labour MPs, among them Michael Foot and Tony Benn, condemned Argyle but his decision was confirmed two days later by the Court of Appeal and it was a week before the defendants returned to court for sentencing. The psychiatric reports confirmed what everyone knew already: Neville, Anderson and Dennis were 'of high intelligence and lack interest in material gain. They are polite and courteous. There are aspects of society that appal them and they edited *Oz* to show the urgent need of reform.' Argyle jailed Neville for fifteen months and recommended that he should be deported, Anderson for a year, and Dennis for nine months 'because you are very much less intelligent than the other two'. As they were led down to the cells another prisoner asked Neville what his sentence was. 'Fifteen months,' said Neville. The man was appalled. 'That's terrible,' he said. 'I got the same, and I tried to murder my wife!' Outside the court more than four hundred young people went berserk. For two hours they staged a sit-in on the steps of the court, burned an effigy of Argyle, chanted 'Roast pig! Roast pig!', threw smoke bombs and fought with the police. Eleven were arrested and police mounted a day-and-night guard at Argyle's country house in Nottinghamshire. Fifteen Labour MPs signed a Commons motion calling the sentences 'an act of revenge by the Establishment against dissenting voices', the National Council for Civil Liberties said they were 'savage and vindictive', and the *New Law Journal* that they were 'indefensibly severe'. John Lennon called them 'disgusting fascism' and they were condemned by the British Humanists' Association and the liberal lawyers' organisation the Haldane Society.

The newspapers exploded with front-page lead stories in *The Times*, *Daily Mail* and *Daily Mirror*. 'OZ: OBSCENE! BUT WHY THE FEROCIOUS SENTENCES?' shrieked the *Daily Mirror*, adding: 'WHY make martyrs of these silly young men?' Yet as Duff Hart-Davis wrote in the *Sunday Telegraph*, 'there is no doubt that ninety per cent of ordinary people would agree with the jury's verdict. The School Kids Issue ... would shock the great majority of the public. It is impossible to believe that any ordinary parent would gladly let young children see the magazine; nor could anyone easily claim that its sexuality was redeemed by beauty or literary merit – both conspicuously absent from the crude and garish production.' The *Daily Mirror* agreed: 'The School Kids Issue of *Oz* was repellent. It was sex without tenderness: lust without love. No rational person could defend it. Every parent would regard it with horror.' Editorials in *The Sunday Times* and even the liberal *Guardian* and *Observer* all agreed that *Oz* 28 was undoubtedly obscene but condemned the prison sentences. An editorial in *The Times*, however, defended even the sentences because 'that issue of *Oz* was directed towards children of secondary school age ... The judge had sufficient justification for severity here.' Mrs Mary Whitehouse told *The Times*: 'The sentences were about right. It was absolutely essential for them to be long enough to make them effective. The line had to be drawn because children were at risk and the people of this country will not take that kind of thing.' Even the youth wing of the Conservative Monday Club issued a statement thanking Argyle 'for having the courage to defend the law against those whose motives certainly have nothing to do with the search for a freer society'.

Nor was the widespread left-wing hatred of Judge Argyle completely justified. Neville said himself that the trial had been completely fair until the judge's summing-up, and Derek Roberts-Morgan wrote in the *Sunday Telegraph*: 'Every unbiased person who has heard [Argyle] at work during this trial must acknowledge that he has bent over backwards to ensure that every possible point of any relevance to the defence has been put fairly and fully to the jury.' Few of those who vilified Argyle had any idea that despite his strong views he was privately kind and generous. He often gave up his lunch break to try to help unemployed defendants find jobs and offered £100 of his own money (£950) as a reward for information leading to the arrest of a mugger who had attacked a woman usher at the Old Bailey.

The trial had taken twenty-seven days, which made it the longest obscenity trial in history, and two days later Mortimer managed to persuade another judge, Mr Justice Griffiths, to grant bail while he appealed against the convictions. For his part in the trial Mortimer earned an estimated £8,300 in legal aid (£77,600 or £2,874 a day), which made his protestations of poverty quite ridiculous. Speaking on London Weekend Television's *Man in the News* programme after the trial he said he was against any sort of censorship at all: 'There can't be a limit to what a writer, if he is truthful, is going to write about. It would be quite impossible for a creative writer to stop in the middle of a paragraph and say, "No, I'm afraid I'm not allowed to say that," or, "this is something I'm not allowed to write about."' But, he was asked, should society not protect children from obscenity and pornography? 'I'm opposed to paternalistic laws because I don't think the law has that object,' he said. 'If you are a parent then it's your responsibility, and you must make the choice as to what extent you want to expose your child and at what stage you want to expose your child to the enormous number of sexual objects and sexual things and so on which surround its everyday life. It is part of living to be shocked and nauseated and disgusted. I think it's absolutely necessary that people should be outraged. I don't think there could be any progress without people being outraged.' Or as he told me in 1993, 'If you said everything which shocks people should be censored then you would have to censor the gouging out of Gloucester's eyes in *King Lear*, and lots of the Bible, and a lot of modern art was shocking at the time that it was done. I also think it's rather *good* for people to be shocked. That doesn't mean to say that freedom is not risky. It's *very* risky, like deciding whether to send your children on a cycling holiday in Europe. They may get mugged or raped or have an accident, but they've got to be free in the end to make their own lives. The risks of freedom in writing and viewing are less than the risks of having government authorities dictating what people should read or write, and the law is inappropriate to decide those things. People have to decide for themselves – and you can always turn the television off.'

Mortimer was so nervous before going into court for the *Oz* defendants' appeal on 3 November that he vomited in the lavatory – a reaction that he was to suffer whenever he appeared before the Court of Appeal or the House of Lords, like an actor about to go onstage – but when he addressed Lord Chief Justice Widgery, Mr Justice James and Mr Justice Bridge he

argued confidently that during the Old Bailey trial Argyle had misdirected the jury no fewer than seventy-eight times. He claimed that
Argyle had denigrated the defence 'experts', had not stressed sufficiently
to the jury that the legal definition of obscenity was that which tended
to deprave and corrupt, not that which they found revolting, and that
Argyle's summing-up had been highly prejudicial. After a three-day
hearing the judges agreed and quashed the sentences because Argyle had
made a 'substantial and serious misdirection'. It was a famous victory
that established Mortimer as the leading radical barrister to brief in any
future case to do with freedom of expression, obscenity or pornography.
'State censorship was absurd, footling and quite oppressive,' Sir Richard
Eyre told Alan Yentob in 2003 and 'when he appeared in the *Oz* trial he
was a champion of liberal values and a hero for our generation'. Two days
later, on the BBC radio programme *The World This Weekend*, Mortimer
called the law on obscenity 'totally ridiculous' and demanded that it be
abolished.

'John was greatly admired by his fellow barristers for winning the
case,' Lord Hooson told me. 'The nature of society began to change with
the *Oz* trial and once you've succeeded in a case like that people tend to
come back to you.' Neil Kinnock, who was to become leader of the
Labour Party twelve years later and a great friend of Mortimer, told me
in 2004 that 'it is easy to forget now how curtailed our society still was
forty years ago. He never made the offensive respectable, but he made it
necessary for respectable people to recognise that the toleration of diversity was the real mark of civilisation. He was in the vanguard and without
him and Roy Jenkins – and Sydney Silverman on capital punishment,
Leo Abse on divorce and homosexuality, David Steel with the Abortion
Act – the changes of the Sixties and Seventies wouldn't have been made.
The big mistake that prudes and cultural conservatives make is to think
that what they call "permissiveness" was created by a bunch of mischief-
making lawyers like Mortimer and louche politicians like Jenkins and
Abse, when actually they were simply codifying conditions that had long
pre-existed.' Another Labour MP, Glenda Jackson, agreed. 'Roy Jenkins
and John Mortimer were engaged in attempting to break down these
ludicrously artificial barriers,' she told me. 'They were on a tide that was
turning. There was clearly a feeling within the country that changes had
to take place because social changes had actually *taken* place. Huge
changes were coming from a young group that had never been reckoned
before.'

On the other side of the political spectrum Norman (later Lord) Tebbit,

who was in 1971 the forty-year-old Tory MP for Epping and was later
to become a Cabinet Minister and Margaret Thatcher's right-hand man,
was less impressed. 'If you contrast the society in which we lived fifty
years ago – when you could walk the streets with a gold wristwatch on
and not think for a moment that you might be mugged for it – with the
one in which we live now,' he told me, 'if you look at the statistics now
of murder, mugging, child abuse and all other sorts of skulduggery,
whatever the Permissive Society is, it is not as Jenkins called it in his
famous remark a *Civilised* Society. It's a distinctly *less* civilised society.
Our standards have gone down and down since then and I think people
like Mortimer and Jenkins were to blame. It was driven then to some
extent by undergraduate perversity, by people who in some cases had not
altogether grown up. I wouldn't say that particularly of Roy Jenkins, but
other people who were involved were typical of naughty boys who wanted
to know how far they could go in being rude, or shouting rude words,
before somebody clipped them round the ear. Then they found they
weren't getting clipped round the ear so they went a bit farther, and then
they found how profitable it was. These guys now are the allies of a
number of people in business who've found that the Permissive Society
is jolly good business and they can sell more smut, more liquor, more of
everything, so there's a rather unholy alliance between the two groups.'

One of Mortimer's fellow QCs, Judge Angus Stroyan, who had been a
contemporary at Harrow, was equally critical of him. 'He wasn't all that
popular at the Bar because he threw his weight around a bit and didn't
mix,' Stroyan told me. 'When I was at Assizes he never dined in mess.
He was a loner, although he did turn up sometimes on circuit with
various girls of whom nothing much more was ever heard afterwards. I
share the view that Mortimer and Jenkins were partly to blame for a
decline of standards in Britain. Certainly Mortimer was very much in
favour of the decline of standards.'

Mortimer was given another smacking surprisingly by one of the
younger generation when he went to the Cambridge Union to join
Neville in a televised debate against the anti-permissiveness campaigners
Lord Longford and Mary Whitehouse. His critic was a twenty-one-year-
old undergraduate, Jeremy Paxman, who reported the debate for the
university newspaper *Varsity* and was later to become a caustic television
interviewer and Mortimer's friend and admirer. He was not an admirer
then. 'You could ... credit Neville with some degree of authenticity,'
sneered Paxman, but 'the same could not be said of Dr Martin Cole or
John Mortimer with their self-conscious use of words like "hang up" and

"turn on" dropping like pebbles into a pond from their middle-aged mouths ... if you suspect someone of not being true to themselves, how can you believe in the truth of their ideas? ... And if we consider the real issues at stake in the pornography question it becomes apparent how much of the stand taken by the trendy liberators, and not least by people like John Mortimer (oh-so-clever with words), is purely a question of fashion.' As for *Oz* magazine, its editors closed it down, Neville returned to Australia, Anderson emigrated to California and Dennis, who Argyle had said was so much less intelligent, built a huge magazine empire and became a multi-millionaire.

On 4 August, the night before the *Oz* defendants were sentenced by Argyle, the new stage version of *A Voyage Round My Father* opened at the Haymarket Theatre. 'It's like having two first nights in a row,' said Mortimer. Michael Codron was delighted when Alec Guinness agreed to play Clifford Mortimer but told me that 'when we opened for the try-out week at Brighton John said to me, "He really isn't angry enough. My father was angry. Alec's too benign." We took Guinness to lunch and I said, "Do you think you could convey anger a bit more?" and he said, "but I *am* being angry. Haven't you seen the way I tap the egg at breakfast?" ' It was certainly a subdued performance by comparison with Laurence Olivier's Clifford on television eleven years later, but Guinness was 'cast-iron box office', said Codron, the reviewers loved him, and the play was an immediate hit and had a long, successful run with Jeremy Brett as the adult John Mortimer, Leueen MacGrath as Kath and Nicola Pagett as Penelope. Peggy Ramsay, however, felt guilty that neither she nor Mortimer had done anything to persuade Codron not to dump Mark Dignam, who they both thought had been excellent in the part at the Greenwich Theatre, in favour of Guinness. 'What kind of theatre are we promoting?' she wrote to another of her clients, John Arden. 'We have GOT to stop this insidious tendency for the author now to be less important than the star.' Guinness, a Catholic, disapproved of Mortimer at first because he was about to divorce but later warmed to him although strangely he made no mention of him in his autobiographies or published diary.

In August John and Penny stayed in the South of France with Tony Richardson, who had made so much money out of the film *Tom Jones* that he had bought an entire French hamlet, Le Nid du Duc (The Night Owl's Nest) near La Garde Freinet. Richardson had been trying for several years to film Robert Graves' Ancient Roman novels *I, Claudius* and *Claudius the God* and persuaded John to write a script even though Edward

Bond and Christopher Isherwood had already tried and failed. By the end of the month John had produced a script which Richardson told Graves had just 'the right style and irony', but five weeks later he reported that the movie industry was lukewarm about a new 'toga film' so he planned to put it on the stage first. In later years the Mortimers often stayed with Richardson, whose house was regularly filled with parties of up to thirty guests at a time, and it became an Easter tradition for John to write the rhyming clues for the annual Nid du Duc treasure hunt.

When Penelope's sad new novel *The Home* was published in September the reviewers raved about it – although Francis King called her heroine an 'often tiresome woman after the breakdown of her marriage'. Penelope told Olga Franklin of the *Daily Telegraph* that although everyone seemed to think she was tough and sophisticated she was in fact 'muddled, desperately shy and spend a lot of my life in a sort of terror about one thing or another. Terror of life I suppose.' She admitted that she was difficult to live with but suggested that John had never grown up. 'Some men take a longer time to grow up,' she said. 'If you find an adult man to marry . . . they are very few and far between. And I find the idea that all men are little boys at heart the most unattractive thing I can think of. And then men are much more concerned about growing old than women are.'

Mortimer seemed unconcerned about Penelope's vulnerability and bitterness and told Lynda Lee-Potter of the *Daily Mail* that he had not found it traumatic to read *The Home*. 'I take it for granted that Penelope will write about me,' he said with a shrug. 'I don't see what else she can do. Writers, after all, can only write about what happens to them. I don't believe there is any such thing as total imagination or total invention. Writing is therapeutic: it gets rid of your memories.' Nor did he feel at all guilty about his behaviour or the end of the marriage. 'I have never felt disturbed by Penelope's books,' he told the *Daily Mail* eleven years later. 'She's a marvellous writer and I don't look back on our marriage with any sense of regret. I am not ashamed of anything. It would be ridiculous to go through life being ashamed.'

On 6 October 1971 Penny was taken to Queen Charlotte's Hospital in Hammersmith to give birth to John's second illegitimate child, a daughter whom they called Emily Kathleen Anne (after their mothers) and who was to become an even more famous actress than Caroline. She was actually born Emily Gollop because her birth was registered under Penny's surname and no one was named as the father, although Penny was to register it again by declaration eight months later after she and

John had married, naming him as the father, as allowed under Section 14 of the Births and Deaths Registration Act of 1953. Soon after the birth, when Penny had returned home and John was in court appealing against the conviction of *The Little Red School Book*, she haemorrhaged badly and was rushed back to Queen Charlotte's, where she thought she was dying. Alarmed, Mortimer abandoned the trial and dashed off to the hospital much to the judge's irritation. In due course the appeal was refused and although the publisher took his case to the European Court of Human Rights that too rejected his final appeal five years later.

1971 had been an *annus mirabilis* for Mortimer and during it he had reached the height of both his professions: he had won the most important of all his trials and the best play he was ever to write was a West End hit. Yet he was increasingly fed up with being a barrister. 'As I grow older I find it more and more unsatisfactory,' he told Lynda Lee-Potter, pointing out that as a defence barrister biased towards his client 'one is always saying only half the truth. In the law courts everybody is giving a performance. The judge is acting being a judge, I'm acting being an advocate. The whole thing is a very stagey outfit.' Despite the huge amount of money he was making he claimed that he still felt insecure. 'I don't think anybody can ever be very happy with a life like mine, which depends on writing a successful play every twelve months,' he said. 'There's no other life where you have to face a crisis every year.' This was self-pitying nonsense and he could not possibly have believed that his rich, privileged life was more stressful than that of an exhausted junior hospital doctor, fireman, soldier, big-businessman or unemployed slum dweller with six children to feed. 'I live in a state of total insecurity,' he whined. 'Every time I finish a play I feel I'll never do it again. I get desperately anxious.' It sounded like spurious Uriah Heep humility.

The only Mortimers suffering serious stress were sixteen-year-old Jeremy, who had lost his home and father, and Penelope, who was finally granted an undefended divorce on 14 December 1971 on the grounds of John's adultery with Penny and the 'irretrievable breakdown' of their marriage. John paid all the costs and Penelope was given the care and control of Jeremy. The judge was told that John was eager to marry Penny as soon as possible because of Emily's birth and ordered sympathetically that the decree should become absolute after just one month but Mortimer repaid Judge Noakes's kindness and understanding by dragging his feet for more than three months. He seemed curiously lukewarm about marrying again and three weeks after Emily's birth, a few days after Penny had nearly died, he told Lynda Lee-Potter that his writing was easily the most important thing in his life and that he would be quite happy to live alone so long as he could write. It was not the most romantic way to start a new marriage.

Nine

Rumpole and the Oral Sex
1972–1976

Mortimer was now earning a great deal of money both from the Law and writing and began to live mainly at Turville Heath, where he would rise early, write for two hours and cook breakfast for his wife and child before driving up to his chambers in the Temple. Penny enjoyed a cosseted life although she did help him by typing his illegible manuscripts, as Penelope had done, and telling him what she thought of his work although he was painfully touchy about criticism. 'Oh God!' he would shout. 'It's awful! You hate it! You've broken my confidence!' They hired a mother's help and John did all the cooking at weekends, when they often had visitors, but he drew the line at changing nappies and left it to Penny to see to Emily if she cried in the night. Luckily she was a contented baby.

At the end of March the National Theatre faced a major crisis when Olivier discovered to his fury that the board was secretly about to choose the forty-one-year-old director Peter Hall to succeed him as artistic director. Olivier was sixty-four, ill, tired and due to retire soon, but he wanted to choose his successor himself, wanted an actor not a director, and feared jealously that Hall might well run the NT better than he had, but he had been dithering for months and the board had had enough of the delay. Ken Tynan also wanted to stop Hall getting the job because they disliked each other and he asked Mortimer, who supported Hall, why he had not warned him and Olivier what was going on. Mortimer said he thought they had been consulted. Angry and impotent, Olivier and Tynan had to give way and never forgave the board for what they saw as its shabby treatment of them even though Hall was not due to join the National for another year nor to take over from Olivier until 1974.

Mortimer found himself involved in another theatrical row when Arnold Wesker wrote a play about a newspaper, *The Journalists*, and the Royal Shakespeare Company director David Jones commissioned it for the RSC, signed a contract, cast it and announced its opening date but was then forced to renege on the deal when the actors refused to perform the play. 'My theory is that they were at that time under the sway of the Workers Revolutionary Party,' Wesker told me, 'and I had created in the play four Tory Cabinet Ministers who were highly intelligent. Trevor Nunn was in charge of the RSC at Stratford, stood by the actors, and it was never produced professionally in Britain, and I was furious and sued them for £25,000 for loss of earnings and damaged reputation. Mortimer agreed to represent me but later said he couldn't because he had forgotten that he was a governor of the RSC. Perhaps he didn't want to blot his copybook with the RSC or he was talked out of it by friends and made up an excuse. They had a really good legal team and dragged the case out for seven years, by which time I was weary and settled out of court for £4,000 and they didn't pay my legal bills. It would have been better if I'd had John Mortimer. He might have won. The other side might have capitulated immediately if they'd known they were up against him.'

When Mortimer got around to marrying Penny at last he bothered to do it only because the judge in an Old Bailey murder case adjourned for a day to let a juryman go to a funeral and Mortimer found that he had an unexpected free day. They married on 21 April 1972, his forty-ninth birthday, at Paddington Register Office, where Jeremy was the best man and Sally, who was only three years younger than the bride, signed the register. The marriage certificate claimed that Penny was twenty-five, a year older than she was, perhaps because John was so embarrassed by the difference in their ages. He never gave the date of his marriage to Penny in *Who's Who* and *Debrett's People of Today* although he made no attempt to hide that of his marriage to Penelope.

After the ceremony they went back to Blomfield Road for the reception, where 'Penny looked about fourteen', Molly Parkin told me. 'She was a little girl and somebody said "it's *gross*, isn't it? It's like an old *paedophile* marrying a *child*." But you should have seen the beauty of the women, like Charlotte Rampling and Shirley Anne Field, who were there. Almost all of us had been John's mistress at some time. The only other person who would find it quite normal to be surrounded by so many gorgeous women was David Bailey, who had the same reputation as John for being a ladykiller.' Molly was dying to ask Charlotte Rampling if she had been his mistress too but 'there was something magnificently glacial about her, the kind of distance that Garbo must have projected and, even though the booze had loosened my tongue sufficiently, courage failed me at the last minute'. There was certainly plenty of booze. 'It was like a *Who's Who* of London and everybody was totally arseholed. I could see Penny's freshness but I don't know whether John was faithful to her. A poet said to me, "Mortimer's a *bastard*. If you bump into him when you're out for the evening you can't go to the loo because he'll jump in and take the number of the girl you're with." I said, "Not now he's married," and he said, "Does a leopard change his spots?" That's the reputation that he's got. Once I saw him with a beautiful ballet dancer and he'd been a lover of hers too. She said, "We're in the same club, aren't we, Moll?" and I said, "And another friend of mine," and she said, "Well, *everybody's* had John, darling. It's a very large club." '

Shirley Anne Field realised that her close friendship with John had to end. 'I never really knew Penny 2,' she told me. 'Eleanor Fazan told me to make a friend of her but I didn't. Perhaps I should have.' Penelope was devastated by John's remarriage. 'I thought, I'm going to live with this the rest of my life, regretting and mourning,' she told Lynda Lee-Potter in 1993. 'It was terribly painful [and] I got afraid of people. My confidence was absolutely zero.' Clive Donner was now married to Jocelyn Rickards and Penelope had 'dozens and dozens of affairs, but nobody I really cared about', she said. 'There were a few toy-boys. I was very fond of them, one in particular, a kid in America, but I grew out of that.'

Penny soon felt sorry for Penelope and tried to be nice to her. 'I always got on quite well with her,' she told Craig Brown of the *Mail on Sunday* in 2001, 'but John was *terrified* of her. I once realised that she wasn't doing anything on Christmas Day, so we asked her down. She ruined the whole day, sighing when anyone pulled a cracker.'

In May the first of Mortimer's five latest half-hour plays, *Mill Hill*, was broadcast on BBC TV with Peter Cook as the kinky dentist who likes to dress up as Sir Walter Raleigh and Geraldine McEwan as the wife who has to pretend to be Elizabeth I. A fortnight later another of his plays, *Alcock and Gander* was screened by Thames Television. At the Haymarket Theatre Michael Redgrave had taken over from Alec Guinness in *A Voyage Round My Father*, was finding it difficult at sixty-four to remember his lines, and relied onstage on a radio-controlled hearing aid through which the prompter fed him his lines. Mortimer loved to tell how one night Redgrave was onstage, picked up a radio-taxi message, and startled the actress who was playing Kath, Jane Baxter, by declaring: 'I must now proceed immediately to number 4 Flask Walk, Hampstead.' Sadly Redgrave's biographer Alan Strachan told me that the story is untrue. Strachan had directed both Guinness and Redgrave and reckoned that Redgrave was by far the best of all the actors who played Mortimer's father, including Olivier later on television. 'Olivier was hammy and far too big for the small screen and Guinness – perversely – was much too miniaturist and altogether missed the darker, angry side of the character. There's a crucial line in the play – "I'm always angry when I'm dying" – which Guinness played almost beatifically. Redgrave, without missing any of the character's puckish eccentricity, created something much more layered, clearly death-haunted and using his wit and his wiles to stave off unvoiced terrors.' The play continued to pack audiences in until Redgrave took it to Canada for a few weeks and then to Australia, where it won more rave reviews.

In July Mortimer had a second play running in the West End, at the Queen's Theatre: *I, Claudius*, his adaptation of the Robert Graves books. Graves, now eighty-seven, thought it was 'a wonderful piece of work' and attended the packed first night and party with his wife Beryl. David Warner played the Emperor Claudius but the production ran for only two months, which baffled Graves though Beryl told his biographer Richard Perceval Graves that it had been 'all right but a bit too clever, almost a farce: good in its way but not into it'. Tony Richardson eventually admitted that he and Mortimer had never quite got it right. He wrote in his autobiography that 'the ambiguity of the central character which Robert could convey by interior monologues defeated us', and abandoned his hope of making a film though the BBC later made an excellent television series starring Derek Jacobi.

As the author of two big West End plays Mortimer was invited to all the smartest theatrical parties, at one of which he met his childhood hero, the unworldly and eccentric Sir John Gielgud, who was bewildered when John and Penny arrived at Tony Richardson's London house with Emily in her carrycot. 'Why on earth didn't you leave your baby at home?' asked Gielgud. 'Are you afraid of burglars?' Mortimer was now so successful as a playwright that he was thinking seriously again of giving up the Law. 'I should have left then,' he told me in 1993, 'because I didn't need to do it any more, but I stayed on because I'd got rather good at it and I enjoyed the forensic excitement of performing in court. Some of the speeches I made to juries were exciting and cross-examining people is very interesting. I cross-examined some solicitor until he fainted in the witness box! The judge gave him smelling salts and said "carry on!".' He did, however, find himself involved in some cases that he would rather have done without, such as one in which he was required to object to the seizure by Her Majesty's Customs and Excise of a consignment of large, battery-operated mechanical penises from Denmark. He won that one after spotting that the chairman of the magistrates had an artificial leg and was able to argue in court that if one man needed an artificial limb another had just as much right to an artificial erection.

In September John and Penny went off on holiday to Italy, where he started work on yet another revealing play, *Collaborators*, which was based on the early years of his marriage to Penelope. Set in the late 1950s, it told of a waspish, ball-breaker wife who suspects that her hard-up, overworked barrister/writer husband is having an affair with his articled clerk, Griselda, and tells him she is going to leave him to marry a producer who wants them to collaborate on a filmscript about their marriage. Bizarrely Mortimer called the alter ego husband Henry Winter – the name he was to give Michael Fenton in his autobiography *Clinging to the Wreckage* – and he recycled many of his personal details and memories. The Winters live in a house in north-west London just like 23 Harben Road. Both drink far too much. The wife, like Penelope, enjoys being depressed and fighting with Henry and is angry that he never says anything serious but is always making jokes. Henry is harassed by numerous noisy, hungry, menacing children and a mountain of unpaid bills and is so useless around the house that when anything goes wrong he tells his wife to 'get a man in'. Their marriage is a vicious game in which they use people like the producer to fight each other but decide to have an affectionate divorce because although they adore each other they can't stand living together. In the end, though, unlike the Mortimers, they stay together and accept bleakly that they are meant for each other.

Penelope made a valiant attempt to rebuild her life by sailing to New York to work for five months on a screenplay of *The Home* for the French director Alain Resnais. There she was befriended by the hag-like, horribly over-made-up, often drunk, sixty-four-year-old Hollywood star Bette Davis, who wanted a part in the film and snarled: '*Ten years* since I had a fuck! What d'you think of that?' Sadly the project came to nothing and Penelope returned to London. Undaunted, she tried to land another film deal by flying to the South of France to meet Dirk Bogarde because Bette Davis had asked her to write a script for the two of them. Nothing came of that, either, but Bogarde became a friend and was to write Penelope numerous letters over the years ahead.

Despite Mortimer's wealth he was still arguing about Penelope's maintenance – 'why should I support you when you're not there to cook my
dinner?' he said – and their lawyers were still locked in combat, but at
least she had the consolation that her children were all doing well.
Madelon was working in Rome as a reporter for the *Daily Mirror* and
happily married to a much older man, the *Mirror*'s popular, twenty-stone,
alcoholic ex-editor Lee Howard. She had just published a romantic
historical novel, *Darling Pericles*, about a thirty-six-year-old Greek prostitute, Aspasia, and her love affair with the aristocratic statesman who
ruled Athens in the fifth century BC – a novel in which the heroine's
father bears a distinct resemblance to Mortimer in that he is compulsively
promiscuous, worships women, believes they are far superior to men and
shuns male company. Caroline's acting had led her to be mentioned often
in the newspapers and in November 1972 twenty-four-year-old Deborah
married a young television producer, Colin Rogers, whose son she was to
have seven months later. Penelope invited John and Penny to the reception at her house in Loudoun Road – John 'looking portly and benevolent,
his wife Penny wearing a little woollen hat'. Sally, now twenty-two,
had dedicated herself to looking after blind and handicapped children,
perhaps because her grandfather had been blind, and Jeremy, now seventeen, was working hard at Bedales to win a place at Oxford and moved
into Penelope's basement with a girl he had met at school and would
one day marry, Polly Fisher, the daughter of a High Court judge and
granddaughter of an Archbishop of Canterbury, Geoffrey Fisher. Penelope, completely free of children at last, returned to the United States for
two months to write her next novel, *Long Distance*, at Yaddo writers'
colony near New York.

John and Penny enjoyed a spring holiday in Tunisia before the opening
of *Collaborators* at the Duchess Theatre in April. John Wood played Henry
Winter, Glenda Jackson his wife, and Mortimer's friend Joss Ackland the
film producer. It was an evening of 'bitchy fun', said the *Sun*'s theatre
reviewer Fergus Cashin, 'a delightful evening with a married couple so
full of pure vitriolic wit that they bring a new dimension to domestic
comedy.' Michael Codron was not as easily pleased. 'The play wasn't
wonderful,' he told me, 'but I managed to get a sensational cast and we
had a very good director, Eric Thompson. It didn't get wonderful reviews
but it was an absolute smash and there was a sequence in it where the
husband and wife say "have you noticed that the word *fuck* could be
substituted for the word *dance* in all the musical numbers of the 1930s?"
They danced and did a *wonderful* sequence of songs singing *fuck* instead

of *dance* – "Shall We Dance", "Dancing on the Ceiling", "You Won't Dance With Me" – and the moment you knew it was about fucking it became hysterical.' In the *Daily Express* however Herbert Kretzmer was not impressed by 'the play's self-regarding style' or by Glenda Jackson's 'special kind of fierceness', of which Milton Shulman said in the *Evening Standard* that her 'set look of cold distaste for her husband would freeze any man into impotence. Even when she breaks into an affectionate dance it is only as sunny as the tinkle of ice cubes.' Equally critical was an American woman who complained to Glenda Jackson about her language. 'She had brought a party of American matrons on an intellectual tour of Europe,' Miss Jackson told me, 'and they'd come to see the play because they'd all seen me in *Elizabeth R* but they were mortified that I allowed my mouth to frame the word *fuck*.'

The play was not a happy experience, wrote Joss Ackland in his diary: 'John [Wood] was far too demented and extrovert and Glenda and I were forced to lose balance and underplay ... Each time we left the stage she and I would put a little tick on the wall as we approached the end of our three-month contracts.' Miss Jackson agreed that 'Joss and I would moan in the wings. I think John Wood had problems with seeing himself as a star, and that always tends to unbalance a play like that which is dependent on just three characters working closely together.' When the Mortimers adopted a new dog, a bitch, they named it Jackson.

While *Collaborators* was breaking the box-office record in its first week at the Duchess Theatre, John and Penny flew to Tunis to celebrate his fiftieth birthday, where many people assumed they were father and daughter even though he still wore his hair youthfully shaggy, greasy and so long that it cascaded over his shoulders. Despite his age Penny was trying to persuade him that they should have another baby as company for Emily but he had suffered more than his fair share of children and resisted stoutly, telling her they could give an only child much more love and time, forgetting how lonely he had been himself as an only child.

In May Mortimer was elected a Fellow of the Royal Society of Literature and began to write the books for two musicals after meeting the lyricist Leslie Bricusse, who had written *Stop the World: I Want to Get Off*. One was about Sherlock Holmes, the other about Henry VIII's six wives, which Bricusse called jokingly *The King and I and I and I and I and I and I*. 'Neither show was destined for success,' he told me. 'We could never cast Sherlock Holmes and I bought John out of both projects, but his

genius is that he can turn to any subject.' Another possibility for Mortimer
was to make another film with his old friend David Niven. 'We went to
stay with him in Cap Ferrat and would always meet him when he came
to England,' Mortimer told me in 2001. 'He'd come to lunch in the
country and was very sweet because we used to ask him for one o'clock
and people would see him walking about the lanes because he thought it
would be rude if he came before one o'clock. He once brought a beauty
queen he'd picked up at London airport and was incredibly charming
and entertaining and would tell his wonderful stories.' Sadly Niven's
second marriage, to a Swedish model, Hjördis Tersmeden, was not a
happy one. 'We kept going out without Hjördis,' said Mortimer, 'and
we went to Monaco to see Prince Rainier and Princess Grace. He was
quite proud of having had this great affair with her, but she was a little
housewifely figure sitting in the corner doing embroidery and Rainier
talked like him in a very English voice: "have a jar".' When Emily was
older she was always to call Niven 'Uncle David'.

Alvin Rakoff was keen to make a movie of *A Voyage Round My Father*
for the cinema with Rex Harrison playing Clifford, Edward Fox as
Mortimer, Lisa Harrow as Penelope and Wendy Hiller as Kath and he,
Mortimer and the film's American producer, Fred Brogger, flew to the
South of France to talk to Harrison about it at his home at Cap Ferrat. 'I
wasn't looking forward to it,' Mortimer told me, 'and I'd just had a bath
and was sitting gloomily on the edge of the bath and the phone rang and
Rex Harrison's voice said, "I just want to say something to you before
you come. I just want to make it clear that you're a complete *shit* and
you always have been. I don't want to say it in front of the other people
so I thought I'd say it on the telephone." My eyes misted over with tears
and then there was a great big laugh and that was Niven impersonating
him. It was so exactly the sort of thing that Rex Harrison *would* do.
Nobody liked Rex. He was a shit, an appalling man. The archetypal Rex
Harrison story was that he was in *My Fair Lady* and George Cukor was
going to direct the film and he said to MGM "I want Rex to be in it"
and they said "no, we want a big star, we want Gary Cooper or someone",
and for a year George Cukor argued that Rex was the only person who
could do it and he kept saying "I'll resign unless we have Rex in it", and
finally they had a great meeting at MGM and Rex Harrison was waiting
in his villa in Portofino, walking up and down, chainsmoking, and the
head of the studio rang up and said, "well, Rex, we've thought for a long
time and George has argued your case for over a year and he's finally
persuaded us and you've got the part." So Rex said, "oh, that's very nice —

but do you think George Cukor is exactly the right person to direct this film?" That's what he was like.'

'Rex was an awful shit,' Rakoff told me. 'A few years later John McEnroe appeared on the tennis scene and I said, "I know that behaviour, that's Rex Harrison!"' One evening they all went out for dinner at a ridiculously expensive restaurant where Harrison kept ordering ridiculously expensive wines. 'He looked wonderful in his white cashmere jacket,' said Rakoff, 'but when the phenomenal bill arrived he just patted his breast pocket and said, "Oh, Alvin, I've forgotten my wallet." He was extraordinarily mean. They didn't take credit cards so Mortimer ended up paying a *fortune* in cash because he'd been in Italy receiving cash for some of his work.' Illegal, tax-free cash? 'Eventually we did get the producer to pay' but not surprisingly he ran out of money and the film was never made.

In August, while Penelope was in America writing her new novel, her mother died in London of bronchopneumonia and kidney failure. She was nearly ninety-seven and left a small estate worth only £3,648.51 (£29,200) to be eked out between Penelope, her brother Paul and Penelope's six children. Penelope had fallen out with both her mother and brother and saw little point in returning for the funeral, but when she finished the novel in little more than a month she dedicated it 'For my mother' even though by the time the book was published her mother had been dead for nine months. The book was another howl of despair, this time about a manic, paranoid, deeply disturbed woman in an asylum and adrift in a torrent of mad, stream-of-conciousness gobbledegook and explicit sexual fantasy. I found it almost unreadable but she felt it was the best book she had written and was exhilarated when the *New Yorker* decided to publish the whole book uncut, which they had done only once before, with J. D. Salinger's *Raise High the Roofbeam, Carpenter*. Suddenly she was rich and celebrated by taking Caroline and Julia to the West Indies for a package holiday in St Lucia, and to add to her euphoria Jeremy won an Exhibition to New College, Oxford, and went up in October 1973 to read English Language and Literature.

In May 1974 there was another rumpus at the National Theatre, where Peter Hall was now the director, when Edward Bond's adaptation of Frank Wedekind's play about the tribulations of adolescence, *Spring Awakening,* included a scene in which a man masturbated onstage. Some of the audience walked out, the Inner London Education Authority deemed the play unsuitable for children, and the first night was 'a dreadful evening', wrote Hall in his diary. 'The audience was stiff and hostile' and the reviews 'patronising and lukewarm'. At the next board meeting several members complained about the play, but Hall reported that 'John Mortimer said he welcomed the masturbating scene as it livened up the proceedings in what he regarded as a boring, old and tendentious play. There was hearty laughter at this sally.'

When Penelope's novel *Long Distance* was published in Britain in June Auberon Waugh called it 'ego-maniac drivel' but the American reviews were so good that she decided to live permanently in New York. What was left for her in England? Jeremy was now nineteen and even David Mercer was about to marry for the third time, this time a German actress, Maria Machado. Penelope sold her houses in Loudoun Road and at Steep, flew to New York, moved into Kurt Vonnegut's old brownstone apartment on East 54th Street and took a job as a creative writing teacher for nine months before moving to Boston, where she became a visiting professor at the university. John was free of her at last, separated by an ocean.

In September he became actively involved in politics for the first time when the actor Stanley Baker persuaded him to join a small group who were advising the Prime Minister, Harold Wilson, about his party political broadcasts during the three-week campaign for the second general election in eight months. His 'expertise was of great help in the treatment of Harold Wilson's TV programmes, and in suggesting many of the passages or themes contained therein', wrote Wilson's personal secretary Marcia Williams in her 1983 memoir *Downing Street in Perspective*. 'Apart from his knowledge of television and his ability to make the most effective use of it, there was the added bonus – for us – that John was such an amusing, clever and entertaining man, whose presence made an enjoyable addition to our small group. Along with Stanley, who had been helping us since 1973, we felt we had an impressive degree of professionalism at our command.' Mortimer in turn found Wilson attractive and jokey and the toothy Mrs Williams charming and fanciable. 'He would give Wilson three or four passages, nice little jewels, on which Wilson could dilate,' Neil Kinnock told me, 'crafted pieces of humorous writing, epigrammatic with a punchline.' Labour won the election with an overall majority of just three seats but Wilson remained Prime Minister and invited Baker and Mortimer to lunch at 10 Downing Street, where he introduced them to Cyprus's head of state, Archbishop Makarios.

At the end of November Mortimer won another accolade when he was elected a Master of the Bench of the Inner Temple, a title similar to that of an Oxbridge Fellow, but his greatest achievement in 1974 was to create the most famous of all his fictional characters, Rumpole of the Bailey. Irene Shubik, the BBC television executive who had produced his play *Infidelity Took Place* in 1967, commissioned him to write an hour-long play about a fat, cynical, sixty-four-year-old, down-at-heel Old Bailey hack barrister, Horace Rumbold – a souped-up version of the previous down-at-heel barristers in *The Dock Brief* and *Infidelity Took Place*. At Oxford, Mortimer told Ms Shubik, Rumbold had been a closet homosexual and like Mortimer himself had won only a poor third-class degree. He was still a junior barrister even though he was the oldest member of his Inner Temple chambers, the head of which was C. H. Wystan, the father of Rumbold's bossy wife, Hilda, whom he called She Who Must Be Obeyed after the hag Ayesha in Rider Haggard's African adventure novel *She*. Rumbold – who lived with Hilda in a state of permanent marital strife in a mansion flat in the Gloucester Road, 25B Froxbury Court – was scruffy, pompous and irascible but endearingly rebellious, treating judges with insolent obsequiousness, calling them 'poor old sweetheart' and prosecutors 'old dear', 'old darling' or 'dear old thing'. When talking about liberty, equality or fraternity he would refer regularly to 'jolly old Jean Jacques Rousseau' or 'my darling Prince Peter Kropotkin'. In his career he had scored only two major triumphs, many years previously, when he had managed to win an acquittal for his client in The Penge Bungalow Murder Trial and won again in The Great Brighton Benefit Club Forgery case thanks to his unexpected under-standing of typewriters. Nowadays his skills include a wide knowledge of bloodstains and *The Oxford Book of English Verse* from which he is given to quoting at length at every opportunity. He also has a fund of scurrilous legal anecdotes and a gargantuan taste for small cigars, steak-and-kidney pudding and Pommeroy's Château Thames Embankment. Then Mor-timer discovered that there was a real barrister called Horace Rumbold so he changed his character's surname to Rumpole 'because he appeared so crumpled, always recovering from hangovers and leading a rather disintegrating life with She Who Must Be Obeyed', he told David Lewin of the *Daily Mail* in 1984, but I was told by a distinguished QC that he told friends that he chose the name Rumpole 'because rump is another word for arse!'. At first he wanted to call the play *My Darling Prince Peter Kropotkin* but Ms Shubik thought that was too obscure, then he suggested *Jolly Old Jean Jacques Rousseau* – just as bad, she said – so they settled on *Rumpole of the Bailey*.

Mortimer wanted Michael Hordern to play Rumpole but he was unavailable on the days that they would want him to record so the director of the play, John Gorrie, suggested a short, fat, ebullient, fifty-four-year-old Australian actor, Leo McKern, whose resonant voice, vast, ripe, bulbous nose and glass eye (following an accident when he was fifteen) seemed just right for Rumpole. McKern had spent three years at the Old Vic, two at the Royal Shakespeare Company, and had been in many films, playing Thomas Cromwell in *A Man For All Seasons*, the Duchess in *Alice in Wonderland* and Thomas Ryan in *Ryan's Daughter*. Even so Mortimer was not keen to cast McKern at first but agreed reluctantly and later admitted that he was so perfect in the part that it was impossible to imagine anyone else in it.

That first Rumpole play was much more serious than the dozens of episodes that were to follow. It showed our hero defending a young black man accused of attempted murder and getting him off by proving that the police have forged his written 'confession' because in fact he can neither read nor write. It told too how Rumpole's adult son Nick disapproves of him, accuses him of being a liar because he makes his living defending people who are probably guilty, and complains that Rumpole has never talked to him seriously but hides behind his jovial legal anecdotes and quotations of poetry. Rumpole is deeply wounded by Nick's accusations and the play ends as he gazes into the middle distance and asks unhappily: 'Who am I, exactly?' None of the regular characters who were to enliven the later Rumpole plays appeared in that first one and 'as with the series that followed, the plot of this first play was slender', Irene Shubik wrote in her 1999 book *Play For Today*. 'It was Rumpole's character and John's satirical analysis, through him, of the law itself and those who live off it and those who break it which were the strength of the scripts.' Mortimer knew that he could not have written the stories had he not been a barrister and told David Lewin that 'we need barristers like Rumpole hacking around the courts, to protect our civil liberties and believing that the police shouldn't make up any more evidence than is absolutely necessary'.

He said that Rumpole was based partly on his father – the clothes, ebullience and poetry – and two barrister friends, James Burge and Jeremy Hutchinson. Burge was a radical advocate who referred often to one of his Russian anarchist heroes as 'my darling old Prince Peter Kropotkin', and to the French philosopher Rousseau as 'my darling old Jean Jacques'. Hutchinson, who had been Gerald Gardiner's junior counsel in the *Lady Chatterley's Lover* case and married to Dame Peggy Ashcroft until their divorce in 1966, was given to calling a horrible judge or prosecutor 'the poor old darling'. Colleagues in Mortimer's chambers at 1 Dr Johnson's Buildings told me that they felt he had used some other barristers' attributes as well. 'I reckon that the model for Rumpole was an incredibly whisky-sodden chap in chambers called John Gardner who was an old hack in probate and divorce,' said Lord Hooson, 'and he had a wife who I'm sure was the model for She Who Must Be Obeyed. There was also a chap called Mickey Bickford-Smith, a marvellous, rumbustious character who became Senior Master of the High Court Bench.' Sir Jonah Walker-Smith, who had recently joined the chambers, mentioned another barrister, James Crespi, 'a vast man of enormous bulk, far fatter than John ever was, who enjoyed the good things of life, eating and drinking. He was wounded when the IRA tried to blow up the Old Bailey and told *The Times*: "It was I with my bulk who saved the Old Bailey"!' There was also of course a lot of Mortimer himself in Rumpole. 'I used to wear the most terrible clothes in court, dropping to pieces,' he told me in 1993, 'but I'm much less stoical than he is. I couldn't stand his life: She Who Must Be Obeyed and all that. He says some of the things I think but that's because I think he's a better person to say it than I am, it's more acceptable. If I say it, it sounds very left-wing but if Rumpole says it, it sounds cuddly.' As for Hilda Rumpole, She Who Must Be Obeyed, Mortimer confessed that she had been inspired by the bossy Conservative Cabinet Minister Margaret Thatcher – Margaret *Hilda* Thatcher – who was then Secretary of State for Education and Science and about to be elected leader of the Tory Party.

Rehearsals for *Rumpole of the Bailey* began in January and McKern never bothered to go and see the Old Bailey because Mortimer's scripts were 'so eminently satisfactory, in atmosphere as in every other way', that he felt it was quite unnecessary, he said in his autobiography. 'On the first reading of the original play ... I knew the man. This happens rarely; it is a strange feeling, and exciting.'

In April Mortimer spoke forcefully at that month's National Theatre board meeting about the NT's increasingly shaky finances. For five years it had been based at the Old Vic while a vast new theatre with several auditoria was being built on the south bank of the Thames at an estimated cost of £16 million (£110 million), but the cost kept increasing and the original completion date of 1973 kept being postponed because of one hold-up after another. By the spring of 1975 the deficit was running at £750,000 (more than £4 million) – and it looked as if it would be yet another year before the new building would be finished. Mortimer had always seen himself as representing the writers, actors and directors on the board rather than the architects, builders and bureaucrats and suggested that the National should forget about the new building and stay on at the Old Vic so that its funds could be spent on higher artistic standards rather than on the running costs of a huge new white elephant. Peter Hall and the chairman, Sir Max Rayne, both agreed with him but by September the first phase of the new theatre, the management offices, was finished and Hall and his staff moved in.

The Mortimers moved too in April into another rented flat in Little Venice at 24B Maida Avenue, a two-bedroom apartment on the ground floor of a four-storey house on the corner of Park Place with a secluded garden and overlooking the canal. By coincidence the tenants in the flat above were Madelon's old boyfriend David Leitch and his wife Jill Neville, whom Mortimer had pursued in vain years earlier. 'John was always devoted to the Canal Zone, as we called it,' Leitch told me. 'It has a history of sexual loucheness and it was a sexy part of London.' Leitch and Mortimer never became friends. 'I always felt that he looked down on me,' said Leitch, 'and that Penny 2 was just there for the night or the weekend. I just don't get on with either of them. He's such an odd bird and there's a lot more there than people might think. The only occasion that Jill and I went to his house at Turville Heath was a particularly disastrous weekend when Penelope 1 turned up for tea — I have an idea it was her birthday and I was surprised to see her because no love had been lost between them when I last saw them together. It was one of those Thames Valley days when suddenly you get these very lowering clouds and we sat in the garden waiting for her and when she finally turned up it was like something out of *Macbeth*. I imagined a lot of very sinister things took place in his and her early lives.' Peggy Ramsay was as surprised as Leitch but for a different reason. 'You're not *still* with that little girl, are you?' she said about Penny to Mortimer. 'I never thought *that*'d last.'

One relationship that did not last was that of Leslie Phillips and Caroline, who was about to appear in a new television series, *Warship*. They split up in October after thirteen years, despite often talking about marriage, because Phillips, a father of four, did not want any more children. Caroline was badly hurt by the end of the affair and became reclusive but was eventually to marry the actor John Bennett.

In September a couple of Graham Greene's short stories that Mortimer had adapted for television were broadcast under the title *Shades of Greene*, one of which starred John Gielgud, and *Rumpole of the Bailey* was eventually broadcast on 16 December 1975. The reviews were excellent and McKern, who had always refused to accept a regular part in a series because he was afraid of becoming typecast, asked Mortimer and Irene Shubik to make five or six more Rumpole plays because Rumpole was such a good character. Ms Shubik tried to persuade the BBC to commission a Rumpole series but the corporation dithered for so long that Mortimer 'fell into a decline', she wrote in *Play For Today*. 'I was surprised by this unexpected behaviour from one who presented such an outwardly jolly personality to the world and was such a success story both as a barrister and a writer.' Later Penny told her Mortimer's 'jolly exterior was deceptive; John got deeply depressed if he wasn't either published or mentioned in at least one of the Sunday papers every week.' After a year of discussions and indecision Ms Shubik resigned from the BBC after fourteen years and took Rumpole, Mortimer and McKern to Thames Television, where she had persuaded the Head of Drama, Verity Lambert, to commission a series for ITV instead.

In January he was back at the Old Bailey to defend another publisher accused of selling an obscene book, this time a Soho publisher, Johannes Hanau, whose 50p paperback *Inside Linda Lovelace* was the tacky sexual autobiography of a twenty-four-year-old American prostitute and porn movie 'star' whose speciality was oral sex and who had made a sleazy film about it, *Deep Throat*. Mortimer asked Jill and David Leitch to testify in court that the book had some literary merit but although they were young, broad-minded and sexually permissive themselves they refused. 'Jill said it was just unalloyed filth and there was absolutely no redeeming literary or human value in it,' Leitch told me. 'It was a saga of the exploitation of a woman and she would have nothing to do with it. The idea that it was worth going into court to fight a battle on behalf of Linda Lovelace was absolutely laughable. She was a sexual slave.'

When the trial started the *Oz* prosecutor Brian Leary was prosecuting again, and again Mortimer trotted out all the libertarian arguments about freedom that he had used five years earlier. Once again he wheeled out what Mary Whitehouse called 'Mortimer's travelling circus of "expert" witnesses' – among them Mervyn Jones, Jeremy Sanford and the aggressively feminist Anna Coote, who was said to have 'a positive attitude to sex'. Once again he suggested to another jury of three women and nine men that by now, surely, in 1976, we were all sufficiently adult and tolerant not to take a bit of sleazy smut seriously but to accept it as a bit of a joke. 'You may be able to save this court ... from making itself ridiculous by using the vast hammer of the criminal law to crush a small sex nut,' he told them, and added jovially: 'You have to ask yourselves whether our society is such, having survived two major wars, that it will actually totter to an end because Miss Lovelace cheerfully indulges in all sorts of sexual shenanigans.' Defending the publishers was twenty-nine-year-old Geoffrey Robertson, the Australian law student who had advised Richard Neville during the *Oz* trial, had recently joined Mortimer's chambers, was to appear in many future cases as Mortimer's junior and to become one of his few male friends. In his book *The Justice Game* Robertson agreed that *Inside Linda Lovelace* was 'a shoddy little book' but during his final speech he made the memorable observation that should there ever be a Sexual Olympics Linda Lovelace would easily be beaten by the sexy novelist Molly Parkin – just as Mortimer had been himself, of course.

Mortimer's jokes and flippant style 'had the judge beside himself with mirth', his fellow QC Sir Tim Cassel told Emma Brockes of the *Guardian* in 2003. Indeed, Judge Rigg found the proceedings so hilarious that at one stage he giggled helplessly behind his notebook when Mortimer's cross-examination referred to a passage in the book about a suspended, seatless chair in which a naked woman could sit and be spun round just above a man lying on his back beneath her. Rigg's summing-up was so tolerant that it made an acquittal inevitable. 'Whether we like it or not,' he said, 'we are living in a permissive society. Sexual matters are treated with a freedom of expression which did not exist ten to fifteen years ago.' After a seven-day trial the notably youthful jury found the accused not guilty. The judge remarked 'if this is not obscene, you may ask yourselves "what is?"' and in a few weeks 600,000 copies of *Inside Linda Lovelace* were sold and from now on even the most degrading, revolting pornography suddenly seemed permissible in Britain. When I asked Mortimer in 1993 if he was proud of the major part he had played in facilitating the deluge of sleazy books and films that flooded into Britain after the Lovelace case, he called it 'a tricky question' and said: 'The fact that I defended those books didn't mean I approved of them any more than if you defend a murderer you approve of murder, but I came to the conclusion that censorship laws are impossible and there's no way of defining a law which is not going to stop free artistic expression. I don't think "anything goes" but what goes is up to private individuals and not the State.' I suggested that British society had been seriously damaged by the brutal trivialisation of sex in books and films since the Lovelace trial. 'Yes,' he said. 'Violence in films is terrible but *all* entertainment has always been violent. A Punch and Judy show is full of violence, and Grimm's *Fairy Tales* and Shakespeare's violent, but I'm not sure there is a direct connection between that violence and violent crime.'

The Times was unimpressed by his argument. Its main leader on the morning after the acquittal forecast under the headline 'THE PORNOGRAPHY OF HATRED' that the verdict 'could well be very damaging for our society. *Inside Linda Lovelace* is indeed pornographic in that it is an erotic book about a vicious girl written in vulgar language, but the most obscene passages have the character of a manual of love making.' It noted that Mortimer always objected to potential jurors who were female, middle aged or middle class since they were more likely to convict and that he had 'a particular gift for amusing irrelevance, which makes the proceedings appear absurd, combined with a passionate devotion to defence of the freedom of pornography'. To show just how far the liberal 'progressives' had gone in their defence of pornography, *The Times* leader recalled the evidence of one of Mortimer's 'expert' *Inside Linda Lovelace* witnesses, Dr Brian Richards – who was in fact not an 'expert' at all but a genial GP from Sandwich – in a trial the previous year in which the defendants had been the magazine publishers Bens Books.

'This is a picture of a female in chains, tied up, and a naked man pointing a sword at the woman's genitals,' said the prosecuting counsel, showing Dr Richards a magazine. 'This is for the public good,' said Dr Richards, 'because it produces a masturbatory situation. I would certainly prescribe this for a patient.' He was shown another photograph, of a naked man beating a woman's genitals with a cat-o'-nine-tails. 'This can stimulate a man,' said Richards. 'It has great therapeutic value.' He was shown a picture of a woman inserting an object into a man's anus. 'Yes, this has therapeutic value for that kind of man,' said Richards. 'I have patients who would be stimulated by this kind of thing.' Then another picture, this time of a man being caned and tied with ropes around his neck and genitals. 'Yes, this is highly therapeutic for masturbation,' said Richards. 'Making a man or woman masturbate is a highly beneficial process.' He was shown yet another picture, this time of a frightened girl manacled and tied up while being lacerated by a man with a bayonet. 'I have known patients who could benefit by masturbating on this,' said the good doctor.

The Times leader concluded that 'the pornographers are sick-minded commercial men who sell images of hatred, and particularly of hatred of women, for vast profit. We need both a law and a law-enforcement which stops them.' Mortimer was so stung by the article that he wrote a letter to the editor in which he said that he was so passionately devoted to free speech that he would defend even *The Times* leader itself should there be any legal attempt to suppress it. *The Times* letters page overflowed for several days with correspondence about the case and a week later the paper carried a powerful article by Ronald Butt in which he questioned whether Mortimer, Robertson and their 'expert' witnesses had consciences. Were they really quite happy, he asked, to ignore the misery of all the exploited women who were forced to pose for degrading pornographic photographs, sometimes with animals? What about the sexual photographs of small Asian children that were so disgusting they would make any decent man or woman weep? 'Do our gallant and flippant upholders of freedom sleep easier when they defend such cases because they know that those who provide the material for such pornography live a long way off?' asked Butt. 'Will there be nothing but wit and weasel words in defence of these, too? . . . The exercise of debating skills is no longer relevant. It is time we let ourselves concentrate on what, with the accumulation of human wisdom, we know to be right and act accordingly.'

Seventeen years later, in 1993, looking back at the social damage that had been done by the Lovelace acquittal, Geoffrey Wheatcroft wrote – in the liberal *Guardian*, of all places – that 'one trial after another found more and more "expert" witnesses testifying to the literary merit of works which had none. This particular treason of the clerks reached its climax with the trial in 1976 of *Inside Linda Lovelace*, a work of pure commercial pornography produced under particularly loathsome circumstances – and whose praises were sung in court by an array of self-appointed illuminati.' In later years Lovelace campaigned herself against the evils of pornography, admitted in her autobiography *Ordeal* that – far from indulging 'cheerfully in all sorts of sexual shenanigans', as Mortimer had put it – she had been a terrified sex slave, grossly abused and exploited, that she had been bullied into becoming an unwilling prostitute, and that her first husband had forced her at gunpoint to make *Deep Throat*. Yet when she died in a car crash in 2002, aged fifty-three, Mortimer wrote an article in the *Evening Standard* in which he showed no remorse for his part in defending the exploitation of her degradation but even claimed that her dreadful experiences simply showed that he had been right and how important it was to allow pornographic films to be made legally rather than by gangsters. The Devil could not have wished for a more devious advocate.

Mortimer and Robertson were such an effective double act that in future they were to be briefed to defend numerous clients who were accused of publishing obscene or pornographic books or films. Mortimer's approach was always to be light-hearted and amused in court. In one trial, about a book in which the authoress suggested various objects that could be shoved up the anus for pleasure, one of the prosecution witnesses, a doctor, warned that this could in fact be dangerous, but Mortimer merely made a joke of it and caused laughter in court by producing an old medical dictionary that listed several unlikely objects that had been found in libidinous patients' rectums, among them a pepper pot marked 'Product of Ramsgate' and a small bust of Napoleon III. Another barrister who regularly acted as Mortimer's junior in these obscenity cases was Ann Mallalieu, who had been the first woman President of the Cambridge Union and was to become a judge and a baroness. They once defended together a book called *The Return of the Enema Bag Rapist* and in 2003 she told Alan Yentob: 'We had some very amusing times. We defended what he referred to in his final speech as "a little spanking magazine", and in Birmingham we defended Gordon Thorne, the King of Porn! But John made jolly sure that the cases that he did were ones that he believed in, if not the material that he sometimes found himself defending, which very often he would have found very offensive. He had always the very best of arguments for why people had the right to choose to look at it if they wanted to. John's great skill as a barrister was in addressing a jury. He never spoke down to a jury, in fact he would almost confide in them. I sometimes felt sorry for the prosecution because he would almost draw the jury into a conspiracy – "we civilised people, we can regard this prosecution as a farce" – and once the jury started laughing you knew the case was in the bag.'

Yet 'John would be the first to admit that he was not a great *lawyer*', I was told by Sir Jonah Walker-Smith, who appeared with Mortimer in several trials where they defended 'pornographers and pornography of little merit, but he got amazing results, acquittals where others probably would not have got acquittals'. Even so, he said, Mortimer 'wasn't a *lawyer's* lawyer. He wouldn't have at his fingertips the names of author-ities, cases, precedents and so forth, but he was a superb jury advocate. He could charm juries, largely through his relaxed manner and also because he could make a joke of things, and the best way in those days was to laugh them out of court. He came across as a very relaxed, nice, tolerant man, and that *did* appeal to juries.'

Judge Angus Stroyan was less impressed by Mortimer. 'In the 1970s his reputation was for defending dirty books,' he told me, 'and they were all *extremely* explicit and quite indefensible. He wasn't a good lawyer. He was competent but a generaliser rather than a particulariser. His general theme was that obscenity was fun, though he never said which particular obscenity was fun and in which particular way. To use a very old-fashioned phrase, he's really a man without any bottom.'

Molly Parkin and Shirley Anne Field would disagree.

Ten

Blasphemy, Bollocks and *Brideshead*
1976–1979

The Labour MP and former Postmaster-General John Stonehouse asked Mortimer and Robertson to represent him when his trial on twenty-one charges of fraud, forgery, theft and conspiracy opened at the Old Bailey at the end of April 1976. He had tried to fake his death in November 1974 by pretending to drown off a beach in Florida, but four days before the trial began he decided foolishly to conduct his own defence and sacked his legal team. It was a huge mistake. Throughout the sixty-eight-day trial he was even more out of his depth than he had been off the beach in Miami and was sentenced to seven years in prison.

Mortimer decided to betray his socialist principles too by dressing four-year-old Emily in a little red hat and blazer and sending her to a private, fee-paying school, Kensington School for Girls, telling Penny glibly that 'you can't sacrifice your child's education just because you're a socialist'. Emily had already started bullying him: in the mornings he would wake, wash and dress her and she would sit on the fridge, dangling her skinny little legs, and squeak 'cook my eggs, you old bugger!' and then spit them at him if they were not cooked to her liking. 'I was awful to him,' she said and told Daphne Lockyer of the *Sunday Express Magazine* in 1998: 'If I'd been brought up entirely by my dad I'd be the most horrible woman now, so indulged. He would hate to be cast as the disapproving patriarch or the rotten spoilsport. If it had been left up to him I'd have got away with murder.' Among the rest of the family Julia had her first baby, Jeremy was about to leave Oxford with a 2:1 degree in English, and although Penny was not yet thirty she was already worrying about getting old. 'We were having dinner with David Niven one night in a Chelsea restaurant and she said, "Oh god, I've got these terrible wrinkles on my face," ' Mortimer told me in 2001, 'and David said, "Even if I took every pill there is in the world I'll still be dead in five years." He was very conscious of dying and the passing of time even though there was no sign yet of the motor neurone disease that would kill him a few years later.'

In March the National Theatre left the Old Vic and moved at last into its huge new building on the South Bank, Mortimer finished writing two short new stage plays, *The Fear of Heaven* and *The Prince of Darkness*, and was commissioned by the Associated Television mogul Sir Lew Grade to write a series of six fictional one-hour plays about the life of William Shakespeare. It was one of the most difficult scripts he had ever written, he said, because so little was known about the Bard, so much had to be made up yet still be possible and historically accurate, and it took him much longer than the six months he had expected. Yet he loved doing it because he had always idolised Shakespeare and knew a great deal about his plays. One rumour circulating soon after Shakespeare died in 1616 had suggested that when he had first come to London from Stratford in 1590, at the age of twenty-seven, his first job had been as a parking attendant looking after the horses outside a theatre, so Mortimer made that the subject of his first episode, *Dead Shepherd*, in which young Will is shown as a wily ostler, friend of Christopher Marlowe, and given to lying and boasting about his life in the theatre. The second episode imagined him as a young actor and playwright in London who has just written *Richard III* at a time when the city is threatened by the plague. The third showed him living in luxury under the wing of his patron and lover the Earl of Southampton and having at the same time a secret affair with the Dark Lady of the sonnets, whom Mortimer imagined as the young wife of a brutal judge addicted to hanging. The fourth had Shakespeare bringing his young son Hamnet from Stratford to London, where he falls ill and dies at the age of eleven. The fifth presented him at the court of Elizabeth I, where he and his fellow players flirt with treason when the rebellious Earl of Essex asks them to perform his play about regicide, *Richard II*. And Mortimer set the last episode after the old queen's death in 1603 when Shakespeare's jealous wife, Anne Hathaway, discovers his secret love poems and starts asking awkward questions about the Dark Lady of the sonnets.

Mortimer went off to Sri Lanka to work on the script and ATV built at Elstree the most expensive British television scenery ever at a cost of

£200,000 (£952,000) on sets that included a cobbled street flanked by exact models of Elizabethan houses and a replica of the Globe Theatre. About £800,000 was spent on the series in all (nearly £4 million) and filming started in June with the dashing, doe-eyed Tim Curry – the star of *The Rocky Horror Show* – as Shakespeare, the swarthy Ian McShane as Christopher Marlowe, Nicholas Clay as the Earl of Southampton, Meg Wynn Owen as Anne Hathaway and Patience Collier as Elizabeth I. John's script was far from perfect and the director, Peter Wood, 'rewrote most of it', I was told by the National Theatre's former literary consultant Derek Granger, who was also a senior producer at Granada Television.

While the first episode of *Will Shakespeare* was about to be filmed Mortimer's two short, mischievous, one-act plays about religion and the Church, *The Fear of Heaven* and *The Prince of Darkness*, opened at the Greenwich Theatre in May under the title *Heaven and Hell* with Denholm Elliott playing the lead in both. In the first Elliott was Lewis Luby, an English atheist who is injured when a balcony in Tuscany collapses, is taken unconscious to a hospital where the ceiling of his ward features a huge fifteenth-century painting of Heaven, comes round from his coma, sees the painting, and assumes that he must be dead and that the huge toe of God in the painting must be proof that God exists. To make matters worse he is terrified that Mary Whitehouse is getting on a bit and may suddenly turn up in Heaven too. In the next bed is another Englishman who Luby discovers jealously has had much more fun during his life and has blithely committed incest, adultery and buggery, whereas Luby has slept with only one woman, his wife. The second play, *The Prince of Darkness*, which also starred Eleanor Bron, told a wonderfully diabolical story about one of those trendy Church of England bishops of the 1970s who were always on television and one of those modern Church of England vicars who had trouble believing in God, sin, Hell, prayer, or most of the Bible but acted instead as a caring social worker for homosexuals, sado-masochists, people who like being beaten, bondage and mackintosh freaks and other deviants. The atheist vicar is disconcerted by the arrival of a new curate who appears to believe in everything that a priest should believe in and performs embarrassingly vulgar miracles, among them the sudden appearance in the vicar's fridge of loaves and fishes and bottles of water that keep turning into wine. The curate, who has been sent to test the vicar's lack of faith, is of course the Devil himself – the Prince of Darkness. 'One of the messages of the play', Mortimer told the *Evening Standard* wickedly a year later, playing yet

again the Devil's Advocate, 'is that if you abolish the idea of sin you take
a lot of fun out of sex. It's a very religious message.'

In November the Greenwich Theatre revived *A Voyage Round My Father*
yet again but Mortimer was upset when fourteen judges of the European
Court of Human Rights in Strasburg decided by thirteen votes to one
that the British courts had been right to ban *The Little Red School Book*
and to reject Mortimer's appeal against its conviction. The book had
undoubtedly been aimed at children, said the judges, and had had
'pernicious effects on the morals of many of its readers'. Mortimer complained to Herbert Kretzmer of the *Daily Express* that 'the puritan
backlash is now absolute and predominant' – an absurd claim considering
it was only ten months since he had won the Linda Lovelace trial. 'Nobody
cares about free speech any more,' he moaned. 'The puritan streak in
England is deathly and terribly depressing. Now we've got this awful,
paternalistic, self-protective society which insists on putting people into
seat-belts and Sikhs into crash helmets. The State is becoming our nanny
and it's all very sad.'

There were more complaints at the National Theatre board meeting
in mid-December that the production of the play that Peter Hall had
chosen for the Queen to see when she had opened the South Bank theatres
in October, Carlo Goldoni's Venetian comedy *Il Campiello*, had been
dreadful and that Albert Finney's uncut *Hamlet* had not been much better.
To Hall's irritation it was suggested that maybe he needed a panel of
experts to help him choose plays in future. Hall responded with a speech
that lasted two hours and was staunchly supported by Mortimer, who
argued that it was the business of the director, not the board, to choose
plays, and was rewarded for his loyalty when Hall commissioned him to
translate another Feydeau farce, *The Lady From Maxim's*.

The new year, 1977, brought him a firm deal at last to write the first
Rumpole series for Thames Television and a brief to appear in a spy case
in February when he applied for bail for two journalists who worked for
the underground listings magazine *Time Out*. Duncan Campbell and
Crispin Aubrey had been arrested under the Official Secrets Act for
endangering national security after Campbell had written an article that
revealed the existence of a secret electronic eavesdropping intelligence
network at the Government Communications Headquarter (GCHQ) in
Cheltenham. Mortimer and Robertson, his regular sidekick, realised that
the best way to free Campbell and Aubrey from Brixton prison was not
to argue in court about freedom of the Press but to appeal to the judge's
snobbery, so Mortimer told the judge that Campbell had just come down

from Oxford and that both men came from blameless, loving, middle-class families and were guilty of nothing but the sort of foolish high jinks that all well-bred Oxford undergraduates had enjoyed since time immemorial. It worked. The two defendants were freed but the third, John Berry, a working-class social worker, was kept in prison. When the case finally came up at the Old Bailey eighteen months later Mortimer was too busy to conduct their defence and handed it over to his Rumpolish friend Jeremy Hutchinson – by now a Labour life peer and vice-chairman of the Arts Council – with Robertson as his junior, and the defendants were acquitted.

Mortimer's fame was now so great that when Penelope returned from Boston in May to live in England again she was appalled to find that he had become a celebrity who seemed to grin out of every newspaper and joked publicly about his marriages to Penny 1 and Penny 2. When he appeared on Terry Wogan's television show he was introduced not just as a famous lawyer and writer but also as a notorious womaniser and told the audience of millions jovially that he had been married when he was 'about fourteen to someone with five children' and that 'I can't feel loyalty to a wife simply because she's my wife. One's only duty and obligation is to oneself.' She waited fifteen years before she took her revenge by writing her autobiography *About Time Too*, but to escape her ex-husband's constant presence in newspapers and on television she left London and bought a cottage in the tiny Gloucestershire Cotswolds hamlet of Chastleton, near Stow-on-the-Wold, where she started to write her first volume of autobiography, *About Time*, took up gardening obsessively – 'I suppose it was some sort of displacement activity,' said Jeremy – and escaped from John's world with huge relief by going into semi-hibernation for thirteen years.

As Mortimer worked on the six episodes of the first Rumpole series and Thames Television began to build permanent studio sets of the Old Bailey, Rumpole's chambers and the Rumpoles' flat in the Gloucester Road, Mortimer took Irene Shubik along to the Old Bailey to see him in action in a bottom-smacking trial. 'We lunched extremely well at a nearby restaurant where John, replete with good food and wine, drew out his brief and skimmed through it some ten minutes before the proceedings were due to start,' she wrote in *Play For Today*. 'Whether this was a revision or the first time he had ever read it, I don't know. He seemed remarkably unworried and casual about the whole thing. His client, who published a magazine devoted to bottom-smacking, smackers and smackees, was on trial for obscenity. The very respectable-looking members of the jury each had a copy of the bottom-smacking magazine in front of them and were several times solemnly referred by the judge to various pictures of bottoms which they equally solemnly examined. It was an instant *Rumpole* in the making.' Ms Shubik was surprised by Mortimer's cavalier attitude towards his legal work. 'He treated the whole thing as a sort of *joke*,' she told me. 'It was terribly last-minute considering that he was one of the highest-paid lawyers. John found the case very funny. Chad Varah [the founder of the Samaritans] was there and saying how good it was for all these people that they could see such a book because otherwise they might go out and smack strangers' bottoms, and the judge was saying with a straight face, "Would the ladies and gentleman of the jury kindly refer to the picture of the bottom at the bottom of page three."' She was also amazed by Mortimer's energy. Not only was he rising before dawn, finishing the Shakespeare plays as well as a book based on them and writing the Rumpole series, he was also writing a series about Rasputin, a new play, another French farce, barristering all day, enjoying long lunches and drinking heavily, yet he seemed to spend each evening 'at some "in" party or first night, usually well reported in the newspaper gossip columns', she said. Mortimer's secret was in fact that he tried to be in bed each night by ten thirty, no matter how much fun the party was, but he came close to cutting out one of his many commitments that summer when he, Peter Hall and the entire National Theatre board nearly resigned because the NT's finances were in such a mess. The deficit was now more than a million pounds because of yet another delay in opening one of the South Bank's theatres, the Olivier; an increase in the number of employees from 450 to 750; and a six-day strike by the stage-hands. The National's financial problems were so serious that a few months later Hall, now Sir Peter, wrote a letter of resignation before tearing it up.

Of all the characters in the first Rumpole play only Rumpole himself, Hilda, their son Nick and Rumpole's gentle barrister friend George Frobisher survived into the first series, for which Mortimer created a lively cast of new characters to inhabit Rumpole's chambers and appear in most future episodes. First was Guthrie Featherstone, a smooth, elegant barrister who becomes an MP, QC and beats Rumpole in the election for a new head of chambers, much to the chagrin of She Who Must Be Obeyed. Next came finicky young Claude Erskine-Brown, Rumpole's disapproving colleague, who wears striped shirts, elastic-sided Chelsea boots and believes that Rumpole's untidiness, vulgar clients and threadbare old wig (bought second-hand from a retired Chief Justice of Tonga) seriously lower the chambers' tone. Then Mortimer invented the sexy, young, French-perfumed Phillida Trant, the chambers' first woman barrister, and old Uncle Tom Rowley, who hasn't had a brief for fifteen years, and the two clerks, Albert and Henry, and Rumpole's dreaded *bête noir*, His Honour Judge Roger Bullingham, a thick-necked, beetroot-faced, choleric old bigot who mutilates the English language, hates blacks, Asians and foreigners, and has rarely sentenced anyone to less than seven years in jug if he can possibly help it. Each episode was also much jollier than the first play.

Will Shakespeare, a book of stories rather than a novel, was published in June to coincide with the broadcast of the television series in the autumn, though that was eventually delayed until the spring of 1978. It had jokey chapter headings – 'Of How Shakespeare Lied About His Life At The Rose Theatre, And How An Honest Man Lost A Capon' and 'Of How Shakespeare's Sonnets Were Demanded Of Him By A Gentleman In Black Garments' – but he told Philippa Toomey of *The Times* that he no longer enjoyed writing novels: 'It's very lonely. Novels come out and nobody gives a party and you never spot anybody reading them [but] go into a theatre and . . . you can hear them laugh and you are part of an enterprise. And you make friends – for a short while.' He told her too that he was depressed by a new puritan backlash against the Permissive Society. Mary Whitehouse had recently initiated a private prosecution against the fortnightly 22,000-circulation paper *Gay News* for printing what she claimed was a blasphemous poem about the possible homosexuality of Jesus Christ, and Mortimer had been briefed to defend the thirty-two-year-old editor, Denis Lemon. It was the first blasphemy case for fifty-five years, since 1922.

The public prosecutor adopted the case so that the trial became most appropriately 'the Queen versus *Gay News*'. It opened at the Old Bailey in July 1977 before a seventy-two-year-old judge, His Honour Alan King-Hamilton, QC, with John Smythe, a committed Christian, prosecuting, Mortimer defending Lemon, and Geoffrey Robertson defending the publishers, Gay News Ltd, as well as acting as Mortimer's junior. The sixty-six-line poem that had inspired the prosecution, 'The Love That Dares to Speak Its Name', had been written by the Professor of Poetry at Amherst College in Massachusetts, fifty-four-year-old James Kirkup, and described Jesus's crucifixion and a Roman centurion's homosexual lust for the body of Christ when he was lowered from the cross. On the first morning Mortimer realised glumly that all twelve members of the jury – seven men and five women – had sworn their oaths on the

New Testament and so were probably Christians, even though he and Robertson had challenged fourteen potential jurors, but he opened the defence by contending that no blasphemy law existed any longer because England was now a multi-religious society. The judge disagreed and Mortimer and Robertson had to listen to Smythe telling the jury that the poem was 'so vile it would be hard for the most perverted imagination to conjure up anything worse'. Even now, thirty years later, the poem seems unacceptably unsavoury. In it the centurion describes how the body of the dead Christ, 'well hung', is lowered from the cross and how he kisses the corpse, licking its tongue, wounds and somehow still-throbbing penis. He claims that Jesus has 'had it off' not only with Herod's soldiers, Pontius Pilate, John the Baptist and Paul of Tarsus but also with all the apostles including Judas ('a great kisser'). The centurion lies naked beside Christ's cold body, ravishes it, and is in turn 'enter'ed by the corpse. It is difficult to believe that any devout Christian would not be deeply offended by the poem.

At the end of the first day Mrs Whitehouse wrote in her diary that 'Mortimer, usually so confident and full of joking assumption that, of course, the prosecution's case is a lot of silly nonsense and no one could really take it seriously, seemed much less so today'. The second day, she wrote, 'was like something out of a fantasy – Mortimer would not concede that the man in the dock *was* Denis Lemon or that the copy of *Gay News* which the judge held up in his hand *was* a copy of *Gay News* or, for that matter, that the paper existed.' Nor was Mortimer mollified when a group of homosexuals demonstrated with posters outside the Old Bailey and a barrister greeted him in the robing room by growling: 'I see you've got your friends from Rent-a-Bum outside today.'

Mortimer's old Oxford contemporary Francis King, now a respected novelist, literary critic, chairman of the Society of Authors and friend of Denis Lemon, agreed to give evidence for the defence as a literary expert even though he did not think much of the poem, and Robertson had again lined up the ubiquitous novelist Margaret Drabble, but King-Hamilton ruled that literary merit was irrelevant in a case of blasphemy, nor did it matter whether the poet, editor or publisher had *intended* to commit blasphemy. When it looked as if no witnesses at all could give evidence Robertson called Drabble and *The Times* columnist Bernard Levin not as literary 'experts' but to give character evidence in support of the paper – in vain. In a final, desperate attempt to save the day Mortimer told the jury in his summing-up, as he had in the *Oz* trial, what a waste of a lovely summer it was for them all to be sitting in an air-conditioned, windowless courtroom and said: 'Perhaps you rubbed your eyes when the charge of blasphemy was read out. Perhaps you thought we'd all been transported in a time machine back to the Middle Ages.' Unwisely he accused Mrs Whitehouse of having brought the prosecution 'out of malice', which the judge said was rubbish, and when the jury retired after seven days to consider its verdict for five hours Mrs Whitehouse and a group of her supporters prayed loudly in the corridor for a verdict of guilty. Their prayers were granted by ten votes to two, which pleased the judge, who said: 'It is perhaps being a little too optimistic in this era of obscenity, but it is possible to hope that by this verdict the pendulum of public opinion is beginning to swing back to a more healthy climate.' He fined Lemon £500 (£2,055), ordered him to pay a fifth of the estimated £8,000 prosecution costs (£32,900) and gave him a suspended sentence of nine months' imprisonment, which the judge admitted in his memoirs five years later had been too harsh because the fine and costs were quite enough. Gay News Ltd was fined £1,000 and ordered to pay the rest of the costs, and *The Times* and *Daily Telegraph* both agreed with the verdicts though Robertson later accused King-Hamilton of being unfair to the defence in his summing-up and the scandal rag *Private Eye* published such a vicious attack on the judge that the chairman of the Old Bailey journalists, C. Doherty, wrote to him to say that they were appalled by the article and that 'in the view of the Press Room staff you are held in the highest esteem as one of the most fair-minded and competent judges to have adorned this famous building'. When the case went to the Court of Appeal seven months later the three judges supported King-Hamilton, praised his summing-up and upheld the convictions, as did the House of Lords when another five judges rejected a further appeal by three votes to two.

'One didn't have to be a Christian to be revolted [by the poem],' wrote Judge King-Hamilton, who was Jewish, in his memoirs, though Mortimer's final speech to the jury had been 'very effective. Horace Rumpole would have been very proud to have made such a speech. I had to interrupt him once or twice, though, for typically Rumpolean observations.' Mortimer was so shocked to lose that he drove to Turville Heath Cottage, where he had recently had a swimming pool built – an amenity that his mother would have found incredibly vulgar – and had a long swim alone until his anger evaporated. The next morning at his flat in Maida Avenue he gave an interview to an *Evening Standard* reporter who found a Chagall on the wall, Schubert on the radio, and the furniture 'rather old and comfortable', like Mortimer himself: 'He doesn't seem to take a great deal of care about his appearance. He is overweight (there is rather more than the suggestion of a paunch) and the long hair hangs lank over his collar.' Mortimer was still depressed by the verdict. 'A new Puritan Age is darkening our doors,' he said morosely. He cheered up a few days later when he gave another interview to Mark Amory for *The Sunday Times Magazine*, who found him giggly and 'not so much plump or rounded as fat', though Mortimer did claim yet again that he worried all the time that he did not earn enough – a ludicrous remark considering he was now earning about £40,000 a year as a barrister and the same again as a writer (a total of about £329,000 a year in 2005).

During the trial Mrs Whitehouse referred admiringly in her diary to the silver-tongued Robertson as the Devil's Advocate but the title was equally applicable to Mortimer, his leader in the case, and a week later, appropriately, an extended version of his play about Satan, *The Prince of Darkness*, opened at the Richmond Theatre before moving in July to the Garrick. Renamed *The Bells of Hell*, this time it starred Tony Britton as the Devil and had a couple of new characters, one a young man who is consumed by an aching lust for Mrs Thatcher.

In August the National Threatre began to rehearse Mortimer's adaptation of *The Lady From Maxim's*, a musical with plenty of jolly songs, in which a married Parisian doctor awakes after a drunken night at Maxim's to find to his horror that he has brought a prostitute home with him and his wife is due back at any minute. The result is the usual French farce chaos of embarrassment, panic, rushing around, misunderstanding, mistaken identity and sexual innuendo. Mortimer's version was to open at the NT's Lyttelton Theatre in October, starring Stephen Moore, Michael Bryant and Edward Hardwicke, with Morag Hood as the lady from Maxim's, and although the original play was notably laboured and unfunny Mortimer won good reviews for his translation although the critics were not so kind about the actors and the production itself.

For many years the theatrical agent who represented Evelyn Waugh's estate, Anthony Jones of A. D. Peters, had been trying to land a deal for a major film of Waugh's favourite novel, *Brideshead Revisited* – about Oxford, religion, male friendship, snobbery and the English class system in the 1920s and 1930s. Derek Granger, one of six senior producers at Granada Television, had been trying for years to persuade Jones to let him make instead a lavish six-part television series. Eventually Jones agreed in 1977 though he and the estate kept tight control over the choice of a writer to adapt the novel and insisted that they should also approve the script. First they stipulated that the screenplay should be written by one of the agency's clients, Alan Bennett, who agreed but changed his mind because he thought it would take too long, so Jones then chose Mortimer, whom Peters had taken on as a client after Peggy Ramsay's death. 'He was a big figure by then,' Granger told me. At first Mortimer had his doubts. 'It's by no means my favourite Waugh novel,' he told Sheridan Morley during an interview for *The Times* four years later, 'and there were certain aspects of it that I found deeply nasty, notably his attitude to the General Strike and the patronising of Rex Mottram. But then I found something fascinating in the preface to one of the later editions, where Waugh says that the success of *Brideshead* tells you more about 1946 than about 1925; it's the memory of a golden age recreated for a very austere time.'

As Mortimer began to adapt *Brideshead* he was briefed to challenge the Greater London Council's refusal to licence two new Soho porn cinemas, a case that he won despite vociferous objections from local residents who said they were afraid of attacks by the pornographers. He was then offered a case so bizarre that he found it irresistible: to make a brief appearance in a lowly magistrates' court in Nottingham to go into battle on behalf of the Sex Pistols punk rock band and the boss of their record label, twenty-seven-year-old Richard Branson of the Virgin Record Company, against a charge of indecency because they had used the word 'bollocks' in the title of their first album, *Never Mind the Bollocks, Here's the Sex Pistols*. The Pistols were notoriously crude and violent, a group of foul-mouthed yobs who belched, swore and spat at their audiences, but when Branson approached Mortimer to defend the case he said breezily: 'What on earth's wrong with "bollocks"? It's one of my favourite words.' Branson telephoned a linguistics expert at Nottingham University, the Professor of English Studies, James Kingsley, who told him that 'bollocks' had been an eighteenth-century nickname for priests and had come to mean 'rubbish' because they tended to talk a lot of it. The single defendant was the manager of Virgin's local shop, twenty-five-year-old Christopher Seale, who was charged under the Indecent Advertisements Act of 1889. When the trial came to court in November with Geoffrey Robertson riding shotgun for the defence as usual Mortimer tried to keep the Pistols themselves as far away as possible because 'one had green teeth!' he told Deborah Ross of the *Independent* in 1999, forgetting the notoriously verdant hue of his own. 'Are we strong enough to tolerate Anglo-Saxon and vivid language even if we disapprove?' he asked the three magistrates but it was Professor Kingsley who clinched the case. He explained the ancient meaning of 'bollocks' and testified that not even a priest could object to it. 'How can you be so sure?' asked the prosecutor. Kingsley rolled down the neck of his polo-neck sweater to reveal a dog collar: he was a priest as well as a professor. With great reluctance the magistrates dismissed the case.

'It always fascinated me how Mortimer managed to be the fashionable left-of-centre lawyer who got involved in all the fashionable cases representing the defence against the Establishment, the Michael Mansfield of his period,' I was told by *The Times* literary editor and publisher Ion Trewin, 'and yet remained an Establishment man himself, the champagne socialist yet also a member of the Garrick Club. It was a wonderful way of publicising himself and getting in the headlines.'

Mortimer's next case, however, was far from fashionable: he flew to Singapore to defend Ben Jeyaretnam, a Christian Tamil parliamentary candidate for the opposition Workers' Party who was being sued for libel by the brilliant but dictatorial Chinese Prime Minister, Lee Kuan Yew, for something he had said during the general election campaign the previous year. Mortimer knew so little about libel that he had to consult his law books but he accepted the brief and flew out to Singapore with Penny in December. Appalled by the island's draconian laws, which still allowed hanging, they did the town and saw the sights. In Bugis Street Mortimer nervously ate a hundred-year-old boiled egg and chatted with a beautiful, deep-voiced transsexual prostitute. In the Raffles Hotel they had dinner with John's old Dragon School contemporary Desmond Neill, who had played the Earl of Northumberland in *Richard II* in 1937. In the Raffles, too, an old man told them that in the glory days of the British Empire he and his friends had always tried to avoid talking to one of the hotel's regular patrons, Somerset Maugham, because 'he was such a tremendously boring old bugger!'

During the trial Mortimer was cycled to court each day in a trishaw to face his opponent, another English QC, Robert Alexander, and a Chinese judge as well as the hatchet-faced Mr Lee, who had taken a double first in Law at Cambridge and was himself a member of the Inner Temple. There was no doubt that Jeyaretnam's remarks had been defamatory, so Mortimer spent an afternoon cross-examining Lee and trying to persuade him to agree that it was rather demeaning for the Prime Minister of a democratic nation to be trying to squeeze money out of another politician because he had expressed a democratic opinion that was spoken only in the heat of a general election that Mr Lee had in any case won by a landslide. It was a cunning argument but swiftly undermined when Jeyaretnam himself demanded £5,000 from a local newspaper in damages for something it had printed about him. He lost the case, was ordered to pay about £35,000 in costs and damages (£144,000) and had to sell his house although he continued his political career and three years later won a seat at last in Singapore's Parliament. During a lull in the case the Mortimers took a break and flew to Bangkok, where they stayed by coincidence in the Somerset Maugham suite of the Oriental Hotel, long considered by many to be the best hotel in the world.

Back in England John found himself in the middle of another row at the National Theatre, where Peter Hall was furious about a critical history of the theatre by John Elsom and Nicholas Tomalin and was trying to persuade the board to stop the NT bookshop selling it. As a notorious defender of the freedom of the Press, Mortimer spoke against any ban but supported Hall when the board passed a vote of confidence in him and extended his contract by another three years.

In February 1978 Mortimer was back in the Appeal Court to protest against the conviction and sentences of Denis Lemon and *Gay News* seven months previously. Armed with more than sixty legal books, a pile of old papers, a heavy cold and his usual gofer, Robertson, he told the three judges, Lords Roskill and Eveleigh and Mr Justice Stocker, that the Old Bailey verdict had made the law of blasphemous libel more stringent than it had been even before the reign of Queen Victoria, and he argued that Judge King-Hamilton had badly misdirected the jury, expecially in his ruling that it did not matter at all whether the poet, editor or newspaper had actually *intended* to insult or attack Christianity. The hearing lasted five days and the appeal was rejected, the convictions upheld, and King-Hamilton's direction to the jury found to have been 'full, clear and correct', though the judges did set aside Lemon's suspended prison sentence and gave leave for a further appeal to be made to the House of Lords.

In March Mortimer told David Gillard of the *Daily Mail* that he listened to the radio much more than he watched TV and singled out especially the Brian Hayes phone-in on LBC 'because he's insulting to everyone who rings up, and I quite like getting sex advice from Anna Raeburn in the middle of the night', but he could not stand the idolised Alistair Cooke's *Letter From America*, which he said was 'paralytically irritating. Hearing a man from Manchester with a spurious American accent rambling on about nothing at all except the weather in Vermont just about drives me up the wall.' It is astonishing that he found any time to listen to the radio for he had just finished the six new Rumpole scripts and the six *Brideshead Revisited* scripts and had delivered six short stories based on the Rumpole scripts to the chief fiction editor at Penguin, Judith Burnley, for a paperback collection to be published to coincide with the TV series in April. He was able to take on so much work only because he wrote too quickly and without enough care. 'He was a lazy, sloppy writer,' Irene Shubik told me. 'Frankly he couldn't write a real plot. It was all anecdotes strung together, and there was never any heart in it. There was always humour but it didn't get any deeper than that, either intellectually or emotionally. And if you asked him to make any changes he'd say "yes, darling, of course" but then he wouldn't do it or only half do it. He was the definitive show-off.'

Judith Burnley agreed that Mortimer was a careless writer. 'He's a bit sloppy,' she told me, 'as he was with his ties when lunching. We'd have long lunches at the White Elephant with masses of champagne, and he was always crumpled and endearingly scruffy and he'd have his breakfast egg all down his tie. He was a great bon viveur and we laughed a lot, and he was *very* flirty and suggested further lunches, but I can believe that story about mould on his teeth and I never thought he was sexy. He still looks like a child and his messy eating is very childlike. He must have had something in his background that made him want to go on being a baby. If you think of him as a cartoon you would think of him in a high-chair throwing the food all around and having it all over his face. I'm sure there must have been something strange in his childhood and about his mother. His "I'm a naughty little dirty baby" persona must have something to do with that. I wonder if he liked sex to be dirty? Maybe he did. If he liked to be punished and smacked that's beginning to add up.'

Mortimer always gave the impression that he no longer committed adultery after his marriage to Penny but it seems that now – seven years after Emily's birth – he succumbed to the seven-year itch, according to a Granada Television employee who told me that a girl who worked there used to boast that whenever Mortimer visited their offices in London he would ravish her in the ladies' lavatory. More disturbing for Granada were Mortimer's *Brideshead Revisited* scripts, which were not what Derek Granger wanted at all. At sixty Granger had won numerous prizes for his work in television, had been Head of Drama at London Weekend Television, head of the play department at Granada, co-produced plays with Laurence Olivier, won a BAFTA award for *Country Matters*, spent a year each producing *World in Action* and *Coronation Street*, produced numerous other current affairs programmes, documentaries and situation comedies, and was about to become a council member of the Royal Court

Theatre, but he was deeply disappointed by Mortimer's scripts. 'Sidney Bernstein, my boss at Granada, a genius and an extraordinarily wise and good man, rang me and said, "I'm not sure about those scripts, Derek,"' Granger told me. 'Then one of the German co-financiers expressed much disappointment in the Mortimer adaptation and said, "Where are the Proustian overtones, Derek?" And then the director of the series, Michael Lindsay-Hogg, said, "What are we going to do about these scripts? Oh, to hell with it. Why don't we just shoot the book?" and that's virtually what we did. We started rewriting from scratch and discarded John's commissioned material so that in the end John didn't write a single word of the television version of *Brideshead*. I wrote it entirely with a young writer from the BBC, Martin Thompson, and Michael Lindsay-Hogg made lots of suggestion, and when he was held to a contract to direct a play in New York and forced to go to America he was replaced by Charles Sturridge, who also made valuable contributions. Michael and I had agreed that we needed Charles Ryder's voice-over, the first-person commentary of the novel, which Mortimer had hardly used, and Charles saturated the story with it and it became one of the drama's main ingredients. It was a crushing task but I don't want to claim enormous credit for writing it because it is *so* close to the book that *Waugh* scripted it, but it had to be brought down to look like a proper filmscript. Many of the passages of the novel are virtually taken in their entirety, though on several occasions Martin and I created dramatised scenes which Waugh did not include in the novel.'

When Thompson, a twenty-nine-year-old freelance writer, joined the *Brideshead* team 'Lindsay-Hogg was already casting and the scripts were way behind the casting!' he told me. 'The decision had been taken to go back to the book and be faithful to it so Derek and I spent many hours tearing pages out of the book, pasting and drafting. It was great fun, the beginning of a fascinating eighteen-month process. I found not long ago a copy of the memo that Evelyn Waugh sent to Hollywood moguls about the way he thought *Brideshead* should be filmed and it vindicates our approach because we followed it almost to the letter. Waugh would have been happy with our version.'

Lindsay-Hogg, now Sir Michael and living in Los Angeles, told me that he had loved the book, knew it well and had always liked Mortimer. 'We'd met socially in the early Seventies because we had a lot of friends in common,' he said. 'I always found him funny and full of charm and bonhomie. I also saw him a lot on television when he usually was speaking for liberal and humane causes. He was always the liberal side in the argument and I was very taken by that aspect of him because it seemed very decent.' But he thought that although Mortimer's script had 'turned the book into a nice little telly play it had set off in the wrong direction, on a perfectly decent road but just the wrong way. He'd cross-cut or parallelled the stories of Charles Ryder and Julia, and the whole great engine of the Waugh novel had been dismantled and there were just little bits and pieces of it and a lot of his own dialogue and his own situations which he'd invented. He was setting it up as the love story of Charles and Julia, which it partly is, but he was trying to contain the book in a way in which it couldn't really be contained. I don't think we used *any* of John's original script. We certainly didn't use the form.'

Granger told me that he did not think it was entirely Mortimer's fault that his scripts did not work. 'He and I had had comparatively brief discussions on method and approach but it was never the close collaboration I usually enjoyed with writers I'd commissioned myself. I found him daunting and we didn't talk on equal terms because although he's too clever to be actually condescending, and he's got a lot of personal charm, it was a bit of the Great Man coming in. John was of course an experienced television writer and *Rumpole* was a huge success and excellent of its type, absolutely first-rate – intelligent, funny, exciting, good narrative – and what he did for us was a very adequate, competent series of one-hour episodes of *Brideshead*, but what it hadn't got was that elegiac, delicate, feathery quality of film nor the enormous detail that we wanted.'

I asked Granger why he had not simply asked Mortimer to rewrite his scripts the way they wanted them. 'Well, John was a very grand writer then. With a writer like Jack Rosenthal we'd rewrite into the night but if you don't know the writer he can say, "Right, I've done it, I'm a superior fellow, I'm a highly credited writer, so that's it." You'd get some rewrites but they would be just little excisions, and it would have been impossible to sack him or say we couldn't use his script because under the contract the estate had script approval and they'd have withdrawn it. And I didn't want to get on the wrong side of John: he can be absolutely ferocious if things go against him. He's enormously self-admiring and can be very difficult and intimidating. All that sweet, self-deprecating thing of his is an outrageous act. Somebody I knew was very surprised by John's fury over a not-very-serious professional thing where his interest was slightly challenged.'

Lindsay-Hogg assembled a stunning cast for *Brideshead Revisited*: Anthony Andrews and Jeremy Irons in the two main roles with Laurence Olivier, John Gielgud, Claire Bloom, Diana Quick, Nickolas Grace and a host of other superb actors in the smaller parts, and the lavish, idyllic, beautifully filmed series was a huge success as soon as the first episode was finally broadcast nearly three years later, in October 1981, and subsequently all over the world. Nobody ever said openly that Mortimer's scripts had been dumped so for more than twenty-five years he was widely acclaimed as the writer of one of the most magnificent of all television series and never denied it. 'He was interviewed endlessly when *Brideshead* was broadcast in 1981,' said Granger, 'and there was one moment when I was really stunned. Ludovic Kennedy was interviewing John on some television arts programme and he said, "Oh, the *script*, John, the feathery *lightness* of it, the shimmering, feathery *lightness* of it," and John said, "Thank you," and I thought, Well, *bugger*! He could have given the rest of us credit for it but it didn't occur to him. Martin and I spent a year and a half writing that script but he never acknowledged it and we were never given writers' credits. There's something extraordinarily tough and vain about him. Most of the people who were in *Brideshead*, like Anthony Andrews, have said "why on *earth* don't you go public about it?" but I always felt that would look rather mean and sneaky. Charles Sturridge says that John actually believes that his version is the one on the screen! I saw a big piece by John in the *Mail* in 2003 in which he said what a joy it had been to write the screenplay and how much enormous care he had devoted to the religious aspect of it even though he was a leftie and an atheist. In the end the series grew longer and longer and we wrote eleven episodes – it was an *enormous* amount of film, the quivalent of eight feature films back-to-back, twelve and a half hours of screen time – and John even got paid for the extra seven episodes that I wrote! I was baffled by that but Granada didn't know what else they could do. "How can we not?" they said. "He's the credited writer and he was commissioned." The series cost £10 million to make (£25 million) and with repeat royalties John would have made a very large amount of money. I don't in any way want to diminish his huge ability, talent and charm but the fact is that we didn't use his scripts.

'About eighteen months later I got a rather beady call from Anthony Jones, who said John had heard that a great many changes were being made to his script and asked for a special screening of all the material that had been shot so far, so John and Anthony saw the material in a small cinema in Soho and that was the last we ever heard. They never reacted at all. They just accepted what they had seen. They could easily have vetoed our version and there could have been an appalling row if they hadn't liked what they saw. It's very odd: he *knows* he didn't write it. It's one of those unspoken secrets and it's always very difficult for me when I meet John because it's like Banquo's ghost coming up before us.'

Lindsay-Hogg confirmed Granger's story. 'John was a big name in the theatre, television and the artistic community,' he told me, 'so nobody ever told him that we had junked his scripts. I never got any reaction from John or Anthony Jones as to whether they liked the finished product, but John was paid for all the extra episodes and would probably have been reluctant to forgo that money – he has a lot of commitments, a big family and an extravagant lifestyle – and he must have made a lot of money out of *Brideshead Revisited* and he may still do well out of it. If he claims something which he didn't do and is lauded for it he has to live with himself for that. It's not for me to criticise him. It's for him to think about.' When Mortimer published his second volume of autobiography, *Murderers and Other Friends*, he devoted more than two pages to his adaptation of *Brideshead Revisited* that give the distinct impression that he had written every word of the script himself and had been a party to the decision to keep Charles Ryder's voice-over narration. He mentioned Derek Granger only once but Lindsay-Hogg and Thompson not at all.

The first episode of the first Rumpole television series, *Rumpole and the Younger Generation* – in which our Horace defends a teenager who is charged with robbery with violence – was broadcast in April 1978 with Peggy Thorpe-Bates replacing Joyce Heron as She Who Must Be Obeyed. Peter Bowles was Guthrie Featherstone, the smarmy head of chambers, and Julian Currie the finicky, disapproving Claude Erskine-Brown. Each episode opened with a lazy bassoon theme tune composed by Joseph Horovitz, mischievous cartoon credits by Rob Page and there were more jokes than there had been in the original play. The reviews were wonderful. 'Destined to be one of the great winners,' said *The Times*. 'Not to be missed,' said the *Sunday Mirror*. 'Leo McKern is superb as the wild and wily barrister.' The second episode a week later, *Rumpole and the Alternative Society*, faltered because Mortimer made the mistake of taking Rumpole out of his chambers and court and sending him off to meet an old flame in the country and *Punch* complained that the denouement 'was feeble stuff' and drew attention to 'Mortimer's ambivalent attitude towards his first profession, half snobbish admiration, half derisive contempt'. But the third episode, *Rumpole and the Honourable Member*, which had our man defending an MP accused of raping one of his party workers, was excellent, as were all the others. In the fourth, *Rumpole and the Married Lady*, the sexy barrister Phillida Trant (played by Patricia Hodge) made her entrance and in the fifth, *Rumpole and the Learned Friends*, Bill Fraser appeared for the first time as the irascible, domineering Judge Bul-lingham, who several lawyers believe was based on Michael Argyle, the judge who had presided over the *Oz* trial. The viewing figures were so good that after three episodes Thames Television's director of pro-grammes, Jeremy Isaacs, asked Irene Shubik to commission Mortimer to write a second series.

It was a charming, funny and perceptive series and such a success that McKern said he had been offered more work in a fortnight than in the previous two years, and Thames agreed to pay him much more for the second series. 'I think of Leo always with great gratitude,' Mortimer told me in 1993. 'I always think of him when I'm writing the episodes. He really is the character and he's wonderful, everything that Rumpole should be.' Mortimer's own fee was also increased handsomely from £1,800 to £2,500 per episode (£8,450). He deserved the rise. 'The amount of invention that went into *Rumpole* was extraordinary,' Ned Sherrin told me. 'It's enchanting.' Arnold Wesker agreed: '*Rumpole* was splendid, charmingly English, idiosyncratic and clever.' A few barristers objected to the series and Lord Hooson told me that one of John's fellow QCs at 1 Dr Johnson's Buildings, Aubrey Myerson, 'nearly had apoplexy when some of the Rumpole stories were on television. He was a stickler for form and correctness in everything and they had several clashes.' Another QC who was not seduced by Rumpole was Judge Angus Stroyan, who told me that few barristers found Rumpole lovable because 'he didn't mix with other barristers. He is always shown as drinking claret by himself, which most people didn't, and not being very kind or matey with his chums in chambers. He was undoubtedly a self-portrait of Mortimer.' According to Geoffrey Robertson the Rumpole series was not just excellent entertainment, it was politically important too. 'It had a very significant effect on the law, the police and civil rights,' he told Alan Yentob in 2003. 'It led to a 1984 reform called the Police and Criminal Evidence Act where police were not any longer allowed to make up statements by defendants in their pocketbooks. They had to sit them down and record them.'

Of the three people who had built the success of the first Rumpole series only one did not benefit hugely from the second: Irene Shubik, who had commissioned the first play, cast McKern, found a home for the series at Thames Television when the BBC did not want it, thrown up her job at the BBC to take it to Thames, commissioned the second series, and was described by Martin Jackson in the *Daily Mail* in March as one of the 'very best TV drama producers'. Mortimer acknowledged how much she had done for him by dedicating the first Rumpole book to her and writing to her in February an effusively affectionate letter of thanks addressed to 'Dearest Irene', calling her 'the onlie begetter' of the series, asking for ideas for the new series, and sending not only his love but as a family friend that of Penny and Emily too. Yet she told me that when Verity Lambert offered her less money to produce the second series and she asked Mortimer to speak up for her and insist that she should share in the success of the series, he failed to do so.

'What astonished me,' Ms Shubik told me, 'was that I fully expected John to support me, but the first thing he said was "poor John", so I said, "what do you mean, 'poor John'?" Here was this man who was a big success and he was worried that Thames Television, who knew they were onto a financial winner with *Rumpole*, might not do it if he didn't kow-tow to Verity Lambert. I just couldn't *believe* it. He could have saved my job, but he's always been out for number one. Maybe I'd been too successful because the critics had mentioned me as part of the success of *Rumpole*. They appointed a new producer for the second series, Jacqueline Davis, a perfectly nice woman, very pretty, but one who had been a lowly production secretary for years before producing a few programmes that nobody's ever heard of, and after the first six *Rumpoles* she got all the residual payments that I should have got. It's cost me a lot. I wanted Thames at least to give me a "series devised by" credit, which would have got me a residual, but John would not support me. It wouldn't have affected what he got and he's made a fortune out of it. I think he thought, Well, it doesn't matter now about her because we've got it going, but we were *friends*, and when I begged him to help me he said, "I can't. Jeremy Isaacs says he can't interefere with his Head of Drama." John was such a *Judas*.' She said that Mortimer even went to Manchester with Ms Lambert to persuade McKern to go on with the series even if she did not produce it. To make matters worse, 'when I introduced John to Judith Burnley at Penguin and suggested that they should publish the Rumpole episodes as short stories Judy wanted me to write an introduction describing how the series came about, but John told me he wanted to do it himself, thereby making it easier to wipe me out of the series. I don't say that was his intention but that's how it worked out. I would have been quite a rich woman, which Jacqueline Davis now is, on my residuals. Financially it was a complete disaster for me and pretty well wrecked my career. I had long periods of unemploy-ment and was hard up, and one ignorant reporter called Verity "the beloved producer of *Rumpole*". I feel quite bitter about it and can hardly bear to talk about it. I was weeping my eyes out once in front of Robin Dalton – "How could he have *done* this?" – and she said, "What are you *surprised* about, darling? John's *known* for that. That's the way he behaves." Just because somebody's fat and smiley it doesn't mean they're nice. You somehow automatically assume that they are.' In *Murderers and Other Friends* Mortimer devoted just two bland sentences to Ms Shubik's row with Ms Lambert and then a whole page to the delectable Jacquie Davis, describing her so fulsomely that despite his atheism he obviously believed in angels.

In May 1979, when the second Rumpole series was screened, the *Daily Telegraph* critic Sean Day-Lewis called it 'quite simply the most classy situation comedy now extant' and reported that Mortimer had said it was 'a tragedy' that Irene Shubik had not stayed on as producer. She went on to join Granada and produce some wonderful television programmes, among them Paul Scott's unforgettable story about an old couple living on in India after independence, *Staying On*, with Trevor Howard and Celia Johnson, and then the whole of Scott's *Raj Quartet* about the last years of British rule in India. 'Celia invited me to her birthday party after we came back from India,' she said, 'and John was there being his genial self and did the "darling" bit to me, and I said – a word I've seldom used – "you're the biggest *shit* I've ever encountered. How could you have done that?" and told him precisely what I thought of him and he sort of quivered and looked devious but never apologised.'

In June the first episode of the Shakespeare series was broadcast and the critics loved it, 'shining like a jewel amid the dross of all those repeats and all that football', said the *Sun*. The series was eventually to be screened in the United States, almost every country in Europe, and was the first British series since *The Forsyte Saga* to be sold to Russia. The comedian Spike Milligan was less adulatory at the end of the month in a face-to-face debate about pornography organised by the *Daily Mirror*. 'We're being swamped by a tidal wave of filth,' said Milligan. 'I feel embarrassed by my daughter being able to see some of the things in these porn shops.' Mortimer admitted that he found pornography 'quite revolting. I always take off my glasses even when, in the course of legal duty, I'm watching blue movies at Scotland Yard so I see very little of it. I think it's bad and vulgar and the ladies look appalling. But ... once you surrender your freedom of choice to some central authority you are surrendering your freedom to people like the police and politicians ... I think pornography is the most harmless form of literature. It should be totally legitimate.'

That summer the Mortimers went on holiday to Italy, which was to become their favourite holiday venue. They stayed in a rented villa at Port'Ercole, eighty miles north of Rome, with the novelist Emma Tennant, who also edited a literary magazine, *Bananas*, with which Penny often helped out part time. 'She's a delightful person and has a very nice, kind nature,' Miss Tennant told me, 'but she did make lots of bitchy jokes about Penelope.' In her diary Miss Tennant wrote: 'This is one of the most enjoyable holidays I've known – but John doesn't seem to believe in holidays: up at five in the morning, he's down at the port with a cognac, a coffee and a croissant by six and when he returns to our little house in the hills he has written an episode of *Rumpole* as well as bringing with him a gleaming fresh fish from the market down there ... He does go to bed early, though. We sit under stars – more white wine – and talk long after the progenitor of *Rumpole* has gone downstairs to bed.'

The first half of 1979 was not as idyllic. The Mortimers did enjoy a Far Eastern cruise but in February the House of Lords rejected the second appeal by *Gay News* and Denis Lemon against their convictions. In May filming of *Brideshead Revisited* started in Malta without Mortimer or his script, the Conservatives won the general election and the dreaded Mrs Thatcher became Prime Minister and began vigorously to dismantle many of the socialist changes that the Labour Party had made to the fabric of British life. She was to win the next two general elections as well and to remain Prime Minister for eleven years while the Labour Party crumbled. Mortimer's worst political nightmare had begun.

Eleven

Rumpole and the Suspicious Wife
1979–1984

Seven years after their divorce John and Penelope's lives were still intertwined even though she came to London little and rarely saw him, for in the same week in May her first volume of autobiography was published, his second Rumpole series was broadcast, and both went on to win major awards. Her autobiography, *About Time*, which covered her life up to 1939 and the age of twenty-one, was devastatingly honest, extremely well written and evocative and won the Whitbread Award for the best book of the year. An admiring review by David Holloway in the *Daily Telegraph* noted that 'her first husband is treated with the same ruthless lack of charity as her parents are', which must have made John decidedly nervous that she might write an equally ruthless sequel about him and their marriage. His own prize was an award from the British Association of Film and Television Arts (BAFTA) as writer of the year for the second Rumpole series, which was screened in the summer of 1979, in one episode of which he made his first regular Alfred Hitchcocky appearance. He was to appear in one episode of each series. In two other stories, which appeared in paperback as *The Trials of Rumpole* and were dedicated to Leo McKern, Rumpole resists his colleagues' attempts to force him to retire and sexy Phillida Trant becomes pregnant by the insufferable prig Claude Erskine-Brown and has to marry him.

With barely a pause Mortimer began to write another filmscript – of Terence Rattigan's *Cause Célèbre* – as well as a play for the BBC about Hitler and Unity Mitford, and the BBC's listings magazine *Radio Times* sent him to Miami with the photographer John Timbers to interview American judges and lawyers for an article about US court procedure which later inspired Mortimer to dispatch Rumpole briefly into retirement in Florida. 'We both thought Miami was pretty tacky and never found anywhere decent to eat,' said Timbers. Even so the Mortimers returned to Florida later for a holiday with Leo McKern, who spooked a nervous waiter by nestling his baleful glass eye on a mound of spaghetti bolognese.

Jeremy had found a job as an editor at the publishers Sidgwick and Jackson – he was later to join BBC Radio and eventually become Head of Radio 4 Drama – and John, Penny and Emily moved flats yet again in Little Venice that summer, leaving 24B Maida Avenue for a spacious upper apartment in a four-storey, semi-detached house just five doors away, around the corner at 15 Park Place Villas, in a bosky street a hundred yards from the colourful canal and shielded by pretty gardens front and back. Mortimer's determination not to have any more children meant that Emily's childhood was as lonely as his had been. At eight she was so shy that she had few friends and a year later tragically lost her best one, nine-year-old Lucy Hoggett, John Piper's granddaughter, when Lucy was killed by a car. Emily rarely invited anyone home, avoided children's parties, and was so embarrassed that her father was so old and drove what she later called an 'incredibly naff' Mercedes that when he took her to school every morning she made him park around the corner. She would let him help with her homework but even that could be embarrassing: when she had trouble writing a story about fairies he wrote it for her and was furious when a teacher sent it back with the brutal comment that 'it lacked that vital spark of imagination'. Emily would amuse herself on her own, making up and acting in little plays just as her father had as a boy, but she did get on well with Tony Richardson's daughters Joely and Natasha when the Mortimers went each summer to stay with the Richardsons in the South of France, where a crowd of famous guests such as Jack Nicholson and Rudolf Nureyev would put on a play which Mortimer would review, pinning his notices up on trees. And when the Mortimers went to Crete on holiday Emily built an altar on the beach, pretended to be an Ancient Greek and worshipped herself – perfect preparation for her later career as an idolised film star.

John's two eldest stepdaughters were on the move, too. Madelon, now forty-one and a widow after the death of her much older husband, Lee Howard, had moved to France. Thirty-six-year-old Caroline, who had recently been filmed topless in a bedroom scene in a television serial, *Murder at the Wedding*, was living with and pregnant by another actor, fifty-one-year-old John Bennett, a married man with a teenage son. His divorce was to come through just in time for them to marry in November two weeks before the baby was born – a son with Down's syndrome whom they named Jake.

As if Mortimer were not busy enough already, he embarked on yet another career in 1979 when he started interviewing the great and the sometimes good for *The Sunday Times*. His subjects were household names – Graham Greene, Lord Denning, David Hockney, Rab Butler, Denis Healey – but perhaps because he was famous himself his articles were bland, discreet, unrevealing chunks of lazily undigested quotes – often just lists of questions and answers – that he had not bothered to blend into vivid portraits. His interview with seventy-five-year-old Greene, for instance, was surprisingly cold and remote even though Mortimer considered him Britain's greatest living author, had adapted his stories for television and was soon to adapt his novel *Dr Fischer of Geneva* for a TV film starring James Mason. Now and then he would of course come up with a memorable quote. 'I've never really got the hang of boiling a kettle,' said seventy-eight-year-old Lord Butler, who had in the 1950s and 1960s been Chancellor of the Exchequer, Home Secretary, Deputy Prime Minister and Foreign Secretary. Sixty-two-year-old Healey told him that the brilliant Tory eccentric Sir Keith Joseph had been 'a wonderful mixture of Rasputin and Tommy Cooper' and that talking to Clement Attlee had been 'like throwing biscuits to a dog'. But otherwise the interviews were generally undistinguished.

Leo McKern loved playing Rumpole but was reluctant to go on too long for fear of becoming typecast. He agreed to do it just once more for a two-hour Christmas special at the end of 1980, *Rumpole's Return*, in which he has become bored by retirement in Florida, returns to London as ebullient as ever, to the consternation of his fellow barristers in chambers, and craftily wins an apparently hopeless murder case. There were some nice touches in the short novel of the same title that accompanied the programme – to Rumpole's disgust Mrs Mary Whitehouse is given an honour by the Queen – but otherwise the book was so laboured and uninspired that Mortimer was obviously already tired of writing the Rumpole stories. It was completely unfunny, often unbelievable, with careless mistakes, and even the dialogue was galumphing and unlikely. Yet by now Rumpole had become hugely popular not only in Britain but also in America and Australia. In the States a group of defence attorneys founded a club named after Rumpole's favourite wine bar, Pommeroy's, which prosecutors and judges were forbidden to join. A Rumpole Society was started in San Francisco and branches soon spread all over the country. 'They have the most extraordinary meetings,' Mortimer told me in 1993. 'They have Hilda lookalike contests, and wear She Who Must Be Obeyed T-shirts, and drink replicas of Pommeroy's wine. When Americans come to London there's a Rumpole walk down Fleet Street to El Vino's and round the Temple, and in Australia there's a skyscraper in Adelaide called The Rumpole Building and a restaurant in Brisbane called Rumpole's which serves all the food which Rumpole would never touch, like rocket and grilled scallops, no steak-and-kidney pudding.'

Mortimer was now fifty-seven and such a cultural icon that he was asked to open the Edinburgh International TV Festival in August 1980. There he met a bubbly, married, twenty-six-year-old freelance public relations woman, Jenny Bailey, and began an affair with her that was to last two years. 'Jenny was a very jolly, funny girl,' I was told by one of her colleagues, 'and it was quite an affair.' Mortimer was fascinating company, she told me in 2004. 'We hit it off big time in Edinburgh. He was such a sweet, wonderful person and used to call me Little Jen. Back in London he would take me to lunch at the White Elephant and the Boulestin, and we'd bump into all sorts of people like David Frost and John never wanted to hide it. My husband asked me about him and I said "I'd never sleep with anyone that ugly" but of course I did. It was more cerebral than physical, but my husband was quite startled when he found out. Yes, of course John had other girlfriends at the same time as me. He wasn't faithful to Penny 2 or me, but I wasn't jealous. He was writing *Clinging to the Wreckage* when we were going out together and he read a bit out to me which I thought was rather childish and surprisingly bad.'

His affair with the 'Young Bailey' was to end in July 1982 hilariously, like one of his favourite Feydeau farces. 'I was managing a boutique in Fulham by then, Filiardo's, which used to be called Brother Sun and Sister Moon,' said Mrs Bailey. 'John came in to buy a scarf which he said was for his wife, but Penny 2 must have found the receipt for it or gone through his pockets and got very suspicious. Quick-wittedly John said "I must have left the scarf in the shop" and rang me to cover his tracks. I had to ring his house and say that he had left the scarf in the shop, and Penny and a friend were on the doorstep at 9 a.m. the next day, the first time she had ever come, and she was very suspicious and demanded to come in. John was going off to interview Mick Jagger in Madrid and phoning me frantically from the airport – "Jenny, is it all right?" – and my assistant Michelle was in a panic – "This woman's on the doorstep, what do I do?" – and I told her to give her a scarf. Penny was *very* suspicious and wanted to know how we had got her telephone number. Michelle said we had a visitors' book. Penny insisted on seeing it. Then, after she had gone, the key to the shop went missing – it was very strange – but the next day the key was pushed through the door. John appeared the next day, very crumpled and flustered, to pay £48 for the second scarf, and as he ran out I said, "You've been found out, you naughty boy! What will Penny think when she reads about all this in your book?" Well, I suppose she knows all about it. I think they lead completely separate lives now and have for a long time.'

Another young married woman who stirred Mortimer's lust was the actress who was playing Phillida Trant in the Rumpole series, thirty-four-year-old Patricia Hodge. His pursuit of her was almost certainly in vain but 'he was very keen on her', said Irene Shubik. 'He was always eyeing her during rehearsals.' Ned Sherrin also noticed Mortimer's enthusiasm and Mike Molloy, who was now editor of the *Daily Mirror*, saw John and Miss Hodge together in a restaurant and stopped at their table to say hello to him. 'She glared at me furiously!' Molloy told me. 'I could see she was utterly charmed by him and looked all dreamy. It was like a snake being mesmerised by a snake charmer!'

Sex reared an uglier head in October when an explicit play at the National Theatre caused an uproar and a deluge of complaints because one scene depicted graphically one man buggering another. Peter Hall had warned the board that the play, *The Romans in Britain* by Howard Brenton, which purported to portray Julius Caesar's invasion of Britain in 54 BC, would be sexually and politically controversial, showing as it did a Roman soldier raping an Ancient Briton and drawing brutal parallels with the British army's presence in Northern Ireland. Several of the actors begged Brenton and the play's director, Michael Bogdanov, to cut the scene but they refused, and since the board had undertaken not to interfere with Hall's artistic decisions it was not until several days before the first night that the board realised just how much trouble the play was going to cause when the leader of the Greater London Council, Sir Horace Cutler, marched angrily out of a preview and threatened to withdraw the GLC's grant to the National. At the next board meeting several members were furious that their advice had not been sought but Mortimer advocated as usual his 'what the hell, anything goes' policy, pointed out that there were even more revolting horrors in *King Lear* and *Titus Andronicus*, and told his fellow members with typical flippancy to 'keep right on to the end of the woad'. His old adversary Mary Whitehouse was not prepared to be so tolerant, complained to Scotland Yard, and when the Director of Public Prosecutions refused to take any action launched a private prosecution against Bogdanov under the Sexual Offences Act of 1956 for 'procuring an act of gross indecency', a charge that could mean a two-year prison sentence. Since Mortimer was himself a member of the board he could not be briefed to defend the National when the trial opened more than a year later at the Old Bailey – where two embarrassed barristers had to re-enact the buggery scene in court, one of them on all fours – so the defence was undertaken by Jeremy (Lord) Hutchinson, the prosecution withdrew for lack of evidence after two days, and the case collapsed. 'The NT board behaved in an exemplary way over *The Romans in Britain*,' wrote Peter Hall in his autobiography. 'A leading theatre in any country is prone to play safe, and there is an inbuilt temptation to make sure that it ruffles nobody's sensibilities [but] without controversial work in the repertory, we would be evading our social responsibilities and becoming merely a fixture of the establishment, unwilling to deal with new and dissenting issues or young writers or to attract young audiences.'

In November 1980 Mortimer made his only visit to the set of *Brideshead Revisited* when he travelled north to Castle Howard in Yorkshire to interview Sir Laurence Olivier for *The Sunday Times*. In his subsequent article he admitted that although he had written the screen adaptation he heard hardly one line of dialogue that had not been changed. One line of that interview was truly memorable, when Olivier told Mortimer just how he had hit exactly the right terrible note during a production of *Oedipus* just after the war when he had had to give a heart-stopping scream as he was being blinded: he had heard that hunters of ermine in the Arctic trapped the little creatures by sprinkling salt on the ice and that when the ermine licked the salt their tongues would freeze to the ice and they would scream in agony. That was the howl that he gave to Oedipus.

Over the next couple of years Mortimer wrote numerous interviews for *The Sunday Times*. Malcolm Muggeridge, a reformed Casanova himself and born-again Christian now that he was seventy-eight, told him that the big mistake of liberals like Mortimer was to see good in everything: 'That has been of great assistance to the devil,' he said. Roy Jenkins, the ex-Home Secretary and Chancellor who had just helped to launch the Labour-breakaway Social Democratic Party, earned Mortimer's approval by saying that 'if pornography were the only evil in society we'd be extremely lucky'. Sir John Gielgud told him that Ken Tynan had complained that Gielgud had only two gestures on stage: left hand up or right hand up. 'What did he want me to do?' asked Gielgud. 'Bring out my prick?' Other subjects included Frederick Forsyth, the Archbishop of Canterbury Robert Runcie and the Labour politicians Tony Benn, Ken Livingstone and Michael Foot, though Mortimer had nothing new or interesting to say about any of them. When he wrote about the ill-educated jockey Dick Francis he did not even hint that much of the literate, sophisticated Dick Francis racing thrillers had actually been written not by him but by his university-educated wife, Mary. When he met the comedian Eric Morecambe he gave no hint at all of the dark, melancholic side of his character. There was the occasional rare nugget: the strict, disciplined moralist Enoch Powell confessed that as a boy he and his gang had vandalised railway carriages; Cardinal Hume said enviously that 'it must be marvellous to have a wife'; and in a memorable 'Casanova Meets Don Juan' encounter in Lausanne seventy-nine-year-old Georges Simenon told Mortimer that he had written most of his Maigret novels in seven days, even though he drank three bottles of wine a day, and discussed the thousands of women he had ravished, boasting unconvincingly that even with the hundreds of prostitutes he had rented over the years 'I always let them have their pleasure first – and of course I was enough of a connoisseur to know if their pleasure was faked'. Not everyone who met Mortimer, however, was impressed by his genial manner and when Philip Larkin wrote a letter to Kingsley Amis in January 1981 he called him 'that arsefaced trendy John Mortimer (argh! s**t! farkks!)'.

The next Rumpole episodes on television, *Rumpole for the Defence*, for which Leo McKern was yet again inveigled back, which was published in book form as *Regina versus Rumpole*, strengthened the suspicion that Mortimer was struggling to reach the high standard of the first series. They were thin, repetitive, padded-out stories that indicated weariness and straining for effect. Sadly that was to be the case increasingly with almost all the Rumpole stories from now on: they began to read as though they had been a chore to write. Wisely he took a break – though he was still writing *Clinging to the Wreckage* – and went around the world to New Zealand, Sydney, Bali and India, where he saw the Taj Mahal, before returning to England in May in time to help Alvin Rakoff make his long-delayed ninety-minute film of *A Voyage Round My Father* for Thames Television with Laurence (now Lord) Olivier playing Clifford, Alan Bates as John, Elizabeth Sellars as Kathleen and Jane Asher as the young Penelope. Olivier asked John to go to his house in Chelsea one evening to read the entire script to him – just as he had read every evening to his father, though this time he was very nervous – and at the end of it Olivier said caustically, just as Clifford might have done, 'That was a bloody awful reading, dear boy, but never mind.' Olivier – who had just been awarded Britain's highest honour, the Order of Merit – asked him if his parents had shared a bed right to the end of Clifford's life, was told they had, and said that he thought that was why they had been so happy together. Shooting began at the end of June 1981, much of it at Turville Heath Cottage and the surrounding area while John was still living in the house, so that he would regularly feel a spooky frisson when he saw Olivier dressed as his father or acting his father's death in the very bed in which Clifford had died. Olivier, now seventy-four, was very frail and his memory was failing badly, which made him furious and frustrated. His lines had to be written on huge blackboards off-camera and by each afternoon he was so tired and bewildered that filming had to be curtailed. Yet his frailty and heavy breathing actually added to the veracity of his superb, touching performance because he was just as sick and feeble as Clifford had been. He was also gloriously contemptuous and angry, as Mortimer always thought his father should be portrayed, though some critics later felt that he was hamming it up. When the play was screened in March 1982 the critics raved and it went on to win an International Emmy award. The film was 'a delightful, movingly affectionate circumnavigation of an extraordinary parent with marvellous language that would be a joy even without such an excellent production', said *The Times*. *The Financial Times* said it was 'a work of great power' and the *Daily Telegraph* called it 'a performance for posterity'. It was, said *Punch*, 'a great television occasion. Faultlessly cast, exquisitely shot, one of those few exercises the viewer never forgets.'

The first of the eleven episodes of *Brideshead Revisited*, the longest and most expensive British TV drama ever, was broadcast at last in October 1981 to more ecstatic reviews and Mortimer was heaped with adulation for his 'lovingly adapted' script, as the *Sun* put it, nominated for the Emmy award for the best scriptwriter of the year, and won an award from the American Alliance for Gay Artists. Yet although Olivier had played memorable parts in both *A Voyage Round My Father* and *Brideshead Revisited* he devoted only fourteen words to the first and four to the second in the autobiography that he published the following year, *Confessions of an Actor*, and none at all to Mortimer himself. Nor, oddly, was there any mention of Mortimer in Noël Coward's diaries when they were also published that year, nor in Michael Redgrave's autobiography when that was published the following year, nor in Alec Guiness's in 1999. None of the great actors who appeared in his plays and films felt he was worth writing about even in passing. Yet he was by now a playwright whose work was constantly being revived.

In January 1982 there was yet another production of *The Dock Brief* (with Nigel Hawthorne and John Alderton) and *The Prince of Darkness* (with John Alderton and Desmond McNamara) at the Young Vic under the title *John Mortimer's Casebook*, and Mortimer's workload was as heavy as ever. He was adapting *Dr Fischer of Geneva* for television; writing a new play, *Edwin*, as well as additional dialogue for a Ray Bradbury film, *Something Wicked This Way Comes*; concocting a one-man show for the National Theatre of Canada, *When That I Was*, about an old actor at the Globe Theatre in Shakespeare's day; churning out more Rumpole stories; and about to defend *Private Eye* in a libel case in the High Court. Now nearly fifty-nine, he told Sheridan Morley in an interview for *The Times* that he had become obsessed by the value of time and furious at the prospect of dying. He had become a grandfather three days earlier when his daughter Sally, who was now married to an artist, Howard Silverman, gave birth to a son, Gus, and for the first time in Mortimer's life he had stopped worrying about money, he said – not surprisingly since he was earning vast bundles of the stuff – but he was now extremely mean with his time. 'Too many months have been wasted writing rubbishy filmscripts,' he said.

Typically, however, he had again taken on much more work than he should, so it was inevitably not always up to scratch. *John Mortimer's Casebook*, for instance, was supposed to include a third play, about the medical profession, but long after rehearsals had begun he had still not finished it. 'The first draft of the new play rambled all over the place so John Mortimer offered to rewrite it,' said Hawthorne in his autobiography twenty years later. 'And again. He just couldn't make it work. And time was running short.' A few days before the previews a final version arrived. Hawthorne and Alderton were horrified: this draft was much longer than the earlier ones and they had only days to learn it. They read it aloud with Mortimer. 'Well,' said Hawthorne, 'that doesn't work either.' Mortimer thought hard. 'There's only one thing that will save the show,' he told Hawthorne. 'Instead of playing a doctor you're a matron.'

'Drag?'

'It's the only thing which will work.'

Kitted out in a blue uniform, frilly cap, wig and padded breasts, teetering terrified around the stage in high-heeled shoes, Hawthorne was horrified to hear that Mortimer had invited Olivier and his wife Joan Plowright to the first night and that they were sitting in the front row. He knew that he had to prevent his eyes catching Olivier's. 'I knew that were they to meet the reptilian gaze of the man ackowledged to be the greatest actor in the world, I wouldn't even finish the play.' Yet at the reception after the show Olivier 'couldn't have been kinder, more friendly or more generous if he'd tried. Unless he was the most terrible liar, he had thoroughly enjoyed the evening, and even been delighted by my drag act at the beginning. Unfortunately, the critics didn't share Olivier's enthusiasm.'

Busy though Mortimer was, he took Penny off to Australia to promote sales of the Rumpole books. They loved it: the restaurants, the wines, even the people. They swam at Bondi Beach, went sightseeing in a tiny seaplane, revelled in the wildlife of the northern Queensland rainforest, visited the Great Barrier Reef, and John made a speech at a lawyers' dinner in Brisbane where the evening ended in drunken chaos. He said he had not been so happy and carefree for ages.

The libel trial of *Private Eye*, its editor Richard Ingrams, and its publishers and printers – all represented by Mortimer – began in the London High Court in March 1982 when the television producer and presenter Desmond Wilcox claimed damages from the scandal magazine for having alleged in 1975, 1980 and January that he had made £22,000 by abusing his position as head of the BBC's general features department. When Wilcox had presented the series *Explorers* in 1975 a tie-in book was published to coincide with it and his name had appeared on the cover as the only author, whereas the chapters inside were in fact the work of two ghostwriters who had based them on the work of the eight original scriptwriters – among them Hammond Innes and Rosemary Anne Sisson – whose copyright *Private Eye* had accused Wilcox of infringing deliberately. It had also accused him of stealing someone else's idea for another BBC series, *The Jews*, and he claimed that the magazine's bully-ing, anti-semitic 'vendetta' against him had driven him out of his job at the BBC. The proceedings started on an appropriately farcical note. 'I appear for Mr Desmond Wilcox, my Lord, and he needs no introduction from me,' said Wilcox's QC, Anthony Hoolahan. 'Well, he does to me,' said the judge, Mr Justice Jupp, 'because I have absolutely no idea who he is.' After a two-day hearing the magazine amended its defence and the case was adjourned until the end of April, when it staggered on for fifteen days. 'John got so bored during the case,' I was told by Ingrams' wife Mary, 'that he was always slipping me £20 to go to the pub to buy a bottle of champagne and put it on ice ready for lunchtime.' The judge eventually found for Wilcox, chided the magazine for its 'campaign of denigration' against him, and awarded him damages of £14,000 (£32,600) and ordered the magazine to pay legal costs of about £80,000 (£186,000), much of which went to Mortimer, who was told by the mischievous Ingrams that to lose such a simple case had obviously required a great deal of highly paid skill.

On the same day Mortimer found himself facing a charge in court himself when he was fined £60 for careless driving after running his BMW into the back of a parked van. The conviction reinforced his dislike of judging, which he was still doing occasionally as a Commissioner, a deputy High Court judge, one of the chores of being a QC, although the end of his legal career was nigh. In his last case as a judge he had to decide whether two little boys should live with their garage-owner father in England or their opera-singer mother in Norway. He begged the parents to make the decision themselves but they insisted that it was impossible, and the responsibility of deciding their futures was such a burden that Mortimer decided seriously that he must soon leave the Bar at last to concentrate on his writing.

At the end of March 1982 *Clinging to the Wreckage* was published and the reviewers rightly loved it. It was beautifully written and funny, 'enchantingly witty [and] should be held as the model for all auto-biographies of our times,' said Auberon Waugh. It went on to be a huge bestseller, to sell extremely well in America too, to win the *Yorkshire Post* Book of the Year award, to be reprinted many times and to earn Mor-timer – according to one knowledgeable literary agent – at least £400,000 over the years. As an apparently factual autobiography, however, it was totally inadequate. For a start, like John's three subsequent volumes of autobiography, it had no index. It was also extremely unreliable, pres-enting lies as facts, skating over details, inventing and exaggerating anecdotes, omitting a great deal, ignoring Penelope and their marriage almost completely, and stopping suddenly with a hurried finish at the end of the 1960s. 'It's hard to find me in it,' Penelope told Elizabeth Grice of the *Daily Telegraph*. 'He seems to think that it's possible to write your autobiography and not write about your *life* at all.' The book was so dubious that it is difficult not to wonder how much was true and whether even his celebrated portrait of his father was a huge exaggeration or even completely untrue. Was Clifford really so vivid? So brave? So clever? Such a monster? Or was he simply another of John's fictional characters? As Charles Champlin wrote in the *Los Angeles Times*, the book had 'the strength and sensitivity of a carefully observed novel'. Maybe that is in fact what it really was.

The Sunday Times sent Stephen Fay to interview him at Turville Heath, where he found Mortimer slouching and looking much scruffier than the average QC, with long, unkempt hair and small silver pendants on a chain around his neck. He looked 'like an actor playing an eccentric barrister speaking lines that he has written himself', said Fay, and he was claiming now to rise for work sometimes at 3 a.m. He was now so famous that he was asked to appear in July on *Desert Island Discs* for a second time, a rare accolade, and again chose a piece by Mozart as his first record – Kiri Te Kanawa singing 'Soave sia il vento' from *Così fan tutte* – and another as his last, Ruggero Raimondi singing 'Qual tremore insolito' from *Don Giovanni*. He picked two pieces by Puccini, too: Pavarotti with 'O soave fanciulla' from *La Bohème* and David Sellar with 'Io de' sospiri' from *Tosca*. In between were Jack Buchanan and Elsie Randolph with 'Fancy Our Meeting', Jacqueline du Pré with Elgar's Cello Concerto in E minor, Bob Dylan's 'Just Like a Woman' and Verdi's 'Veglia, o donna, questo fiore' from *Rigoletto*. The book he chose was also Rumpole's favourite, *The Oxford Book of English Verse*, but he could not be bothered to think of a new luxury to take to his island and again chose a bath, as he had when he had first appeared on the programme in 1968.

Meanwhile another row was brewing at the National Theatre, where Peter Hall was determined to stage and direct himself an untried new American musical, *Jean Seberg*, about the life and death of a minor American actress who had played the lead in Otto Preminger's film about Joan of Arc but had done little else before committing suicide in Paris in 1979. Many members of the National board, including Mortimer, felt that it was quite wrong for the NT to produce a new play that could easily be staged in the commercial theatre, let alone a musical, and that was no more than a try-out before it opened on Broadway. Usually Mortimer supported Hall but this time he denounced the project at the quarterly board meeting in July and demanded that his opposition should be noted formally in the minutes. Hall ignored the criticisms and when the show opened in December 1982 it was a disaster, 'one of the most frightful stagefuls of junk ever seen in London,' wrote Bernard Levin. Hall confessed in his autobiography that it was the most notorious flop of his career and it lost the National about £750,000.

Mortimer's new three-character play, *Edwin*, was given its first performance on BBC radio in October with Emlyn Williams playing the main character, Sir Fennimore Truscott, a part that was to be played a

year and a half later in a television version on Anglia with Sir Alec
Guinness as Truscott, a retired High Court judge who misses his life in
court so much that when he accuses his neighbour Tom Marjoriebanks
of seducing his wife he puts Marjoriebanks 'on trial' for adultery. As the
'trial' proceeds Sir Fennimore comes to suspect that his son Edwin is
actually Marjoriebanks's son, until eventually it transpires that Edwin is
the son of neither but in fact the fruit of the loins of Sir Fennimore's
gnarled old gardener, Cattermole. It was an amusing idea – unless of
course you were Jack Bentley, who had only recently stopped having to
support Mortimer's own son, Ross, who was now twenty-two and had
just been told by his mother that Mortimer was his real father. The play's
jaded, cynical depiction of the judge, court procedure and the Law
underlined just how disillusioned Mortimer had become with the Bar
and how ready he was to retire as a barrister himself.

Early in 1983 he heard that his delightful old chum David Niven,
who was seventy-three and suffering increasingly from motor neurone
disease, was approaching the final stage of his dreadful illness, which was
robbing him relentlessly of the use of his muscles and voice. Mortimer
went to say goodbye to him in Switzerland at his big wooden chalet in
Château d'Oex, near Gstaad, and was appalled to see how gaunt, wasted
and frail he was. 'Fundador!' croaked Niven. 'What about a jar?' They
sat and shared the last of their many bottles of white wine, recalling
hilarious old anecdotes as the sun went down and the snow froze hard on
the lawn and Niven's famous voice grew fainter and fainter as he battled
with his terrible affliction. 'I think it's having talked far too much during
my life that's taken my voice away,' he croaked. They were never to see
each other again. 'What a bastard God is,' Mortimer told me in 2001, 'a
real bastard.'

Back in England he undertook a nationwide author tour in April to
promote his two latest books, *Rumpole and the Golden Thread* and a
collection of his *Sunday Times* interviews, *In Character*. The new Rumpole
was dedicated to the beautiful Jacqueline Davis, who had now become
a friend as well as the producer of *Rumpole*. In one story Guthrie
Featherstone is made a judge and in the subsequent election to choose
his successor as head of chambers Rumpole is beaten yet again by Sam
Ballard much to Hilda's fury. In another tale the delectable Phillida
Erskine-Brown becomes a QC to the shame of her husband, Claude, who
is still a junior barrister.

Mortimer celebrated his sixtieth birthday and eleventh wedding anniversary with a supper and firework party in a marquee together with his

Turville Heath neighbour John Piper, who was eighty. 'It was a *huge* party,' Celia Brayfield told me, 'and *everybody* was a celebrity, from Bob Geldof and Paula Yates to Barbara Castle. John was incredibly affable – he always called me "Beauty" – and the minute he saw me he would always say "ah, *Beauty*!" but only because he'd forgotten my name. He had several of those parties and towards the end of one of them I said to Penny "that was such a wonderful party" and she said, "do you know, before you arrived John was sitting in the middle of the tent *crying* and saying 'nobody's going to come'." It had never occurred to me that he had that level of insecurity.'

Five days later he was in court again to oppose a plan by the local education authority to close the village school at Turville but his fight was in vain. He and Geoffrey Robertson also defended that year two members of the euthanasia organisation Exit who were accused of aiding and abetting suicides by giving each a sleeping pill, bottle of whisky and plastic bag. One defendant was given a long prison sentence but the other, who wore a bobble hat and claimed that he received ethereal instructions through a hole in the top of his head, was acquitted. Some time later Robertson was alarmed when he fell ill with pneumonia, answered the doorbell and found the freed Exit defendant standing on the doorstep, wearing his bobble hat, saying he had heard Robertson was not well, and asking if there was anything he could do to put him out of his misery.

Mortimer's main project in 1983 was the filmscript for *Dr Fischer of Geneva*, which was to be directed by Michael Lindsay-Hogg, the director of *Brideshead Revisited* who had dumped his script then and was about to junk this one too. '*Dr Fischer* was also not an entirely happy experience,' Lindsay-Hogg told me, 'because John had invented other characters and once again had gone away from the central thrust of the book. Richard Broke, the producer, and I didn't think the script was going to work and we asked Graham Greene himself what he thought of it, and he said it had gone in the wrong direction, away from the book – the same thing as *Brideshead*. Graham had a *keen* dramatic sense, had written *The Third Man* movie and knew a lot about film structure, so he, Richard and I spent three or four days going back to the book in London. John came for a drink with Richard and me at Claridge's and we talked. Everybody liked John – he's affable, bright, funny and naughty – and because we didn't want to offend him we didn't tell him that we were talking to Graham or that we were going to go another way. In the end Richard got the credit for writing the script, there was an argument about it and another producer, John Pringle, said to Mortimer "what are you talking about? It happened to you before on *Brideshead*. Michael Lindsay-Hogg told me," and from that day to this Mortimer has never spoken to me because of what he took as a slight or a betrayal. I bumped into him once at a dinner Tina Brown gave in Oxford and there were about forty of us there, so John managed to avoid talking to me, and Penny 2 gave me a very curt "hello" before turning away to talk to someone else. I'm sorry he doesn't talk to me any more. I suspect that he's a slightly trickier figure than he presents himself. And it's interesting that in his scripts for both *Brideshead* and *Dr Fischer* John chose to take away from the books the very qualities that make the books so interesting and put little slaps of wallpaper on which weren't nearly as interesting. If you're going to do an adaptation of a book you want to stay as truthful to the book as you can.'

Mortimer had also been commissioned by Peter Hall to translate yet another Feydeau farce for the National Theatre, *A Little Hotel on the Side*, a doggedly unfunny comedy about an extremely ugly builder's attempt to seduce his best friend's pretty young wife in a sleazy and apparently haunted hotel in Paris in 1899. It was an embarrassingly corny play with some dreadfully facetious double entendres, girls running around in their underwear, and the usual Feydeau misunderstandings, mistaken identities, chaos and confusion. The clumsily lecherous would-be seducer, Benoit Pinglet, was obviously closely related to Peter Sellers' Inspector Clouseau and Gordon Kaye's René in the television series *'Allo 'Allo!*; the domineering Madame Pinglet could well have auditioned for the part of Hilda Rumpole; and the play itself could have come from a particularly dire episode of *The Benny Hill Show*; but somehow it found its way onto the stage of the Olivier Theatre the following year with Graeme Garden playing Pinglet and a cast of twenty-two directed by Jonathan Lynn. Mortimer also found time to select a series of old criminal cases for a new Penguin paperback edition of a fascinating 1941 collection of contemporary accounts of controversial *Famous Trials* – such as those of the murderers Dr Crippen, Madeleine Smith, George Smith and Herbert Armstrong and the wartime traitor William Joyce, 'Lord Haw-Haw'. And he continued to interview the famous for *The Sunday Times* – the American evangelist Billy Graham, the multi-multi-millionaire thirty-one-year-old Duke of Westminster, the ex-Prime Minister Edward Heath – but even when he wrote about other novelists such as Ruth Rendell and William Golding, who had just won the Nobel Prize for Literature, the subsequent pedestrian articles revealed little.

His most significant interview that year was for the *Spectator* when he went to the House of Commons in October to meet Neil Kinnock. Kinnock had just been elected at the age of forty-one to succeed Michael Foot as leader of the Labour Party after another Labour defeat in the general election in June when Margaret Thatcher tripled her majority in the Commons. Despite her 144-seat majority Kinnock told Mortimer that he had no respect for her at all. 'She has the references of a five- or ten-year-old child,' he said. 'Her answers seem contrived and over-rehearsed. I don't rate her highly at all.' Perhaps he should have done, for she was to beat him in the next general election four years later and after losing yet again in 1992 he was forced to resign as Labour leader. Mortimer was not pleased that Kinnock had a minder sitting in on the interview: Patricia Hewitt, his Press Secretary, and 'made it *very* evident that he was brassed off with her being there', Kinnock told me at his European Union commissioner's office in Brussels in 2004, 'but I liked him instantaneously. He was immensely jolly, a witty, well-motivated person who had been prepared to take pretty courageous stands in court.' They got on so well that Kinnock invited him to continue the interview without Hewitt at his house in Ealing, where Mortimer was impressed that the Leader of the Opposition drove a second-hand Cortina and loved watching rugby and the comedians Tommy Cooper and Russ Abbott. He also met Kinnock's wife, Glenys, who was to become one of his most affectionate platonic friends and even closer to him than Kinnock. 'I can remember warming to him immediately,' she told Veronica Groocock of the *Independent on Sunday* in 1999. 'He's one of the easiest people to feel relaxed with [and he] has that twinkle in his eye and a kind of outrageousness about him ... He's always the same: warm and kind, although I can imagine he's capable of being otherwise. He wouldn't have been a very successful lawyer if that were not the case.'

'Glenys was at first daunted by meeting this great person,' said Kinnock, 'but it took him about four minutes to charm her up from the grass. They laugh at each other's jokes *all* the time, which is something I can't claim. When we stay with him in Tuscany, near Siena, he goes off every day to a nearby village, to a bar on the corner of the main road where all the big lorries rumble past and the Lambrettas, motorbikes and tourist traffic. This is a bar where you can contract severe carbon dioxide contamination in the course of one drink but John *loves* it. Glenys decided to feed this obsession of John's for watching six-axle trucks going past so she started saying, "Oh John! You're not going to *believe* this: there's the most *fantastic* blue Volvo coming along," and John would immediately join in a serious discussion about these *bloody* trucks going past, as if they were in an art exhibition or a particularly spectacular ballet! It's absurd but it's very funny.' In Italy too the Kinnocks and Mortimers would often go together to the opera at San Gimignano.

I asked Kinnock whether Mortimer, as a renowned champagne socialist, ever had any real political influence in the Labour Party. 'Not in policy terms,' he said, 'but he's one of the people whose civilised radical views always helped to set the context over the last forty-odd years. I've never consulted him politically but he is phenomenally well read and erudite. I realised after a couple of years that he was prepared to trade analysis and gossip on things artistic in return for my providing him with gossip and analysis about politics!' – and 'John *loves* scandal and gossip,' said Celia Brayfield.

David Niven died at his Swiss chalet on 29 July and John delivered the eulogy at a packed memorial service in October at St Martin-in-the-Fields, where Olivier, now very frail indeed, read from the Book of Revelation. Niven's joyous yet often tragic life, John had once said, was 'Wodehouse with tears' and he spoke movingly of 'our joy in knowing a man who gave us so much happiness' and quoted a remark that the Hollywood director Ernst Lubitsch had once made to Niven, that 'nobody should try and play comedy unless they have a circus going on inside. Perhaps that was the secret of David's style,' said Mortimer. 'He seemed so elegant and cool, he was so handsome and well dressed, but inside the band was forever striking up, the children were clapping with delight and the clowns were always about to be brought on.'

The ascendancy of right-wing Thatcherism in Britain inspired a powerful backlash against Mortimer and the other 'anything goes' liberal midwives of the Permissive Society who were attacked on several sides in November by the Lord Chief Justice, Lord Lane; the director of the Confederation of British Industry, Sir Terence Beckett; Madelon's first boyfriend, Christopher Booker; and even by Mortimer's regular 'expert witness' Bernard Levin. Lane claimed that the social fabric of Britain was seriously threatened by a huge increase in crime, drugs, pornography and mistrust of the police that had been encouraged by the trendy liberals, and Booker applauded him in an article in the *Daily Mail* for alerting the nation to the 'horrific picture of immoral Britain today' which had been encouraged by 'a general blurring of boundaries which established right and wrong which is leading to a rapid erosion of family life'. Mortimer was so stung by these attacks on the permissive revolution that he had done so much to bring about that he defended himself and Jenkins in a full-page article in *The Sunday Times* but his arguments were weak, unconvincing and irrelevant. Bizarrely he denied that there was anything wrong with Britain's soul because, he said, British television was still the best in the world; because young editors in publishing were still prepared to be exploited for very low wages; because Emily, now twelve, did two hours of homework every evening; and because the countryside views at Turville Heath were still 'as good as anything in Europe' as if that had anything to do with it. Foolhardily he boasted that his own family life had not yet disintegrated, dangerously overlooking Penny's possible reaction should she discover for sure that he was still buying scarves for other women, especially since she had just become pregnant again against his wishes. He concluded his article by claiming that Britain was the most beautiful, peaceful, tolerant and politically mature country in the world without explaining why such wonderful people kept voting Conservative rather than Labour.

On Boxing Day 1983 he flew to Singapore to defend again his old client Ben Jeyaretnam, the Workers' Party politician and only opposition MP who was still being pursued by the vengeful Prime Minister, Lee Kuan Yew, and accused this time of misusing his party's funds, a charge that could mean a long prison sentence. 'Ah!' cried the elderly Chinese lady in the barristers' robing room at Singapore's Central Court, who recognised Mortimer immediately and exclaimed with delight: 'Ah, there you are, Lumpore of the Bairey!' The trial was hot, humid and tiring and over lunch he told a *Times* correspondent that it was about time he left the Bar. The judge acquitted Jeyaretnam on all but one of the charges and fined him just £300, but the judge was then sacked by the government and Jeyaretnam was tried again, convicted, imprisoned, fined, deprived of his seat in Parliament and disbarred as a solicitor even though Singapore's highest court, the Privy Council in London, ruled that he had been treated unlawfully. As if that were not enough, Lee Kuan Yew was to sue Jeyaretnam yet again for libel in 1989 and 1997. Exhausted both physically and emotionally, Mortimer flew back to London via Tokyo and Los Angeles, where he stopped off to promote yet another Rumpole television series, to take a quick holiday, and decided definitely to leave the Bar knowing that he had enough writing projects to keep him busy and rich for the next five or six years.

He began to work on his first novel for twenty-nine years, which he called *Paradise Postponed* because it was inspired by his disappointment that the socialist Utopia of which he had dreamed for so long had still not come about in Britain. The novel was set around Henley and Turville

Heath and asked whether he was mad even to dream of Utopia. His central character was one of the post-war generation of young, right-wing Thatcherites, Leslie Titmuss, an ambitious, determined, working-class boy – apparently based on Mrs Thatcher's forceful minister Norman Tebbit – who fights his way to the top of the greasy political pole to become a forthright, populist Conservative Cabinet Minister and stern, puritannical symbol of the new ruthless Tory Britain that Mortimer professed to hate so much. Ranged in the novel against Titmuss is one of those trendy, left-wing, turbulent priests of the 1960s, the Reverend Simeon Simcox, a rich yet committed campaigner, protester and CND marcher, the rector of the nearby village of Rapstone, whose dreams of a socialist paradise are shared by his wife although she would never dream of inviting a member of the working class to tea. Yet when the Revd. Simcox dies he leaves £2 million to Titmuss, who represents everything that he abhorred. This bizarre bequest amazes his two sons, who Mortimer admitted later were based on two different sides of himself, 'the nasty flashy part' and 'the nice, quiet, middle-class chap' – and, like Mortimer, Simcox has a secret illegitimate child.

It was not a good novel, perhaps because Mortimer was writing sim-ultaneously a twelve-part version of it for television so that the book is jerky and episodic, like a restless TV script, with irritating flashbacks and too many characters, most of them cardboard. It was written in a slow, dreary, humdrum style and was neither funny nor witty, but its anti-Thatcherite tone was highly topical and most of the reviewers were fulsome when it was published the following year. 'This is the work of a very skilled comic dramatist,' said *The Times Literary Supplement*, and the *New York Times* said the book was 'thoroughly delightful' with 'a sense of the absurd, a shrewd eye for human foibles, and an infallible sense of comic timing'. I must have been reading a different book.

Mortimer's other major project in 1984 was his adaptation for tele-vision of John Fowles' novel *The Ebony Tower*. 'Mortimer clinched the rights over Anthony Andrews' head,' Derek Granger told me. 'He called Anthony and was quite savage, and Anthony was very surprised and hurt.' Olivier was to play the main part, of an old artist living with two lovely girls in a French forest, even though he could barely remember any of his lines, which had to be draped on the trees round about. When the director once asked him when he would begin to speak he replied with dignity: 'When I approach the dialogue.' The two beautiful girls were played by Greta Scacchi and Toyah Willcox, and since they were sometimes required to be naked Mortimer turned up several times on the set, though very sensibly 'his wife was always with him and he never made a pass at me', Ms Scacchi told me. 'I was twenty-three and it was one of my first films, and he was very lovable and warm, with a formidable brain, and the piece was beautifully adapted.'

Twenty-six-year-old Toyah Willcox was one of Mortimer's *Sunday Times* interviewees that year: she told him that although she had had orange hair as a teenager and had hung out with bikers she had remained a virgin until she was twenty. Lauren Bacall, now sixty but still husky-voiced and feisty, told him that she too had been 'a nice Jewish virgin' when she made her first film at the age of nineteen, *To Have and Have Not*, with her future husband Humphrey Bogart in 1944. Christine Keeler, now forty-two and living on social security in a flat in a vandalised council tower block in Chelsea, confessed that she deeply regretted her part in the scandalous Profumo Affair twenty-three years earlier. And when Mortimer had dinner with Raquel Welch at the Savoy Grill he was stunned by her beauty and perfect bosom even at the age of forty-four.

In the first week of June, with Penny due to give birth at any time, Mortimer announced that he was retiring at last from the Bar at the age of sixty-one. 'I always felt that when I grew up I would have to choose between being the advocate and the writer,' he told David Lewin of the *Daily Mail*. 'The advocate has to be passionate with detachment and persuasive without belief. The writer cannot help exposing himself, however indecently.' Like Rumpole he had always been a defence barrister except for one case when he had prosecuted some police officers. 'Naturally they got off,' he told Lewin. 'I never wanted to use my superior wits or whatever it is to send someone to prison.' Seven years later he told Andrew Duncan of the *Sunday Express Magazine* that he had long thought that 'the world of actors was real and that the Bar was a fantasy – everyone dressing up and pretending to be something they weren't. [And] I hated the servility – "if your Lordship pleases" [and] nowadays judges are getting very young and don't know much about anything.'

I asked him in 1993 whether he was particularly proud of anything he had achieved during his legal career. 'No,' he said. 'I didn't change anything. I made a slight change to the divorce law when I induced the English courts to recognise a Muslim form of divorce where my client had said to his wife "I divorce thee, I divorce thee, I divorce thee" on the Tube station at Aldgate East! That divorce wouldn't be valid if he was domiciled in Britain but it was in his case because he was only here on a trip. I cleared that little matter up but that's very dull and I can't say it's given me a glow of pride. I suppose finding people in a mess and guiding them into less of a mess has given me the most satisfaction. And I'm a QC for life and I don't think they can take that away from me unless I do something *really* awful!' He was in fact about to do something really wonderful: a delightful novel called *Summer's Lease*.

Twelve

Rosie, Russia and the Royal Court
1984–1992

Penny's second daughter was born on 14 June at Queen Charlotte's Hospital in Hammersmith and named Rosamond Lucy May. Like her father and Emily she was to have an unusual and lonely childhood because at sixty-one Mortimer was a grandfather and reluctant to find himself a father again and Emily was nearly thirteen and a pupil at the most intellectual girls' school in Britain, St Paul's at Hammersmith – another private, fee-paying academy to shame Mortimer's allegedly socialist principles. Rosie was a sickly baby who was so seriously ill during her first year that she was in and out of hospitals and her parents feared for her life, but miraculously her malady suddenly disappeared and she grew up to be quite unlike her quiet, studious, girly sister, to prefer toy cars, Lego and football to dolls, and to go on to become a horsy, headstrong tomboy who was naughty at school and called Emily 'Doris' because she thought she was boring.

Mortimer was by now such a celebrity that he was invited to become president of BBONT – the Berkshire, Buckinghamshire and Oxfordshire Naturalists' Trust – and accepted the post, and the council of the English Theatre Company, which ran the fringe theatre in Sloane Square, the Royal Court, asked him to become its chairman. He declined and the job went instead to Matthew Evans, the managing director of the publishers Faber and Faber.

In February 1985 the Mortimers escaped the English cold by flying to Morocco, where they were to spend several weeks every winter from now on in the same hotel just south of the Atlas mountains, near Marrakesh, where John would sit by the swimming pool writing his latest book or play and occasionally ride an old horse around nearby mud-hut villages. In March Alvin Rakoff started to film the television series of *Paradise Postponed*, which was to run for eleven hours and cost £6 million to make (£12 million). David Threlfall played Leslie Titmuss, Michael Hordern was the dotty Revd. Simeon Simcox, and Annette Crosbie the daft Dorothy Simcox. 'After two weeks shooting John said Threlfall should be fired,' Rakoff told me, 'but I said if he was fired I'd go too.' Eventually Mortimer admitted that Threlfall was so good as the cold, pushy, sarcastic Titmuss that, like Leo McKern as Rumpole, it was impossible to imagine anyone else playing the part. '*Paradise Postponed* is all about the decline and fall of the middle classes,' he told Sarah Bond of the *Daily Express*. 'It begins after the war when everyone looked forward to a wonderful new world which never came about. We ended up with the same old world.' This was nonsense: Britain in 1985 was a huge improvement on that of 1945, even from Mortimer's own liberal, socialist viewpoint. Was not the birth of the National Health Service a major improvement? The abolition of hanging? The decriminalisation of homosexuality and abortion? The loosening of the laws against censorship and obscenity? The decline in class consciousness and racial discrimination? The growth of tolerance and a genuine meritocracy? The thawing of the Cold War? The diminishing threat of a nuclear holocaust? Mortimer's apparent pessimism was little more than a pose to publicise the series.

'It was a long shoot, eight months,' Rakoff told me, 'and it was not a happy set-up because it was a very thin story spread over twelve episodes and it shows. The script didn't quite work – it had a lot of waffle in it and we kept trying to sharpen it – and John, the producer and I had to do a lot of rewriting. Even when we started shooting, the actors had to kick the dialogue around in order to make it fit. It wasn't easy like *A Voyage Round My Father*. Everyone thought they'd get *A Voyage Round My Father* multiplied by twelve but they didn't, they got twelve rather weak episodes. John is a very literate writer, wonderful at characterisations, but his visual sense is not all that wonderful and in all his adaptations he needed help visually. He also dashes things off rather quickly and his scripts were always unbearably long. When I suggested that we reduced the twelve episodes he was opposed to that. It was a huge mistake to have that many episodes, which weakened the impact. If we'd done it in four or six parts we could have gone from being quite successful to being a really whopping, *huge* success, but he couldn't see it and he can be tough. You can't be in our business as long as John without having some degree of ruthlessness and I saw him being pretty firm. Maybe he went along with the idea of twelve episodes for the money. I could never understand his need to make so much money. He was never poor and I'm sure he doesn't need money: he owns half the county by now! All the time we were working together he was buying another piece of land at Turville Heath. You'd think he'd been raised *poor* but his father sent him to expensive schools. I found it very strange. There's an avariciousness there which nobody can explain, and also a need to be the centre of attention. When he was younger he looked vaguely like a Down's syndrome child, with that slack jaw and long vacant face, and that's possibly the reason for this need always to be the centre of attention.' Another problem for Rakoff was that the producer was Mortimer's favourite television beauty, Jacquie Davis, with whom Rakoff had many rows, and often she ended the day in tears. 'I don't need a producer at all,' said Rakoff, 'but he brought in this lady and I found her unhelpful. And what sort of producer ends her days often in tears? What sort of professional behaviour is that?'

While they were shooting the series Mortimer had an operation on his foot for a snapped Achilles tendon. 'He was told that if he didn't have this operation there was a possibility he wouldn't be able to walk again,' said Rakoff, 'and he was very worried about it and went on about it, asking for advice, but it's not easy giving advice to the sort of man he is. They wouldn't guarantee that the operation would work but they did guarantee that if he didn't do it he'd be crippled. Luckily it was a success.' After the operation, however, he developed deep-vein thrombosis, had to take rat poison to thin his blood, and spent weeks in a wheelchair. When the doctors told him to give up alcohol during the treatment he ignored them. What was the point, he asked, of giving up all the things you enjoy so that you can live a couple of years longer in a geriatric hospital in Weston-super-Mare?

With the *Paradise Postponed* novel due to be published in September, Mortimer was honoured with an honorary Doctor of Literature degree from Susquehanna University in Pennsylvania and a rare tribute from *Butterworth's Law List*, the lawyers' *Who's Who*, which saluted Rumpole's fame by including a mischievous, fictitious entry for him and his non-existent chambers. There were also two big Sunday newspaper profiles. 'When the official history of English drama in the second half of this century comes to be written,' said Geoffrey Wansell in the *Sunday Telegraph*, 'John Mortimer QC may well find himself occupying a place of distinction alongside Harold Pinter, John Osborne, Tom Stoppard and

Samuel Beckett [for he] is a playwright of exceptional talent ... If anyone has inherited the place of the late Sir Terence Rattigan as the creator of elegant, thoughtful and intelligent drama it is Mortimer – although, as a friend says, "He can seem so frivolous that some people never quite take Mortimer seriously as a writer.'" The *Observer* in an anonymous profile in August compared his prolific output to those of Chesterton and Belloc, although 'he is more versatile than either [and] the epitome of the good-natured man'. It added that he was once described by a disapproving QC as 'the soft underbelly of the law' and that he admitted to occasional depression and 'to feeling a bit low, particularly in the afternoon' – which was hardly surprising considering that he drank so much champagne and wine in the middle of the day that he told me in 1993 that he always got drunk at lunchtime.

He continued to write interviews for *The Sunday Times* – Lord Scarman, Gloria Vanderbilt – and the Bishop of London, Dr Graham Leonard, warned him sternly but rather too late that sex outside marriage was a sin. By now Mortimer had become fond of the opera and was delighted when the general director of the Royal Opera House at Covent Garden, Sir John Tooley, asked him to translate *Die Fledermaus* for them and gave him four years to do it. The *Sunday Telegraph*'s literary editor, Miriam Gross, translated it literally from the German for him and he embarked on the long, painstaking job of putting it all into credible English that fitted the music and rhythms precisely. Now that he could no longer perform in court he found a new outlet for his love of acting by appearing now and then in his own one-man stage show, *Mortimer's Miscellany*, a farrago of jokes and anecdotes which he was to present in small theatres and halls for many years, usually with the help of a couple of actresses such as Joanna David and Angharad Rees. He continued to appear on television in at least one cameo role in each new Rumpole series and had a brief part as himself in a TV mini-series based on Fay Weldon's novel *The Life and Loves of a She-Devil*.

When *Paradise Postponed* was published in September Nicholas Shakespeare interviewed him for *The Times*, described him looking like 'a benign but unkempt pasha' and reported that he had discovered to his surprise that he had really enjoyed writing a novel again: 'There's nothing between you and the reader, no actors, no producers. It's been a marvellous pleasure writing prose. It's really what I want to do.' Over the next twelve years he was to write five more novels and numerous Rumpole stories but not one play for the stage.

It was rare for Penelope to steal the limelight from John but she did explosively in March 1986 when her warts-and-all biography of the Queen Mother was published and caused an uproar because she alleged that the old national darling was a sly, shrewd, coldly ambitious, calculating actress who had been jealous of the Duchess of Windsor, Wallis Simpson, because she had wanted to marry Edward VIII herself instead of her husband, George VI, whom Penelope said she had found 'totally repellent'. During the furore she announced boldly that she was a republican – unlike John, who happily accepted three months later an honour from the Queen, a CBE.

Another Rumpole book and series, *Rumpole's Last Case*, followed in 1987 despite the advice of the bestselling scribbler Jeffrey Archer, who bounced excitedly up to Mortimer at a book fair. 'Kill Rumpole!' he barked. 'It'll make a terrific story!' In the new book Rumpole actually left She Who Must Be Obeyed at last and dossed down in his chambers, relishing his glorious new freedom, but he soon returned – as did Leo McKern, who swore after every new series that he would never do another but failed to resist three more.

In July 1986 Mortimer became a grandfather for the second time when Jeremy's girlfriend Polly had their first child, Felix, and to protect his descendants' cultural heritage he joined other local celebrities – George Harrison, Robert Hardy and Mary Hopkin – on a committee to save the art deco Regal Cinema in Henley from demolition to allow a Waitrose supermarket to be built on the site. He had no hesitation, however, in making major changes himself to Turville Heath Cottage now that it was fifteen years since his mother's death. Apart from installing the swimming pool he added a conservatory to the side of the house, a two-bedroom guest-house cottage by the back door and bought thirty more acres of meadow and woodland.

In August the Mortimers flew south for their annual summer holiday in Tuscany, where there were now so many English residents and tourists that he dubbed it 'Chiantishire'. Each year now he was to rent a large villa with a big pool thirty miles east of Siena, near Arezzo, from Richard Ingrams' banker brother Leonard and to invite numerous friends to join them. He still wrote every morning but stopped at lunchtime to enjoy to the full the Italian food, wine, restaurants, art and culture that he loved – and Emily, who was now fourteen, quickly adopted Italian ways and pinched a policeman's bottom.

They returned to England in time for the first television instalment of *Paradise Postponed* in September and a chorus of acclaim from most critics, who praised its characters, warmth, wit and beautiful filming. One

British reviewer, however, Herbert Kretzmer of the *Daily Mail*, said the first instalment was 'sluggish and confusing and an unexpected disappointment' because there were too many characters and too much was shown in flashback. Nevertheless Melvyn Bragg fronted an admiring London Weekend Television profile of Mortimer on *The South Bank Show*, the newspaper interviewers flocked to his door and he told them exactly why he disliked so much Mrs Thatcher's lower-middle-class government and ministers who resembled Leslie Titmuss. 'I don't think there has ever been a government I dislike as much as this one,' he told Miriam Gross. 'It's the first time that people haven't even paid lip-service to what, to me, are the real English values, the values of Dickens – the idea that you should try to improve society, that you should feel compassion for the less fortunate, and that this should be your predominant political feeling.' When Alan Franks of *The Times* accused him of being a snob he admitted it and confessed 'I deprecate it greatly'. Yet when he himself interviewed the apparently ungentlemanly Norman Tebbit – who was now chairman of the Conservative Party and castigated by Labour MPs as 'the Chingford Skinhead' and 'a semi-housetrained polecat' – Mortimer was disconcerted to find him charming, sardonically funny, utterly honest, and as much an agnostic as he was. 'He's like an unshaven footman tittering behind a rather soiled white glove,' he told Caroline Bridgwood of the *Sunday Mirror*.

A second collection of his interviews was published at the end of 1986, *Character Parts*, he went to Buckingham Palace to collect his CBE – 'Regina meets Rumpole,' quipped Prince Philip – and more honorary degrees were heaped upon him: a Doctorate of Law from Exeter University, a Doctorate of Literature from St Andrews. In February Fleet Street rumbled with rumours that Neil Kinnock had put him forward for a life peerage but Mrs Thatcher had vetoed it because Mortimer was so rude about her. 'I thought he should go into the House of Lords,' Kinnock told me. 'If the Lords has a purpose it is to have artists and scientists of Mortimer's capability. I took it pretty much for granted that he would go to the Lords because there's a spectrum of issues on which somebody like Mortimer would be great. He would not be a good constituency MP: dealing with housing repair complaints wouldn't have been his forte. He hasn't got a lot of time for party politics and he would have bloody hated the incessant pettiness of a lot of it. It can be as bad as the Bar.'

In January he flew off again to Australia to promote his two latest TV series and books, *Paradise Postponed* and *Rumpole's Last Case*. When he returned to Britain he finished writing a revue about Shakespeare which was to be produced at a gala evening at the National Theatre in May to celebrate Olivier's eightieth birthday and began *Summer's Lease* and yet another collection of Rumpole stories and scripts, *Rumpole and the Age of Miracles*. His reputation was now so high that his publishers reprinted three of his earliest novels – *Charade, Like Men Betrayed* and *The Narrowing Stream* – and some of his fame was already rubbing off onto Emily, now fifteen, who was asked by *The Sunday Times Magazine* to write an article about what is was like to be a teenager. In it she said she was convinced she would get three A-grade A levels, win a scholarship to Oxford, have 'countless impassioned affairs' with older men, marry in a vast white wedding gown with a veil longer than Princess Diana's, and become the most famous actress in the world. Every one of those dreams – except perhaps the flings with old fogeys – were to come at least partly true. She was not yet ready, however, to admit publicly that although John was wonderfully tolerant and liberal – Penny was the family disciplinarian – she was always excruciatingly embarrassed when she went to a London nightclub and he would come in at midnight to collect her wearing his gardening cap and squeaking: 'Emily, darling, where are you?'

In May Mrs Thatcher announced a general election to be held on 11 June and Mortimer, who had recently been castigated by the Industry Secretary John Butcher as 'an up-market punk who has made money for fifteen years by eroding the self-confidence of the British', told Caroline Bridgwood that 'it's the worst decade since I've been alive. Very selfish, very money orientated, and it'll be a ghastly world if Mrs Thatcher wins the General Election.' He prayed that Kinnock would win because 'he would make an admirable Prime Minister' and told Jane Adams of *Today* glumly: 'I don't know if I can stand another five years of Thatcher. I hope an election will mark the end of her, but I have my doubts. The majority of people are against her, you know.' He was wrong. She beat Kinnock by an even bigger majority than before, 376 seats to 229, to make her the first Prime Minister for more than a hundred and sixty years to win three elections in a row. One of the casualties was Roy Jenkins, who lost his seat after thirty-nine years in Parliament, never to return as an MP – a defeat that Mortimer did not regret because he blamed Jenkins and his breakaway Social Democratic Party for splitting the Labour Party and the anti-Tory vote.

Depressed by the result, Mortimer flew to New York for the *Daily Telegraph* to interview the seventy-eight-year-old doyen of Anglo–American broadcasters, Alistair Cooke, to mark his two thousandth BBC *Letter From America* radio programme. Nine years earlier he had sneered at Cooke and his programme but now he praised his gentle voice, the 'perfect timing' of his broadcasts, and said he had enjoyed listening to his stories about all the famous people he had met during his career. Experienced in American politics though Cooke was, he was no more successful than Mortimer as a political prophet, telling him that it was 'inconceivable' that President Reagan would be succeeded by his Vice-President, George H. Bush, when he retired the following year. 'It'll be a Democrat,' he said. He was wrong. Bush became the next president in 1988.

The Kinnocks licked their wounds by joining the Mortimers again that summer in Tuscany, where John worked tirelessly on *Summer's Lease*, possibly the best of all his novels. It told very readably a funny, unusual story about a fortyish English solicitor who rents a villa in Tuscany exactly like Ingrams' for his family's summer holiday but makes the mistake of inviting his harassed wife's appalling seventy-seven-year-old roué father, Harverford Downs. Downs is the third unforgettably vivid comic character that Mortimer created in his fiction: a lecherous, malicious, unscrupulous yet hilarious rogue who is writing a pretentious weekly newspaper column called 'Jottings from Tuscany' in which he recalls with sleazy nostalgia his sexual misbehaviour in Chelsea in the 1960s, when – like Mortimer – he wore jeans and gold chains even though he was in his fifties, chased blonde miniskirted girls who were young enough to be his daughters, and suffered from an irritating wife who refused to turn a blind eye to his infidelities. The plot is enlivened further by the mysterious disappearance of the villa's English owner, a possible murder, a criminal racket involving water shortages in Chiantishire – and a painting by the fifteenth-century artist Piero della Francesca, *The Flagellation*, in which Christ is shown being beaten.

In Italy Mortimer also found time to film a television travelogue, *Mortimer in Tuscany*, for which he interviewed two local British celebrities, the aesthete Sir Harold Acton and the novelist Dame Muriel Spark, and he started yet another collection of Rumpole stories and plays, *Rumpole and the Age of Miracles*, in which Hilda walks out of the Rumpole marriage, Phillida Erskine-Brown becomes a judge, and one of Rumpole's clients is accused of trying to drown his wife in the bath because she has always made him sit at the tap end – a scenario that echoed one of his own real court cases, suggests most married couples bath together and conjures up the mind-boggling vision of Mortimer trying to squeeze his enormous bulk into the same tub as Penny.

In September Jeremy, who was now thirty-two, at last married Polly Fisher, the mother of his fifteen-month-old son, after they had lived together for eleven years. His sister Sally had just had another boy and Polly was to give Mortimer yet another grandchild, his fourth, when her first daughter, Dora, was born a year after the wedding.

Summer's Lease was published in April 1988 and greeted by the usual fanfare of literary lunches, bookshop signings and media interviews, including an appearance on Terry Wogan's television chat show where Mortimer was miffed to discover that he was not the main guest. Top of the bill instead was the black American feminist writer Maya Angelou, who Mortimer muttered ungallantly 'has been raped the requisite number of times'. To promote the book further *Mortimer in Tuscany* was broadcast in May but the reviewers dismissed it as a bland, blatant plug for *Summer's Lease*. 'Glib and glossy,' said *The Times* sourly, 'less a potted guide to Tuscany than an oleaginous commercial for a product never quite glimpsed.' The *Daily Mail* was equally sniffy and reported that Muriel Spark 'proved remarkably unresponsive to the Mortimer charm', but a fortnight later the paper's star interviewer, Lynda Lee-Potter, was taking him to the Savoy Grill for lunch and listening to him explaining why he had never really grown up and how insecure he always felt. 'It's the worst side of vanity, refusing to grow up,' he admitted, and 'saying things not because I mean them but just to start an argument.' Criticism or a bad review always devastated him, he said. 'It goes back to being an only child, you think you have to make an impression. It's that thing of "look at me, I'm dancing on the table". I lurch from insecurity to insecurity [and] I don't like confident people.'

By the middle of 1988 left-wing intellectuals were so depressed by what they saw as Mrs Thatcher's callous, intolerant, illiberal, monetarist philosophy and the predominance in Britain of powerful right-wing commentators in the media who supported her that Mortimer, Harold Pinter and his wife Lady Antonia Fraser founded a left-wing, radical-chic philosophy group and think tank that sounded like some Mexican revolutionary movement, the 20th June Club. It was to meet regularly for supper and highbrow political chat at the Pinters' luxurious London house at 52 Campden Hill Square – the very house in which Lady Antonia's first husband, the Tory MP Sir Hugh Fraser, had held meetings of a *Conservative* philosophy group in the 1970s that were attended by Mrs Thatcher and helped to bring her to power. Among the first 20th

June Club members were Melvyn Bragg, Margaret Drabble, Richard Eyre, Germaine Greer, David Hare, Michael Holroyd, Anthony Howard, Margaret Jay, Peter Nichols, Salman Rushdie and Geoffrey Robertson, and later meetings were addressed by Labour luminaries such as Barbara Castle and Denis Healey. Pinter insisted that the club's membership and activities should be kept secret, as though it were the Ku Klux Klan, which caused hilarity in the right-wing media when its existence was exposed a fortnight later. LADY ANTONIA'S INFIDELITY, crowed the cover of the Tory magazine the *Spectator* and for months there were derisive jeers in the Press about 'literary luvvies', 'champagne socialists' and 'Bollinger Bolsheviks,' many of whom, including Mortimer, were to sign a 'Charter 88' manifesto demanding a British Bill of Rights and a written constitution.

There was another meeting in December when the irascible Pinter appalled Mortimer by glaring at Geoffrey Robertson's girlfriend Kathy Lette and barking: 'I haven't got you on my list. Who are you, anyway?' She was in fact a brash, loud, foul-mouthed Australian writer who had just arrived in Britain, had recently published her second raunchy chick-lit book, and was so keen to write and talk about sex and contrive unfunny, sleazy puns that she gave Down Under a whole new meaning. 'What do cold beer and cunnilingus have in common?' she asked. 'You can't get either of them in London.' She seemed surprised that few English people took to her even though she was to marry Robertson two years later and they were to become Mortimer's close friends. The Pinters decided to throw the giggling media off the scent by holding their next meeting, in March 1989, at the fashionably expensive River Café on the Thames at Hammersmith. The Mortimers took along their friend Ann Mallalieu and other newcomers included the politician Harriet Harman and the novelists Angela Carter and Ian McEwan. Pinter was elected chairman and the assembled thinkers discussed the plight of Salman Rushdie, who had recently been sentenced to death by a Muslim *fatwa* because of his blasphemous novel *The Satanic Verses*. McEwan, Drabble and Mortimer said that the best thing that they could do for Rushdie was to shut up rather than make a fuss and incite further Muslim fury, but Pinter 'chose this moment to announce that tomorrow's broadsheets in Europe and the US would carry a letter signed by a thousand loony-marys expressing solidarity with our fellow writer', wrote the playwright Peter Nichols in his diary, an extract from which was published in the Oxford magazine *Arete* in November 2004. 'Ann Mallalieu now accused our coven of airy-fairy nonsense and Antonia, who'd been anxiously observing hubby's efforts to control this unruly class, demanded "with the greatest possible respect" what right Ann had to say that when she wasn't even a member of the group. At which Harold got even more chairman-like and asked: "Madam, I don't even know why you're here as you weren't invited." Penny Mortimer burst in to say Ann was in fact her guest and her name was on the invitation list but Antonia, with even greater respect, said she wasn't. This started an unstoppable ding-dong between Penny and Antonia [and] tempers hadn't cooled by the time we had to break up at 11 p.m.'

Pinter apologised to Penny two days later, saying, 'I'll never act as chairman again. I only behave like a ruffian,' but a fortnight after that he became enraged again at the club's next River Café meeting when he spotted a BBC journalist claiming a table that he had booked weeks earlier. Pinter ordered him to leave. The journalist refused, so Pinter threw him out but he returned, determined not to be menaced by this glaring apparition in his trendy black pullover and heavy horn-rimmed glasses. Pinter ejected him again and the journalist, instead of telling the owners exactly where they could put their poxy restaurant, agreed to leave and return instead another night. Pinter's reaction to Press attacks became ever shriller and after one he trumpeted: 'We are going to meet again and again until they break the windows and drag us out.' Nor was his glowering boorishness at an end. He, Lady Antonia and the Mortimers fell out seriously after meeting in a pub in the Portobello Road where Pinter became incandescent because Penny said she had seen a recent film, *Scandal*, about Christine Keeler's affair with the Minister for War, John Profumo, in 1963. Pinter was furious that she had dared to watch such a movie and exploded so violently and offensively – apparently because he and Lady Antonia were nervous that someone might make a scandalous film about them too one day – that Mortimer told him to 'piss off'. Penny was not the first Mrs Mortimer to be less than enthusiastic about the self-important Pinters: in her second volume of autobiography Penelope described a trendy socialites' party 'where the hostess delivered a lantern lecture on cunts [with] Antonia Fraser, exquisite as usual, sitting the entire evening on a small sofa, her expression placid, as though about to moo'. A couple of years later, during an interview with Andrew Duncan for the *Sunday Express Magazine*, Mortimer 'wondered idly' why Lady Antonia, who claimed to be a socialist, continued to use a courtesy title to which she was entitled only because her father was the Earl of Longford: 'Curious,' he said.

The Pinters realised that the 20th June Club might be taken more seriously and run more smoothly if they adopted a lower profile, so they handed the organisation over to Penny Mortimer – who had recently taken up the surprisingly un-left-wing pursuit of hunting on horseback – though they continued to attend meetings at yet another fashionable literary luvvies' venue, the Groucho Club in Soho, and the group kept going in a desultory fashion until 1992, when the Tories won yet another election, their fourth in a row, even after dumping Mrs Thatcher for John Major, and the 20th June Club collapsed, hopelessly disillusioned, like a wrinkled balloon.

Once again the Mortimers and Kinnocks repaired for their 1989 summer holiday to Tuscany, where Mortimer was approached in a restaurant by an angry English couple and their pretty, blonde, heavily pregnant daughter. 'Look at her!' cried the mother. 'It's entirely your fault!' Mortimer denied that he had ever met the girl. 'It's still your fault!' insisted the mother. 'She read your book about Tuscany and you made it sound irresistible!' It turned out that the father of her child was the owner of Mortimer's favourite Bar Dante in Radda, whom eventually she married.

Back in London in September Mortimer interviewed the crusty, right-wing, Thatcherite novelist Kingsley Amis for *The Sunday Times* over lunch at one of their favourite restaurants, the Savoy Grill, to talk about his latest comic novel, *Difficulties With Girls*. Amis denied that it was homophobic – 'the gay couple are two of the more sympathetic characters in the book' – and said of another of the book's characters, an adulterer called Patrick, 'if you're like Patrick and want to go to bed with everything that moves, you run the risk of losing what's most precious to you' – a warning that was a bit late for Mortimer. When the interview was published it contained a splendid misprint when it quoted Amis as saying that the only time he had ever got really angry was when he had hit his son with a hammer. His son? Martin Amis? The novelist? Could a blow on the head with a hammer at an early age perhaps explain why Kingsley found his boy's books so unreadable? In fact Amis senior had said that he had hit his thumb, not his son, with a hammer.

A few days later Mortimer interviewed the glamorous, giggly, fifty-five-year-old film star Joan Collins at her London hotel for the *Telegraph Weekend Magazine* to coincide with the publication of *her* novel *Prime Time*. She revealed that as a child she had wanted to be a detective, claimed that she enjoyed writing so much that she had not been so excited by anything since she had her first baby, and denied that her most famous TV soap, *Dynasty*, was some sort of camp joke but admitted that occasionally 'my tongue gets into my cheek'.

In September 1988 Richard Eyre succeeded Peter Hall as director of the National Theatre and Mortimer – who was now co-editing a book called *Famous Trials of Marshall Hall* on top of all his other work – decided to leave the board after twenty-one years even though Eyre was a friend. 'He just felt he'd done long enough,' Sir Richard told me in 2004. 'He wasn't forced to step down.' Hall took his three final National productions – Shakespeare's late plays *The Winter's Tale, The Tempest* and *Cymbeline* – on a tour of Russia and Mortimer went as well to write about it for the *Daily Telegraph*. 'I spent a couple of weeks in Moscow,' he told me in 1993, 'and I got to know quite a lot of writers and theatre people and had a *wonderful* time. It was the spring of the Gorbachev era, just at the end of the Afghan war, full of hope, and I was an honoured artist, they made a fuss of me, and I got so many roubles a day, a chauffeur and a car. Moscow is a place for having a really good time.' He was however startled to find in his room at the huge Peking Hotel in Mayakovsky Square two men in blue suits lying on his bed, watching television, munching pickled cucumbers, and reluctant to leave although they went eventually. He loved the beauty of the city but was depressed to discover in Gorky Street a big shop window displaying just three tired cabbages and to learn that his young woman translator had to live in a tiny flat with her husband, child, mother and stepfather, though he perked up when she asked him brightly whether he would like a bonk only to learn disappointingly that she thought a bonk was a drink. From Moscow the company moved a thousand miles south to Tbilisi in Georgia, where the actors had to perform without costumes or scenery because the props did not arrive in time, the actresses were all propositioned by randy locals, Mortimer was kissed alarmingly by a huge Georgian man who stuck his tongue deep into his ear, and the director of the opera house declared that he wanted to put on much more music by Vayber – Andrew Lloyd Vayber.

In November 1988 the government proposed to abolish the TV licence fee that paid for the BBC and suggested instead a scheme of commercial subscription, which infuriated Mortimer, who argued in the *Mail on Sunday* that the Thatcherite philistines who had already undermined the British film industry were now trying to destroy the BBC and sabotage its high standard of quality programmes, which would be swamped by old American films, serials and game shows. He repeated the accusation the next day during a heated debate on Channel 4 television with a Home

Office Minister, Tim Renton, who called him foolish and ignorant. Mortimer appeared on television as himself when *Rumpole and the Age of Miracles* was screened in November and he surfaced as a judge at a legal lunch. In another episode Caroline played a journalist in one of her last three brief television appearances before she retired three years later, in 1991. As the year ended he was also deeply involved in rehearsals at Covent Garden for his translation of *Die Fledermaus*, which was to be staged in January and his script to win praise from the critics.

Another burden was added to his workload when Roy Jenkins, now Lord Jenkins and president of the Royal Society of Literature, press-ganged him into becoming the RSL's new chairman in March. Mortimer asked for a short delay to decide whether he had time for it but the notoriously smug, arrogant Jenkins announced the appointment without his or the RSL council's agreement and presented him with a fait accompli. Mortimer was furious but could not withdraw without looking churlish. He was right to be wary of taking on the job because the RSL was about to begin a long battle to persuade the owner of its premises at 1 Hyde Park Gardens, Stephen Blumenthal, to extend its lease, which was due to expire in four and a half years. Mortimer took his revenge by calling Jenkins 'Woy' behind his back because he could not pronounce the letter r. 'Politically they were very close – one was a champagne socialist, the other a claret socialist! – but they didn't get on at all,' I was told by another member of the RSL's council, David Hughes, who was to become a vice-president for life in 1998. 'John didn't get on with Woy because of Woy's pomposity as much as anything. You had the sense that if Mortimer could take him down a peg or two he would.' Another council member, George Bull, 'said that Mortimer and Jenkins were like two dogs circling each other,' I was told by Hughes' wife Elizabeth, who was then the RSL's deputy secretary. 'I don't think there was a huge amount of love lost between them. John thought Roy was pompous and he *was* very pompous.'

Mortimer's style of chairmanship 'was very different from that of anybody else', said David Hughes. 'The meetings were always at tea-time on the second Tuesday of every month, there'd be a nice tea provided, and he would come in after a good lunch looking extremely jolly for reasons which are not hard to find. You couldn't say for sure that he was drunk but there was every sign that he'd had quite enough! He was certainly merry and shambling, in a good mood. He was very anxious to get through the business as relaxed as possible and he was never very good at consulting other councillors. He would say "well, that's decided, then" after a minimum of discussion. He'd already decided what was the best thing.' Another councillor, John Sutherland, 'used to say that he absolutely *loved* being on the council of the RSL just to see John take a meeting,' said Mrs Hughes, 'because it was so relaxed and John would say, "oh, we don't need to bother with that, really, do we?" Also he was very sharp when he needed to be, absolutely on the ball, especially over the Hyde Park Gardens lease. It went on and on and on, lawyers, surveyors, property experts, and John went to all the meetings even though it wasn't his area of legal expertise.' His literary expertise was not quite as impressive: 'At one time we needed money badly and John and Jenkins took [the rich literary patron] Mrs Heinz out to lunch to ask her to get some but neither was able to tell her what the RSL was all about! The two people who should have been able to explain it best just spluttered and were incapable of doing it!'

He did however launch his chairmanship by writing to every Fellow and member to ask if anything should be changed at the RSL. The replies were caustic and tended to claim that it was too genteel, snobbish, detached and ineffectual. 'Everybody always found John very convivial and nice,' said David Hughes, 'except that he was very snappy with the staff on occasion. He really snapped the head off one young assistant in her early twenties who had only just started there. I was never very easy with him because he's not a man's man, and I often suspected that the faint haze of faraway drunkenness might be a veil to conceal from himself the fact that he was slightly nervous and shy.'

In April Mortimer flew out to Tuscany with the producer and director of *Summer's Lease*, who were about to begin ten weeks of filming. The director, Martyn Friend, had previously directed two instalments of *Rumpole* and the producer was Mortimer's stepson-in-law Colin Rogers, who had previously produced the John le Carré series *A Perfect Spy*. To Mortimer's delight John Gielgud agreed to play Haverford Downs and wrote to his friends Pat and Michael York: 'I have a very amusing part to play, which I hope I may do justice to.' He did, and was superbly mischievous and jaunty as the dreadful Downs in his silk cravat, white jacket and straw hat with a cigarette dangling constantly from his lips. The other main parts were played well too by Susan Fleetwood, Rosemary Leach and Michael Pennington.

'It was wonderful to make,' Friend told me, 'and although it seems quite slow now Gielgud's performance is terrific' – it was to win him the Best Actor Emmy in 1990 – and 'he took the part by the throat. You'd think he was a young actor in his first part, wanting to make good. I found him very easy to work with and although he was eighty-five and I was forty-five he asked for direction, which put me at ease. He was also funny. We were shooting a scene where he was dressing for dinner and I said, "We'll get you coming out of that door with the sound of a loo flushing," and he said, "So you want the old queen coming out of the closet, do you?"'

In June Gielgud suffered a recurrence of an old prostate problem but insisted on carrying on for a week until the pain became too much. 'He acted with terrific verve,' said Friend. 'As an exhibition of raw courage I haven't seen an example like it. One could tell that he was in acute discomfort but he did not want to let the side down and had to be forced to fly back to England for an operation.' He was away for ten days. 'It's the kind of thing that a producer dreads,' said Rogers. 'It was a huge risk taking an actor that old abroad, but he was such a pro that all he was anxious about was getting back to the film.' Gielgud later told the publisher Ion Trewin that although Mortimer wrote very literate scripts the actors 'had to play around with the dialogue because it was not absolutely apt for the character'. Friend and Rogers were surprised by this claim. 'That's not true,' said Friend. 'John wrote wonderful dialogue.' Rogers agreed and said that 'the two Johns got on well together and enjoyed each other's company'. One day Gielgud and Mortimer were chatting about the missing aristocrat Lord Lucan when Mortimer said that Lucan had apparently been murdered by a contract killer for £3,000. 'Good Lord!' said Gielgud. 'Is that all it costs to have a man killed? If Donald Wolfit had known that he would have taken out a contract on me years ago.'

Another of Gielgud's old rivals, Lord Olivier, died on 11 July after a long battle with cancer and was buried in Westminster Abbey, much to Gielgud's irritation because he felt the abbey should be reserved for monarchs and great leaders.

Mortimer started work on an anti-Thatcherite sequel to *Paradise Postponed* which again he wrote simultaneously as both a novel and a television script, called it *Titmuss Regained*, and he and Jacquie Davis set up their own television company, New Penny Productions, to produce it. 'I thought it was very cruel to Penelope 1 to call themselves that,' said Irene Shubik, 'but John thought the whole New Penny/Old Penny thing was very funny.' In the new book Titmuss was now a pallid, sardonic, outspoken, devious Cabinet Minister in his fifties, married for the second time, and his ruthlessly right-wing policies have changed the face of England drastically. Swathes of beautiful countryside have been raped by motorways, new towns and shopping malls. Farm labourers' cottages have been tarted up and sold for vast prices to commuters working in computers, advertising or merchant banking. Every pretty old town centre is now disfigured by windy, soulless, pedestrian shopping precincts, congealed litter from Chinese takeaways, brutal concrete multi-storey carparks. Small corner shops have been driven out of business by vast out-of-town supermarkets; butchers and fishmongers by boutiques and health-food shops; cosy traditional pubs by poncy wine lodges. Yet when Titmuss hears of a plan to build ten thousand houses close to his country mansion he sets out to scupper it.

The novel, sadly, was as pedestrian as the precincts: an uneasy mess of cynical politics, romance and social satire that never really came together, with numerous flashbacks, even more irritating flashforwards, and tedious lectures. The end is pathetically limp and uninspired, and as for the book's dreadful style you have only to try to read the first sentence of chapter fourteen to realise that Mortimer was an amazingly careless writer: 'In the place on the Rapstone Nature Area, once known, although the fact is forgotten except by Hector Bolitho Jones and a very few former villagers now lodged in the Hartscombe Old People's Home, as Hanging Wood, there were, when Hector was a boy, at least fifty badgers.' Nor was the new Rumpole book, *Rumpole à la Carte*, much better: three of the six stories were so laboured, unlikely and repetitive that Mortimer was obviously straining to produce each new Rumpole book. 'I don't think he's a good novelist,' said David Hughes, himself a prizewinning author of more than a dozen highly praised novels. 'He's a slack and lazy writer. The Rumpole stories are pathetically banal and poorly written but I can quite see their appeal because the character is splendidly conveyed. To have thought of the character and present him with such skill is in itself an achievement. But he doesn't seem to rewrite much, which the best novelists do. He's low on self-criticism and high on self-satisfaction.' Yet Mortimer's reputation was now so inflated that he kept collecting more honorary degrees: a D.Litt. from Nottingham University, a D.Univ. from Brunel.

Now that Emily was seventeen and had left school after sitting A-level exams in English, History and Russian she decided to spend a gap year in Moscow before going up to Oxford to read English and Russian at the end of 1990, and Mortimer gave up the Maida Vale flat and retreated to the country, where he found he could write much more easily than in London. 'I wake up every morning delighted that I don't have to go to court,' he told Heather Dixon of the *Yorkshire Post*.

The *Summer's Lease* television series was screened in November and December 1989 but aroused the derision of the sixty-seven-year-old Tory politician and author Lord Lambton, who lived in Tuscany and wrote dismissively in the *Spectator* that Mortimer's parodies of middle-class mediocrity in the book and programme 'are exactly what I would expect from a professional class, left-wing parlour pink who has for years ... courted the company of millionaires'. The *Daily Express* sent Sharon Churcher to bait Mortimer with questions about his wealth, 'champagne socialism', sixty-acre estate and hypocritical decision to send Emily to private schools. 'I'm not rich at all,' claimed Mortimer, adding that his estate was only forty acres, not sixty, that there was nothing wrong with enjoying champagne – 'Stalin probably drank champagne' – and that Rosie, who was now five, was going to an ordinary village school. Ms Churcher did not ask what on earth Stalin might have to do with it but wrote: 'So thoroughly convincing are John Mortimer's bumbling mannerisms, self-deprecating wit and helter-skelter appearance that a stranger might mistake him for a harmless, slightly loony eccentric on the loose from the pages of one of his own novels ... His upper body has ballooned out of kilter with the spider legs on which he proceeds in a stately roll. His teeth apparently have been attacked at random angles with a chisel and his rose-pink-striped shirt threatens to part from his trousers, such are the magisterial dimensions of his paunch.' He told her that he would like to spend less on champagne and more in tax. 'He sounds serious,' she wrote, 'but there again, as with the characters in *Summer's Lease*, the truth is unfathomable.'

In January he became a grandfather for the fifth time when Polly had a second daughter, Beatrix. In February he took Penny and Rosie off to Marrakesh for their two-week winter holiday, and in March he told Scarth Flett of the *Sunday Express* that of all the fictional characters he had created Titmuss was his favourite because 'he has taken the Conservatives out of the the upper classes' – directly contradicting what he had told Miriam Gross of the *Sunday Telegraph* and Alan Franks of *The Times* four years earlier when he had sneered at Mrs Thatcher's Tory government because it was so lower middle class. Did he really mean what he told interviewers or believe anything at all, or was it all just camouflage? Did he really prefer Titmuss as a character to Rumpole and Haverford Downs or did he say so simply because he had a new Titmuss book to publicise? 'There is an endearingly bumbly, rumpled air about him,' wrote Ms Flett. 'His waistcoat is mis-buttoned, his brown leather shoes could do with a polish and his wayward hair is in need of a comb.' A cynic might ask why Mortimer always chose to look like a cuddly tramp when meeting interviewers and why his wife did nothing to smarten him up. He did not fool Scarth Flett. 'It is a deceptive image,' she wrote. 'His dress is entirely contrived.'

He continued to travel constantly and took another trip to Australia to promote his latest books, but on his return he was so appalled by the condition of the aircraft that he abandoned his usual mask of bumbling geniality and had a noisy row with the captain, telling him that he had 'the honour to be the pilot of undoubtedly the worst airline in the history of flying. The seats are falling to pieces, the carpets are disgusting, the loos are blocked, the place smells of disinfectant, the food shouldn't be given to hens, the hostesses look like officers from prison camps and there's no champagne.' He then raised his voice and addressed the other passengers: 'Listen to this. You are about to enjoy the worst flight the free enterprise system can produce.'

Thames Television agreed to fund New Penny Productions' first three-part mini-series of *Titmuss Regained* and Mortimer, Jacquie Davis and Martyn Friend, the director, went to Paris to persuade Kristin Scott-Thomas to play Titmuss's wife after Mortimer had admired her vague, beautiful performance in Evelyn Waugh's *A Handful of Dust*. 'When we had lunch with her in Paris we knew immediately that she was the one to play the part,' Friend told me. 'We shot the series partly in London and all the countryside stuff was done near Turville.' Less glamorous was a trip that Mortimer made to Slough to interview the head of the Muslim Institute, Dr Kalim Siddiqui, to ask why he was such a strong supporter of the *fatwa* that called for Salman Rushdie to be killed for writing *The Satanic Verses* and was taken aback to discover that despite his thirst for Rushdie's blood Siddiqui was a portly, bearded, jolly little man who was always laughing and had once been a sub-editor on the *Guardian*.

In June Mortimer took on yet another onerous job, as chairman of the council of the Royal Court Theatre, the post he had turned down six years previously. To make more time for it he resigned his presidency of BBONT and was wise to do so for the Royal Court, which dedicated itself to producing daring new plays, was to take up a huge amount of time. The current chairman, Matthew Evans, was resigning in 'despair', partly because of a lack of communication between the artistic director, Max Stafford-Clark, and the council. There were rows at council meetings about accepting commercial sponsorship from companies such as Barclays, doubts about its Arts Council funding, and the theatre needed to raise at least £800,000 (1¼ million) to repair the rotting beams under the stage, the precarious wooden fly-tower, the leaking roof, the shabby dressing rooms, and to muffle the noise of the underground trains that was so loud that at times the actors were inaudible. 'The Royal Court does take up a lot of time,' Mortimer told me in 1993, 'because it went through quite an upheaval, but it *is* great fun and lovely for me because it's a beautiful theatre, and I'm stage-struck, and it's very important because it encourages new writing.' He took over in June and 'with typical shrewdness and managerial know-how', I was told by Derek Granger, who had recently resigned from the council after twelve years' service, 'he introduced the idea of a small four- or five-strong executive committee of the most businesslike board members so that he didn't have to be regularly hamstrung with the cumbersome and unwieldy full group of the fifteen or so regular members. He was an effective and relaxed chairman and brought a necessary period of calm and healing after a tremendously turbulent period at the end of Max Stafford-Clark's period as artistic director.'

To film a new Rumpole episode, *Rumpole at Sea*, in which Horace and Hilda sail off on a second honeymoon, Thames Television took the actors and crew on a cruise ship that sailed in October 1990 around the Greek islands and Adriatic. 'We went from Piraeus to Venice via Dubrovnik and other places,' I was told by John Timbers, who went along to take publicity photographs. 'Penny wasn't with John, and whenever there was a party he was there jiving away, always doing an energetic version of the Twist and always dancing with the prettiest PA. He says he doesn't take exercise but he doesn't need to what with the shagging and dancing! He drank Tequila Slammers – tequila, ice and then you slam the glass down – and although I've seen him jolly he never got out of control or falling-down drunk.' Mortimer was never much of a dancer but Leo McKern was very light on his feet and would drag him onto the dance floor in the Dolphin Saloon and they would waltz together like Tweedledum and Tweedledee.

Emily returned from her gap year in Moscow, where she had lived with a twenty-eight-year-old, moustachioed Russian poet, Denis Novikov, even though he was ten years older and could not speak English. As they crossed Red Square one night holding hands in the moonlight he had said: 'It's such an honour to be walking across Red Square with a girl whose father defended the Sex Pistols.' She considered marrying him but knew she ought first to get her degree at Oxford, where she had passed the entrance exam and been offered a place at Lincoln College even though her A-level results had been poor: one A, one D and an unclassifiable U.

Mortimer insisted that the D and U papers should be marked again but the new examiners gave them exactly the same marks. Even so the college still accepted her, she went up to Oxford in October, pined for Denis, started a magazine called *Babel* and fell in love again with a handsome actor, Tom Ward. Meanwhile back at Turville Heath Rosie, now a feisty six, kept trying to interrupt her father's work, and as he and she were taking a bath together one day said suddenly: 'I don't love you, Dad.'

'That's very sad,' he said.

'Yes,' she said, 'but it's *interesting*.'

When her parents gave a lunch party at Turville Heath Cottage for a galaxy of famous actors, politicians and writers Rosie sat on the stairs and moaned, 'I'm bored, bored, bored, bored, bored, *bored*!'

The year ended joyously for Mortimer when Margaret Thatcher resigned as Prime Minister after eleven years in power, driven out by her Cabinet colleagues, and when the unlikely John Major replaced her Mortimer dared to dream again that Kinnock would soon become Prime Minister and Britain would be ruled again by socialists. There was still, however, strong opposition in Britain to Mortimer's liberal, permissive opinions and as the old year died the chairman of the Broadcasting Standards Council, Lord Rees-Mogg, attacked the BBC for its unrelenting diet of sex and violence on television and laid the blame for it on the fact that it was now run by 'children of the Sixties' whose sense of decency and morality had been corrupted by the Permissive Society. Mortimer responded by attacking Rees-Mogg in a full-page article in the *Evening Standard* under the headline 'DON'T TRUST ANYONE WHO REGRETS THE SIXTIES'. The Sixties had been an era of huge achievements, he argued, when Britain had abolished hanging, legalised homosexuality, become much more tolerant, understanding and critical of authority, and had produced wonderful films, drama and popular music – an argument that was precisely the opposite of the one he had used seven years earlier to publicise *Paradise Postponed* by whingeing that nothing whatever had changed for the better since 1945. He even had the nerve now to suggest that Britain had been better in the Sixties because there had been fewer divorces and bastard children, ignoring his own part in boosting both statistics. Yet again it is difficult to dispel the suspicion that often he did not really mean what he said and wrote.

Encouraged by Mrs Thatcher's downfall, Mortimer became increasingly political, writing articles in April in the *Guardian* and *Evening Standard* urging that a United Nations peacekeeping force should go into Iraq and use force against the dictator Saddam Hussein. *Today* reported that Neil Kinnock had once again nominated Mortimer as a working peer, yet again, mysteriously, he did not go to the House of Lords, perhaps because he had disapproving or sceptical enemies within the machinery of the honours system. 'It's disgraceful that he didn't,' said Lord Hooson. 'They were *crackers* not to make him a life peer. He would have been excellent because the Lords is just the right place for a fellow like him.' Sir Jonah Walker-Smith agreed: 'John would have been superb as a peer, and if you make Ann Mallalieu a peeress why not John? He *should* have been a peer and it's a great pity he never was.' Equally political and heated was the atmosphere at the Royal Court Theatre thanks to a row over who should replace Stafford-Clark as Artistic Director when his contract expired in a few months. Although he had agreed to leave he was now reapplying for the job and Mortimer would have been happy to reappoint him but many on the council wanted a change and were angry that he was allowing Stafford-Clark to reapply. One councillor, Jocelyn Herbert, accused him of packing the selection committee with Stafford-Clark supporters and wrote: 'Mortimer's behaviour was appalling about this.' The dispute dragged on for seven months while the committee interviewed several candidates and dithered for so long that the director Lindsay Anderson said Mortimer and the committee were 'craven' and should resign. The leading candidate to replace Stafford-Clark, Stephen Daldry of the Notting Hill Gate Theatre, became so fed up with the delays that in October he said he was withdrawing his application. 'Once I'd understood the political game playing I thought I'd just do the same,' he told Philip Roberts, who was writing a history of the Royal Court. 'It was horrible for John primarily but I thought this is a playpen. I'll get in the playpen and start throwing a bit of sand about and see what happens.' Alarmed, the committee quickly decided on a feeble compromise: Daldry was appointed Artistic Director Designate but Stafford-Clark was allowed to remain in tandem with him as Artistic Director for another eighteen months. Some council members were unimpressed by this cop-out and loudly critical of Mortimer, and then the Arts Council complained that the theatre was not presenting enough plays to justify its grant. It was a rough start to his chairmanship.

By May 1991 he had become so unusually political that he joined Kinnock and the Labour ex-Cabinet Minister Barbara Castle on the platform of a packed village hall at Usk in south Wales to speak in support of a Labour candidate who was standing there in a by-election for the parliamentary seat of Monmouth, Huw Edwards, a thirty-eight-year-old university lecturer in social policy. Monmouth was held by the

Tories with a majority of 9,300 and Mortimer was there to persuade middle-class voters to swing to Labour by telling them why he had always voted Labour. 'The poor bloody candidate wasn't afraid of the audience,' Kinnock told me, 'but he was terrified of us behind him, the poor sod! We were praying for him to be effective and Mortimer told a string of jokes but every one with a civilised sting: "What do we stand for? Why are we here? Why are we campaigning for this young man?" Barbara, who was a great mate of the Mortimers, spoke last and you could see her getting ignited, determined to do better than John because she was competition personified. She made an incandescent speech, it was a great night, and we all went off and had a few gins, a meal and few laughs. Huw was very very nervous, so when we got to the hotel for a meal I was thinking up all the songs that included 'you' in them: "It had to be Huw", "Only Huw", "Huw are My Sunshine", "If Huw were the Only Boy in the World", and this went on and on because although John's singing is as bad as Michael Foot's he's encyclopaedic about the pop songs of the Thirties. Nowadays he "sings" some Cole Porter number while he does a kind of sitting-down dancing.'

Edwards, who was still an MP in 2004, but lost the seat back to the Tories in 2005, told me that he was a bit embarrassed by the singing 'but it relieved the tension after the longest day of the campaign. The by-election was very significant. It was an affluent rural seat but we won with a majority of 2,300. The loss of Monmouth to Labour possibly delayed the general election another year.' With typical exaggeration and laziness Mortimer claimed in *Murderers and Other Friends*, without bothering to check, that Labour won the seat by ten thousand votes, but Kinnock was so impressed by his performance on the platform that the *Sunday Telegraph* reported that he was thinking of making Mortimer his Lord Chancellor should he win the next election. A week later the *Sunday Express* repeated the rumour and added mischievously: 'Wouldn't it be a wonderful thing for the man who has made so much money out of poking fun at the country's judges to find himself suddenly in charge of the lot of them?' Kinnock told me, however, that he had never thought of appointing Mortimer to the job. 'I would have sent him to the Lords but for Lord Chancellor you need not just a good lawyer but also someone with a history of party political engagement.' Mortimer told me that he would have hated being Lord Chancellor, 'having to sit there all day. I did this wonderful interview with Lord Hailsham when he was Lord Chancellor and I said, "You look so bored sitting on the Woolsack and scratching yourself and falling asleep and looking up at the stars and scratching your legs. How do you keep yourself amused?" And he said, "Well, I whisper 'bollocks' to the bench of bishops!" I had no intention of doing that.'

Another suggestion was that Kinnock would make Mortimer his Minister for the Arts but he told me that 'a minister for the arts needs to be someone who really can convincingly cross swords with the Treasury and mobilise opinion across their own party and in parliament. As an *adviser* to a minister for the arts Mortimer would be pure gold. Pity he's never been properly used.' At the end of the year, when Kinnock was described by Edward Pearce in the *Guardian* as 'an adolescent fool', Mortimer wrote a loyal letter to the editor to defend his friend, though he admitted that Kinnock's speeches were not always brilliant and that he tended to lose his temper in the Commons.

One new job that Mortimer did take on that year was the presidency of the Howard League for Penal Reform, which lobbied continually for a reduction in the prison population. 'Britain is now number one in Europe for sending the most people to prison,' he told the *Daily Mail*. 'Too many are serving time for what are relatively minor offences. Putting people inside does not improve them – prisons are the universities of crime.' His new post allowed him to make a regular jest at the expense of his political *bête noire* Michael Howard, the Employment Secretary and future Home Secretary whom Mortimer was to blame for increasing the prison population: jokingly he would refer to the Howard League for Penal Reform as the Penal League for Howard Reform. He wheeled out another of his favourite jokes when Richard Eyre came to dinner in June, telling him about a man who came home drunk one night and fell asleep on the stairs, where his prankster sons found him, took some chicken giblets from the fridge and stuffed them into his flies before going up to bed. 'Some time later,' wrote Eyre in his diary, 'the wife comes downstairs, looking for her husband, and sees the dog bent over him, apparently eating his genitals. She screams, falls downstairs, breaks her arm, and sues her sons for damages.'

As the row at the Royal Court rumbled on Mortimer found himself in July having to referee another fight at the Royal Society of Literature, where several council members were angry that their president, Lord Jenkins, had with his customary arrogance high-handedly fiddled the vote to elect four new Companions of Literature, the RSL's highest honour. All agreed on Muriel Spark, Anthony Burgess and Kathleen Raine but Jenkins had also unilaterally 'elected' the travel writer Patrick Leigh-Fermor instead of the candidate the majority preferred, the poet

Seamus Heaney. Leading the protest were the crime novelist P. D. James and Jeremy Treglown, ex-editor of *The Times Literary Supplement* and that year's chairman of the judges for the Booker Prize, and the RSL's next council meeting overruled Jenkins and declared his behaviour unconstitutional. They also instructed Mortimer to write to the Secretary of State for Education and Science, Kenneth Clarke, to protest against the choice that year by the University of London Schools Examination Board of Frederick Forsyth's thriller *The Day of the Jackal* as an A-level English set-book. Clarke agreed that the book was not sufficiently literary but said that he had no power over exam boards.

With so many outside interests and responsibilities – Mortimer even agreed to be a judge for that year's *Sunday Express* Book of the Year Award, which I ran – it is remarkable that he found any time to write, but even on holiday in Tuscany again in August he was working on another novel, *Dunster*, which was to turn out to be very much better than *Titmuss Regained*. Its protagonist, Philip Progmire, is a timid accountant for a London television company, Megapolis, that has commissioned his old friend Dick Dunster to write a series about war crimes. Progmire and the lively, irreverent Dunster have not seen each other for years – not since Dunster stole Progmire's wife and married her. She is not the only reason Progmire hates Dunster – a mischievous, irritating troublemaker who prides himself smugly on always telling the truth, no matter how rude or uncomfortable it is nor whom it might hurt – and when he produces a script accusing Progmire's boss, Sir Crispin Bellhanger, of having committed a war crime Sir Crispin sues him for libel with unexpected results. It is an excellent novel that turns into a thriller – amusing and moving as well as gripping, intriguing and very readable, with a splendid ending – and most of the reviewers agreed when it was published in 1992.

No fewer than two of Mortimer's new television series were screened in October, *Titmuss Regained* and a sixth helping of *Rumpole*, yet still he scribbled on, working already on the seventh and final Rumpole series. He was himself the main character in another television programme, a reconstruction of the *Oz* trial written by his old sidekick Geoffrey Robertson, now a QC himself, in which Mortimer was played by Simon Callow, Richard Neville by Hugh Grant and the judge by Mortimer's almost-ex-stepson-in-law Leslie Phillips. 'I never spoke to Mortimer about it, either before or after,' Callow told me. 'My performance was based on film clips.' The theatre critic and literary agent Giles Gordon asked Mortimer what he had thought of Callow's 'rather underpowered' performance. 'I hope I had more energy than that,' he said.

In November 1991, two years after the Communist Party in Czecho-slovakia had been overthrown in a 'velvet revolution' and the playwright Vaclav Havel been elected president, Mortimer flew to Prague to stay with the sister of the woman who had always translated his books into Czech, Jaraslova Moserova, and was appalled to discover that Czech judges earned only £250 a month (£4,260 a year) and that his hostess, who introduced him to the new chief judge of the supreme court, earned 15p an hour as a gynaecologist, about 21p in 2004. The judge took him to lunch in a restaurant where Mortimer asked how different it had been under the Communists. 'Cheaper!' said the judge.

It had been a memorable year but also alarming because he discovered that he had glaucoma when 'one of the retinas fell off my left eye', he told me two years later, 'so I can only see out of my right one. It happened when I was in the office of a television company giving prizes to young playwrights and suddenly I couldn't see half of the people there. They did an operation the next morning to stick it back on again but it doesn't work properly. That's frightening because it's exactly what happened to my father, so I'm always frightened that I'll go blind. With one eye I can't judge distances very well and it intereferes with my reading. I have to have drops in my eyes, they get quite tired, and I don't read nearly as much as I did or should do.'

Straight after Christmas, which he said he always loved as long as there were children around, he took the family off to Morocco again, where they met in their hotel a kindred spirit: a frail, rich, old upper-class Englishman who was dying of cancer and his brash, tattooed, working-class boyfriend, who was helping him to end his life with style, eating lobster and drinking pink champagne. The old man had been given only a month to live but had decided defiantly to make the most of his last few days rather than endure some dreadful hospital treatment that might prolong his life by a miserable few months – just as Mortimer would have done himself in the same situation. Back in England the old man wrote to him but a month later he was dead.

When *Dunster* was published in March one reviewer declined to join the chorus of praise: Ian McIntyre, a former controller of BBC Radios 3 and 4, who wrote waspishly in *The Times* that Mortimer was 'a considerable show-off. When I read, in a savage cameo of one of the Megapolis directors, that he "began a little snuffling giggle" at one of his own jokes, I wondered if he had caught the habit from his creator. Unremitting smartness can be wearing. I reckon that on a good day Mortimer gusts up to about Force 7 on the Ned Sherrin scale. The writing only really calms down when Mortimer stops trying to impress and settles to his plot.' He concluded contemptuously that 'Mortimer manages to fit in the regulation number of unbuttonings and unzippings. I did not keep a note of the incidence of copulation, but I am sure it will work out neatly at not less than one bout for each episode of the television series. He has been called many things in his time, from a former practising barrister to a champagne socialist, but nobody could ever call John Mortimer uncommercial.' In fact, surprisingly, *Dunster* was never televised.

Mortimer was still doing his best to help Neil Kinnock win the general election that John Major announced would be held in April 1992. WHY ARE WE SO BEASTLY TO NEIL KINNOCK? asked the headline over an article he wrote in the *Evening Standard* that asked why so many newspapers were biased against Kinnock, whom they had called a 'windbag' and 'ignoramus'. Two weeks later he tried again under the headline DON'T BE SCARED TO VOTE LABOUR, claiming that life had been wonderful under Clement Attlee's Labour government from 1945 to 1951. It was no good. Even though Kinnock had abandoned many of Labour's unpopular left-wing policies and was convinced he would win, the electorate voted the Conservatives back into power for the fourth time in a row. Kinnock resigned as Labour leader and went on to build a new career in Brussels as a European commissioner while his wife became a member of the European parliament. 'I was very depressed when Neil lost,' Mortimer told me a year later, 'and I think that was the end of the sort of Labour Party which I've known and loved all my life. Whatever emerges is going to be different. Whatever you think about Neil Kinnock, at his best he was representing the old ideals of the Labour Party of Attlee and Nye Bevan, who changed the whole face of England. I'd love to see the Conservatives vanish but I don't feel that great pull towards this present Labour Party. I'm not quite sure what it's standing for or what it's about. It's very sad.' He was not to see another Labour government for five years, and when it came he hated it.

Thirteen

A National Treasure
1992–2003

Many of the Kinnocks' 'friends' abandoned them after he lost the election but the Mortimers 'were lovely', Kinnock told me. 'They got in touch instantly with "don't let the bastards get you down" messages and said "now you can come to the theatre more often".' They all went off to Tuscany and 'there are few pleasures that exceed sitting on that verandah', said Kinnock, 'in that beautifully situated Tuscan farmhouse with sixteen at the table, terrific food, endless flows of any kind of booze anybody has ever thought of, and conversation that is sometimes quite profound, often joshing, great storytelling, jokes that vary from the new and uproariously funny to the ancient. You can hear a joke ten or a dozen times – I'm not kidding! – and it's never told in exactly the same way and Pen will say, "oh John, everybody's heard this!"'

Not everyone was enamoured of Mortimer and his genial manner. The foodie guru Sir Clement Freud took him out for lunch to interview him for *The Times* and was not impressed when he made his chauffeur wait outside while he guzzled champagne, wine, dessert wine and grappa and refused to move his arms from the table as the waiter tried to remove his plate. Freud thought Mortimer was arrogant and insensitive and wrote: 'His mind is in very much better shape than his body. He walks like Uncle Fester.' Others were cynical when he joined a campaign to turn Turville's empty village school into a retreat for inner-city children from London. Several of the local glitterati joined the campaign, including the Jeremies Irons and Paxman, but many who actually lived in the village felt that a rowdy kids' hostel would ruin their tranquillity. Not Mortimer:

he wrote a worthy article in the *Evening Standard* generously supporting the plan but omitted to mention that he did not actually live in the village himself but two peaceful miles away. It was to be four years before the local council endorsed the scheme.

That summer Mortimer made his final Hitchcocky appearance in the last Rumpole episode of all when he played a lawyer at a legal lunch in the Temple and said, 'Madeira, bishop?' 'It took the whole bloody morning,' he told me. 'I could have written the whole *script* in that time! As an extra you discover how actors are treated: nobody tells them what to do or takes a blind bit of notice of them.'

Ticking away like a timebomb throughout 1992 was Penelope, who was seventy-four, living in London again in a ground-floor flat in Cricklewood, had had half a lung removed because of cancer, and had decided to write a second volume of autobiography in which she was to savage Mortimer and expose the true nature of their marriage. 'Penelope was a total nightmare,' I was told by her editor at Weidenfeld and Nicolson, Ion Trewin, 'a woman who was really embittered by life. She was not well, really looked her age and was still smoking. She insisted that I should go to her house regularly but it was terribly inconvenient to get to. She would send me a chapter and then I'd go out and discuss it but she found it very difficult to accept praise and never took anyone's word for anything, so whatever I said was then tested out on other people like Jeremy, who read everything. I'd say, "I think you've got that chapter absolutely right, that's great," but the next time she'd say, "I've rewritten that chapter because so-and-so said something." It was so *frustrating*. I said to her once, "I don't know whether I'm the right person to edit you because we seem to agree about things and then you change your mind," and she said, "Oh no no, I need you, you're very valuable." She was a passionate gardener – no flower was out of place, no weed would have dared show its face – and I said "you have a nice garden" but she dismissed it and said "oh, it's easy to do". There was an awful lot in the book about John and his infidelity, so I asked her how he would react. "I'll tell him," she said. "He can hardly complain," and I think Jeremy became an intermediary. I don't think John was in a position to *stop* her writing it. He was hardly likely to sue her. She never made very much money from her writing and I think he bailed her out financially until late in her life. It was a way of buying her off too.'

Since Mortimer was the villain of Penelope's autobiography it seems appropriate that his own next book should be *The Oxford Book of Villains*, which he edited for the Oxford University Press with the help of Emily and several other researchers. Published in September 1992, it was an anthology of short factual and fictional pieces about murderers, crooks, seducers, cads, con men, hypocrites, traitors, spies and tyrants, and included a couple of extracts from his own Rumpole stories. He was to edit a similar anthology the following year for W. W. Norton, *Great Law and Order Stories*.

On 6 October Denholm Elliott died at seventy, inevitably of Aids, at his home in Ibiza, and after Mortimer spoke at his memorial service in London in January the mourners repaired to the Ivy restaurant where Elliott's cousin Forest Ellvers approached him for a chat. 'As I'd been with him at Harrow and he'd been to my house not so very long before I thought I'd go along and have a word,' Ellvers told me. 'He was talking to somebody, glanced at me, thought *oo-ah*, and looked away. I waited about ten minutes for him to speak to me but he was obviously keeping me waiting intentionally and I thought, no, I don't really like you. I have difficulty disliking people but I wasn't very fond of him, and Denholm would have been very upset if he'd known about him and his wife.' Mortimer had another nasty reminder of mortality when a BBC radio reporter came to interview him and offered to read out the obituary they planned to broadcast when he died. 'Put it away, for God's sake!' he cried.

In February he and Penny took Emily to Morocco, where several English holidaymakers in their hotel cut him dead until they discovered that Emily was not Woodrow Wyatt's lubricious young daughter Petronella, as they had thought, and that he was not sleeping with her. When he returned to England he indulged his love of acting by appearing at the Oxford Playhouse with Jacqui Dankworth, Mel Smith, Griff Rhys Jones, Tim Brooke-Taylor and a troupe of tap dancers, Zoots and Spangles, as the compère of a charity show. He read some poetry too, cracked a few jokes and recited *The Party's Over* in the manner of Noël Coward.

At the end of March he flew again to Moscow to spend a sunny week with Emily, who was there for her third undergraduate year to improve her Russian and take an acting course at the Moscow Arts Theatre. With her was her Oxford boyfriend Tom Ward, with whom she was living in a tiny flat in a crumbling block. Emily's old Russian boyfriend, Denis, took them to eat at the Writers' Union, where Mortimer was robbed, though this did not bother him unduly because 'if you've got a handful of dollars you can live in great luxury in Moscow', he told me two weeks later. 'My books don't sell there like they do in Czechoslovakia, but they do some of my plays so I had some roubles to collect. It's a very beautiful

town and incredibly changed. GUM, which used to be for buying
voluminous knickers and very dreary greatcoats, now has Christian Dior,
Galerie Lafayette, Benetton, everything, and the Russians are queuing
outside. They're either hard-currency prostitutes, taxi drivers or crooks
and they all look extremely well dressed and fed. The beggars consist of
gipsy children and old ladies, pensioners who are very badly off, but
they're no more predominant than they seem to be in London and you
can buy anything. You go to the market and there are banks and banks
of fruit and caviar. The whole thing is an endless market. Emmy can do
it all. You come out of the hotel and she ignores the taxis but just holds
up her hand and the first car stops – they're just people going home –
and she sticks her head in and drives a bargain for how much it'll be to
get her where we want to go. And the palatial Metropole Hotel, which
is just by Red Square and probably the most expensive hotel in the world,
$350 a night, is marvellous. We had a great dinner party in Emmy's
very small flat and had very good conversations with Russians about
Shakespeare and life and literature, and when you come back to England' –
he chortled – 'everyone's talking about Charles and Di! Nobody wants
to go back to communism.' I asked Mortimer whether it bothered him
as a socialist that most Russians had rejected socialism. He laughed
nervously. 'We know all the disadvantages of communism but the advantage was that there was full employment if you didn't get into political
trouble. You lived a very secure life from the cradle to the grave, everything was found for you, even your holidays.' He was playing Devil's
Advocate again, this staunch champion of free speech and liberty, defending an indefensible political system that had depended on repression.

Back in England he started to write a television series about an English
art house like Christie's or Sotheby's, *Under the Hammer*, for which he set
one of the episodes in Moscow and included a part for Emily to play, a
jazz singer. The series was to star Richard Wilson and Jan Francis as
two art experts working for a London auction house, Kinsky's, and
investigating paintings and artefacts that may be forgeries. Shooting the
first episode was like a repeat of *Summer's Lease* because Gielgud appeared
as an antique collector and Colin Rogers was again executive producer.
In another episode Judy Cornwell played one of Wilson's old flames.
'There were these charming scenes where they reminisce about the affair
they'd had,' she told me, 'and it was pure John. He was hovering around
the set and I told him what a joy it was to have properly structured
paragraphs and good language to read. It was lovely quality work.' Critics
praised the series but when he recycled the episodes as paperback short

stories – which he dedicated to Jacquie Davis – they were poorly written, laboured, unconvincing and read as though he had forced himself reluctantly to pad out the original scripts.

In April 1993, to mark his seventieth birthday, I took him out for a very liquid champagne lunch and an interview near Turville Heath at his favourite local restaurant, the Stonor Arms, where our conversation was punctuated by his disconcertingly shrill, nervous giggle. Penny had forbidden him to talk to me at Turville Heath Cottage because a previous interviewer had sneered that the place was furnished 'like an upmarket old people's home'. Being seventy, he told me, 'I don't feel any different from when I was forty or even thirty. I can't see out of one eye but I've never been particularly healthy so it doesn't make much difference. I do swim a bit up and down the swimming pool but that's all. This worrying about health is another sickness of the modern age. The Russians are wonderful: they don't give a *fart* about their health! I don't have any resolutions but if I can do a new television series and write a new book every year then it'll be fine. I really do love working. I'm fundamentally very lazy so I have to work very hard. The best feeling in the world is having finished a piece of work. It's marvellous. I do it by getting up very early, but about this time of day it's over for me. I get very *very* thirsty.' He giggled. 'I get drunk at lunchtime and sleep in the afternoon, and that's it. You should have seen me in the Writers' Union in Moscow!'

His proudest achievements, he said, had been *A Voyage Round My Father*, *The Dock Brief*, *Clinging to the Wreckage*, *Paradise Postponed*, 'and I'm proud of having written *Rumpole*. I think my father would have approved of what I've done.' He admitted that he was tempted to live somewhere warm and sunny like Tuscany or Morocco – but it would be unfair to take Rosie, who was now almost nine, away from her school 'and we've got horses, dogs, chickens and a garden. And I'm very English. England's very beautiful, and at their best the English people are admirable. They're very interesting to writers because they never say anything they mean. Americans say what they mean and it's very boring. With the English you have to deduce what they mean from what they don't say. Everything in England is hidden under the surface and the English are very stoical and never talk about their feelings, so that when it does all come bubbling out it's much stronger.'

As for the prospect of death, 'I *try* not to think about it. It's *awful*. I don't believe in immortality, apart from the immortality that my father has because he is remembered and I wrote about him, and my children have strong traces of him, and me, and my mother too. My father said immortality was like living for ever in a great transcendental hotel with nothing to do in the evenings.' He laughed. 'But I'd like to live another ten years, then I shall give it up and pack it in.' What about being an atheist? 'Well, I *do* flirt with religion in that I'm always discussing it with bishops and cardinals but I've never really had great religious feelings. When I think about God I don't like him or the way he carries on, if he exists. I don't know why you'd create a world and then allow seven million Jews to be gassed and not do anything about it. I've never found the answer to that from any religious person. But on the other hand an entirely materialistic life can be a bit drab and I think you could try and find religious mystical feelings in ordinary life, and that's especially true in the country, a sort of Wordsworthian pantheism. And in music and some poetry. I'm not at all hostile to religion, I love country churches, and the vicars round here are people who are doing good things and I'd *hate* them to all vanish. But there's no chance of a deathbed conversion.'

I asked whether he still had any unfulfilled ambitions. 'I'd love to write a proper, really good stage play,' he said, 'and I can't think of one, so that's thoroughly frustrating. I've been rather siphoned off into television and although it does have some excitement it doesn't really quite have that high charge of the theatre.'

Finally I suggested that after all these years he must be thoroughly fed up with being interviewed. 'No, because they're never the same,' he said. 'I love doing them with people who have done their homework, like you.' So what was the stupidest question he had ever had to answer? 'I get asked about the Rumpoles' sex life quite a lot in America.' Rumpy-pumpy? He chortled. 'Yes! I think that Mrs Rumpole would be quite keen on it but Rumpole's experience of sex is extremely limited.'

To mark his birthday the Ministry of Transport sent him a new three-year driving licence even though he had told them he was blind in one eye, fuzzy in the other, could no longer judge distances, had never been a good driver, and had once driven into a wall without any excuse at all. This did not bother the Ministry of Transport which included with his new licence a jolly note that wished him 'Happy Motoring!' Wisely he decided never to drive again and employed a chauffeur.

As chairman of the Royal Society of Literature one of his main concerns was to preserve the teaching of Shakespeare and other authors in English schools which were rapidly abandoning great, traditional literature, and he, P. D. James and the critic John Carey went to see the Secretary of State for Education, John Patten, to express their concern and anxiety.

He also led an authors' protest against a government plan to impose Value Added Tax on books. 'It would wound our culture,' he said, 'and add to the philistine reputation of a government which would not be forgiven.'

Since his parents had both lived in South Africa when they were young he took Jeremy to Johannesburg on a pilgrimage into their family's past and met half a dozen relatives at a dinner before going on to Cape Town, Durban and Pietermaritzburg, where they found his grandparents' graves.

Penelope's second autobiography *About Time Too* caused a sensation when it was published in October and attracted huge headlines and articles, revealing as it did all the vividly gory details of their marriage and John's behaviour during it. She sent him an advance copy but he never replied or reacted publicly to the book until after her death six years later. 'John isn't used to any kind of criticism,' she told Elizabeth Grice of the *Daily Telegraph*. 'He reacts with utter terror and misery. If he is distressed it is not *my* distress that he is distressed about, it's the *cause* of the distress being made public.' Her four eldest children, who she said rarely saw John any more, 'had no problem with the book', she told Julia Llewellyn Smith of *The Times* but John's children, Sally and Jeremy, 'probably found it at best embarrassing, at worst distressing'. Penny 2 was so appalled by the book that she burned it. 'It was a really nasty book,' Mortimer told Ginny Dougary of *The Times* eight years later. 'Penny was really hurt by it,' especially when Penelope told Lynda Lee-Potter of the *Daily Mail* that Rosie was slow to learn to speak because Penny was always away hunting or fishing. Discussing John's failure to react to the book, Penelope said: 'He's frightened of Penny, but he could have made a surreptitious phone call or sent a fax. Knowing John he's dug his head firmly in the sand and is trying to pretend it doesn't exist. A lot of John's trouble is that Penny creates a scene and he will do anything for a quiet life. She just doesn't want to face up to the fact that I ever existed. He's scared of her. She lives her own life – there's a lot of hunting, shooting and fishing. She's in with all the country nobs. She's got a cottage down in Cornwall, none of which is John's sort of scene.' Considering the numerous violent scenes during Penelope's own marriage to John, her suggestion that Penny was a difficult woman was most amusing. She also told Lee-Potter that she felt 'a bit sharp sometimes that John is so rich on the rubbish he writes [whereas] I'm skint. John gives me a bit, but that's taxed [and although] I made quite a lot of money when I was married I always used to spend it on the kids or extras. John would refuse to buy a freezer or whatever, so I'd use it for that.'

When the fuss eventually subsided Peter McKay wrote in the *Standard* under the headline THE OTHER SIDE OF CUDDLY JOHN that 'John Mortimer will ride it out, but perhaps the book will encourage those who have long envied his success – and those who have never quite been convinced of his authenticity – to unsheath their swords.'

On the day that Penelope was talking to Lynda Lee-Potter, John was savaging the new Tory Home Secretary, Michael Howard, whose firm, authoritarian attitude towards criminals and prisons – and his wish to remove defendants' ancient right to silence – appalled Mortimer's liberal instincts. Writing as president of the Howard League for Penal Reform he sent a letter to *The Times* attacking Howard's 'banal utterances on criminal policy' and reminding him that Winston Churchill – who was obviously not always as gaga as Mortimer had fibbed that he had been at Harrow – had once said that 'the treatment of crime and criminals mark and measure the stored-up strength of a nation and proof of the living virtue in it'. It was the start of his long campaign to attack and denigrate Howard at every opportunity. 'John and I have been on panels opposing each other on this,' the right-wing novelist Freddie Forsyth told me in 2004. 'He is passionately anti-prison and didn't like it when I said to him, "So what would you do with the burglar who's just committed his *fiftieth* burglary? You've got to lock him up because the public comes first, not the underworld." There's a whole wing in the legal profession who take this view – Louis Blom-Cooper, Geoffrey Robertson, an entire coterie in Cherie Blair's chambers – and cannot reconcile punishment with their beliefs about freedom. Their views are terribly bad for society. John's never been beaten up or robbed! Turville Heath is a rather low-crime area, and he's never been duffed up or his wife raped, so he takes a very benign view of the professional underworld.'

As Emily approached her final exams at Oxford in 1994 she asked her father to help her draft some essays for a thesis that she had to write for her degree. He did but was mortified when she read them and said: 'That's awful. It sounds like you're writing for the *Daily Mirror*.' She was so worried about her finals that she asked if he would love her less if she got only a third-class degree. 'I will love you much more if you get a third,' he simpered. She did better than a third – just – but passed with only a 2:2 and felt ashamed because she had been considered clever enough for a first, but by then it hardly mattered because she had been spotted in a college play, Kafka's *The Trial*, by a theatrical agent who was struck by her gawky, elfin looks and already building the foundations for her career as an actress. At Oxford she had appeared in several other college productions, among them *Hamlet* and her father's translation of *A Flea in Her Ear*, and even before her final exams the agent landed her a part to play the title role as a prostitute's daughter opposite Nigel Havers in a wigs-and-crinolines romantic television adaptation of Catherine Cookson's, *The Glass Virgin*, another part in the series *Sharpe's Rifles*, and another in a Ruth Rendell television mystery, *Heartstones*. John was delighted that she had inherited his love of acting and was already off to a flying start.

Betraying his socialist principles yet again, he sent Rosie, now ten, to board at the Dragon School because, he said, she was lonely, and her absence freed Penny, who now had six horses, to indulge fully her enthusiasm for riding, hunting, shooting and fishing and to launch over a chic lunch in London at the Ivy – along with Ann (now Baroness) Mallalieu and Sir Denis Forman, the ex-Granada Television executive – the Leave Country Sports Alone group to oppose increasing demands to ban blood sports in Britain. At the age of forty-six she rode to hounds mainly with the smart Bicester Hunt but 'still looks like a highly strung girl blinking through big glasses [and] her checked shirt and big sweater seem straight out of the Land's End catalogue', wrote Pauline Peters in the *Evening Standard*. To further her campaign she stood as a Labour candidate for the local council but lost.

In April 1994 Mortimer's secret son, Ross Bentley, now thirty-two, lost the man he had long thought was his father when Jack Bentley died at the age of eighty. Mortimer must have seen the long obituary in *The Times* a week later but seems to have made no attempt to contact Ross or his mother even though he could do so now without upsetting anyone. It was to be ten more years before he acknowledged Ross yet he continued to be fascinated by the subject of bastardy because that summer he started work on another novel, *Felix in the Underworld*, in which the hero is haunted by the possibility that he has an unknown illegitimate son. Felix is a genteel middle-class novelist who is pursued by a woman who claims he is the father of her ten-year-old son and is suspected of murder, goes on the run, and finds himself joining the growing number of homeless people who sleep on the streets of London and live in cardboard boxes behind the Savoy Hotel. Mortimer's research for the book drove him to talk to them – 'nice, gentle people,' he said – and to claim that begging was 'a perfectly honourable profession' even though charity workers kept warning the public that giving to beggars actually increased the problem and their dependence. 'I'm very much in favour of giving money to beggars,' he told *The Times* when the book was published nearly three years later. 'I feel no moral outrage. After all, I beg the entire time. For the Royal Court I'm holding out my hand for £5 million' – as if that did not involve a completely different principle.

That summer he also adapted Dickens' *A Christmas Carol* for the Royal Shakespeare Company to stage in December, embarked on another six Rumpole stories, and when his second autobiography, *Murderers and Other Friends*, was published in September it turned out to be a witty, well-written album of snapshot portraits of friends, acquaintances and incidents throughout his life though too much of it repeated stories he had already told in *Clinging to the Wreckage* and numerous interviews and articles. He gave as usual a couple of newspaper interviews over lunch at the Stonor Arms, whither he was conducted from Turville Heath Cottage in his chauffeur-driven Mercedes since Penny was still forbidding reporters to enter the house in case they might ridicule her lack of taste. Bravely he told Henry Porter of the *Guardian* that he would not mind at all if some critical author started snooping around his life to write his biography, though he could hardly say anything else since he had spent decades defending the freedom of writers to publish anything they chose, no matter how intrusive or offensive it might be, and insisting that in fact they had a positive duty to shock people. Helena de Bertodano of the *Sunday Telegraph* was told by Jacquie Davis that he was 'both ruthless and charming' and that he and Penny often had loud shouting rows, and he confessed that despite what de Bertodano called his 'veneer of bluff charm' there was 'a great well of aggression inside me. Only when I think of Michael Howard does it come out in force.' He was certainly less than benign when he went on a nationwide tour to promote the book and became so deeply irritated by the tarted-up hotels where he stayed and their plastic-smile receptionists, slow computers, unworkable key-cards, unopenable bedroom windows and endlessly humming electrical gadgets that he wrote an article for the *Mail on Sunday* complaining about almost every aspect of modern life, from bar codes in shops and cash machines in banks to men with pigtails and mobile phones. Cuddly old John, the national treasure, was fast becoming a grumpy old man. He was also increasingly frail and unsteady and turned his father's old engine room and garage into a bedroom, bathroom and dressing room so that he no longer had to climb the stairs.

His adaptation of *A Christmas Carol*, with Clive Francis as Scrooge, opened in December at the Barbican Centre in London to widespread praise. 'People think it's just a jolly Christmas story,' he told Heather Neill of *The Times*, 'but it's much more than that: it's a denunciation of poverty.' He completed his new collection of Rumpole stories, *Rumpole and the Angel of Death*, three of which were much better than most, in which Phillida Erskine-Brown has become Dame Phillida and a High Court judge while her poor old husband Claude trails far behind. One of the stories, 'Rumpole and the Rights of Man', was quite ludicrous and unbelievable, and in some of the yarns you can see the 'surprise' denouement coming long before the end, but Rumpole was by now so popular all over the world that it hardly mattered. He was mentioned even during the trial for murder in America that year of the football star and actor O. J. Simpson when a defence attorney remarked in court: 'As Mr Rumpole would put it, I think we have a case of premature adjudication.'

His extra-mural activities kept him as busy as ever and in March he submitted on behalf of the Royal Court an application to the National Lottery for a grant of £14 million to undertake major improvements to the theatre including an enlargement of the auditorium upstairs, better dressing rooms and offices, and the construction of a restaurant under Sloane Square and a balcony to overlook it. The lottery fund approved an even bigger grant, £15.8 million, on condition that the theatre raised another £7 million itself, which involved him in a mammoth, time-consuming fundraising effort and numerous rows in council between those who accepted that the only way to raise so much money was to approach big businesses for sponsorship and those who felt that this would sully the theatre's artistic purity. Another dispute that rumbled on and on began when the American woman playwright Timberlake Wertenbaker complained that the new black leather seats in the theatre would give women thrush, though eventually her protest was voted down, and while building went ahead the two Royal Court theatres moved to the West End and took over the Duke of York's and the Ambassador's for four years until the work was finished.

One way Mortimer helped to raise money for his pet projects and charities was to perform his stage show, *Mortimer's Miscellany*, and another possibility presented itself when his literary agent, Michael Sissons of Peters, Fraser and Dunlop, appointed a public speaking agent, Juliet Lewis, who told Mortimer she could arrange several lucrative engagements for him. 'Why should I pay commission to Michael whenever I make a speech?' he said. 'Just tell me privately whenever you get an offer for me to speak and I'll pay the ten per cent to charity instead.' Mrs Lewis was shocked by this underhand suggestion that she should cheat her employers and told him that she could not possibly do so.

As both John and Penny became prominent in the campaign to prevent the abolition of blood sports they received that summer death threats from animal rights activists who sent them hate mail, hidden razor blades and even an envelope stuffed with faeces. Threatening messages were left on their answerphone and the police told them to be wary of packages and to look under the car for bombs. Mortimer had himself long objected strongly to people who enjoyed blood sports but Penny's vociferous enthusiasm for hunting, shooting, fishing and stalking, which she was to take up the following year, changed his mind for him.

By 1996 his fame was beginning to be eclipsed by Emily's even though she was only twenty-four. She appeared in several television programmes, including episodes of *The Saint*, *A Dance to the Music of Time* and *Prime Suspect*, in which she had to simulate fellatio and said later that she did not regret the scene although 'I don't think I gave very good head'. She made her first two films, *The Ghost and the Darkness*, which was shot in South Africa with Val Kilmer and Michael Douglas, and *The Last of the High Kings*, which was shot in Ireland. Over the next year she was to play Kat Ashley in *Elizabeth* and Miss Flynn in *Cider With Rosie*, the script for which was written by her father. In July she appeared for the first time on the professional stage in *Lights* at the Royal Court and in October at the Royal Lyceum in Edinburgh playing Portia in *The Merchant of Venice*. In her first two years as an actress she earned enough to buy herself a flat in London's newly chic area of Notting Hill and suddenly she was the flavour of the year. Almost every month she was photographed, interviewed and gossiped about in newspapers and magazines. She modelled for *Tatler*, which called her 'eminently beddable', appeared with her father in *Hello!* – although Penny refused to let the reporter and photographer into the house – and like him loved being famous. 'I would like to become a celebrity,' she told the *Daily Express* naffly. 'I was really happy when I got recognised by the people in the toy shop down the road.' John too was to tell Victor Davis of the *Mail on Sunday* that if he had to choose between fame and fortune he would choose fame because 'it's nice when people congratulate you on something'. In fact he had both in abundance already and admitted that he was so rich that he never needed to work again. Father and daughter shared another trait too: both were outrageous liars, she confessed to the *Daily Mail*, *The Times* and *Harpers & Queen*. 'He'll always tell a lie if it makes things more interesting,' she said. 'He fibs and never feels bad about it.'

In February he went on a tour of the United States to promote *Rumpole and the Angel of Death* and was confronted one night in New York by a

mugger who growled, 'Gimme fifty dollars!' Bravely Mortimer decided
to negotiate. 'What about twenty-five?' he suggested. 'Okay,' said the
mugger, 'gimme twenny-five,' took the money and disappeared into the
darkness. Back in England, where the Home Secretary, Michael Howard,
was doing his best to deter muggers and other criminals by introducing
fixed sentences that could not be reduced by bleeding-heart liberal judges,
Mortimer launched another attack on him in the *Daily Express* accusing
him of trying to rubber-stamp justice in Britain.

Another liberal QC, his old legal gofer Geoffrey Robertson, was among
the Mortimers' guests in Tuscany that summer of 1996 with his brash
Australian wife Kathy Lette, who had by now become one of John's
closest friends despite her poorly written books and tiresomely relentless
taste for concocting sleazy puns and sexual innuendo. 'She's such a tonic,'
Mortimer told the *Independent on Sunday* magazine in 2002. 'I've never
seen her not smiling and laughing, she's outrageous and does outrageous
things, and generally she keeps people alive.' The Mortimers had also
become intimate with Tony Blair's inexplicably influential Rasputin,
Peter Mandelson, who was on the list of a hundred and fifty 'celebrities'
whom they invited to Turville Heath in September to celebrate Penny's
fiftieth birthday and bop frenetically with the likes of the TV newsreader
Anna Ford, Bob Geldof, Tory politician Lord Gowrie, Richard Ingrams,
Ann Mallalieu, Jeremy Paxman, Salman Rushdie, Lord Snowdon and
Alan Yentob.

Yet despite the Mortimers' efforts to hobnob with New Labour's
leaders, John had by the end of the year fallen out with Blair over hunting
and his prissy pursuit of political correctness in every field of life. He
told the *Daily Express* that although he still wanted New Labour to win
the next election – anything to get rid of the Tories – he had all but lost
faith in his old party and was 'not as close to the leadership as I used to
be'. Even so, when John Major called a general election to be held in May
1997 Mortimer voted Labour as always and chose to watch the results on
television at a London party given at Christopher's restaurant by the Tory
Daily Telegraph so that he could jeer at his hosts by cheering loudly every
time Labour won a seat. 'It was not the sort of thing you do at a *Torygraph*
party,' I was told by Anna Deedes, wife of the paper's chief executive,
'but Mortimer does like to draw attention to himself.' Eventually the
fashion editor, Hilary Alexander, could stand Mortimer's noisy exhibitionism no longer, marched over to him and ordered him to leave. One
witness claimed that she actually told him to fuck off. 'I was so annoyed,'
she told me, 'that I told him that if he thought Tony Blair was so

marvellous why was he drinking our booze and not theirs? He was surprised, angry and embarrassed but he left. He's probably not often challenged.'

He spent the rest of the evening carousing and galumphing at a Labour celebration at the Festival Hall and was overjoyed when the Conservatives were voted out of power at last after eighteen years and Blair became Prime Minister with a whacking majority of 254 seats. Perhaps paradise would not be postponed for much longer. 'I am so happy,' he told the *Daily Telegraph*. '*Everyone* is so happy. We don't have to worry about what Michael Howard is doing. We don't have to worry about politics any more.' He was soon to be disillusioned. To his dismay Blair's government turned out to be no more socialist than the Tory one and his first two Home Secretaries, Jack Straw and David Blunkett, just as illiberal and authoritarian as Howard.

When *Felix in the Underworld* was published a month later it turned out to be a ludicrous yarn — badly written, embarrassingly facetious, utterly unbelievable and with huge flaws in the plot — but he was now so well established as a writer that critics as distinguished as Ruth Rendell and Elizabeth Buchan greeted it with enthusiasm and Allan Massie claimed unconvincingly in the *Scotsman* that 'Mortimer is our finest comic novelist, one of the few writers who can make me not only smile, but laugh aloud'. In an interview with Angela Levin of the *Daily Mail* Mortimer confessed that although he was now less aggressive and unpleasant than he had been in middle age he was still devious, manipulative, and not a good person and forecast glumly that when he died the newspaper placards would read RUMPOLE MAN DIES, 'which means I shall be fused with him for ever and ever'.

He was visited at home that summer by the actor Michael York's wife Pat, who asked him to let her photograph him nude for an exhibition of naked people and corpses that she planned to mount in St Petersburg. He declined but Penny was delighted to cooperate and was snapped feeding her chickens naked except for a pair of wellington boots, much to the amazement of their ancient Italian gardener. Equally bizarre was a letter that Mortimer received from a complete stranger in Frankfurt who was making his will and wanted to leave everything to him.

He was still writing non-stop: a new TV play, *Coming Home*; two filmscripts, *Tea With Mussolini* and *Hons and Rebels*; and another Titmuss novel, *The Sound of Trumpets*. But he was understandably furious when BBC Radio 4 decided not to serialise the Rumpole stories because in Blair's new touchy-feely, politically correct Britain some dim BBC committee had decided that they denigrated women – an extraordinary accusation considering Mortimer's long, slavish admiration of women. He was writing *Tea With Mussolini* for Franco Zeffirelli, a sentimental little comedy based on Zeffirelli's autobiography about the wonderfully daffy, snooty English ladies who lived in Florence in the late 1930s, admired the fascist dictator because he made the trains run on time, and were interned there as enemy aliens during the Second World War. At that time one part had been cast, Joan Plowright, with the possibility of Cher as a Jewish-American millionairess, but before the others were cast Shirley Anne Field, now fifty-nine and prodded by her American agent, phoned Mortimer when they both happened to be in Los Angeles at the same time. 'He said "darling", as if we had talked only yesterday, "how wonderful to speak to you. Let's have lunch together,"' she told me. 'We had lunch at the Ivy and he said I'd be perfect for the part of the arty one. He said I was now just the right age and he would speak to Zeffirelli about me but I never heard any further.' Judi Dench eventually played the part opposite Maggie Smith. He never gave her a job, of course, because Penny knew that she had been one of his old flames and would have 'created' merry hell if he had. He flew to Rome to spend ten days discussing the film with Zeffirelli and was delighted to meet there a woman friend of Penny's who was every Devil's Advocate's dream because she was risking the fires of Hell by having a steamy affair with a priest who worked in the Vatican and whom she had met at Alcoholics Anonymous.

His health was declining rapidly. At seventy-four he was now so fat that he could no longer put on his socks, he had two bad falls that ripped a knee muscle and caused an ulcer on one leg that would not heal for years, his legs became so weak that he had to be pushed around in a wheelchair, especially at airports, and he started to suffer from asthma and to worry that he was developing Alzheimer's disease because his memory was deteriorating. But he still flew off in August for his summer holiday in Italy, where he emulated Haverford Downs of *Summer's Lease* by contributing three weekly articles to the *Mail on Sunday* magazine entitled not 'Jottings From Tuscany' but 'Notes From Tuscany', in which he wrote about his joy at sitting again on the smelly pavement outside the Bar Dante in Radda, the pleasure of welcoming a houseful of guests, listening to Kinnock warbling Elvis Presley songs and Zeffirelli singing arias and telling him that the conductor Arturo Toscanini had been a genius but also 'a complete bastard'. He went to Siena again and reminisced about the Palio horse race, and the open-air opera *Il Trovatore* in the square at San Gimignano, and visited Muriel Spark, whom he considered

Britain's best living novelist, at her house at Civitella della Chiana, which he learned with diabolical delight had been a church before becoming a brothel.

On 31 August 1997 Diana Princess of Wales was killed in a car crash in Paris and Mortimer flew back to London to describe with awe for the *Daily Mail* the mountain of flowers, teddy bears, poems, balloons and astonishing scenes of public mourning outside Kensington Palace and to write for the *Evening Standard* an elegiac report of the silent grief of her funeral. He was beleaguered by tragedy and death that autumn, for he flew back to Italy in October to report for the *Mail on Sunday* the aftermath of an earthquake that had badly damaged the vast, glorious Basilica of St Francis in Assisi and destroyed many of its beautiful works of art, in an article in which he castigated God for not saving a lovely, eight-hundred-year-old temple that had been built as a tribute to his own glory. Then he spoke at Laurie Lee's memorial service at St James's, Piccadilly, where he recalled how Lee had launched his own career as a writer at the Crown Film Unit during the war.

In December he flew to Washington to be the guest of honour at a banquet given by Rumpole-loving judges of the Supreme Court where all the women wore She Who Must Be Obeyed badges. That month too he reduced his enormous workload by resigning as chairman of the Royal Society of Literature after resisting successfully for eight years its eviction from its elegant premises in Hyde Park Gardens, though it did move eventually to Somerset House three years later.

That winter he took Emily and Rosie to Goa on holiday and nearly drowned in rough sea after ignoring a red flag of warning. Back in England he and Penny joined an estimated 250,000 demonstrators who marched (or in his case was wheeled) through London to protest against a bill to ban fox-hunting, and found themselves embarrassingly beside the two Tory politicians he had always attacked vociferously, Lord Tebbit and Michael Howard. Afterwards Penny went off on a hunting and shooting holiday in Devon, leaving him alone at Turville Heath with his chauffeur/handyman Peter Hayes to keep an eye on him. In April he celebrated his seventy-fifth birthday with the Kinnocks in Brussels, where they gave him a big dinner party and a European Union bow tie and braces. Tony Blair tried to heal the growing rift between himself and Mortimer by giving him a knighthood in June, and although he accepted it – despite writing three years previously that there was 'no damned merit' in the honours system – the bribe failed to work.

The newly titled Sir John's disillusionment with Blair and his prissy

New Labour gospel of political correctness came to a head on a lovely summer evening when the Blairs invited the Mortimers for dinner at the Prime Minister's official country residence, Chequers. Smoking was now banned in the great house where Winston Churchill had once chain-smoked huge Cuban cigars and knocked back the champagne, whisky and brandy by the gallon. Penny, now Lady Mortimer, herself a chain-smoker, asked Cherie Blair whether she would mind if she lit up a fag outside on the terrace, in the open air. 'I'll allow you just one if you *have* to,' snapped Mrs Blair, 'but it's a *filthy* habit' – yet as Penny told Rachel Sylvester of the *Daily Telegraph* indignantly Mrs Blair did not hesitate in the middle of another Chequers dinner party to whip out a breast and feed her baby, Leo, at the table to the astonishment of the guests. The Mortimers' dislike of New Labour was enhanced when Penny found herself sitting at dinner next to Blair's spin doctor Philip Gould, whom she had never met but who remarked: 'John really is getting old, isn't he? Why do you stay with him, for love or duty?' Stunned by his rudeness, she replied mildly 'probably both' but wished later that she had been quick enough to say, 'for the wonderful sex but I don't suppose you'd know about that.' The Mortimers were never invited back. They had little time either for Blair's fifty-eight-year-old Lord Chancellor, Lord Irvine. 'Little Derry Irvine's a pain in the neck, isn't he? So pompous,' Mortimer told Mary Riddell of the *Daily Mail* magazine in November. His long love affair with the Labour Party was finally over. Yet he saw no shame in accepting a knighthood from a Prime Minister whom he despised and trotted off to the less than socialist College of Heralds to choose a coat of arms with the help of the chief herald, Garter King at Arms. They settled on a crest showing a dormouse perched on a shield and sipping a glass of champagne above the Latin motto *Aestas Gliris* – *The Summer of a Dormouse* – a quote from Byron's *Journals* describing the shortness of life that was to be the title of his next book. Mortimer paid £3,025 for the crest, framed it and hung it in the hall at Turville Heath.

He returned to Rome for the shooting of *Tea With Mussolini* at the Cinecittà studios before going up to Edinburgh to take part in a debate with Sir Richard Eyre about the future of television. Penny was meant to go with him but changed her mind and flew instead to Hollywood to see Emily, who was working there on a film, so John persuaded a beautiful young black girl called Tabitha to go with him to Edinburgh for a night at the Balmoral Hotel and pretend to be his wife. Suggestively he told her that the biblical King David had in old age been kept warm in bed at night by a lovely girl called Abishag, and Tabitha responded saucily that in that case for him she would change her name to Tabishag. When they flew to Edinburgh Tabitha travelled using Penny's name and later she accompanied him to the opera regularly when Penny was unavailable.

Despite his various woes he was delighted when capital punishment in Britain was finally abolished completely, even for treason, piracy and arson in Her Majesty's dockyards, at the end of July, and his daughters too were a source of pride in his old age. Emily had like her mother recently been photographed naked – for an episode of the television series *Midsomer Murders* – and had just landed a part as one of Hugh Grant's blind dates, the Perfect Girl, in the movie *Notting Hill*, whose scriptwriter Richard Curtis knew her because he lived near Turville. From now on she was to appear in at least two films or television plays a year and knew she had achieved her dream of becoming a 'celebrity' when the *News of the World* splashed a story about her love life across two pages. Her ex-lover Andrew Mitchell told the paper how bitter he was that she had just dumped him for another actor, twenty-six-year-old Paul Bettany, with whom she had been filmed in another naked clinch when they both appeared in the television play *Coming Home*. Mitchell reported gallantly that she was very good in bed and enjoyed making love in the open air even though she was very skinny, gauche and walked 'like Bambi'. She was soon to dump her new boyfriend too for Alessandro Nivola, the man she would marry, a twenty-six-year-old, Yale-educated, Sicilian-American actor whom she met on the set of Kenneth Branagh's musical film of *Love's Labour's Lost*. As for Rosie, a tempestuous teenager who fought constantly with her mother, she was now at yet another posh fee-paying boarding school, co-educational Bryanston in Dorset, where she was so embarrassed by her father's age, frailty and weakness for telling the same old stories again and again that she told people he was her grandfather and when he went to her school she said: 'You can come and see my dormitory provided you don't speak.' She could be equally brutal towards her mother but when she yelled at her 'fuck off and die!' Penny waved her cigarette and champagne glass at her and croaked in her husky chainsmoker's voice: 'I'm trying as hard as I can, darling.'

In August the Kinnocks, Eyres, Jeremy Irons and his wife Sinèad Cusack, Geoffrey Robertson and Kathy Lette joined the Mortimers again in Tuscany, where Kinnock would dance around the big living room wearing a cowboy hat and regaling them with old pop songs. 'There's a lot too much eating and a lot too much drinking, wild dancing and all of us behaving in ways that do not befit people of our age,' Glenys Kinnock told Veronica Groocock of the *Independent on Sunday*. 'It's a let-your-hair-down time. We have an evening sitting around seeing who can remember the most songs from the 1950s, or dancing over the furniture to Sixties music' – a pastime unlikely to endear them to the furniture's owner, Leonard Ingrams. 'John just sits and laughs at it all. His singing is not something you encourage.'

In September Penny left him alone again at Turville Heath to go off for another holiday cruising around Turkey on John Paul Getty's yacht while Mortimer started work on a three-part adaptation for television of another Evelyn Waugh novel, *Decline and Fall*, which never reached the screen. He gave a couple of newspaper interviews to mark the publication of the third Titmuss novel *The Sound of Trumpets* and the screening of his television adaptation of *Cider With Rosie* in October. Both reporters were allowed to sneak into the house now that Penny was away and he told Sabine Durrant of the *Guardian* bravely that he rather liked being on his own. Ms Durrant claimed that by now he had become 'a national treasure', that everyone who met him loved him, and reported that he was 'quite doddery now' and that what with his 'large, round stomach and long, thin legs' he had to lean on her when he walked. He admitted that he was a liar and that Penny had told him that he sounded utterly insincere when he told every woman he met how beautiful she was. Alice Thomson of the *Daily Telegraph* found him 'frail and sunken in his crumpled pink Oxford shirt, baggy corduroys and trainers' and unhappy about being alone in the evenings. The government was losing its soul, he told her: 'I had such high hopes for Mr Blair. He doesn't seem to have any firm ideas. No one wants to lead any more – they just hide behind focus groups, spin doctors and the "People". It's an insidious disease.' When Penny returned from her cruise she took off again for a shooting holiday in America and then to the Labour Party conference in Brighton to lobby against the projected ban on fox-hunting. As John aged she seemed to spend less and less time with him and Mary Riddell of the *Daily Mail* magazine also reported that he was lonely on his own at Turville Heath.

The Sound of Trumpets won a chorus of praise from the critics – deservedly so since it was an amusing, pointed satire and splendidly incorrect politically. Leslie Titmuss, now in his fifties and retired from the political battlefield with a peerage, has become deliciously cynical, devious and mischievous as he pulls the strings in a local by-election for his old seat and decides that the Conservative Party is now so left-wing and New Labour so right-wing that as an old Thatcherite it is his duty to help the New Labour candidate to win, and in the process he manipulates the poor booby so unmercifully that he destroys him and his career. 'Yes, I've

heard that I was Mortimer's model for Titmuss,' Lord Tebbit told me
equally mischievously in 2004, 'and I was aware that he was not one of
my admirers. Thank God he didn't call the book *The Sound of Strumpets*!
Mind you, if he had I might have been able to sue him.' The novel drew
a vividly sardonic portrait of Tony Blair's Britain, where you could no
longer get your teeth into a solid, old-fashioned ploughman's lunch in a
pub but had to nibble a bit of goat's cheese and sun-dried tomatoes and
the local vicar referred to Jesus as if he were the New Labour MP for
Nazareth East. It also included a couple of startlingly vulgar passages
such as the tacky scene in a disco where a public schoolboy approaches a
girl he has never met and suggests 'why don't we dance a bit and then
we might consider a fuck in the toilet?' – and they do, after which 'the
girls were all panting to be taken into the toilet'. Like the girl at Granada
TV all those years ago, no doubt.

Mortimer started work on a screenplay of David Niven's hilarious
autobiography *The Moon's a Balloon* and television adaptations of *Aesop's
Fables* and a book by Eric Newby, *Love and War in the Appenines*. He was
also having to referee more rows at the Royal Court because by the end
of 1998 the Arts Council had come up with an extra grant of £2½ million
but the theatre still needed to raise another £3 million in less than six
months to complete the repairs and renovations, otherwise it would go
bankrupt. A business charity, the Jerwood Foundation, offered to donate
all £3 million if the building were renamed the Royal Court Jerwood
Theatre but there was uproar on the council, where several members felt
that the theatre's tradition would be sullied if it were named after a
commercial sponsor who might then insist on choosing the plays as well.
There were protest meetings and Timberlake Wertenbaker demanded
Mortimer's resignation. He was strongly tempted to comply but brokered
a compromise by which the theatre kept its old name and Jerwood signed
an agreement not to interfere with artistic decisions but the two auditoria
were named the Jerwood Upstairs and Jerwood Downstairs. Wertenbaker
was still dissatisfied and resigned but Mortimer told *The Times* that 'this
is the age we live in. Like it or dislike it, we have got to live in it. They
are living in a dream world if they think the arts are so valued that you
can shame the government into coming to your rescue.' He made the
most of the Jerwood windfall by having a lift installed from the foyer to
the first floor. 'He joked that this was exclusively for him because his legs
had gone and without it he couldn't get down the stairs fast enough
when he needed a pee!' I was told by the *Daily Telegraph*'s arts correspondent, Nigel Reynolds.

Mortimer flew to Florence for the Italian premiere of *Tea With Mussolini* and was mugged by an eighteen-month-old baby when he was approached by a woman beggar with an infant who had been trained to snatch wallets. It reached into the inside pocket of his jacket, grabbed the wallet, and Mortimer had to wrestle with the baby to retrieve it. Later he began to think that maybe Tuscany was losing the charm that had kept him returning for so many years and to realise that he was himself partly to blame for the crowds of tourists and holidaymakers who were attracting the criminals.

In April the Secretary of State for Culture, Chris Smith, asked him to chair a committee to suggest whose statue should be raised on the one empty plinth in Trafalgar Square that had stood vacant since 1841. Originally the site had been intended for a statue of William IV on horseback but the money to pay for it had never been raised. The committee called a crowd of witnesses whose suggestions ranged from Christ, Churchill or Nelson Mandela to Dickens (Mortimer's favourite), the Queen Mother, Mrs Thatcher, the Beatles, Princess Diana, David Beckham and the Unknown Slave. They might equally have raised a statue to the Unknown Juryman, for Mortimer was increasingly concerned that the Labour Home Secretary, Jack Straw, was about to tear up Magna Carta by removing the ancient legal principles that a defendant is innocent until proved guilty and entitled to be tried by a jury. The government was even about to agree to hand British citizens over to judges in other European countries that did not have the sort of safeguards against injustice that Britain had, such as habeas corpus, which stipulated that no suspect could be held in police custody for more than sixty hours without being charged. The Mortimers were themselves the target of criminal threats from animal rights activists who continued to bombard them with so many anonymous telephone calls and death threats that the police gave them a hotline number to ring in an emergency.

Penelope's refusal to stop chainsmoking finally killed her when she died of lung cancer in October 1999 in a hospice in Kensington. 'It's better to die happy than to live cautiously,' she had once remarked and amazingly, despite her heavy smoking and drinking, she had lasted for eighty-one years. Sadly she did not die happy but was bitter to the end. John went to say goodbye when he knew she was dying but they spoke like strangers, unable to forgive each other. 'She knew she was killing herself,' Jeremy told me, 'but I don't think she cared about death. There was a self-destruct button there and she never got over my dad. She was obsessed by him.' She left a net estate of £275,296 – £85,000 to Madelon,

£2,000 to each of her eleven grandchildren, the rest to be divided equally between Caroline, Julia, Deborah, Sally and Jeremy. Jeremy also inherited her royalties and became her literary executor, and her children gave John a small memento: Penelope's light metal stick with a claw for picking things up without having to bend down. It was a sad little metaphor for the end of their long, passionate relationship.

Mortimer's hard work for the Royal Court finally paid off when the theatre reopened, beautifully renovated, at the end of February. 'He had earned quite a reputation for getting the Royal Court through a very difficult period,' I was told by one witness. 'It was almost entirely due to him and you've got to be a pretty ruthless bastard to do that.' His job done, he resigned the chairmanship and celebrated by writing his first stage play for nineteen years, *Naked Justice*, a sharply cynical attack on the precarious nature of justice and the judicial process about three High Court judges who are sharing the judges' lodgings in a northern town. Mortimer based one of them, Fred, on himself: a liberal, tolerant, merciful judge who no longer tries criminal cases because he is too reluctant to pass severe sentences. The second judge, Keith, is a strict disciplinarian renowned for imposing harsh sentences and about to try for murder a seventeen-year-old black boy who has apparently signed a confession. Fred knows that Keith will be so biased against the boy that the jury will convict him whether he is guilty or not and he blackmails Keith by warning him that unless he gives the boy a fair trial and summing up he will reveal that Keith was homosexual at Oxford. Terrified of being exposed, Keith is so scrupulously fair that the boy is acquitted – unjustly, because when he is freed he turns out to be guilty after all. Fred's tolerance and gentleness have allowed a killer to escape justice.

In March Penny abandoned John again to go off with the TV personality Miriam Stoppard and ninety other women to ride bicycles around Israel and Egypt for charity while he wrote another play for television, *Don Quixote*, and when she returned she set off again with a group of friends for a fishing holiday in Cuba. John was on his own so often nowadays that Andrew Billen of the *Evening Standard* asked him why anyone should believe that he had been any more faithful to Penny than he had been to Penelope. Mortimer did not answer the question but remarked genially that Billen would have made an excellent cross-examiner. In fact a really excellent cross-examiner would have insisted on an answer.

After dithering for nearly a year Mortimer's Trafalgar Square committee failed to suggest any one statue but recommended feebly that a temporary sculpture should stand on the plinth for a year before being replaced by another and then another each year. A week later John Gielgud died aged ninety-six and Mortimer wrote a fulsome tribute in the *Evening Standard* saying that he had been England's greatest living actor and the best company of any thespian he had known. Five months later he wrote another eulogy for Alec Guinness, who died in August at the age of eighty-six, writing in the *Independent* that he was the last great character actor and reporting that when he had asked Sir Alec a couple of years previously why he no longer acted, as Gielgud still did, Guinness replied in his sepulchral voice: 'Johnny always enjoyed acting. Many of us thought it was a rather silly profession.'

Mortimer was garlanded with a tribute of his own in October when the National Film Theatre screened the first Rumpole play, *Rumpole of the Bailey*, though he was disconcerted to see that Irene Shubik had been invited too. 'He seemed dismayed to find me there,' she told me, 'and said with feigned innocence, "Oh darling, *where* have you been? You've been abroad, haven't you?", implying that was why he hadn't seen me for so long. Afterwards he gave a talk in which he was forced to mention what a great producer I was. He was with Geoffrey Robertson and his ghastly show-off wife, Kathy Lette, who acted as though my partner Andrew and I did not exist. Their bratty kids were also in evidence, but Penny was not there.' Ms Lette had recently taken part in a series of public readings entitled *The Vagina Monologues* and shared with her fellow performers a cake tastefully shaped like a large vagina. Also present that night was Alvin Rakoff. 'I hadn't seen John in about ten years, since we did *Paradise Postponed*,' he told me, 'and I went to embrace him in a manly heterosexual fashion and you could see him recoil. John was always very reticent about showing his emotions.' It would take an entire posse of psychiatrists to hunt down Mortimer's fear of other men. Was he sexually abused as a child or assaulted by another man? Only he could say.

A week later he published *The Summer of a Dormouse*, a collection of random jottings about his life – loosely assembled as a sort of diary of the years 1997 to 1999 – that slid backwards and forwards in time and repeated many of the stories he had told over and over again. It was nevertheless serialised at length by *The Sunday Times* because it included some amusing new anecdotes and was a genial, optimistic celebration of life even though he was by now an invalid and despite the indignities of being old, which he described vividly and poignantly. He gave the same title to a radio play about growing old and being obsessed by Byron that accompanied the book. Jan Moir interviewed him for the *Daily Telegraph* and he claimed that even at seventy-seven he still lusted after young women. On a regular basis? 'On a *daily* basis!' he giggled. When he met a fanciable new woman he did not expect actually to have sex with her, he said, much to Ms Moir's relief, but 'there is always that kind of edge that you *might* have sex with them. It is just a promise in the air that hovers gently over lunch.'

Although Leo McKern was now too old at eighty-one to make any more Rumpole episodes and Mortimer said he could not imagine anyone else in the part, he embarked on yet another volume of six stories, *Rumpole Rests His Case*, in one of which Horace defended successfully a ferociously right-wing politician on a charge of smoking marijuana even though he hated his politics. In another yarn Rumpole defended an asylum seeker but the final tale ended ominously with him in hospital after a heart attack and possibly close to death.

Naked Justice opened in Leeds in January 2001 with Leslie Phillips playing Fred the blackmailing judge and Nicholas Jones as his victim, Keith, and Mortimer was exhilarated to hear again the sound of a paying audience laughing at something he had written. 'No other medium gives you that extreme experience,' he told Judith Palmer for her book *Private View: Artists Working Today*. To mark his first stage play in two decades Craig Brown interviewed him for the *Daily Mail*'s magazine *Night and Day* and wondered whether there was something spurious about Mortimer's genial mask. 'This is a man who is so liberal that he even enjoys the company of his enemies,' wrote Brown. 'Almost everyone he talks about tends to be "sweet" or "lovely" or "charming". Those he is not so keen on are "rather nice", and the lowest of the low are "quite nice". But does his own niceness extend too far? Before I ever met him, I remember feeling that there was something a bit, well, *squashy* about him, something a bit too all-incorporating, as though the whole world, good and bad, was, in the final reckoning, just a charming entertainment put on for his benefit.' Graciously Penny allowed Brown into the house and admitted that she had just been painted in the nude and he rewarded her by describing her as 'good fun, a keen horsewoman, very friendly, with a mischievous sense of humour'. She told him that John moaned daily that he was now just 'a sad person whose talent has gone and who's going to go bankrupt and is never going to write anything again and is anyway going to die soon. He thinks he must never say no to work because otherwise we'll go bankrupt. He'll never have enough money not to worry about it. That's what keeps him writing.' Mortimer confessed that he was ashamed of some things he had done, especially of the callous way he had sometimes dropped people. 'I've been concentrating on myself,' he said, and, 'I've never really had that great male friendship.' He concluded by launching a tirade against Blair and New Labour: 'I hate the endless control this government tries to exert over every aspect of your life. It can't make the health service work, it can't make education work, it can't make anything work, so it covers it all up with unnecessary legislation. The end was reached when a government committee said we should walk more. What's it got to do with the government whether you walk or not?' A couple of months later Mortimer returned to the attack to castigate Jack Straw for planning to allow juries to be told of a defendant's previous convictions, to rail at other ministers for vilifying all asylum seekers, and to claim that British jails were in such a terrible state that the prisons minister, Paul Boateng, should resign.

He had so enjoyed being involved in the theatre again that he wrote another stage play, *Hock and Soda Water*, a surreal semi-musical with lots of songs from the 1920s and 1930s in which an old man looks back with nostalgia and regret on his life and failures and discusses with himself both as a boy and as a middle-aged man the lessons they have yet to learn and warns them of the opportunities that they have yet to lose. As always in his plays there were elements of autobiography: as a boy the old man played as a one-man band and wanted to be Fred Astaire although he never could dance or sing; he loves Byron's poetry, can no longer pull his socks on and admits that he has told lots of 'small, unimportant' lies all his life. He even discovers late in life that one of his old girlfriends has secretly had his illegitimate son. Make the most of your life, he tells his former selves, and don't waste time, but of course it is all too late. The play was to have its premiere in Chichester in November with Richard Johnson playing the old man, Alan Cox his middle-aged self, and Sam Harding himself as a boy.

In February Mortimer was granted the rare accolade of a third appearance on *Desert Island Discs*, a feat achieved by only seven other people, all of them performers rather than writers – Arthur Askey, Robertson Hare, Earl Hines, Stanley Holloway, Celia Johnson, John Mills and Emlyn Williams – and it was now that he broke down when he chose Brahms' Fourth Symphony, one of Michael Fenton's favourite pieces, and the tape had to be stopped until he recovered. His seven other records were Fred Astaire with 'Funny Face', 'Signore, ascolta' from Puccini's *Turandot*, 'Dio, che nell'alma infondere' from Verdi's *Don Carlos*, Dinah Washington singing 'Our Love is Here to Stay', Mozart's 'Soave sia il vento' from *Così fan tutte*, Louis Armstrong with 'C'est si bon', and 'Hab' mir's gelobt' from *Der Rosenkavalier* by Richard Strauss. As his luxury he chose a picture by Velázquez but his inspiration flagged when it came to a book and he chose the same as he had in 1982, *The Oxford Book of English Verse*.

In May Tony Blair called a general election and for the first time in his life Mortimer could not bring himself to vote Labour. In an article in the forcefully Tory *Daily Mail* he urged voters to abstain but they ignored him and Blair was returned to power with another huge majority over the Tories of 247, almost as big as in 1997. Mortimer was to fail again five days later when the equestrian Olympic gold medallist Richard Meade faced expulsion from the Royal Society for the Prevention of Cruelty to Animals for allegedly flooding the RSPCA with new pro-hunting members so that they would oppose its support for a ban on fox-hunting. Mortimer wrote a defence for another barrister, Hugh Tomlinson, to put to the hearing but it was rejected and Meade expelled. Mortimer was unable to stand up and speak at the hearing himself because his legs were now so weak and ulcerated that they needed daily dressings and regular electronic treatment administered by two of his neighbours, identical blonde sisters, Vicky Lord and Jackie Paice, who were both married to members of the pop group Deep Purple and whom he dubbed the Heavenly Twins.

In November he resigned as a governor of the Royal Shakespeare Company after thirty-seven years because he was worried that he might lose everything, even his house, if the RSC's plan to spend £100 million on new theatres at Stratford came to grief and the governors were held personally responsible financially. When the new Rumpole book was published Penny, who was soon to go off on another charity bicycle ride, this time across Jordan, allowed two more journalists into the house to interview him. Nigel Farndale reported in the *Sunday Telegraph* that 'Sir John has ... a dark, bitchy side' and was amazed when Mortimer told him that he was tolerant of hypocrites because 'I don't think it matters too much to your beliefs if you can't live up to them'. This seemed to Farndale to be 'an extraordinary moral code. Does he consider himself to be a moral person? "No, not especially,"' said Mortimer, "I am, in a way, too detached to be moral. I really regard myself as an observer, someone on the sidelines watching it all. Not judging."' It was a claim that he contradicted blatantly a few days later when he told Ginny Dougary of *The Times* that he judged President Bush to be a 'dickhead'. She asked if he had any great regrets. 'Missed opportunities of love affairs,' he lamented. And what about his epitaph? 'The defence rests,' he said.

The success of *Hock and Soda Water* in November reawakened his delight in the theatre and in December he began a two-week run of *Mortimer's Miscellany* at the tiny King's Head Theatre in Islington before taking it on a nationwide tour with the support of a pianist, flautist and two actresses at each performance – among them Joanna David, Nicola McAuliffe, Rohan McCullough, Jean Marsh and Angharad Rees. 'A regular dose of adulation in essential,' he told Judith Palmer.

During his performances – inspired no doubt by Kathy Lette – he liked to remark that sexually he preferred the Plumber Position: 'You stay in all day and nobody comes.' He would also jest that marriage was like a Florida hurricane: 'It begins with a lot of blowing and sucking and you end up losing your house.' Reviewing the show in the *Evening Standard* Nicholas de Jongh called it 'an endearing trip down memory lane . . . an old-fashioned evening of armchair anecdotage' during which 'Sir John is a dry, droll raconteur, at home and happy in limelight's beam. He sits in his three-piece suit, an actress on either side, and reminisces with all the spontaneity of an ad-libber who scorns a script. There's no particular chronology to Mortimer's recollections. He keeps dipping into his colourful rag-bag of memories – some familiar, some fresh, all quirkily Mortimerish.' De Jongh felt however that Mortimer was a poor reader of poetry and that the actresses displayed a 'dreadful, affected winsomeness'.

Emily, who was spending much of her time in Los Angeles with her future husband, Alessandro Nivola, brought him home for Christmas and gave him an overcoat that he decided to wear in the house on Boxing Day. Mortimer grumbled that it was depressing to see someone wearing an overcoat inside the house, to which Nivola replied that it was equally depressing to see Mortimer staggering about 'wearing a dirty old dressing gown with bandages falling off his legs' – a feisty reply that sealed Mortimer's approval of him. He was impressed too by Emily's film career: she had recently made a teen slasher movie, *Scream 3*; had played Bruce Willis's girlfriend in *The Kid* and a leather-clad hit-woman gangster in a British thriller, *The 51st State*; and was about to impersonate Princess Diana in a television spoof called *Jeffrey Archer: the Truth*. Many of her parts, however, were startlingly raunchy. She had taken her kit off on screen yet again for a full-frontal display in *Lovely and Amazing* and was about to make an erotic film in which she was to be smeared in custard, brown sauce and blue ink, smacked on her bare bottom, and ravished naked on all fours roughly from behind by Ewan McGregor as well as on a rowing boat, in a coal wagon, and underneath a lorry for a film called *Young Adam*. The Mortimers did not even seem to mind when she caused a stir in the US by saying 'cunt' in public. 'I get less and less demure as time goes on,' she said. 'I start saying "cunt" a lot and you really aren't meant to say "cunt" in America at all. It's a great word. I think it's almost a term of endearment.' Mortimer was equally tolerant with Rosie, who was as bolshie as ever, marched out of Bryanston in the middle of her sixth-form studies and was now swotting in London for her A-level exams at a crammer in Swiss Cottage. Like Emily she was 'discovered' miraculously when the co-owner of a model agency saw her coming out of Swiss Cottage tube station in February, aged only seventeen, and signed her up. Her A-level results that summer were dreadful, two Cs and a D, but within weeks she was being photographed by *Vogue* and Lord Snowdon, appearing on fashion show catwalks, and within months had bought herself a flat on the Portobello Road.

Mortimer began to translate *Così fan tutte* but was still unhappy with *Naked Justice*, rewrote parts of it, and the new version opened in Birmingham in February with Leslie Phillips as Fred again and Simon Ward as Keith. John Timbers was hired to take the production pictures and told me: 'John was charming the knickers off the young press office girl up at Birmingham. I've no idea how he's managed to seduce so many women. I've watched him operating many times and I think he's actually amoral. I honestly don't think he understands.'

On 30 March the Queen Mother died at the age of a hundred and one and Mortimer was drafted in again by the *Evening Standard* to report a royal funeral. His own longevity was also becoming impressive and two weeks later Penny and ten of his women friends gave him a rowdy surprise party in a barn on his seventy-ninth birthday, ordered a huge birthday cake with his photograph on the icing, invited two hundred guests and hired the rock band Deep Purple. The women called themselves the Mortimettes, dressed up in fishnet stockings, top hats and tailcoats, lined up to dance like high-kicking chorus girls and sang him the Gershwin song 'They Can't Take That Away From Me' with new lyrics – 'the way you wear your wig' – written by Richard Curtis and Tom Stoppard. 'We were all vying madly for his attention,' Kathy Lette told the *Independent on Sunday*. 'He's such a babe magnet,' she twittered, and as an extra birthday present she took him to Stringfellow's lap-dancing club in London where he spent an evening drooling over the nearly naked girls and tucking banknotes into their garters. 'I find that all rather surprising,' Shirley Anne Field told me, 'it's schoolboy stuff.' Fay Weldon agreed: 'I went to a lap-dance once,' she told me, 'and I was really pleased to get out into the healthy air! It's not sexy at all. I can't stand a stripper, and this sort of sauciness is sadly outmoded. Young men in their teens like this sort of thing but once you're eighteen you ought to go right off it because it's not an erotic experience.' As Mortimer had said himself during the *Oz* trial in 1971, 'laughter is something which is never present in strip clubs or at erotic shows. Those breathless old men in mackintoshes are viewing the ceremony with the most extreme seriousness, and a good giggle would break the spell at once,' but now in old age he was for some reason mesmerised by Ms Lette, whose style was not to everyone's taste. Patricia Delano told me that she was once with Kathy Lette in a mixed group of people, including a senior Australian judge, and apologised for having a cold and a hoarse voice. 'Kathy said, "I know the best cure for that: you should gargle with spunk." Nobody was amused and the judge looked shocked.' Shirley Anne was amused about the Mortimettes. 'He has this harem of older ladies – it's rather funny, really!' she said. 'Penny's clever to surround him with these older chorus girls: it makes him feel good and everybody feels like "aren't we naughty, breaking all the rules?" but nobody's breaking *any* rules. It's a very odd way of carrying on but I do think Penny's become a good support for him.'

Mortimer's old friend Barbara Castle died in May aged ninety-one and he wrote in the *Daily Mail* a nostalgic tribute to her and the Old Labour ideals that they had shared before their party was hijacked by Blair and his smug spin doctors. Death was lurking increasingly in the shadows: at the end of July Leo McKern died aged eighty-two and Joss Ackland's wife Rosemary succumbed to her terrible motor neurone disease, the dread muscular curse that had killed David Niven. The death of Labour's traditional beliefs was another cause of mourning and deepened by Blair's appointment of a new Home Secretary, David Blunkett, who turned out to be even more authoritarian than Straw and Howard and agreed that foreign arrest warrants should apply to British citizens who could be seized, sent abroad to moulder in some alien prison without charge or time limit, and stand trial under unjust laws. Although Mortimer and Frederick Forsyth, a staunch Conservative, were opposed politically they agreed about the continual erosion of ancient British liberties and signed together a letter to *The Times* urging Parliament to reject the acceptance of European Union arrest warrants in Britain. 'He was now hugely disillusioned and *incandescent* about Labour,' Forsyth told me.

The government had still not repealed the anti-blasphemy law that had brought *Gay News* down and in July, on the twenty-fifth anniversary of the trial, Mortimer and Robertson both put their names in support on a leaflet that reprinted James Kirkup's poem 'The Love That Dares to Speak Its Name', which was still illegal in Britain. It was handed out in

Trafalgar Square by demonstrators, led by the gay campaigner Peter Tatchell, who took turns to read out all eleven verses and to demand that they should be arrested or the law repealed. A police film of the demo was sent to the Director of Public Prosecutions but no further action was taken and today the poem is available in full on several internet websites. It seemed that the anti-blasphemy law had been left to die.

The row over fox-hunting rumbled on and in September Mortimer and his wheelchair joined a huge Countryside Alliance demo in London to protest against a possible ban and New Labour's general negligence towards the countryside.

In November he rescued Rumpole from the brink of death where he had left him last and let him escape from the nursing home after his heart attack in the first of six more stories in his last Rumpole collection, *Rumpole and the Primrose Path*, which he dedicated to Kathy Lette. In one tale, 'Rumpole and the Right to Privacy', our hero defends successfully a small newspaper against a rich businessman's claim that it has invaded his privacy and tells him that he can hardly whimper about his right to privacy when he has himself given numerous intimate newspaper interviews about himself. 'Rumpole, like Jeeves and Sherlock Holmes, is immortal,' wrote P. D. James in the *Mail on Sunday*. 'He has ascended to the pantheon of literary immortals,' said the *Daily Telegraph*. 'An absolute delight,' said *The Times*. *The Financial Times* sent Julia Llewellyn Smith to interview him at one of his favourite London restaurants, J. Sheekey's, and she found him 'tufty-haired, sallow-skinned, with fleshy jowls, a tiny crooked mouth and hooded eyes hidden behind huge glasses'. He looked, she said, 'like an old koala in a tweed suit. Half-blind and wobbly legged.' Once again he railed against the government: 'They have gone totally raving mad, totally dotty. The idea of following Bush into a war with Iraq. It's barmy. It's all about Iraqi oil.' As for David Blunkett, he 'is probably the worst Home Secretary we've ever had. He even outdoes Michael Howard.' Like Nigel Farndale a year previously she discovered that 'Mortimer's carefully crafted reputation as a jovial old cove conceals a bitchy streak', which became evident when he mentioned that he had once met the Tory politician Edwina Currie at a dinner where 'she talked about gonorrhoea throughout'.

'She's vulgar,' said Ms Llewellyn Smith.

'Yes, she *is*!' said Mortimer. '"Common", we used to say when I was a boy.'

As vulgar and common as some of his own less than elegant friends?

In December Mortimer spoke at Leo McKern's memorial service where he bumped into Irene Shubik again. 'He was all "darling, how beautiful you look, aren't you elegant?" and was once again forced to say what a good producer I was,' she said. His own health was deteriorating rapidly. The sight in his second eye was weakening and his suppurating legs were now so feeble that Penny gave him a powered wheelchair for Christmas. They hired a housekeeper, Maria, to help Peter Hayes look after him when Penny was away, which was often, but John was bravely determined to enjoy life to the very end, continued to travel, go to lunches and parties, perform his stage show and defiantly to swallow gallons of champagne, pouring his first glass, he claimed, at 6 a.m. every day.

A great deal of bubbly was drunk on an icy 4 January 2003 when Emily, now thirty-one, married thirty-year-old Alessandro Nivola at Turville church in front of a congregation that included Billy Connolly, Sinèad Cusack, Anna Ford, Edward Fox, Bob Geldof, Neil Kinnock, Ewan McGregor and Jeremy Paxman. Rosie was chief bridesmaid and afterwards Emily laid her wedding bouquet touchingly on the grave of her childhood friend Lucy Hoggett, who had been killed by a car when she was nine. The reception was held in a marquee at Turville Heath Cottage where the guests danced to Nivola's favourite Mexican punk band from Los Angeles and watched fireworks.

Roy Jenkins died the next day aged eighty-two and although he had recently incensed Mortimer by calling Blair 'a good Prime Minister and possibly a great one', Mortimer wrote that Jenkins had been the best Home Secretary of his lifetime because he had helped to civilise Britain's laws on hanging, homosexuality, abortion and obscenity. This tribute did not however stop him still poking fun at Jenkins' inability to pronounce the letter r: he liked particularly to tell how Jenkins went into European politics after losing his seat in the Commons and made a speech when he left in which he said 'I'm going into Europe without rancour' but pronounced 'rancour' with a w.

In February Mortimer and his wheelchair joined yet another march through London, this time to protest against the possibility of Britain going to war beside the United States against the Iraqi tyrant Saddam Hussein even though he had urged the United Nations to do just that in 1990. In an *Evening Standard* article he explained his reasons and was attacked for it in the same paper a few days later by the Jewish American journalist Barbara Amiel, the wife of the proprietor of the *Daily Telegraph*, Conrad (Lord) Black. Calling Mortimer a fool, she wrote: 'Speaking of the 11 September attacks in New York, Mortimer wrote that the motive for that terrible event "is Israel's treatment of the Palestinians" [but] this is nonsense. Not even Osama bin Laden has argued that the motive for al Qaeda's action is the Palestinian conflict. Bin Laden and the terrorists that he inspires have always stated that . . . they want the depraved infidels of Christendom and their allies swept from their worldly ascendance. It's a fantasy to reinterpret this as support for the suffering Palestinians. As for Mortimer's notion that there has been no pressure put upon Israel to make peace: he must be joking. The entire Oslo peace process was nothing but relentless pressure on the Israelis by America and it culminated in Israeli Prime Minister Barak's offer to return ninety-five per cent of the disputed territories to the Palestinians. Arafat refused.'

In April 2003 yet another of Mortimer's old friends died, John Paul Getty, but he managed himself to negotiate safely his own eightieth birthday even though Kathy Lette risked over-exciting him by taking him to a restaurant in Covent Garden, School Dinners, where the wait-resses were dressed in skimpy schoolgirl tunics. To stimulate him beyond endurance she took him also to another 'erotic' London venue, Club RUB, which 'should be huge fun', she twittered. 'It's all quite naughty: they whip you with lettuce and things.' Lettuce? What, no hairbrush? Club RUB's internet website confided that it was 'a regular monthly fetish club. Strict fetish dress code applies.' The thought of fat old Mortimer in 'strict fetish dress' is a vision to savour.

And then in June I sent him a letter asking if he would mind if I wrote his biography − if he might even cooperate with it − and jovially he agreed. It was the start of a bizarre episode that made me realise for the first time that he was not at all the man I had always thought he was and led me eventually to write a book dramatically different from the one I had intended. I discovered that he was not a sweet old darling after all.

Fourteen

The Bitter End
2003–2005

When I asked John about writing his biography he encouraged me to do it and agreed to cooperate. In the twenty-three years that I had been the literary editor of the *Sunday Express* we had become friendly acquaintances. I had reviewed his books, he had written to thank me, he had been a judge for the *Sunday Express* Book of the Year Award that I ran, had made the main speech at the prizegiving lunch and had written afterwards to say how much he had enjoyed it and how worthy the prize was. When I left the *Sunday Express* in 1992 and sued the paper for constructive dismissal he wrote affectionately to say how much he admired my work and that he supported my case. When I interviewed him for the *Daily Telegraph* in 1993 he sent me a charming card, showing three naked girls fondling each other's breasts, to thank me for 'a warm and generous interview'. Even Penny, he said, She Who Put Her Foot Down, had approved. It had really cheered up his birthday, he said, and when his publishers gave him a lunch at the Savoy for more than thirty guests he took a copy of my article along to show them. When I edited a new short story magazine, *Raconteur*, in 1994 he wrote a story for it and when I congratulated him on his knighthood he replied with another friendly card. So we were hardly strangers and when he agreed that I should write the book – when in effect he authorised me to do it – I sent my publisher a proposal for what I called an authorised biography.

The project began to collapse when Mortimer's literary agent, Michael Sissons, demanded to see a copy of the proposal, accused me aggressively of lying because I had called the book 'authorised', tried to dictate which company should publish the book and eventually wrote to say that John had now decided not to cooperate after all. I wrote to John to say that I was devastated by this decision because I had already spent three expensive months researching the book and buying every one of his and Penelope's books and plays, but despite our cordial relationship over so many years he never replied or explained why he suddenly dumped me as callously as later I discovered he had dumped others over the years. Instead I received an astonishingly offensive fax from Sissons which accused me falsely yet again of lying, and he sent it by open fax to my London club, where his libellous remarks could have been read by a dozen witnesses. The fax concluded by saying that although Mortimer would no longer cooperate neither would he dissociate himself from the book – yet a few weeks later he appointed one of Sissons' agency's own authors, Valerie Grove, to write a rival authorised biography, and soon he was telling his family and friends not to talk to me but only to Valerie. The barrister who was widely revered for his staunch defence of free speech and the right of authors to publish anything at all was now trying to censor me. Even men who were much admired for their independence and moral courage – Sir Richard Branson, Richard Ingrams, Richard Neville – were frightened off. There were honourable exceptions: Jeremy Mortimer and Neil Kinnock talked to me at length, Jeremy because he felt he owed it to his mother that I should know the truth about her, Kinnock because he had agreed to see me before John tried to nobble him and felt he should honour his promise. Mortimer's attempts to censor this book became so farcical that when he was lunching one day at the Wolseley restaurant in Piccadilly he spotted the publisher Ion Trewin across the room and sent a waiter over with a note that said 'Don't talk to Graham Lord' only to discover that it was Trewin himself who was editing and publishing this book.

Ironically Mortimer did me a huge favour because his devious be-haviour showed me an unattractive side of his character that I had never suspected and freed me to write a ruthlessly honest biography completely independent of any control by him or Sissons. Twenty-seven potential witnesses refused to talk to me but eighty did and many came up with startling revelations that Mortimer and Sissons would never have let me publish in an authorised biography. Poor old authorised Valerie Grove: how is she ever going to be able to tell the complete truth about Mortimer with Sissons harrumphing and snorting over every paragraph?

In July 2003 Alan Yentob's television tribute *Imagine: John Mortimer Owning Up at 80* was broadcast by the BBC. 'He stands, whether you agree with it or not, for freedom – freedom of expression,' Jeremy Paxman told Yentob. Oh, really? As for 'owning up at eighty', Mortimer owned up to nothing and there was no one on the programme to suggest that he was anything other than the twinkly, heroic sweetie he had long been thought to be: no Wendy Craig, Shirley Anne Field, Derek Granger, David Leitch, Michael Lindsay-Hogg, Molly Parkin, Irene Shubik or Judge Angus Stroyan. 'He's a brilliant anecdotalist,' said Sir Richard Eyre, 'but if you're around him a lot the anecdotes recur and generally they've been worked up and embellished a little more.' In other words they're lies? Some of the interviewees did hint that he had a few teeny character defects. 'He likes to be centre stage,' said Baroness Mallalieu, 'and if he is centre stage then everything is fine. John needs constant reassurance and it astonishes me that someone with John's ability should need constantly to be told that it's all satisfactory. Every morning on holiday he says "my career is at an end"!' Penny, chainsmoking, waving a glass of wine, looking barmaid-blowsy and recently returned from yet another long charity bicycle ride, this time through Romania, declared in a rasping smoker's voice that 'he gets *crucified* by reviews. One bad review cancels out nine brilliant ones. He's looking for it to *prove* that he's no good.' Richard Eyre confirmed it – 'there's a compulsive desire to be admired, approved, for what he writes' – and Penny added: 'He'd like to be Pope, wearing robes with women kneeling at his feet and kissing his ring. That's his idea of Heaven on earth, writing in his study with the door slightly open and three very lovely women sitting round the table in the kitchen quietly talking about how wonderful he is.' There was certainly plenty of that in Yentob's programme. 'We all adore him,' gushed Kathy Lette. 'He's just God's gift to womankind, the thinking woman's crumpet.' Baroness Mallalieu declared that he '*likes* women and there are not many men of his generation who actually *like* women. If you ever walk into a room where John is he makes you leave it feeling better.' Especially if you're gullible enough to think that the old fraud actually means what he says. 'He flatters outrageously,' admitted Penny, waving a whole packet of cigarettes. 'You'll hear him say "oh, darling, you're looking *so* beautiful", and you look at her and she's a real old *hag*!' There were plenty of those around him.

In September he became a grandfather yet again when Emily gave birth to a son, Sam, in London nine months to the day after her wedding, three days after her film *Young Adam* opened and four days before the opening of her next, *Bright Young Things*. Rosie had by now decided that modelling was 'insipid' and wanted to write for television instead, and

Mortimer's own new production was a short book in which he gave all his grandchildren some gentle, waffly advice about life, *Where There's a Will*, which was published in November. Once again he padded it out with far too many of his old anecdotes. 'I have always envied the way in which he recycles his jokes with the same relentlessness with which Anita Brookner recycles her novels,' Francis King told me, and at times the book was decidedly smug. It was also often surprisingly illogical for a writer with a sharp legal brain: he declared, for instance, that fox-hunting harmed no one 'unless you wish to count the fox' but that was surely the whole point of the abolitionists' objections and the same could be said of dog and cock fighting, bear and badger baiting, bestiality and numerous other cruel pastimes that have long been illegal.

To be scrupulously fair, *Where There's a Will* was also often amusing, mischievous, iconoclastic and splendidly politically incorrect. To mark its publication he gave a couple more newspaper interviews, one to Emma Brockes of the *Guardian*, who was told by the increasingly ludicrous Kathy Lette that Mortimer was 'a total babe magnet, a literary love god', and by Sinèad Cusack that he and Penny 'have great, sparky arguments. They don't hold back.' Derek Laud, who interviewed him for the *Mail on Sunday*, discovered just how big a snob the allegedly socialist Mortimer had become when he saw on his mantelpiece a row of old Christmas cards from Prince Charles. He was invited to speak at a Foyles literary lunch in London where he told an *Evening Standard* reporter that he was appalled that Michael Howard might be about to become leader of the Conservative Party. 'It is one's worst absolute nightmare,' he groaned. 'He was the worst Home Secretary we ever had [and] mostly in favour of sending everyone to prison.' Hang on: had he not said recently that Straw and Blunkett were both even worse than Howard?

Joss Ackland asked Mortimer to speak at his beloved wife Rosie's memorial service in December and Claire Bloom and Greta Scacchi to read extracts from her diaries. 'John combined humour and sadness and had us in tears,' Ms Scacchi told me, 'and he spoke without even a note.' He was finishing a Rumpole novel that was finally to describe the greatest triumph of the old hack's legal career, the Penge Bungalow Murders, began to write the script for a television biography of the saucy, moon-faced British TV comedian Benny Hill, and contributed an absurdly sexist article to the *Daily Mail* in which he suggested that women should run the world because they are more sensible, rational and down-to-earth than men. Without offering any evidence at all he claimed that women are stronger, more understanding, harder working, better friends and company, more realistic, open-minded and law-abiding, and do not indulge themselves by having long, drunken lunches and seducing their secretaries – obviously assuming that all men behave like him. By contrast, he claimed, men live in a world of hopeless, egocentric fantasy. So how come most great leaders, philosophers, scientists, inventors, doctors, writers, painters, composers and musicians have been men? He claimed yet again that his idea of hell was an all-male dinner yet he had for many years been a member of the men-only Garrick Club and was to speak two months later at an all-male, black-tie Garrick dinner in honour of Peter Hall. Yet again it is impossible to know whether Mortimer really meant anything he ever said or wrote.

Kathy Lette, who had recently added sophistication to Salman Rushdie's stag night by devising for it a lesbian theme – and was about to publish a novel, *Dead Sexy*, that was accompanied by huge posters sniggering 'it's long, it's thick and will keep you up all night' – once again organised a special birthday treat for Mortimer's eighty-first by throwing a party at which a stripper-cum-conjuror produced a handkerchief from various parts of her body, finally coaxing one from her vagina. 'John sat in a wheelchair absolutely entranced,' I was told by a guest. 'When she pulled it out of her vagina she handed it to John, who tucked it into his top pocket and looked very pleased with himself. His wife wasn't there.'

Early in June I learned from three sources that Wendy Craig had given birth to Mortimer's son Ross Bentley in 1961 and that Ross and many people in the theatre knew that John was his father. I spoke to her on the telephone and asked for an interview but although at first she sounded half-willing I received instead a letter from a solicitor warning me that she might sue for invasion of privacy if I published the story. She telephoned Mortimer, whom she had not seen for forty-three years, to say that I might be about to reveal the story and he met Ross for the first time three weeks later, on 20 August, invited him to lunch to meet Penny, Emily and Rosie, and spiked my guns by confessing all to Tim Walker of the *Sunday Telegraph*, a friend of Michael Sissons' journalist daughter Kate. The paper ran the story on its front page and inside on 12 September but Wendy Craig was not a party to this decision to go public, I was told by her agent Daphne Waring, and refused to make any comment or talk to any newspapers. Mortimer, by contrast, seemed to revel in his naughty new notoriety and every Sunday paper carried huge stories in its later editions. MORTIMER'S JOY AT WENDY CRAIG LOVE CHILD, shrieked the headline over the *Sunday Telegraph* report, in which he claimed that Wendy had never told him in 1961 that she was pregnant and insisted that he had had no idea of Ross's existence, that neither was ashamed of anything, and that they were both very happy. He claimed that Wendy's husband, Jack Bentley, had made her swear to tell no one that he was Ross's father and that she had not told Ross until he was in his twenties. He also claimed inaccurately that Ross bore a striking resemblance to Emily: luckily for Emily she resembled her mother and looked nothing like her father or Ross.

The Monday papers went wild – RUMPOLE AND THE SECRET SON bellowed the *Daily Mail*, DELIGHTFUL SHOCK FOR AN INCOR-RIGIBLE FLIRT AND CHARMER chuckled the *Daily Telegraph* – and carried big photographs of Wendy and Ross then and now. 'It was a very pleasant surprise,' Mortimer told Sarah Chalmers of the *Daily Mail*. 'But I'm very pleased, he's very pleased and we've all become great friends. The real story here is what a happy ending we have found.' The *Daily Express* even ran a simpering leader under the headline SIR JOHN'S SO CHARMING that read: 'What grace and good manners Sir John Mortimer has shown in his reaction to the news that he and actress Wendy Craig have a son. In such a charmless age we could do with more of his unstuffy brand of grown-up behaviour.' The *Daily Express* columnist Vanessa Feltz praised him for his 'customary elegance' but attacked Wendy Craig, grossly unfairly, for 'letting down all those women who adopted her so lovingly as a role model, not by having an affair but by denying it and allowing a festering lie of forty years' standing to cause unimaginable pain to others'. The media frenzy went on for a week. The papers published photographs of Ross showing that he had the same jutting, wonky jaw as Mortimer. They reported that Ross had never got on with Wendy's elder son, Alaster, had read history at Reading University, ran a computer software company, and lived in a mews cottage in Paddington with his thirty-five-year-old girlfriend Kate Forster, a chef, and their fifteen-month-old daughter Iris. Nobody seemed to disapprove of Mortimer's behaviour. He had suddenly become a national hero, Jack the Lad, nudge nudge, wink wink: Rumpy-pumpole of the Bailey. Kathy Lette told Richard Kay of the *Daily Mail* that she was 'so jealous' of Wendy Craig because she 'would adore to have John's love child – as would every other woman I know in London. Having a child with this literary love god could only be a case of designer genes.' Dear oh dear. Amanda Platell wrote in the *Daily Mail* under the headline WHY WE WOMEN JUST LOVE AN UGLY MAN ... that 'none of us is beyond flattery and, strangely enough, a big, fat, ugly man has a much better chance of charming his way under our defences and into our lives because when we meet him we couldn't possibly imagine going to bed with *that*.' Mortimer became so proud of his roguish reputation that soon he was leering at the end of his stage show that 'if anyone wants a love child they should stay behind afterwards'.

Nobody seemed to care about the agony and heartbreak that Penelope and Bentley had suffered when they discovered that Wendy was pregnant. Nobody recalled that Penelope had described her nightmare so vividly in *The Pumpkin Eater*, or the stress and grief that had driven her to endure years of misery, psychiatrists, asylums and attempted suicide. And it seems astonishing that Mortimer, who had been addicted all his life to gossip, did not know about Ross's existence when I and so many people in the theatre did. Even the authorised Valerie Grove claimed in *The Times* that she had known about Ross for months – yet apparently Mortimer didn't.

Two newspaper journalists did question the media's fawning over Mortimer: Tom Utley, writing under his pseudonym Tom Kemp in the *Daily Telegraph*, and the *Daily Mail* columnist Peter McKay. 'I am not so sure why Sir John should be quite as smug as he seems to feel,' wrote Utley. 'When footballers or politicians are caught deceiving their wives, the tabloids call them "love rats". But when Sir John's marital sins come to light, everyone agrees that this only goes to show what a wonderful, charming, all-round good egg he is.' He added: 'I find it baffling that Sir John, with his great Rumpole of a brain, failed to draw any connection . . . Most of us, when women produce children nine months after we have gone to bed with them, think that there may be at least some possibility that we had something to do with it. But the idea doesn't seem to have occurred to Sir John. Perhaps he didn't care enough about the mother of his child even to know that she had produced a baby . . . he got to escape all the horrors, the crippling expense and the guilt of fatherhood. He never had to change Ross's nappy. He never had to spend a moment fretting by the boy's sick-bed, or trying to break up his fights with his siblings. At the age of eighty-one, he finds himself presented with a perfectly formed son, brought up entirely at other people's expense. And then he dares to congratulate himself on how nicely his boy has turned out. No wonder the smug git smiles so much.'

Ross told the papers that he had felt very much at home as soon as he walked into Turville Heath Cottage and met John and his family. 'It's wonderful to have such a highly talented father,' he said, and the rest of the family 'were terribly nice and welcoming. There was absolutely nothing awkward about it all. Everyone made me feel so welcome and comfortable and relaxed.' No one asked Jeremy, who was now head of Radio 4 drama at the BBC, whether he also felt 'joy' at the sudden discovery that he had a half-brother whose birth had devastated his mother's life. And what about Penelope's five daughters, who had had to share their mother's misery for so many years? Even Emily admitted to John Harlow of *The Sunday Times* that meeting Ross had been startling, confusing and bizarre 'and it brings up an awful lot of stuff'. As for Penny, she must surely have wondered what other unsavoury secrets might be lurking behind her husband's smirk. How many other bastards might there be? Given his careless promiscuity for decades there might well be dozens. When John died would she suddenly find that he had left all his money to strangers? She must have found herself staring suspiciously at anyone with a wonky jaw.

Shirley Anne Field was surprised by Mortimer's claims that he had never known about Wendy's pregnancy or Ross's birth. 'I was upset at the airbrushed version painting him as the heroic figure and making Wendy look like some fallen, silly, Mills and Boon, disgraced heroine,' she told me. The *Mail on Sunday* approached Shirley Anne and published the following Sunday a devastating, two-page attack on Mortimer, based on her evidence and written by Laura Collins, under the headline MOR-TIMER KNEW OF HIS SECRET SON FOR 40 YEARS. In 1961, Ms Collins wrote, Jack Bentley had 'made a series of menacing phone calls to Mortimer's first wife, Penelope, in which he described the baby as "this brat" who was going to make them all suffer – particularly Wendy as he would serve as a constant reminder of her betrayal. The emotional fallout nearly destroyed Wendy and Bentley's marriage and brought Penelope to the brink of suicide.' Ms Collins asked Mortimer how he could possibly not have known about Ross. 'It is absolutely not true that I knew about any child until very recently,' he insisted. 'The suggestion that I did is completely untrue. *The Pumpkin Eater* was really about Penelope's relationship with Wendy's husband Jack Bentley. It was a work of fiction. I've answered your questions, there's nothing more to say.' In fact *The Pumpkin Eater* was not of course only about Penelope and Bentley but also about John and Wendy. Penelope and Jeremy admitted that it was entirely autobiographical, Mortimer himself had confessed that he was the model for the shit of a husband in every one of her novels, and Penny 2 had told Alasdair Riley of the *Evening Standard* in 1973 that she had read *The Pumpkin Eater* when she met John and that he had indeed been the horrible husband in the book.

Astonishingly not one other newspaper followed up Shirley Anne

Field's allegation that Mortimer was lying, probably because he instructed the widely feared libel solicitors Carter-Ruck to send a menacing letter immediately to the *Mail on Sunday* claiming that the article was untrue, thus muzzling the rest of the Press. Wrote Peter McKay about Mortimer in his *Daily Mail* column: 'writers are often the first to demand that information about public figures should be aired. Except when they are the victims.'

Instead of trying to discover the truth the *Sunday Telegraph* published an oleaginous interview with Mortimer by Emily Bearn, under the cosy headline RUMPY-PUMPY OF THE BAILEY, that called the *Mail on Sunday* article 'a malignant feature in a tabloid'. She reported that he seemed too frail to have to handle accusations that he was lying. 'His voice has become so soft and tiny that when I first called him on the telephone I thought I was speaking to an old lady,' she wrote. 'His appearance has been likened to a bag of spanners and today, perched behind his desk with bare feet and a dirty white shirt missing two buttons, he does the description proud.'

There was an intriguing footnote to this enormous barrage of publicity which erupted just days before *Rumpole and the Penge Bungalow Murders* was published. In Mortimer's previous novel, *Felix in the Underworld*, the novelist hero is told by his publicist that if he tells the newspapers about his secret mistress and bastard son the publicity would be great for his new book.

Apparently unfazed by the scandal or the fact that her husband had to meet the Press wearing a dirty shirt with two buttons missing, Penny took off for the Labour Party conference in Brighton to harangue the delegates about fox-hunting, leaving John to publicise the new book, which told at last the story of Rumpole's most famous courtroom victory many years earlier, in the 1950s, when he had been a junior barrister just down from Oxford and defended successfully at the Old Bailey a young man who seemed certain to be hanged for murdering two heroic Second World War bomber pilots, one of them his father. It was one of the best of all the Rumpole stories – highly readable, gripping and unusually well written, an astonishingly fresh, inventive tale considering that Mortimer was eight-one, and to add to the pleasure Rumpole describes how he was ensnared into marrying Hilda Wystand, She Who Must Be Obeyed.

Sales of Mortimer's books, however, were declining. 'I don't think the rest of the crew at Penguin thought much of them,' his ex-editor Judith Burnley told me. 'They were good middlebrow fiction and a success but I don't know if there's a market for them now. Publishers don't publish midlist books any more because now they're only interested in lead titles which are on the market for three weeks and then vanish. I don't think that John would get published at all now – I'm really serious – and if they got a manuscript from Graham Greene they'd reject it.' There were rumours that Rumpole was about to be revived on television with Albert Finney as Horace but how could anyone replace Leo McKern convincingly? 'It would be an absolute mistake,' Irene Shubik told me. 'It's past its sell-by date.' Horace Rumpole 'served us well', wrote Geoffrey Robertson in *The Justice Game*, 'although today he would be bankrupted by wasted costs orders and his face would not fit the glossy chambers brochure.'

Even Mortimer himself seemed suddenly less popular despite all the love-child excitement. In October he was due to give a talk on 'Life, Love and the Law' in London but it had to be cancelled when only a sixth of the tickets were sold. 'The world is going to the dogs,' he told the *Independent*, and from his point of view it was. His political nightmare came true when Michael Howard was elected leader of the Conservative Party and announced that if he won the next election he would build more prisons, jail more criminals, see that they were given longer sentences, and ensure that they endured a tougher prison regime. For Mortimer in fact 2004 was a seriously depressing year when many of his hallowed beliefs were challenged. In April the House of Lords agreed to abolish trial by jury in cases where it would be 'impractical'. Harrow, which he had loathed so much, announced that it was to spread its influence, ethos, uniform and even school songs as far away as China by opening a branch in Beijing. In June the wise, tolerant *Daily Telegraph* columnist W. F. Deedes wrote a piece about permissiveness, sex, violence and obscenity on television under the headline MARY WHITEHOUSE MAY HAVE HAD A POINT AFTER ALL. In July Deedes was echoed by Tony Blair, who attacked the permissiveness and amorality of the 1960s – with their flabby liberalism, irresponsibility and lack of strong values and discipline – for causing much of the lawlessness and many of the social ills of modern Britain. A leader in the *Daily Telegraph* declared that 'by rejecting what Mr Blair called "the 1960s consensus" and advocating a return to "rules, order and proper behaviour", Labour is admitting that the Left's founding values have failed.' In another leader three weeks later the *Telegraph* reckoned that the Sixties did not deserve their glamorous reputation: 'Not unlike the 1930s, it was a low, dishonest decade, in which many of the values, traditions and standards that had made this country so admired were unceremoniously dumped. The dragon's teeth then sown, with the best intentions, are still being reaped today.' It was announced that shoplifters and other small-scale thieves were to be given £80 on-the-spot fines rather than a trial and that more criminals would be tagged electronically so that they could be tracked day and night by Big Brother satellite. In October there was uproar from MPs and viewers' groups when *Nine Songs*, a film in which the actors had explicit sex together and which showed in vivid close-up acts of penetration, masturbation and oral sex, opened on general release in ordinary cinemas. Two days later David Blunkett announced that in future a jury could be told of a defendant's previous convictions before they decided whether he was guilty. In November the Lord Chancellor, Lord Falconer, announced that cases in the Court of Appeal would in future be televised in an experiment that might well spread to all law courts. Fox-hunting was outlawed at last from the middle of February 2005 and a couple of days later, when the Queen opened a new Parliament, she announced that Blair's government would enact thirty-two intrusive new bills to strengthen state security and extend government control of its citizens, from forcing them to carry identity cards to ordering how they should treat their pets. 'We are in danger of having a police state without the police,' said Michael Howard (of all people) in the Commons. At the beginning of December the Metropolitan Police Commissioner, Sir John Stevens, declared that house-holders should be entitled to use much more force when encountering a burglar in their houses even if that meant killing an intruder. Even Mortimer's fear that the government would abolish the annual £121 TV licence and make the BBC financially dependent on advertising or business sponsorship came closer when a government committee announced in December that it was a strong possibility. A few days later Stephen Pollard's biography of David Blunkett reported that Blunkett thought Michael Howard had been a better Home Secretary than Jack Straw, and when Blunkett was succeeded by Charles Clarke the new Home Secretary announced that he was going to give himself draconian new powers to confine and control suspected terrorists even though they had never been tried or convicted. It was a bitter end to a sorry year as so many of Mortimer's chickens came squawking loudly home to roost.

At the end of 2004 he had four small consolations. Ross announced that he was to marry his girlfriend, Kate, in February and that Jeremy had agreed to be his best man. David Blunkett resigned as Home Secretary after revelations about his own secret illegitimate son by a married woman. Tony Blair was frantically trying to delay the implementation of the Hunting Act so that pro-hunting protesters would not damage his chance of winning the next general election. And on 1 January 2005 a cause dear to Mortimer's heart, a British Freedom of Information Act, came into force to compel bureaucrats and public bodies to open their files to the public. But were these consolations enough? When Mortimer looked back over his long life he must have realised that not everyone was impressed and that many people who knew him well were lukewarm about his achievements. Actors, producers and directors were unanimous that *A Voyage Round My Father* would endure long after his death and that Rumpole had been a gloriously original creation, but no one expected any of his other plays or novels to last. 'I don't like his plays very much,' Michael Lindsay-Hogg told me, 'and his novels are slipshod. He's lazy but he has to write a lot because he has to earn a lot of money.' Robin Dalton agreed: 'I don't think he's a terribly good writer. The problem with John as a writer is that he's greedy. He takes on everything for the money. He just wants to be rich and famous, not a great writer.' Ion Trewin reckoned that if Mortimer was remembered in the theatre at all it would be as 'a real old hack, very accomplished at what he did but not a great, original playwright. He's a journalist, a reporter who knows how to dramatise something suitable for whatever medium he's chosen.' As for his books, even the Rumpole stories, Mortimer is already forgotten by the younger generation even though he was given in April 2005 a Lifetime Achievement prize at the British Book Awards ceremony, where his daughter Emily made an embarrassingly gushing speech. Six months earlier I asked a thirty-something assistant at Waterstone's bookshop in the Brompton Road in London if he had a copy of the latest paperback reprint of *Clinging to the Wreckage*.

'Who's John Mortimer?' he asked.

I was astonished. Waterstone's is renowned for its staff's wide literary knowledge. 'He's a writer,' I said.

'What does he write?'

'Lots of novels, stories, plays. He published a novel just two weeks ago about Rumpole of the Bailey, *Rumpole and the Penge Bungalow Murders*.'

'Ah, yes. I've heard of Rumpole. What's the chap's name again?'

'John Mortimer.'

'How do you spell Mortimer?'

'M-O-R-T-I-M-E-R.'

'So he's the Rumpole man.'

As far as that young man was concerned Mortimer might be dead and buried already.

Even the importance of his legal triumphs was being questioned by

those who felt that his courtroom performances in the 1970s had helped
to corrode many of Britain's proudest values and to coarsen the nation's
social fabric, encouraging among other vicious developments what Lord
Tebbit listed as 'the growth of single-parent families, single mothers
with several children by different fathers, teenage mothers, and the
flaunting of homosexuality so that kids are confused about the nature of
family life and their own role in society. Society should be deeply concerned about these feral children but now they just seem to be regarded
as a by-product of everybody having a wonderful time.'

As for Mortimer's apparently genial, tolerant camouflage, he was by
no means universally admired whatever his gushing groupies might like
to think. 'He's an old bitch, isn't he?' said David Leitch. 'He puts people
down and he's quite ruthless. He's a horrible, horrible man. Everyone
says "what a marvellous man" but he's an absolute shit.' A television
producer who asked not to be named told me: 'John's an awful shit
pretending to be a nice guy. He's ambitious, absolutely ruthless, and has
a huge ego.' Francis King told me: 'I have always liked and admired him
but I suspect that, as with many charmers, the underlying reality is
colder and harder than the first impression.' Richard Ingrams' ex-wife
Mary, who had come to know the Mortimers well during her marriage,
told me that she had heard nothing from them when her drug-addict
daughter Jubby died tragically in her thirties in 2004 even though the
story of Jubby's death was widely reported. 'John and Penny are very fair-
weather friends,' she said. Freddie Forsyth's wife, Sandy, who had known
Penny for forty years, told him when he first met Mortimer: 'Be careful.
He's not quite the beaming, Pickwickian figure that you might think.'
Forsyth told me that 'Mortimer's been quite abrasive, and he's treated a
lot of women very badly, and if you *thought* you were a friend, and things
went badly for you, you would never know whether he would stand by
you'. Even Neil Kinnock admitted that 'there is a down side to John: he
can be irascible and acid', and another witness told me that 'Penny's as
tough as nails. She's the one who rules the roost.' Poignantly his daughter
Rosie, now just twenty-one and living in Emily's flat in London, told
Sharon Feinstein and Laura Collins of the *Mail on Sunday* at the end of
June 2005 – in an interview that appeared under the headline MY DAD
THE CAD – that 'he's very self-obsessed . . . and it leaves him not caring
that much about other people.'

Mortimer's admirers congratulate themselves that they have been
befriended by a man so delightfully liberal, tolerant, amusing, charming
and freedom-loving but his detractors suggest that beneath that cuddly,

twinkly camouflage, beneath all the jolly charm, genial jokes and polished anecdotes, there lurks a very different, much less lovable character. Could that really be true? As Mortimer had said himself so often in court, 'Ladies and gentlemen of the jury: that is of course entirely a matter for you alone to decide.'

Acknowledgements

I must thank Sir John Mortimer himself for giving me two long interviews and encouraging me to write this book before inexplicably he changed his mind and withdrew his cooperation. I should also mention his literary agent, Michael Sissons, whose interference sank the original project but freed me to write the book in half the time it would otherwise have taken and to make it much more interesting and truthful than any authorised biography could possibly be.

I owe a real debt of gratitude to Sir John's son Jeremy, who talked to me candidly about his mother, Penelope Mortimer, and gave me permission to quote from her books; to Sir John's stepdaughters Julia Mankowitz and Deborah Rogers, who kindly answered a few questions; to Sir John's political hero Neil Kinnock, who described their friendship and Sir John's impact on Labour Party politics; to Sir John's political *bête noire* Lord Tebbit; to Simon Callow, Judy Cornwell, Glenda Jackson and Greta Scacchi, who told me about their appearances in his plays; and to dozens of Sir John's friends and acquaintances who talked to me remarkably openly about him and his work.

His schooldays at the Dragon and Harrow were outlined graphically by several of his contemporaries: Dr Ted Bott, Sir Rupert Buchanan-Jardine, Sir Dermot de Trafford, Forest Ellvers, David Henley-Welch, Captain Anthony Hunter, Tony Murray, Richard Ollard, Mark Ramage, Bryan Routledge, Godfrey Royle, Brian Straton-Ferrier, Judge Angus Stroyan QC, Richard Willis and Sandy Wilson.

His two years at Oxford were recalled by his fellow undergraduates Arthur Bone, John Browning, Patrick Freeman, Francis King, John Holmes, James Michie and James Silvester.

His startlingly energetic love life was described in explicit detail by four of his many ex-mistresses – Jenny Bailey, Shirley Anne Field, Jane

McKerron and Molly Parkin – as well as by a very close acquaintance of another of Mortimer's lovers, Denholm Elliott's wife Susan.

His work as a barrister was explained by his chambers colleagues Lord Hooson QC and Sir Jonah Walker-Smith as well as Judge Angus Stroyan QC.

His writing – of novels, stage plays, revues, filmscripts, television plays and series – was examined by Leslie Bricusse, Judith Burnley, Michael Codron, Sir Richard Eyre, Martyn Friend, Derek Granger, David Hughes, Verity Lambert, Sir Michael Lindsay-Hogg, Alvin Rakoff, Ned Sherrin, Irene Shubik, Martin Thompson, Ion Trewin, Fay Weldon and Arnold Wesker.

Among many other witnesses who talked to me I am grateful to Hilary Alexander, Christopher Booker, Celia Brayfield, Andy Croft, Robin Dalton, Anna Deedes, Patricia and Tony Delano, Huw Edwards, Barbara Fenton, Ben Fenton, Frederick Forsyth, Dr Alan Gildersleve, Felicity Green, Elizabeth Hughes, Mary Ingrams, Philip Knightley, David Leitch, Lady Olga Maitland, Mike Molloy, Philip Oakes, Wole Soyinka, Emma Tennant, John Timbers and Andrew Vicari.

Two television programmes were particularly useful: Melvyn Bragg's excellent *South Bank Show* profile of Mortimer in 1986 and Alan Yentob's 2003 BBC1 documentary *Imagine*, and my research was greatly enhanced by the generous help of Juliet Bankes of the Corporation of London Records Office; Roger Beaton of the Bank of England; the Revd. Amanda Bloor; Elizabeth Boardman and Liz Kay, archivist and librarian respectively of Brasenose College, Oxford; Elaine Cleary; Martin and Patty Fennell; Kevin Gabbott of the Office of National Statistics; Rita Boswell Gibbs and Margaret Knight, archivist and librarian of Harrow School; Jeni Giffen; Rachel Hollings; Lord Hutchinson; Elizabeth Hyder of BBC Radio 4; Andrew Jarvis of the Principal Registry of the Family Division of the High Court in London; Luke Leitch; Brian MacArthur; Peter McKay; Sylvia Morris of the Royal Shakespeare Company Archive; Nigel Reynolds; Alan Strachan; Gay Sturt, Rosemary King and Charmian Hearne, archivist, librarian and secretary of the Dragon School, Oxford; and Peter Watson.

I also owe a huge debt to Steve Torrington, the chief librarian of the *Daily Mail*; Amanda Brewer and Lee Chilvers of *The Times* library in London; Dr Clare Rider of the Inner Temple Archives; and the staffs of the wonderful British Library at St Pancras, the British Newspaper Library at Colindale, the Chelsea Reference Library, the Holborn Library, the London Metropolitan Archives and *Private Eye*. And I must thank

Peter Hope Lumley's family for permission to quote from his notes for his unpublished autobiography; Emma Tennant for permission to quote from her unpublished diary; and Ben Fenton and Richard Willis for providing me with some rare photographs.

Finally I owe more than I can say to Juliet for her loyal support and fortitude. She says that whenever I write a biography I become just like my subject: 'It was great sleeping with David Niven for two years – but being kissed by John Mortimer ... ?' I dare not tell her who my next subject is going to be.

Bibliography

Joss Ackland, *I Must Be in There Somewhere* (Hodder and Stoughton, 1989)

Kingsley Amis, *Memoirs* (Hutchinson, 1991)

Stephen Bailey, *Living Sports History: Football at Winchester, Eton and Harrow* (University of Manchester Institute of Science and Technology internet paper, 2004)

Michael D. Barr, *Lee Kuan Yew: The Beliefs Behind the Man* (Curzon, 2000)

Ronald Bergan, *Dustin Hoffman* (Virgin, 1991)

Michael Billington, *The Life and Work of Harold Pinter* (Faber and Faber, 1996)

Melvyn Bragg, *Laurence Olivier* (Hutchinson, 1984)

Richard Branson, *Losing My Virginity* (Virgin, 1998)

Mick Brown, *Richard Branson: The Inside Story* (Michael Joseph, 1988)

Chris Bryant, *Glenda Jackson* (HarperCollins, 1999)

P. H. M. Bryant, *Harrow* (Blackie and Son, 1936)

John Calder, *Pursuit* (John Calder, 2001)

Simon Callow, *Love is Where it Falls* (Nick Hern, 1999)

John Campbell, *Roy Jenkins* (Weidenfeld and Nicolson, 1983)

Humphrey Carpenter, *OUDS: A Centenary History of the Oxford University Dramatic Society, 1885–1985* (Oxford University Press, 1985)

Humphrey Carpenter, *Robert Runcie: The Reluctant Archbishop* (Hodder and Stoughton, 1996)

Colin Chambers, *Peggy: The Life of Margaret Ramsay, Play Agent* (Nick Hern, 1997)

The Cherwell (1940–2)

Peter J. Conradi, *Iris Murdoch: A Life* (HarperCollins, 2001)

Michael Coveney, *Maggie Smith: A Bright Particular Star* (Gollancz, 1992)

Jonathan Croall, *Gielgud: A Theatrical Life 1904–2000* (Methuen, 2001)

Andy Croft, *Comrade Heart: A Life of Randall Swingler* (Manchester University, 2003)

Andy Croft (ed.), *Randall Swingler, Selected Poems* (Trent Editions, 2000)

Russell Davies (ed.), *The Kenneth Williams Diaries* (HarperCollins, 1994)

Desmond Devitt (ed.), *A Diversity of Dragons* (Desmond Devitt, 2003)

Madelon Dimont, *Darling Pericles* (Heinemann, 1972)

The Draconian (Dragon School, 1932–7)

Margaret Duggan, *Runcie: The Making of an Archbishop* (Hodder and Stoughton, 1983)

Susan Elliott with Barry Turner, *Denholm Elliott: Quest For Love* (Headline, 1994)

John Elsom and Nicholas Tomalin, *The History of the National Theatre* (Jonathan Cape, 1978)

Encyclopaedia Britannica (Encyclopaedia Britannica, 1974)

Martin Esslin, *Pinter the Playwright* (Methuen, 1992)

Richard Eyre, *National Service: Diary of a Decade* (Bloomsbury, 2003)

Marcia Falkender, *Downing Street in Perspective* (Weidenfeld and Nicolson, 1983)

Mia Farrow, *What Falls Away* (Doubleday, 1997)

Stephen Fay, *Power Play: The Life and Times of Peter Hall* (Hodder and Stoughton, 1995)

Georges Feydeau, *A Little Hotel on the Side* translated by John Mortimer (Heinemann Educational, 1977)

Georges Feydeau, *Cat Among the Pigeons* translated by John Mortimer (Samuel French, 1970)

Georges Feydeau, *The Lady from Maxim's* translated by John Mortimer (Heinemann Educational/National Theatre, 1977)

Georges Feydeau, *Three Boulevard Farces* translated by John Mortimer (Penguin Plays, 1985)

Shirley Anne Field, *A Time For Love* (Bantam, 1991)

Clive Fisher, *Gielgud Stories* (Futura, 1988)

John Fowles, *The Journals: Volume 1* (Cape, 2003)

Natasha Fraser-Cavassoni, *Sam Spiegel* (Little Brown, 2003)

Michael Freedland, *Dustin: A Biography of Dustin Hoffman* (Virgin, 1989)

Sigmund Freud, *The Essentials of Psychoanalysis* translated by James Strachey (Penguin, 1953)

Nancy Friday, *Men in Love* (Hutchinson, 1980)

David Frost, *An Autobiography: Part 1* (HarperCollins, 1993)

Martin Gilbert, *Finest Hour: Winston S. Churchill 1939–1941* (Heinemann, 1983)

Cheryl Glickhauf-Hughes and Marolyn Wells, *Treatment of the Masochistic Personality* (Jason Aronson, 1995)

Arnold Goodman, *Tell Them I'm On My Way* (Chapmans, 1993)

John Goodwin (ed.), *Peter Hall's Diaries* (Hamish Hamilton, 1983)

Tim Goodwin, *Britain's Royal National Theatre* (Nick Hern, 1988)

Giles Gordon, *Aren't We Due a Royalty Statement?* (Chatto and Windus, 1993)

Richard Perceval Graves, *Robert Graves and the White Goddess, 1940–1985* (Weidenfeld and Nicolson, 1995)

Valerie Grove, *Laurie Lee: The Well-Loved Stranger* (Viking, 1999)

Alec Guinness, *A Positively Final Appearance* (Hamish Hamilton, 1999)

Peter Hall, *Making an Exhibition of Myself* (Sinclair-Stevenson, 1993)

Rex Harrison, *A Damned Serious Business* (Bantam, 1990)

The Harrovian (Harrow School, 1937–1940)

Harrow Magazine (Harrow School, 1937–1940)

Nigel Hawthorne, *Straight Face* (Hodder and Stoughton, 2002)

Denis Healey, *The Time of My Life* (Michael Joseph, 1989)

John Heath-Stubbs, *Hindsights* (Hodder and Stoughton, 1993)

Bevis Hillier, *Young Betjeman* (John Murray, 1988)

Anthony Holden, *Olivier* (Weidenfeld and Nicolson, 1988)

Sir Michael Hordern with Patricia England, *A World Elsewhere* (Michael O'Mara, 1993)

Tim Jackson, *Virgin King: Inside Richard Branson's Business Empire* (HarperCollins, 1994)

Eric Jacobs, *Kingsley Amis* (Hodder and Stoughton, 1995)

C. H. Jaques, *A Dragon Century 1877–1977* (Blackwell's, 1977)

Iain Johnstone, *Dustin Hoffman* (Spellmount, 1984)

James H. Jones, *Alfred C. Kinsey* (W. W. Norton, 1997)

Francis King, *Yesterday Came Suddenly* (Constable, 1993)

Alan King-Hamilton, *And Nothing But the Truth* (Weidenfeld and Nicolson, 1982)

Vivienne Knight, *Trevor Howard: A Gentleman and a Player* (Muller, Blond and White, 1986)

E. D. Laborde, *Harrow School Yesterday and Today* (Winchester Publications, 1948)

Margaret Laing, *Edward Heath: Prime Minister* (Sidgwick and Jackson, 1972)

Peter Lewis, *The National: A Dream Made Concrete* (Methuen, 1990)

Roger Lewis, *The Life and Death of Peter Sellers* (Century, 1994)

Leo McKern, *Just Resting* (Methuen, 1983)

Richard Mangan (ed.), *Gielgud's Letters* (Weidenfeld and Nicolson, 2004)

Patrick Marnham, *The* Private Eye *Story* (André Deutsch, 1982)

Esther Menaker, *Masochism and the Emergent Ego* (Jason Aronson, 1996)

James W. Moir (ed.), *Harrow School Register 1885–1949* (Rivingtons, 1951)

Kenneth More, *More or Less* (Hodder and Stoughton, 1978)

Kevin Morgan, *Against Fascism and War* (Manchester University, 1989)

Sheridan Morley, *A Talent to Amuse* (Pavilion, 1969)

Sheridan Morley, *John G: The Authorised Biography of John Gielgud* (Hodder and Stoughton, 2001)

Penelope Mortimer, *About Time* (Allen Lane, 1979)

Penelope Mortimer, *About Time Too, 1940–1978* (Weidenfeld and Nicolson, 1993)

Penelope Mortimer, *A Villa in Summer* (Michael Joseph, 1954)

Penelope Mortimer, *The Bright Prison* (Michael Joseph, 1956)

Penelope Mortimer, *Daddy's Gone A-Hunting* (Michael Joseph, 1958)

Penelope Mortimer, *Saturday Lunch With the Brownings* (Hutchinson, 1960)

Penelope Mortimer, *The Pumpkin Eater* (Hutchinson, 1962)

Penelope Mortimer, *My Friend Says It's Bullet-Proof* (Hutchinson, 1967)

Penelope Mortimer, *The Home* (Hutchinson, 1971)

Penelope Mortimer, *Long Distance* (Allen Lane, 1974)

Penelope Mortimer, *The Handyman* (Allen Lane, 1983)

Robert F. Moss, *The Films of Carol Reed* (Macmillan, 1987)

Andrew Motion, *Philip Larkin: A Writer's Life* (Faber and Faber, 1993)

Michael Munn, *Trevor Howard: The Man and His Films* (Robson, 1989)

Notes on the School Buildings (Harrow School, 1937)

Garry O'Connor, *Alec Guinness: The Unknown* (Sidgwick and Jackson, 2002)

Garry O'Connor, *Paul Scofield* (Sidgwick and Jackson, 2002)

Laurence Olivier, *Confessions of an Actor* (Weidenfeld and Nicolson, 1982)

Judith Palmer (ed.), *Private View: Artists Working Today* (Serpent's Tail, 2004)

Tony Palmer, *The Trials of Oz* (Blond and Briggs, 1971)

Molly Parkin, *Moll* (Gollancz, 1993)

Graham Payn and Sheridan Morley (eds), *The Noël Coward Diaries* (Weidenfeld and Nicolson, 1982)

Roy Plomley with Derek Drescher, *Desert Island Lists* (Hutchinson, 1984)

Giles Radice, *Friends and Rivals* (Little Brown, 2002)

Beryl Reid, *So Much Love* (Hutchinson, 1984)

Theodor Reik, *Masochism in Modern Man* (Grove Press, NY, 1941)

Tony Richardson, *Long Distance Runner: A Memoir* (Faber and Faber, 1993)

Philip Roberts, *The Royal Court Theatre and the Modern Stage* (Cambridge University, 1999)

Geoffrey Robertson, *The Justice Game* (Chatto and Windus, 1998)

Geoffrey Robertson and Andrew Nicol, *Media Law* (Sweet and Maxwell, 2002)

Alan Ross, *Blindfold Games* (Collins Harvill, 1986)

Sam Rubin and Richard Taylor, *Mia Farrow* (Robson, 1990)

Miranda Seymour, *Robert Graves: Life on the Edge* (Doubleday, 1995)

Ned Sherrin, *A Small Thing – Like an Earthquake* (Weidenfeld and Nicolson, 1983)

Irene Shubik, *Play For Today: The Evolution of Television Drama* (Manchester University Press, 2000)

Ed Sikov, *Mr Strangelove: A Biography of Peter Sellers* (Sidgwick and Jackson, 2002)

Andrew Sinclair, *Spiegel: The Man Behind the Pictures* (Weidenfeld and Nicolson, 1987)

Donald Spoto, *Laurence Olivier* (HarperCollins, 1991)

Robert Stephens with Michael Coveney, *Knight Errant: Memoirs of a Vagabond Actor* (Hodder and Stoughton, 1995)

Alan Strachan, *Secret Dreams: A Biography of Michael Redgrave* (Weidenfeld and Nicolson, 2004)

Robert Tanitch, *Guinness* (Harrap, 1989)

John Russell Taylor, *Alec Guinness: A Celebration* (Pavilion, 1984)

Ann Thwaite (ed.), *My Oxford* (Robson Books, 1977)

Anthony Thwaite (ed.), *Selected Letters of Philip Larkin 1940–1985* (Faber and Faber, 1992)

Kathleen Tynan, *The Life of Kenneth Tynan* (Weidenfeld and Nicolson, 1987)

Kathleen Tynan (ed.), *Kenneth Tynan Letters* (Weidenfeld and Nicolson, 1994)

Nicholas Wapshott, *The Man Between: A Biography of Carol Reed* (Chatto and Windus, 1990)

Arnold Wesker, *As Much as I Dare* (Century, 1994)

Mary Whitehouse, *A Most Dangerous Woman?* (Lion, 1982)

Mary Whitehouse, *Quite Contrary* (Sidgwick and Jackson, 1993)

Sandy Wilson, *I Could Be Happy* (Michael Joseph, 1975)

Ian Woodward, *Glenda Jackson: A Study in Fire and Ice* (Weidenfeld and Nicolson, 1985)

Carl Zuckmayer, *The Captain of Köpenick* adapted by John Mortimer (Methuen, 1971)

NOVELS BY JOHN MORTIMER
Charade (Bodley Head, 1947)
Rumming Park (Bodley Head, 1948)
Answer Yes or No (Bodley Head, 1950)
Like Men Betrayed (Collins, 1953)
The Narrowing Stream (Collins, 1954)
Three Winters (Collins, 1956)
Paradise Postponed (Penguin, 1985)
Summer's Lease (Viking, 1988)
Titmuss Regained (Penguin, 1990)
Dunster (Viking, 1992)
Felix in the Underworld (Viking, 1997)
The Sound of Trumpets (Viking, 1998)
Rumpole and the Penge Bungalow Murders (Viking, 2004)

SHORT STORIES BY JOHN MORTIMER
Will Shakespeare (Hodder and Stoughton, 1977)
Rumpole of the Bailey (Penguin, 1978)
The Trials of Rumpole (Penguin, 1979)
Rumpole's Return (Penguin, 1980)

Rumpole for the Defence, first published as *Regina v. Rumpole* (Allen Lane, 1981)
Rumpole and the Golden Thread (Penguin, 1983)
Rumpole's Last Case (Penguin, 1988)
Rumpole and the Age of Miracles (Penguin, 1988)
Rumpole à la Carte (Penguin, 1990)
Rumpole on Trial (Viking, 1992)
Under the Hammer (Penguin, 1994)
Rumpole and the Angel of Death (Penguin, 1995)
Rumpole Rests His Case (Viking, 2001)
Rumpole and the Primrose Path (Viking, 2002)

NON-FICTION BY JOHN MORTIMER
(as 'Geoffrey Lincoln') *No Moaning of the Bar* (Geoffrey Bles, 1957)
Clinging to the Wreckage (Weidenfeld and Nicolson, 1982)
In Character (Allen Lane, 1983)
Character Parts (Viking, 1986)
Murderers and Other Friends (Viking, 1994)
The Summer of a Dormouse (Viking, 2000)
Where There's a Will (Viking, 2003)

NON-FICTION BY JOHN AND PENELOPE MORTIMER
With Love and Lizards (Michael Joseph, 1957)

BOOKS EDITED BY JOHN MORTIMER
Famous Trials, first edited by Harry Hodge and James H. Hodge (Penguin, 1984)
Famous Trials of Marshall Hall (Penguin, 1989)
The Oxford Book of Villains (Oxford University Press, 1992)
Great Law and Order Stories (W. W. Norton, 1992)

STAGE PLAYS BY JOHN MORTIMER
The Dock Brief (1957)
What Shall We Tell Caroline? (1958)
I Spy (1958)
(Sketches) *One to Another* (1959)
The Wrong Side of the Park (1960)
Lunch Hour (1960)
(Sketches) *Triangle, Conference, Collector's Piece, Cleaning up Justice* (1960)
Collect Your Hand Baggage (1961)
Two Stars for Comfort (1962)
The Judge (1967)
A Voyage Round My Father (1970)

Mill Hill (1970)
Bermondsey (1970)
Gloucester Road (1970)
Marble Arch (1970)
Knightsbridge (1970)
I, Claudius (1972)
Collaborators (1973)
The Fear of Heaven (1976)
The Prince of Darkness (1976), renamed *The Bells of Hell* (1977)
Edwin (1982)
When That I Was (1982)
A Christmas Carol (1994)
Naked Justice (2001)
Hock and Soda Water (2001)

TELEVISION SERIES BY JOHN MORTIMER
Will Shakespeare (1978)
Rumpole of the Bailey (1978)
The Trials of Rumpole (1979)
Brideshead Revisited (1981)
Rumpole and the Golden Thread (1983)
Paradise Postponed (1986)
Rumpole's Last Case (1987)
Rumpole and the Age of Miracles (1988)
Summer's Lease (1989)
Titmuss Regained (1991)
Rumpole à la Carte (1991)
Rumpole on Trial (1992)
Under the Hammer (1993)
*Although Mortimer is credited as the author of the TV adaptation of
   Brideshead Revisited his scripts were never used.

TELEVISION PLAYS BY JOHN MORTIMER
The Dock Brief (1957)
I Spy (1958)
What Shall We Tell Caroline? (1959)
David and Broccoli (1960)
Lunch Hour (1960)
Twenty-Four Hours in a Woman's Life (1961)
The Encyclopaedist (1961)
Collect Your Hand Baggage (1963)
The Choice of Kings (1966)
The Exploding Azalea (1966)

The Head Waiter (1966)
The Other Side (1967)
Infidelity Took Place (1967)
A Flea in Her Ear (1967)
Desmond (1968)
A Voyage Round My Father (1969)
Married Alive (1970)
Only Three Can Play (1970)
Swiss Cottage (1972)
Mill Hill (1972)
Bermondsey (1972)
Gloucester Road (1972)
Marble Arch (1972)
Knightsbridge (1972)
Alcock and Gander (1972)
Rumpole of the Bailey (1975)
Shades of Greene (1975)
Special Duties (1975)
Unity (1978)
Rumpole's Return (1980)
Rumpole for the Defence (1982)
Dr Fischer of Geneva (1982)
Edwin (1984)
The Ebony Tower (1984)
Urania Cottage (1994)
Cider With Rosie (1998)
Coming Home (1998)
Don Quixote (2000)
Love and War in the Appenines (2001)
Benny Hill (2003)

FILMSCRIPTS BY JOHN MORTIMER
Ferry to Hong Kong (1959)
Lunch Hour (1961)
The Innocents (1961)
The Dock Brief (*Trial and Error* in USA) (1962)
Guns of Darkness (1962)
The Running Man (1963)
Bunny Lake is Missing (1964)
John and Mary (1969)
Something Wicked This Way Comes (1982)
Tea With Mussolini (1999)
Così fan tutte (2003)

TELEVISION SKETCHES BY JOHN MORTIMER
That Was the Week That Was (1963)
Not So Much a Programme, More a Way of Life (1965)
BBC3 (1966)

STAGE PLAYS TRANSLATED OR ADAPTED BY JOHN MORTIMER
A Flea in Her Ear by Georges Feydeau (1965)
Cat Among the Pigeons by Georges Feydeau (1969)
The Captain of Köpenick by Carl Zuckmayer (1971)
The Lady from Maxim's by Georges Feydeau (1977)

BALLET SCENARIO BY JOHN MORTIMER
Home (1968)

OPERA TRANSLATION BY JOHN MORTIMER
Die Fledermaus (1989)

RADIO PLAYS
Like Men Betrayed (1955)
No Hero (1955)
The Dock Brief (1957)
I Spy (1957)
Three Winters (1958)
Call Me a Liar (1958)
Personality Split (1964)
Education of an Englishman (1964)
A Rare Device (1965)
Mr Luby's Fear of Heaven (1976)
Edwin (1982)
The Summer of a Dormouse (2000)

Index